NEW
ENGLISH
KEY NOTES

Leaving Certificate 2018 – Higher Level

Series Editors: Pat O'Shea
Tony Lake

MENTOR BOOKS

Published in 2016 by

Mentor Books
43 Furze Road
Sandyford Industrial Estate
Dublin 18
Tel: 01–295 2112 / 3
Fax: 01–295 2114

Website: www.mentorbooks.ie
e-mail: admin@mentorbooks.ie

Edited by: Daniel McCarthy
Design and Layout by: Kathryn O'Sullivan

ISBN: 978-1-909417-66-3

Printed in Ireland

Contents

Contents: Poetry Notes

Contents: Poetry Notes

Note to Students

The purpose of *New English Key Notes* is to offer some practical assistance and advice to students preparing for Leaving Certificate Higher Level English – Paper 2. The notes presented here explain and analyse the three elements of the literature syllabus:

• Single Text (*King Lear*)   • Comparative Study   • Poetry.

New English Key Notes aims to promote a clear-minded, analytical approach to the exam. The range of aspects considered in these notes is not intended to be either exhaustive or prescriptive. Essential phrases are in **bold type**.

Single Text: This sections includes a Scene-by-Scene Summary and Commentary on *King Lear*. Key Points are listed at the end of each scene, stressing the most important aspects in relation to plot development, characterisation, themes, style, etc. Following Exam Guidelines, a variety of Exam Topics are addressed. Finally, the Characters of the play are also examined in terms of their traits and dramatic function. Key Adjectives are listed at the end of each section to highlight each character's most striking qualities.

Comparative Study: This section examines three popular, accessible texts: *The Plough and the Stars, Children of Men* and *The Great Gatsby* in terms of the three prescribed comparative modes:

A. Cultural Context

B. General Vision and Viewpoint

C. Literary Genre.

Key Points of Comparison / Contrast are listed at the end of each section. With such a wide range of texts from which to choose, the aim here is to encourage a coherent comparative approach to the three texts chosen. Sample Answers are provided at the end of each mode. Finally there are Guidelines for Answering Exam Questions.

Poetry: This section discusses the poems of eight poets individually. Key Points are listed at the end of each poem. The Sample Answers given here are considerably longer than the responses expected of students in the exam itself (most responses are three to four A4 pages). The lengthy answers given here are designed to suggest a wide range of areas of possible discussion and to discourage rote learning of such answers. The emphasis throughout this section is on the central importance of personal engagement grounded in the text. Finally there are extensive Guidelines on Answering Exam Questions.

The last section explains **Key Literary Terms**.

King Lear

Introduction

King Lear is believed to have been written around 1605. While the opening scenes of the play suggest a fairytale-like plot with its extremes of good and evil, it is soon apparent that *King Lear* is one of the darkest and most tragic of Shakespeare's tragedies. The vision of the play is, in many respects, extremely pessimistic.

Similar to all of Shakespeare's tragedies, *King Lear* portrays the downfall of a once-great man. Like all of the other tragic heroes, Lear's downfall is caused by a fatal flaw. While Macbeth is ambitious, Othello jealous and Hamlet indecisive, Lear is rash. This rashness is immediately apparent in the opening scene where Lear declares his intention of dividing up his kingdom. His decision to abdicate the throne seems to be motivated by a sense of weariness with the 'cares and business' of kingship. He claims that in dividing the kingdom at this point, he wishes to prevent 'future strife', but, ironically, this is precisely and inevitably what his selfish decision to renounce the throne causes. Seeming to decide the manner in which he will divide the kingdom on a whim ('Which of us shall we say doth love us most?'), Lear compounds the dangerous foolishness of his decision to step down from the throne. The flattery his 'love test' invites immediately flows from both Goneril and Regan, whose desire to out-do each other in their declarations of 'love' prefigures the deadly rivalry that will later consume and destroy them both. Cordelia, the only daughter that genuinely loves Lear, refuses to massage her father's ego such is her disgust at the contrived nature of her sisters' expressions of love. An outraged Lear impetuously disowns and disinherits his one true daughter, dividing his kingdom between Goneril and Regan.

Lear pays an extremely high price for his foolishness. Having given Goneril and Regan power and authority over him, Lear is now at their mercy and neither love nor compassion feature among their qualities. The callous sisters coldly strip Lear of his remaining power and dignity and their unnatural ingratitude ultimately drives Lear to insanity. On the positive side, Lear grows through his suffering, paradoxically acquiring 'reason in madness' and gradually becoming a better and wiser man. While he is eventually reconciled with Cordelia, the play ends in a heartbreakingly tragic manner with Lear carrying the body of the lifeless Cordelia onto the stage.

The play explores such universal themes as the parent-child relationship, love, ingratitude, the abuse of power, growth through suffering and redemption. The universality of these themes is underscored by the fact that the sub-plot (the story of Gloucester and his sons) reflects and reinforces the key themes in the play.

Scene-by-Scene Summary and Commentary

ACT 1 Scene 1

The opening scene introduces us to most of the characters in the play. It is dominated by Lear's abdication (i.e. his resignation from the throne) and by the artificial love-test which will decide the manner in which the kingdom is divided. As king, Lear was seen as God's representative on earth and was not expected to surrender (give up) his power and authority. While Lear believed that he would ensure future peace and harmony by dividing the kingdom at this point ('. . . that future strife may be prevented now'), this unwise decision would ironically ensure the opposite since it would inevitably lead to rivalry and conflict in the future. Furthermore, the ridiculous manner in which he sets out to divide the kingdom is a recipe for disaster. The love-test reflects Lear's foolishness and egotism (self-centred nature) – he believes that he can measure love in words and demands that his daughters express their love for him in a very public manner. Lear's foolishness will plunge the kingdom into chaos, in the process causing unimaginable suffering both for Lear himself and for a range of other characters. While Lear must inevitably pay the price for his faults and failings, the price he ultimately pays is strikingly out of proportion to his initial blunder.

When Lear asks which of his daughters loves him most, he inevitably invites flattery and both Goneril and Regan are happy to pander to his ego (flatter him) in order to advance themselves. Goneril hypocritically proclaims that she loves her father 'more than words can wield the matter'. There is an obvious irony in Regan's observation that she is 'made of the self metal' as Goneril since both sisters love power far more than they love Lear. From the outset, we see the sibling rivalry between these equally false sisters when Regan immediately tries to outdo her sister in her profession of love for Lear: 'In my true heart I find she names my very deed of love, only she comes too short . . .' While these expressions of love are exaggerated and insincere, the sentimental old king is easily duped (fooled). **Goneril and Regan are each awarded a third of the kingdom following their artificial professions of love for Lear.**

Lear has already decided that Cordelia, his favourite daughter, will get the best share of the kingdom. However, when he asks her what she can say 'to draw a third more opulent' than her sisters, he is stunned by her simple response: 'Nothing'. Disgusted by her sisters' hypocrisy, Cordelia refuses to flatter Lear: 'I cannot heave my heart into my mouth. I love your majesty according to my bond: nor more, nor less'. She goes on to logically ask: 'Why have my sisters husbands if they say they love you all?' Cordelia's refusal to indulge Lear sets in motion a series of disastrous events. While it is true that the whole tragedy might have been avoided had Cordelia simply humoured the whimsical (impulsive) Lear, she has high personal standards and will not stoop to using 'the glib and oily art' of flattery to secure her share of the kingdom. She may also have inherited some of her father's pride and obstinacy (stubborness). While Cordelia's expression of love sounds cold and unfeeling, she, unlike her sisters, truly loves her father as a daughter should. **Her refusal to take part in Lear's foolish game reflects her spirit and courage.**

In refusing to flatter Lear, Cordelia inevitably incurs his wrath (provokes his anger). We see Lear's rash and fiery nature when he disowns the daughter he always loved most: 'Here I disclaim all my paternal care, propinquity and property of love'. Furthermore, he jeopardises (endangers) her marital prospects by also disinheriting her. Lear's response to Cordelia's plain speaking is harsh, extreme and wildly disproportionate to the perceived wrong that has been done to him. Lear's misjudgement of Cordelia is one of the root causes of the tragedy, and will haunt him for much of the painful personal journey he will shortly be forced to undertake.

Lear's foolishness is again cast into sharp

relief (brought into clear focus) by his stated determination to 'retain the name and all the additions to a king' even after he has given up the crown. He naively believes that he can keep the title and trappings of kingship after he has walked away from the responsibilities of leadership – this, of course, is utterly unrealistic on Lear's part.

It is at this point that we see Kent's remarkable loyalty, bluntness and moral courage. Kent idolises Lear, regarding him as his king, father, master and patron. However, he is unwilling to remain silent in the face of Lear's shocking rashness and bravely comes to Cordelia's defence. We see how unreal Lear's self-image is when he warns Kent not to come 'between the dragon and his wrath'. Lear sees himself as an all-powerful being, before whom everyone should quake. Lear is spiritually blind at the start of the play, unable to see himself or others in a true light. Kent is the only person in the court brave enough to stand up to Lear, bluntly telling him that he is 'mad' and that he is bowing to flattery. He rightly believes that his unmannerly behaviour towards his king is, in the circumstances, justified. Kent begs Lear to 'check this hideous rashness', reminding him that he has only ever regarded his own life as 'a pawn' to wage against Lear's enemies. Aware of Lear's spiritual blindness, Kent pleads with him to 'see better', before plainly telling him: 'I'll tell thee thou dost evil'.

Kent is one of the most admirable characters in the play, consistently speaking his mind regardless of the personal consequences. Like Cordelia, he too pays a high price for daring to challenge Lear. Accustomed to a lifetime of unquestioning obedience, Lear is enraged by Kent's intervention and banishes him. In a few dramatic minutes, Lear seems to cut himself off from those who love him most. Before leaving the court, Kent expresses the hope that the gods will watch over Cordelia and that Goneril and Regan's actions will match their words of love. He is a good judge of character and, in contrast to the gullible Lear, does not accept flowery declarations of love at face value.

Lear now turns to address Cordelia's suitors. Pointing out that she is now without a dowry and is the object of his 'hate', he asks Burgundy and France if they will 'take her, or leave her'. It is difficult to believe that Lear is talking about his own flesh and blood here, such is his heartless tone. Burgundy and France are sharply contrasting characters. Burgundy is practical and mercenary-minded and has no interest in marrying Cordelia without the promised dowry. However, France is more sensitive to Cordelia's plight, pointedly asking how Lear's favourite daughter ('your best object') can possibly have fallen from favour in such a dramatic manner. We see Cordelia's nobility and spirit when, acknowledging that she lacks the 'glib and oily art' of flattery, she asks Lear to explain that she has not lost favour because of any dishonourable act on her part. France is very impressed with Cordelia's personal qualities and is prepared to marry her despite her lack of a dowry. He tells Burgundy that 'she is herself a dowry'. In his eyes, love has nothing to do with money or territory: 'Love's not love when it is mingled with regards that stand aloof from the entire point'. Addressing her as 'Fairest Cordelia', France declares that she is 'most rich, being poor'. France's love for Cordelia is sincere, and sharply contrasts with the 'love' of Burgundy, which is entirely based on material considerations.

While Cordelia impresses us with her honesty, courage and composure, we also admire her judgement. She sees through her sisters' hypocrisy and tells them so as she leaves the court: 'I know you what you are...' Remarkably, despite Lear's dreadful treatment of her, she remains concerned for him: 'I would prefer him to a better place'. She shrewdly predicts that Goneril and Regan's true intentions will be revealed in time: 'Time shall unfold what plaited cunning hides'.

After Cordelia and France leave, Goneril and Regan reflect on the dramatic events that have occurred. They are genuinely taken aback (shocked) by Lear's poor judgement and rashness. Goneril states that Lear 'always loved our sister most; and with what poor judgement he hath now cast her off appears too grossly'. She points out that Lear has always been fiery and impulsive: 'The best and soundest of his time hath been but rash'. Reflecting on Lear's lack of self-knowledge, Regan tells her sister that 'he hath ever but slenderly known himself'. Goneril and Regan's observations are obviously not rooted in any loving concern for Lear, but in their fear that his rash and fiery nature may cause difficulties for them in the future. **Here we learn that Lear's flaws – his rashness and lack of self-knowledge – are deeply ingrained in his character.**

By the close of the opening scene, Goneril and Regan are already conspiring (secretly plotting) against Lear. Goneril appears to be the dominant sister: 'Pray you, let us hit together'. Having used cunning and flattery to gain their share of the kingdom, they immediately plan to take Lear's remaining power from him. They see no good in their own father and intend to 'do something' about him quickly. Goneril and Regan are particularly unappealing characters because they are utterly ungrateful and callous (unfeeling). While Lear was cruel to Cordelia, he acted on the spur of the moment. In contrast to Lear's unthinking cruelty, Goneril and Regan's evil actions are coldly pre-meditated. **Of course, Lear's tragedy is that he has cut himself off from his one loving daughter and given his two scheming daughters power and authority over him.**

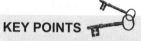

KEY POINTS

- Lear is a deeply flawed character – he is gullible, arrogant, morally blind and rash.
- The love-test invites flattery, and Goneril and Regan do not hesitate to tell Lear what he wants to hear, their artificial expressions of love ensuring them of their share of the kingdom.
- We see Lear at his worst when he disowns and disinherits the loving Cordelia and when he banishes the loyal Kent.
- Cordelia is honest, noble and courageous.
- Kent is loyal, blunt and courageous.
- France displays true love for Cordelia, being prepared to marry her without a dowry.
- Goneril and Regan are cunning, hypocritical and ungrateful – by the close of the opening scene they have formed an alliance and are already plotting against Lear.

ACT 1 Scene 2

This scene opens with a soliloquy from Edmund (a soliloquy is basically a speech in which a character is thinking aloud to him/herself – its value lies in the insights it offers into the character's innermost thoughts). **This soliloquy helps us to better understand Edmund's character and motivation, revealing him to be proud, ambitious, defiant and ruthless.** We learn of Edmund's devious plan to trick his father, Gloucester, into giving him Edgar's inheritance: 'Legitimate Edgar, I must have your land'. Edmund believes in the law of the jungle, the survival of the fittest: 'Thou, Nature, art my goddess . . .' He is as cold and calculating as Goneril and Regan. He does not feel bound by any moral code or natural law, and will achieve his goals by whatever means are necessary. In that sense, **Edmund is a Machiavellian character, believing that the end justifies the means.** We see his pride when he defiantly rejects the label that society has attached to him because he was born outside of wedlock: 'Why bastard? Wherefore base? When my dimensions are as well compact, my mind as generous and my shape as true as honest madam's issue'. It is difficult not to feel a grudging admiration for Edmund's determination to succeed in life and so rise above his lowly status in society. Edmund is a clever schemer and – at this point in the play – a likeable villain.

As the play develops, we see the obvious similarities and parallels between the main plot (the story of Lear and his children) and the sub-plot (the story of Gloucester and his children). Just as Edmund is as unscrupulous as Goneril and Regan, so is Gloucester as gullible as Lear. Gloucester also shares Lear's rashness and moral blindness. Edmund exploits Gloucester's superstitious and credulous (gullible/unsuspecting) nature. His plan is simple – he arouses his father's interest in a letter he is reading by pretending to hide it. Edmund then uses this letter to destroy his brother, Edgar's, reputation. The letter seems to suggest that Edgar is plotting to murder his aged father because he is impatient to inherit his estate, and that he is looking for Edmund's assistance. Rash like Lear, Gloucester never stops to think and ponder the authenticity (genuineness) of this letter. He immediately condemns Edgar: 'Abhorred villain! Unnatural, detested, brutish villain!' Gloucester's inability to see the truth about his sons is an indication of his moral/spiritual blindness. By pretending to defend Edgar, Edmund simply further convinces Gloucester of Edgar's guilt. Edmund manipulates his father with consummate (expert) skill, convincing him to eavesdrop on a conversation between Edgar and himself. Gloucester agrees in order to find out about Edgar's true intentions.

Gloucester is a superstitious character and blames all kinds of problems in the world of men on the stars: 'These late eclipses in the sun and moon portend no good to us'. Edmund laughs at his father's superstitious nature. For Edmund the idea of blaming various problems on the stars is simply ridiculous ('the excellent foppery of the world'). He believes that life is shaped not by the stars, but by people themselves. Edmund believes in the power of his own will – he believes that his destiny lies in his own hands.

The success of Edmund's scheming has much to do with the gullibility of both Gloucester and Edgar. Edgar is presented as a noble, but credulous character. When Edmund tells Edgar that Gloucester is angry with him, Edgar rightly concludes that someone has tarnished his reputation ('Some villain hath done me wrong'), but never suspects that his good name has been destroyed by his brother's lies. At the close of this scene Edmund delights in the ease with which he has manipulated both Gloucester and Edgar. He exploits his father's gullibility and his brother's nobility in order to advance his own selfish plans: 'A credulous father and a brother noble . . . on whose foolish honesty my practices ride easy'. Edmund may have been unfortunate in terms of the circumstances of his birth, but is determined to achieve his goals through his scheming: 'Let me, if not by birth, have lands by wit'. He has no scruples (conscience) and will do whatever is necessary to bring about his own advancement: 'All with me's meet that I can fashion fit.'

KEY POINTS

- Edmund is ambitious, scheming and unscrupulous (without conscience).
- He manipulates both Gloucester and Edgar with expert ease.
- Gloucester shares certain characteristics with Lear, being both gullible and rash.
- Edgar is noble, but rather credulous.
- From the beginning there are clear similarities between the sub-plot and the main plot.

ACT 1 Scene 3

It is not long before Goneril reveals her true nature. With her share of the kingdom secured, she has no need to flatter or indulge Lear any longer. **This scene introduces us to the key theme of filial ingratitude** (the ingratitude of the child towards the parent). Goneril had earlier agreed to provide hospitality for her father and his followers, but has no intention of honouring this agreement. She encourages her servant Oswald to be disrespectful towards Lear: 'Put on what weary negligence you please'. She wants to provoke a confrontation with Lear so that she can assert her authority over him. Goneril resents the fact that Lear still behaves as if he were king despite having given away all of his power, and cannot disguise her contempt for him: 'idle old man that still would manage those authorities that he hath given away'. The hypocrisy of her declaration of love for Lear in the opening scene is underlined by her disdainful remark: 'Old fools are babes again'. She speaks of her father with a total lack of love and respect. Lear is about to start paying the price for his earlier foolishness. Goneril is the dominant sister and sends a message to Regan, urging her to follow her lead in relation to Lear: 'I'll write straight to my sister to hold my very course'.

KEY POINTS

- Goneril's filial ingratitude quickly becomes apparent.
- She encourages her servants to neglect Lear in order to provoke a confrontation with him.
- Goneril ensures that Regan treats Lear as she has done – she is the more enterprising, more dominant sister.

ACT 1 Scene 4

Kent returns in disguise to help Lear. He is so devoted to Lear that he is prepared to serve him as a lowly servant despite Lear having treated him so harshly: '. . . thy master, whom thou lovest, shall find thee full of labours'. Lear still acts as if he were king, demanding that his dinner be served without delay. However, Goneril's servants have been ordered to make Lear and his followers feel less welcome and one of Lear's knights clearly perceives the changed atmosphere: 'Your highness is not entertained with that ceremonious affection as you were wont'. He speaks of 'a great abatement (lessening) of kindness'. Oswald is deliberately disrespectful towards Lear when he describes him as 'My lady's father'. **The idea that his status in life is now defined in relation to his daughter infuriates Lear.** Angered by Oswald's insulting attitude towards Lear, Kent trips up the disrespectful servant.

The Fool plays an important role in Lear's personal development by relentlessly reminding him of his foolishness. Lear calls him 'a bitter fool' because he speaks the bitter truth. Kent recognises the Fool's wisdom when he remarks: 'This is not altogether fool, my Lord'. The Fool bluntly tells Lear that he was foolish to give up his crown: 'Thou hadst little wit in thy bald crown, when thou gavest thou golden one away'. He rightly points out that Lear has given his daughters power and authority over him: 'Thou madest thy daughters thy mother'. Goneril angrily speaks of the 'all-licensed fool' because he seems to have a licence to say whatever he likes.

When Goneril appears, she takes Lear to task (scolds him) for the rowdy (noisy and disorderly) behaviour of his knights ('men so disorder'd, so debosh'd and bold') She demands that Lear control his men and reduce their number. **Lear's knights are the last reminder of his royal power and Goneril is determined to strip her father of his remaining power and authority.** Moreover, Lear's knights might, in certain circumstances, pose a military threat to the new regime (government). Goneril later dismisses fifty of these knights 'at a clap'.

Goneril's bitter attack stuns Lear: 'Are you our daughter?' Not only does Lear struggle to recognise Goneril, he struggles with his own identity: 'Who is it that can tell me who I am?' Accustomed to automatic respect and unquestioning obedience, Lear had always seen himself as an almost superhuman figure. Now that he is being treated with undisguised contempt, he is shaken to the very core of his being. This incident marks the beginning of Lear's battle to retain his sanity. Lear dismisses Goneril as a 'degenerate bastard', foolishly believing that Regan will treat him better: 'Yet have I left a daughter'. He describes Goneril's ingratitude as a 'marble-hearted fiend' and uses animal imagery ('detested kite', 'wolvish visage') to highlight her lack of humanity. **Lear now sees Cordelia's 'sin' as a 'most minor fault' – the first sign that he is growing through suffering.**

Albany arrives on the scene and urges Lear to be patient. However, Albany seems to be a weak, ineffectual character, who has neither been consulted nor informed about Goneril's plans for Lear: 'My lord, I am guiltless, as I am ignorant of what hath moved you'. While Albany appears to be sympathetic towards Lear, his attempted protest on the latter's behalf is ignored by Goneril, who despises her husband's 'milky gentleness'.

Lear is furious with himself when he realises his earlier foolishness: 'O Lear, Lear, Lear! Beat at this gate that let thy folly in and thy dear judgement out!' However, we once again see Lear's rash and fiery nature when he curses Goneril with sterility: 'Into her womb convey sterility! Dry up in her the organs of increase, and from her derogate body never spring a babe to honour her!' If she is to have a child, Lear hopes that it will be an unnatural, thankless child so that she too will feel the pain of filial ingratitude, which he describes as being 'sharper than a serpent's tooth'. Lear is filled with shame that his daughter can treat him with visible contempt, but realises that he is to blame for his present predicament, having given her the power to belittle him. Lear laments his moral blindness: 'Old fond eyes, beweep this cause again, I'll pluck ye out, and cast you with the waters that you lose, to temper clay'.

KEY POINTS

- The ever-loyal Kent returns in disguise to serve Lear as a lowly servant.
- The Fool continues to relentlessly remind Lear of his foolishness and wrongdoing.
- Goneril openly criticises Lear's knights, demanding that Lear control their behaviour and reduce their number. She wishes to strip him of the remnants of his power, authority and kingly dignity. She goes on to dismiss fifty of Lear's knights 'at a clap'.
- Lear is so profoundly shocked by Goneril's humiliating scolding that he struggles to recognise her ('Are you our daughter?') and indeed struggles to recognise himself ('Who is it that can tell me who I am?'). This is the first step in Lear's mental disintegration.
- We again see the rash and fiery side to Lear in the manner in which he curses Goneril with sterility.
- Albany appears to be a well-intentioned, but weak and powerless character.

ACT 1 Scene 5

Lear sends Kent ahead to Regan's castle with a letter announcing his imminent arrival. He is unaware that Goneril has already sent a letter to Regan, urging her to follow her course of action in relation to Lear. After Kent departs, Lear reflects on the injustice he has done Cordelia: 'I did her wrong'. Here we see Lear taking another step on the road to self-knowledge. Helping him along this road is the Fool, who continues to be unrelenting in his efforts to make Lear more self-aware. **While Lear foolishly believes that Regan will treat him better than Goneril, the Fool perceives that both sisters are fundamentally alike:** 'She will taste as like this as a crab does to a crab'. We see the Fool's caustic (biting/sarcastic) wit when he reminds

Lear of the error of his ways in abdicating and leaving himself without a home and at the mercy of his daughters. He tells Lear that even the humble snail has a house 'to put his head in; not to give it away to his daughters, and leave his horns without a case'. He informs Lear that he has grown old without growing wise: 'Thou shouldst not have been old till thou hadst been wise'. Lear is now painfully aware of the depth of Goneril's unnatural thanklessness: 'Monster ingratitude!'

By the close of this scene, Lear can sense the insanity rising within him, pleading with the heavens to keep him sane: 'O let me not be mad, not mad, sweet heaven! Keep me in temper: I would not be mad!'

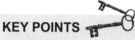

KEY POINTS

- Kent is sent to Regan's castle with a letter informing her of Lear's imminent arrival.
- The Fool continues to remind Lear of his foolishness so that he may become more self-aware.
- Lear displays further signs of personal growth when, reflecting on Cordelia, he acknowledges, 'I did her wrong'.
- Sensing his incipient (the beginning of) insanity, Lear pleads with the heavens to keep him sane.

ACT 2 Scene 1

The opening lines of this act underline the foolishness of Lear's decision to divide the kingdom, with Curan asking Edmund if he is aware of the growing rivalry between Cornwall and Albany: 'Have you heard of no likely wars toward, 'twixt the Dukes of Cornwall and Albany?' **This scene brings Edmund's cunning nature into clear focus.** Meeting Edgar, Edmund insists that his brother is in real danger and is not safe in their father's castle. Tricking the unsuspecting Edgar into participating in a fake sword fight, Edmund inflicts a wound on himself to dupe the malleable (easily influenced), credulous Gloucester into seeing him as loyal and loving, and Edgar as treacherous and unnatural. Shouting aloud to attract his father's attention, Edmund draws

attention to his injury, before going on to paint an utterly dark picture of Edgar, claiming that he had tried to enlist his assistance in murdering Gloucester. Pretending that he reminded Edgar of how 'strong a bond the child was bound to the father', and that he wanted nothing to do with his brother's 'unnatural purpose', Edmund easily convinces Gloucester of Edgar's villainy. Gloucester immediately concludes that Edgar is a 'murderous coward' who must be hunted down and brought to justice: 'Let him fly far: Not in this land shall he remain uncaught, and found – dispatch'. **The similarity between Lear and Gloucester is immediately apparent – both are easily manipulated and rash.** Just as Lear makes an exile of Cordelia, his one true daughter, Gloucester makes a fugitive of Edgar, his loyal and loving son. In another rash act, Gloucester disinherits Edgar as Lear had disinherited Cordelia, telling Edmund that he is now his heir: '. . . of my land, loyal and natural boy, I'll work the means to make thee capable'. **Both Lear and Gloucester foolishly give children, who prove to be thankless and cruel, power and authority over them.**

Edmund is a quick-thinking opportunist, turning every situation to his own advantage. When Regan asks if Edgar (Lear's godson) was consorting (keeping company) with Lear's disorderly knights, Edmund immediately replies that he was indeed accompanying them. Edmund

avails of every opportunity to further tarnish (blacken) his brother's reputation. At this point we learn that Regan will extend no welcome to Lear, telling Cornwall that she will 'not be there' if he and his knights look to stay with her. **As plot and sub-plot converge, we see clear lines of division emerging as Edmund wins his way into the service of the Duke of Cornwall and becomes aligned with the other evil characters.** Impressed by the 'child-like office' Edmund has displayed in defence of his father, and by his 'virtue and obedience', Cornwall declares: 'Natures of such deep trust we shall much need: You we first seize on'.

KEY POINTS

- The foolishness of Lear's decision to divide the kingdom is underlined by the rumour of a possible war between Cornwall and Albany.
- Edmund's opportunism and quick thinking are clearly visible in this scene.
- This scene sees plot and sub-plot converge, leaving the forces of evil combined when Cornwall invites Edmund to enter his service.
- Similarities between plot and sub-plot are very evident in this scene.

ACT 2 Scene 2

When Kent meets Oswald at Gloucester's castle, he cannot disguise his contempt for him and gives him a tongue-lashing before drawing his sword. Kent's hatred of Oswald is intensified by his knowledge of the letter that he carries from Goneril to Regan, urging her sister to treat Lear as she has done: 'Draw, you rascal; you come with letters against the king; and take Vanity the puppet's part against the royalty of her father'. When Kent starts beating him with the flat of his sword, the cowardly Oswald cries out for help, attracting the attention of Cornwall, Regan, Edmund and Gloucester.

Kent's fierce loyalty to Lear and his determination to protect the king's honour at all costs underlie his blunt responses to Cornwall, which inevitably incur the latter's wrath. Bluntness is a striking feature of Kent's character: 'Sir, 'tis my occupation to be plain'. It is his bluntness and 'saucy roughness' that

results in Kent enduring the humiliation of being placed in the stocks (normally a punishment for common criminals).While Cornwall is a brutal character, his wife Regan is even more cruel. When Cornwall declares that Kent will remain in the stocks, 'till noon', the vengeful Regan overrules him, demanding that he remain stocked 'till night . . . and all night too'. **Unconcerned for himself, Kent points out that, in placing the king's messenger in the stocks, Cornwall and Regan are disrespecting Lear's royalty:** 'You shall do small respect, show too bold malice against the grace and person of my master, stocking his messenger'. Gloucester remonstrates with Cornwall: 'Let me beseech your grace not to do so'. He goes on to echo Kent's earlier observation about the stocking of his messenger being grossly disrespectful to Lear: '. . . the king must take it ill that he is so slightly valued in his messenger'. While Gloucester's intervention is weak and ineffectual, it is at least a protest. In registering his disapproval of Cornwall and

Regan's actions, we see that Gloucester is essentially a decent, well-intentioned character with a sense of justice. He tells Kent, 'I am sorry for thee, friend' and promises him: 'I'll entreat for thee' (plead on his behalf).

At the close of this scene we see Kent in a reflective mood in the stocks. We learn that Cordelia has made contact with him and is aware of Lear's plight. Kent plans to co-operate with Cordelia in restoring the kingdom to its previous state of order. Kent is a philosophical character who looks forward to the wheel of fortune turning full circle: 'Fortune, good night: smile once more; turn thy wheel'.

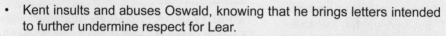

KEY POINTS

- Kent insults and abuses Oswald, knowing that he brings letters intended to further undermine respect for Lear.
- Cornwall is a brutal character who orders that Kent be placed in the stocks.
- Regan is the dominant partner in this marriage, overruling Cornwall, and insisting that Kent be left in the stocks for a much longer period. These characters are well-matched as both are fundamentally evil and cruel.
- Kent is a strong character who is devoid of (without) self-pity. When placed in the stocks his primary concern is that his stocking represents a gross insult to Lear's royalty.
- While Gloucester's protest against the stocking of Kent is weak and ineffectual, he is a decent character with a sense of justice.
- Cordelia has made contact with Kent who intends to co-operate with her in her planned efforts to restore the kingdom to a state of order.

ACT 2 Scene 3

In this brief scene we see that Edgar has been forced to adopt the disguise of a mad Bedlam beggar in order to avoid arrest: 'I will preserve myself; and am bethought to take the basest and most poorest shape'. His father's unjust treatment of him has reduced Edgar to the level of a hunted fugitive who cannot escape from the country because the ports are heavily guarded: 'Poor Turlygood! Poor Tom! That's something yet: Edgar I nothing am'.

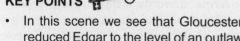

KEY POINTS

- In this scene we see that Gloucester's rash and foolish behaviour has reduced Edgar to the level of an outlaw who is forced to adopt the disguise of a mad Bedlam beggar in order to avoid arrest.
- Edgar seems to be a resilient character, capable of taking the vicissitudes (varying fortunes/ups and downs) of life in his stride.

ACT 2 Scene 4

In this dramatic scene, Lear is pushed to the very brink of insanity by the ingratitude of his daughters. He is deeply shaken when he arrives at Gloucester's castle to find his messenger, Kent, in the stocks. Lear struggles to come to terms with this public display of disrespect towards him: 'They durst not do it; they could not, would not do't; 'tis worse than murder to do upon respect such violent outrage'. The Fool takes this opportunity to once again remind Lear of the depth of his foolishness: 'Fathers that wear rags do make their children blind, but fathers that bear bags shall see their children kind'. When Kent details the treatment he received at the hands of Regan and Cornwall, Lear struggles to retain his mental and emotional balance: 'O how this mother swells up towards my heart! Hysterica passio, down, thou climbing sorrow, thy element's below!' While the Fool fears for Lear, his loyalty to his master is unwavering: 'But I will tarry; the fool will stay'. **When Lear is informed that neither Regan nor Cornwall will come to greet him, he is enraged, but can only rant powerlessly:** 'Vengeance! Plague! Death! Confusion!' Seeming to realise his powerlessness, Lear pathetically makes excuses for Regan and Cornwall and adopts a more conciliatory approach: 'The king would speak with Cornwall; the dear father would with his daughter speak. At this point he again senses and struggles to resist his rising insanity: 'O me, my heart, my rising heart! But down!'

When Regan and Cornwall finally appear, Lear complains to Regan about how Goneril has treated him, using animal imagery to again convey the unnaturalness of her ingratitude: 'O Regan, she hath tied sharp-tooth'd unkindness, like a vulture, here'. **Lear is shocked when Regan tells him to return to Goneril and apologise for his behaviour. What follows is quite pathetic as Lear kneels before Regan, pleading with her to take him in:** 'On my knees I beg that you'll vouchsafe me rainment, bed and food'. When Lear explains how Goneril has cut his retinue by half, he cannot contain his rage and again curses Goneril: 'All the stored vengeance of heaven fall on her ingrateful top!' When Regan suggests that Lear will curse her in a similar manner when 'the rash mood' is on him, he immediately rejects the idea of such a possibility: 'No, Regan, thou shalt never have my curse'. **Naively, he tells her that she is more aware of the natural bond that links parent and child and of the debt of gratitude she owes him:** '. . . thou better know'st the offices of nature, bond of childhood, effects of courtesy, dues of gratitude'.

All of Lear's delusions are shattered when Goneril arrives and Regan, in a public display of unity, takes her by the hand. When Cornwall tells Lear that it was he who put Kent in the stocks, Regan cuts short any further questions on the matter with a particularly callous remark: 'I pray you, father, being weak, seem so'. She again suggests that Lear should return to Goneril with his reduced retinue. The prospect of returning to Goneril nudges Lear ever closer to insanity. Describing Goneril as 'a disease that's in my flesh', Lear declares that he can stay with Regan, 'I and my hundred knights'. Regan quickly interposes, asking Lear why he needs so many knights and telling him that she will welcome no more than twenty-five of his followers. When Lear pathetically remarks, 'I gave you all –', Regan callously replies: 'And in good time you gave it'. **The two sisters now combine to humiliate Lear and strip him of his remaining shreds of dignity by whittling down the number of knights he is to be allowed.**

What follows clearly indicates that Lear's personal growth will be a lengthy, uneven process. Having attempted to measure love in terms of words in the opening scene of the play, Lear now attempts to measure it in terms of the number of knights each sister will allow him to retain. Addressing Goneril, Lear foolishly declares: 'Thy fifty yet doth double five-and-twenty, and thou art twice her love'. When Regan asks why he needs even a single knight, Lear's response is rational and clearly argued as he emphasises the importance of human dignity: '. . . our basest beggars are in the poorest thing superfluous: allow not nature more than nature needs, man's life is cheap as a beast's'. Now fully aware of the depth of his daughters' ingratitude ('unnatural hags'), Lear strives not to break down mentally and emotionally. He raves about the revenges he will have, but is, of course, powerless. He begs the gods to touch him with 'noble anger' so that he does not break down in tears. Lear knows he is now very close to losing his mental equilibrium: 'O fool, I shall go mad!'

Feeling that he has no option but to leave Gloucester's castle, Lear and his remaining followers move towards the gates of the castle. **Regan makes no attempt to stop her aged father leaving the relative comfort of the castle as he faces out into the stormy, exposed moors.** When Gloucester announces that Lear is 'in high rage' and points out the extremely harsh conditions that await him on the moors, Regan coldly replies: 'O, sir, to wilful men, the injuries they themselves procure must be their schoolmasters', before declaring: 'Shut up your doors'. We again see that Regan and Cornwall are well matched when the latter remarks, 'My Regan counsels well'.

KEY POINTS

- Lear is horrified and incredulous at the sight of his messenger (Kent) in the stocks – this action constitutes a gross and open insult to his royalty.
- The Fool continues to remind Lear of his foolishness. However, the Fool is unwaveringly loyal to Lear. Even though he fears for his master, he declares that he will remain with him.
- Lear is further shocked when Regan and Cornwall refuse to greet him when he arrives at Gloucester's castle. Initially enraged, he adopts a quieter approach when he seems to realise his powerlessness.
- Lear foolishly believes that Regan will treat him better than Goneril, but his delusions are quickly shattered when Goneril arrives and Regan takes her by the hand. Lear now realises that both sisters have been acting as one against him.
- The anguish he feels as a result of his daughters' filial ingratitude pushes Lear to the very brink of insanity.
- Lear senses and strives to resist the insanity rising within him.
- Lear leaves Gloucester's castle in a state of high dudgeon (in anger).

ACT 3 Scene 1

This scene opens with Kent asking a gentleman (who seems to be a supporter of the king) about the whereabouts of Lear. The gentleman informs Kent that Lear is out in the middle of the storm, raving at the elements and trying to outdo them in their fury. The gentleman reports that Lear 'strives in his little world of man to out-scorn the to-and-fro conflicting wind and rain'. **The outer, physical storm mirrors the inner storm that is raging in Lear's mind. Through the gentleman we learn of the Fool's unswerving loyalty to Lear. The Fool endures the harshness of the storm alongside his** master, trying to distract him from 'his heart-struck injuries'. Kent speaks of a division between Albany and Cornwall, although at this point this division is not yet out in the open ('. . . the face of it be cover'd with mutual cunning'). **Kent has many important roles in the play, one of which is maintaining the link between Cordelia and Lear.** It is Kent who informs the gentleman (and the audience) that the King of France is aware (through his spies) of Lear's plight. He also tells us of the French force that has landed in Dover for the purpose of rescuing Lear. '. . . from France there comes a power into this scattered kingdom'. Kent asks the gentleman to make his way to Dover as quickly as possible and tell Cordelia of Lear's 'unnatural and bemadding sorrow'. Kent ensures that Cordelia will know the message he carries comes from him by giving the gentleman a ring that Cordelia will recognise to be his. This scene ends with Kent going off to search for Lear.

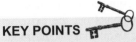

KEY POINTS

- The gentleman informs Kent of how Lear is raving at the elements, trying to outdo them in their fury.
- The ever-loyal Fool remains with Lear through the worst of the storm, trying to cheer him up and distract him from his anguish.
- Through Kent we learn of a growing rift between Albany and Cornwall and of a French force that has landed in England for the purpose of rescuing Lear.
- Kent acts as a link between Lear and Cordelia, keeping the latter updated on her father's situation.
- The counter-movement against the forces of evil has begun.

ACT 3 Scene 2

Lear is out on the moors in the eye of the storm, raving at the elements and urging them to destroy the universe that has created his ungrateful daughters: '. . . strike flat the thick rotundity of the world! Crack nature's moulds, all germens spill at once that make ingrateful man!' Here we see that Lear remains as egocentric (self-centred) as ever, calling out for the universal destruction because of his own intense pain. Concerned for his master, the Fool urges Lear to seek shelter from the storm, even if that means asking his daughters to forgive him: 'Here's a night pities neither wise men nor fools'. **Lear feels that the elements have joined forces with his 'two pernicious daughters' to inflict further suffering on him. Yet there are signs that he is growing through his suffering as he now sees himself as 'a poor, infirm, weak and despised old man'** – a self-image far removed from that in the opening scene when he arrogantly saw himself as an all-powerful dragon to be feared by all. Lear seems to sense that he is close to losing the balance of his mind, and tries to remain patient: 'No, I will be the pattern of all patience, I will say nothing'.

When Kent enters the scene, he underlines the unparalleled ferocity of this storm: 'Since I was a man such sheets of fire, such bursts of horrid thunder, such groans of roaring wind and rain I never remember to have heard'. **This violent tempest reflects both the storm in Lear's mind and the chaos in wider society.** As he reflects on his situation, it is difficult to disagree with Lear's assessment of himself as 'a man more sinned against than sinning'. That Lear has done wrong is incontrovertible (undeniable), but the punishment meted out to him is disproportionate to his wrongdoing. Lear is very conscious of his changing mental state: 'My wits begin to turn'. **He is now on the verge of insanity. Yet there are further indications of his personal growth in his compassion for the Fool:** 'Poor fool and knave, I have one part in my heart that's sorry yet for thee'. Kent's humanity and sympathy for Lear are evident when he guides him to a hovel in which he can shelter. This scene concludes with the Fool predicting that great disorder is coming to England: 'Then shall the realm of Albion come to great confusion'.

KEY POINTS

- The storm on the moor reflects both the tempest in Lear's mind and the chaos in wider society. Disorder in the world of man is mirrored by disorder in the world of nature.

- Lear's egocentric nature is still to be seen in his appeal to the elements to destroy the universe that created his 'pernicious daughters'.

- There are signs that Lear is growing through suffering in his vision of himself as 'a poor, weak, infirm and despised old man' and in his compassion for the Fool.

- The Fool remains with Lear through his darkest hours, trying to cheer him up. His concern for his master is genuine, and his unwavering loyalty very admirable.

- Kent's observations on the storm highlight its unequalled ferocity and, by extension, the inhuman callousness of Lear's unnatural daughters who have closed their doors against their aged father on the night of the worst storm in living memory.

- Kent's sympathy for Lear is to be seen as he guides him to shelter.

ACT 3 Scene 3

This scene opens with Gloucester expressing his disquiet (unease) at the manner in which Lear is being treated by his daughters and sons-in-law: **'I like not this unnatural dealing'.** This is obviously very ironic because Gloucester is utterly unaware of the 'unnatural dealing' of his own son, Edmund, to whom he is expressing his concerns. Edmund's falseness and hypocrisy are strikingly evident in his response: 'Most savage, and unnatural!' When Gloucester asks his guests if he can go to assist Lear, they take control of his house, warning him of the dire consequences that would follow any attempt he might make to support Lear in any way.

Gloucester goes on to confide in Edmund all that he knows about the developing military situation. He tells him about the rift between the dukes and, more importantly, about a letter he has received informing him of the French landing: 'These injuries the king now bears will be revenged home; there's part of a power already footed . . .' Despite the threats hanging over him, Gloucester departs to help Lear: **'If I die for it, as no less is threatened me, the king, my old master, must be relieved'.** Up to this point Gloucester has been a weak, foolish, ineffectual character – unlike Kent he did not have the courage to speak out against Lear's cruel, unjust treatment of Cordelia in the opening scene. **But now Gloucester displays a new strength of character, risking his life to help Lear.**

No sooner has Gloucester confided all in Edmund than the latter instantly decides to tell Cornwall everything. He does this in the hope of being rewarded for his 'loyalty' and in the full knowledge that his father will face death as a result of his callous, unnatural betrayal of him. **Edmund's ruthless philosophy is summed up in his declaration at the close of this scene: 'The younger rises when the old doth fall'.**

KEY POINTS

- Gloucester expresses his concern at the manner in which Lear is being treated, and is threatened with death if he attempts to assist the king.
- Gloucester confides in Edmund, telling him all that he knows about the counter-action against the new regime, as outlined in a letter informing him of the French landing at Dover.
- This scene sees a dramatic development in Gloucester's character – a man who was foolish and ineffectual in the early stages of the play now displays strength and courage in his determination to assist Lear.
- Edmund's utterly callous character is apparent in his decision to betray his father to Cornwall in order to advance himself.

ACT 3 Scene 4

This scene opens with Kent guiding Lear into a hovel. Kent's deep affection for Lear is evident in his response to Lear asking him if he will break his heart: 'I'd rather break mine own'. **In his state of mental and emotional torment, Lear is barely aware of his physical discomfort: '. . . the tempest in my mind doth from my senses take all feeling else save what beats there. Filial ingratitude!' When Lear reflects on the ingratitude of his daughters to whom his 'frank heart gave all', he realises that this is the cause of his insanity: 'O that way madness lies; let me shun that; no more of that.' We see further evidence of Lear's new sense of humanity as he ushers the Fool into the hovel ahead of him: 'In boy, go first'. Lear's personal growth is also to be seen in his new awareness of the poor whom, as king, he had neglected.** As he reflects on the plight of the 'poor naked wretches' that surround him, Lear reproaches (blames) himself for neglecting these, most needy of people: 'I have ta'en too little care of this!' **Most remarkably, Lear now preaches the doctrine of social justice,** suggesting that the wealthy should share some of their riches with the poor: 'Expose thyself to feel what wretches feel, that thou mayest shake the superflux to them and show the heavens more just'.

When Edgar, disguised as a madman enters the hovel, it is clear that Lear has now lost his sanity as he sees Poor Tom's destitution (poverty) and misery entirely in terms of his own experience: 'Hast thou given all to thy daughters? And art thou come to this?' When Kent respectfully explains that Poor Tom has no daughters, the old, fiery Lear is again to be seen: 'Death, traitor! Nothing could have subdued nature to such a lowness but his unkind daughters'. Lear can only see himself in Edgar and the pity he feels for Edgar, he also feels for himself. This scene offers the audience a contrast between Edgar's feigned (pretended) madness and Lear's genuine insanity, which is again to be seen when he calls Poor Tom 'a noble philosopher'. Lear once more uses animal imagery to convey the inhuman behaviour of his daughters, but now sees that he was partly responsible for making them what they have become: 'Judicious punishment! 'Twas this flesh begot these pelican daughters'.

With Lear once again displaying his ingrained flaws of egocentricity and rashness, we see that his personal growth is gradual and uneven – just as he seems to develop on a personal level, we see his old faults surface again. But the uneven nature of Lear's development adds to the realism of the play - while people can certainly learn from experience and become better and wiser individuals, it would be unrealistic to suggest that someone who is rash by nature could develop into a model of self-restraint and composure. Paradoxically, it is when Lear loses his sanity that he acquires true wisdom. Looking at the half-naked Edgar, Lear sees man reduced to his essence: '. . . unaccommodated man is no more but such a poor, bare, forked animal as thou art'. Wishing to reduce himself to the basic level of Poor Tom and the poor that surround them, Lear starts to tear off his clothes, symbols of material wealth and possessions that are now meaningless to him. The Fool remains with Lear, still endeavouring to boost his master's spirits as he encourages him to take shelter from the raging storm: 'Prithee nuncle, be contented; 'tis a naughty night to swim in'. However, the Fool has patently (clearly) become more serious in this scene as he seems to be filled with foreboding (anxiety).

When Gloucester arrives in the hovel to assist Lear, he condemns ungrateful children who mistreat their fathers: 'Our flesh and blood, my Lord, is grown so vile that it doth hate what gets it'. **Gloucester's loyalty to Lear is very admirable because, in attempting to assist his king, he puts his own life at serious risk:** '. . . my duty cannot suffer to obey in all your daughters' hard commands'. Kent perceives that Lear is drawing ever closer to complete insanity: 'His wits begin to unsettle'. Gloucester identifies with Lear's torment in that he too has been deeply pained by filial ingratitude: 'Thou say'st the king grows mad; I'll tell thee, friend, I am almost mad myself'. Of course, Gloucester is still blind to his misjudgement of his own sons, and of the grave injustice he has done Edgar.

KEY POINTS

- Lear welcomes the storm as a distraction from his inner suffering ('This tempest will not give me leave to ponder on things would hurt me more').

- Lear recognises that it is his daughters' ingratitude that lies at the root of his present mental problems, and strives not to think about their thanklessness ('O that way madness lies; let me shun that; no more of that').

- This scene provides us with much evidence of Lear's personal growth – we see his humanity in his kindness towards the Fool, whom he ushers into the hovel ahead of him, and in his newly developed social conscience which is apparent in his acknowledgement that, as king, he neglected the poor. Most dramatically, Lear now declares that the rich should share some of their wealth with the poor.

- When Edgar, disguised as Poor Tom, enters the hovel, Lear's flaws remain very much in evidence – he sees Edgar's plight entirely in relation to his own situation, asserting that only the new arrival's 'unkind daughters' could have reduced him to such a level of misery. In this scene it is apparent that Lear's growth to self-awareness will be gradual and uneven.

- Kent's concern and affection for Lear are immediately evident as he guides his master to a place of shelter and tells him that he would rather break his own heart than cause Lear any additional suffering.

- Gloucester demonstrates admirable loyalty to Lear, risking his own life to assist his king.

- The Fool remains with Lear, but is noticeably more serious as he seems to be very fearful for the future.

ACT 3 Scene 5

Edmund has already supplanted (displaced) Edgar as heir to his father's earldom, but is now impatient for his inheritance. We see the full extent of Edmund's ruthlessness in this scene when he betrays his father in the full knowledge that Gloucester will face severe punishment for his support for the king. The scene opens with Cornwall clearly intent on exacting revenge on Gloucester: 'I will have my revenge 'ere I depart his house'. Edmund hypocritically claims that it pains him to reveal his father's 'treason': 'O heavens! That this treason were not, or not I the detector!' In reality, Edmund does not hesitate to tell Cornwall of the letter implicating Gloucester in the French landing. In an aside, Edmund expresses his hope that Gloucester will be found comforting Lear, so that he will appear even more treacherous in Cornwall's eyes. His hypocrisy is again evident when he tells Cornwall: 'I will persevere in my course of loyalty, though the conflict be sore between that and my blood'.

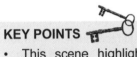

KEY POINTS

- This scene highlights Edmund's ruthlessness and hypocrisy as he continues with his unscrupulous, immoral pursuit of wealth and power.
- Cornwall appears to be as gullible as he is vengeful, being easily manipulated by the cunning Edmund.

ACT 3 Scene 6

Early in this scene, Kent states that Lear is now completely mad: 'All the power of his wits have given way to his impatience'. This scene is intriguing in the sense that it brings the three 'madmen' of the play together: Lear, who is genuinely insane, Edgar who has been forced to assume the disguise of a madman in order to avoid arrest and the Fool, the 'official madman' of the play whose verbal contributions combine the meaningless and the insightful. In his madness, Lear announces that, as king, he is going to put the 'she foxes' that are his daughters on trial: 'Arraign her first; 'tis Goneril . . . she kicked the poor king, her father'. He sees Edgar, in rags, as a 'robed man of justice', declaring that he, along with the Fool and Kent will sit in judgement of his cruel daughters. Both Kent and Edgar are deeply moved by the sight of this once-great king now reduced to the level of a madman. The concerned Kent urges Lear to be patient, clearly perceiving that anger exacerbates (worsens) his mental condition: 'O pity! Sir, where is the patience now, that you so oft have boasted to retain?' For his part, Edgar struggles to maintain his disguise as his tears flow in sympathy for the tormented old king: 'My tears begin to take his part so much, they'll mar my counterfeiting'. Lear cannot begin to understand his daughters' inhumanity, declaring that Regan is to be dissected in an attempt to see what 'makes these hard hearts'.

When the loyal Gloucester enters the scene, he tells Kent of a plot to kill the king, and instructs him to take the king to Dover, where he will find 'welcome and protection'. Gloucester stresses the urgency of the situation, urging Kent to take Lear to Dover immediately, and warning that a half an hour's delay would cost all of them their lives. As he reflects on Lear's suffering, the admirably philosophical Edgar concludes that his own pain pales into insignificance when compared to that of the king: 'How light and portable my pain seems now when that which makes me bend makes the king bow'.

The Fool says little in this, the final scene in which he plays a part. There is no room for the Fool's witticisms in this dark scene and, having done his best to help make Lear more self-aware, his dramatic function is fulfilled, and he is neither seen nor spoken of again.

KEY POINTS

- Lear is now completely insane – a fact twice confirmed by Kent ('All the power of his wits have given way to his impatience', '. . . his wits are gone').
- This scene brings the three 'madmen' of the play together in a scene which powerfully conveys the depth of Lear's torment.
- In his insanity, Lear puts his cruel daughters on trial.
- Both Kent and Edgar are deeply moved by Lear's intense suffering.
- The loyal Gloucester arrives to assist his king, informing Kent of a plot to kill Lear.
- Edgar dismisses his own pain when he sees the depth of Lear's anguish, showing himself to be a strong, philosophical character devoid of (without) self-pity.
- With Cordelia's forces gathered in Dover, the country is on the brink of war.

ACT 3 Scene 7

This is one of the most dramatic scenes in the play, indeed in any of the Shakespearian tragedies. It is memorable for the unspeakable savagery that sees Gloucester's eyes being cut from his head in an act of barbaric retribution (revenge) following Edmund's betrayal of his father. When Gloucester returns to his castle, he finds his enemies awaiting him, impatient to exact vengeance on him. Regan sets the tone for the appalling cruelty that follows when she declares: 'Hang him instantly!' Goneril prefers the idea of Gloucester experiencing more protracted (prolonged) suffering: 'Pluck out his eyes.' Cornwall urges Edmund to leave since '... the revenges we are bound to take upon your traitorous father are not fit for your beholding'. When he addresses Edmund as 'my lord of Gloucester', we learn how Edmund has been rewarded for betraying his own father.

Gloucester reminds his vengeful enemies that they are his guests, but his pleading is in vain. Since Goneril and Regan have no respect for the natural bond that ordinarily connects parent and child (Regan callously refers to Lear as 'the lunatic king'), they (along with Cornwall) are unlikely to be influenced by the natural bond

that should link a host and his guests. Gloucester addresses Regan as 'Unmerciful lady', which only prompts her to pluck his beard – a gesture expressing her disrespect for him. Bound to a chair, Gloucester courageously resigns himself to his fate: 'I am tied to the stake and I must stand the course'. When Regan questions him as to why he brought Lear to Dover, Gloucester's response is (in the light of what happens shortly after this exchange) charged with irony: 'Because I would not see thy cruel nails pluck out his poor old eyes, nor thy fierce fangs in his anointed flesh stick boarish fangs.' Here animal imagery is once again employed to highlight the inhumanity of Lear's unnatural daughters.

Gloucester believes in the idea of divine justice, declaring that he will see 'the winged vengeance overtake such children'. At this point, Cornwall, in an act of unimaginable barbarity, cuts one of Gloucester's eyes from his head. Anxious to outdo her husband in her cruelty, Regan demands that the second eye also be gouged out since 'one side will mock another; the other too'. However, one of Cornwall's servants now feels compelled to intervene, and draws his sword. As the servant and Cornwall fight, Regan stabs the servant in the back – but not before he has inflicted a mortal wound on Cornwall, whose visible pleasure in his sadistic torture of the helpless Gloucester is sickening: 'Out, vile jelly! Where is thy luster now?' In his darkness and pain, Gloucester calls out for Edmund, prompting Regan to heap mental torment onto his physical agony by delightedly informing him that it was Edmund who betrayed him: 'Thou call'st on him that hates thee; it was he that made the overtures of thy treason to us, who is too good to pity thee'. **It is hugely ironic that Gloucester acquires moral vision at the** **very moment that he loses his physical vision: 'O my follies! Then Edgar was abused. Kind gods, forgive me that, and prosper him!'** In a final act of cruelty, Regan orders the blind Gloucester to be thrown out at the gates, from where he can 'smell his way to Dover'.

The way in which the servants care for Gloucester's wounds, along with the courageous intervention of the servant who gave his life in an attempt to protect Gloucester, serve as reminders of man's humanity and better qualities.

KEY POINTS

- Gloucester's eyes are gouged out by Cornwall in an act of monstrous savagery.
- Edmund's villainy is now exposed and out in the open.
- The brave intervention of one of Cornwall's servants serves as a ray of light, a reminder of man's finer instincts in a particularly dark scene.
- It is one of the great ironies of the play that Gloucester acquires moral vision at the very moment that he loses his physical sight.

ACT 4 Scene 1

The opening lines of this scene reflect Edgar's optimism and lack of self-pity: 'The worst returns to laughter'. However, within seconds of this very positive observation, Edgar is horrified to see his blinded father being led by an old man. Gloucester's concern for the old man reflects his growing concern for others: 'Thy comforts can do me no good at all; thee they may hurt'. His burgeoning (rapidly growing) self-awareness is accompanied by a profound sense of despair: 'I have no way and therefore want no eyes; I stumbled when I saw . . .' Gloucester longs only to see his son Edgar again: 'Might I but live to see thee in my touch, I'd say I had my eyes again!' Ironically, the son he loves is within touching distance, but cannot yet reveal his true identity to the world at large. Gloucester now has a very dark view of the gods, believing that they kill men for their amusement: 'As flies to wanton boys, are we to the gods; they kill us for their sport'. He asks the disguised Edgar to guide him to Dover, but first requests the old man to 'bring some covering for this naked soul' (the disguised Edgar), another indication of his new sense of compassion and awareness of the needs of others. Gloucester is keenly aware of the strange times in which they live 'when madmen lead the blind'. Edgar finds it increasingly difficult to maintain his disguise because he is so deeply moved by his father's suffering: 'I cannot daub it further'. Like Cordelia, Edgar bears no ill feeling towards the father who wronged him.

One of the most interesting developments in Gloucester's character is his new sense of social justice which prompts him, as it did Lear, to call for the redistribution of wealth: 'So distribution should undo excess, and each man have enough.' In this scene, Gloucester is so overwhelmed by despondency that all he wants is to be brought to the cliffs of Dover, where he intends to take his own life.

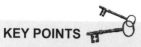

KEY POINTS

- While Edgar is a resilient (strong) and optimistic character, he is deeply shocked to see his blinded father being guided by an old man.

- We see considerable evidence of Gloucester's personal growth in his concern for the old man and in his desire to see wealth redistributed more fairly.

- Gloucester, overwhelmed by despair, sees no point to his life and only wants to reach Dover so that he can commit suicide by throwing himself from the cliffs.

ACT 4 Scene 2

The most striking aspect of this scene is Albany's dramatic personal transformation. He is so changed from the weak and ineffectual character we encountered earlier in the play as to be virtually unrecognisable. No sooner has Goneril mentioned 'our mild husband' than Oswald brings her attention to the 'new' Albany: '. . . never man so changed. I told him of the army that was landed; he smiled at it'. According to Oswald, Albany's loyalties appear to have totally changed: 'What most he should dislike seems pleasant to him; what like offensive'. **For all her bad points (and they are many), Goneril is a strong character, possessed of spirit and determination.** The French have landed, and she immediately takes control of the situation. Dismissing her husband's 'cowish terror', Goneril herself takes up arms in preparation for the imminent battle, sending Edmund ahead to help Cornwall organise his forces. After Edmund (now the Earl of Gloucester) leaves, Goneril admits to her love for him, contrasting him with the husband she despises: 'O the difference of man and man! To thee a woman's services are due.'

When Albany enters the scene, it is immediately clear that he is no longer the feeble character who was seemingly content to live in his wife's shadow. He tells Goneril exactly what he thinks of her, making no attempt to hide the feelings of contempt she inspires in him: 'O Goneril, you are not worth the dust that the rude wind blows in your face'. Albany declares that Goneril's unnatural behaviour (towards Lear, her father) will earn its own appropriate reward: 'She that herself will sliver and disbranch from her material sap, perforce must wither and come to deadly use'. Like Lear, Albany uses animal imagery to highlight the utterly unnatural behaviour of both Goneril and Regan, describing them as 'tigers, not daughters'. Goneril still refuses to accept that she is now dealing with a very different man to the one that she had dominated and controlled for so long: 'Milk-liver'd man!' Albany's hatred of his wife is so intense that he declares that he could physically tear her limb from limb: 'Were it my fitness to let these hands obey my blood, they are apt enough to dislocate and tear thy flesh and bones . . .' He describes her as 'a fiend' in 'woman's shape'. When Albany learns that Cornwall has been killed, he sees his death as an example of divine justice at work: 'This shows you are above you justicers, that these our nether crimes so speedily can venge!'

Goneril is not, in one sense, pleased with the news of Cornwall's death because, with her husband dead, Regan could emerge as her rival for Edmund's affections. Having learnt of Edmund's betrayal of his father and of his leaving his father's castle so that Cornwall and Regan could more freely torture him for his act of 'treason', Albany dedicates himself to avenging Gloucester's eyes: 'Gloucester, I live to thank thee for the love thou show'dst the king and to revenge thine eyes'. **This scene sees the forces of good gaining an unlikely ally in the shape of the dramatically transformed Albany.**

KEY POINTS

- In this scene Albany has clearly undergone a dramatic personal transformation – he is now an utterly different character from the feeble, subservient character we saw earlier in the play.
- Albany dedicates himself to avenging Gloucester's eyes.
- Like Gloucester, Albany believes in the concept of divine justice.
- Goneril now views Edmund as a suitable, indeed desirable, partner, but anticipates competition from Regan.
- The death of Cornwall, along with the dramatic transformation of Albany's character, are positive developments in terms of the battle the forces of good, led by Cordelia, will shortly face against the forces of evil.

ACT 4 Scene 3

This scene is set in the French camp at Dover. Kent asks the gentleman who had brought his message to Cordelia about her reaction to his report. The language and imagery used to describe Cordelia suggests that she is a royal, saintly figure: 'It seem'd she was a queen over her passion . . .', 'There she shook the holy figure from her heavenly eyes'. Kent again expresses his belief in the power of fate: 'It is the stars, the stars above us, govern our conditions'. Kent updates the audience on Lear's condition.

It seems that, in the midst of his bewilderment, Lear has moments of clarity: '. . . sometimes in his better tune remembers what we are come about.' Kent explains that Lear feels too ashamed of his cruel mistreatment of Cordelia to approach her:

'. . . burning shame detains him from Cordelia.' On the positive side, the fact that Lear is guilt-ridden over the wrongs he did his one true daughter is another indication of his personal growth.

KEY POINTS

- Cordelia is depicted as the personification of love, goodness and forgiveness in her response to Kent's report on Lear's condition.
- Kent once again displays his philosophical disposition as he restates his belief in the stars.
- Lear's shame at his grossly unjust treatment of Cordelia is another sign of his personal growth.

ACT 4 Scene 4

This scene vividly highlights Cordelia's loving, forgiving nature, while also revealing a steely side to her character as she prepares to lead her forces against the evil powers that now rule the kingdom. In Cordelia's words, Lear is now 'as mad as the vex'd sea'. He is wandering about, covered in flowers (a sign of insanity in all Shakespearian dramas) and singing aloud. Cordelia is again seen as the epitome (personification/embodiment) of loving forgiveness, declaring that she would give all of her 'outward worth' to the person who could help Lear to regain the balance of his mind. She understands her father's nature and orders that he be found before his 'ungoverned nature' prompts him to take his own life. Cordelia also impresses us with her composure and determination as she faces into a critical battle. When she is told that the British forces are marching towards them, she remains calm and unruffled, pointing out that her army stands ready: ''Tis known before; our preparation stands in expectation of them'.

At the close of this scene, Cordelia insists that her presence in England is not motivated by ambition for conquest or power, but by concern for her aged father and his rights: 'No blown ambition doth our arms incite, but love, dear love and our aged father's right'.

KEY POINTS

- This scene showcases Cordelia's kind, loving and forgiving nature.
- Cordelia also shows a new side to her character – a real determination to rescue her father from her evil sisters, who even now are plotting to kill Lear.
- Cordelia declares that she is not in England for any ambitious reason, but only out of concern for her aged father.

ACT 4 Scene 5

This scene sees Regan in conversation with Oswald, Goneril's personal servant and messenger. When Regan enquires about Albany's forces, Oswald, ever loyal to his evil mistress, replies that Goneril is the more capable military leader: 'Your sister is the better soldier'. **While the previous scene highlighted Cordelia's forgiving nature and the power of love, this scene reflects Regan's callous nature and the power of evil and jealousy. Regan regrets the fact that Gloucester was not killed earlier because, in his blinded state, he turns people against the present regime: 'It was great ignorance Gloucester's eyes being out to let him live.'**

This scene brings the growing rivalry between Goneril and Regan into clear focus. The evil sisters are now locked in what will prove to be a deadly conflict for Edmund's affections. It is rather ironic that sisters driven primarily by hatred and ruthless ambition should now find themselves at loggerheads over their love for the one man. Regan tells Oswald that she knows that Goneril 'does not love her husband', before going on reveal her jealous streak when she says that she has seen Goneril flirting with Edmund: 'She gave strange oeillades and most speaking looks to noble Edmund'. Utterly unprincipled, Regan pleads with Oswald to show her Goneril's letter, before going on to openly declare her love interest in Edmund: 'My lord is dead; Edmund and I have talked; and more convenient is he for my hand than for your lady's'. She asks Oswald to deliver a note from her to Edmund, while also requesting that he inform Goneril of what she has just said. Regan's cruelty is again to be seen at the close of this scene when she tells Oswald that he will be rewarded if he kills Gloucester: 'If you do chance to hear of that blind traitor, preferment falls on him that cuts him off'. The cowardly Oswald agrees to do what Regan asks, untroubled by the idea of serving two mistresses.

ACT 4 Scene 6

This is a very significant scene in a variety of ways. Firstly we see how Edgar restores his suicidal father's will to live by tricking him into believing that he has jumped from the cliffs of Dover and has survived because the gods wished him to live. While Edmund had deceived Gloucester early in the play, his actions were motivated by selfish ambition. In total contrast, Edgar's deception of Gloucester in this scene is motivated by loving concern.

Edgar tricks Gloucester into believing that he is on the very edge of the cliff, vividly describing his dizziness as he looks at the sheer drop from the top of the cliff, depicting the fishermen on the beach as being no bigger than mice, and even speaking of 'the murmuring surge' of the sea below. Taking his father by the hand, Edgar tells Gloucester that he is now within a foot of the edge. While Gloucester remains as credulous as ever, Edgar feels a little guilty at his deception, but justifies it on the basis that it is for the worthy cause of ridding his father of his despair: 'Why I do trifle thus with his despair is done to cure it'. When Gloucester falls forward, Edgar adopts the voice of a different persona – a man on the beach who witnessed Gloucester's 'fall' – and declares to the disoriented old man, 'Thy life's a miracle', before going on to claim that 'the clearest gods, who make them honours of men's impossibilities, have preserved thee'. (It is interesting, but not entirely surprising given his innate optimism, that Edgar retains his belief in the miraculous capabilities of 'the clearest

gods'). Gloucester believes this explanation of his 'survival' and announces that from this moment on he will 'bear affliction' and endure life's sorrows and difficulties until the gods decide it is his time to die.

The second major episode in this scene is the meeting of Lear and Gloucester. In his insanity, Lear continues to show signs of personal growth. Speaking of Goneril and Regan, Lear observes, 'They flattered me like a dog . . . they are not man o' their words: they told me I was everything; 'tis a lie, I am not ague-proof'. **The uneven nature of Lear's personal development is again to be seen in an outburst typical of the old, arrogant Lear:** 'Ay! Every inch a king: When I do stare, see how the subject quakes'. **What is particularly striking about this scene is the sense that the mad Lear sometimes makes.** He wisely tells the blind Gloucester,

'A man may see how this world goes with no eyes', before going on to deliver some sharp insights into the double standards and corruption that lie at the heart of the justice system: 'Through tattered clothes small vices do appear: Robes and furred gowns hide all. Plate sin with gold, and the strong lance of justice hurtless breaks; arm it in rags, a pigmy's straw doth pierce it'. He is also very sharp in his insights into the falseness of politicians: 'Get thee glass eyes; and like a scurvy politician, seem to see the things thou dost not'. **Edgar aptly sums up the wisdom that Lear, in his insanity, displays when he speaks of Lear's 'reason in madness!'** Lear even reveals a philosophical capacity when he reflects, 'When we are born, we cry that we are come to this great stage of fools'. Lear then lapses into nonsensical ramblings, prompting Gloucester to express his deep sympathy for the tormented old king: 'A sight most pitiful in the meanest wretch, past speaking of in a king'. He now sees his own suffering as insignificant compared to Lear's and reiterates his willingness to let the gods decide when he is to die, praying that he will never again be tempted to take his own life: 'You ever-gentle gods, take my breath from me; let not my worser spirit tempt me again to die before you please!' Gloucester also reflects that Lear has one daughter who redeems nature 'from the general curse which twain (the two evil, unnatural sisters) have brought her to'.

Having already saved his father's life once, Edgar is now called upon to save it a second time when the cowardly Oswald enters the scene, proclaiming to Gloucester: 'That eyeless head of this was first framed flesh to raise my fortunes'. As the despicable Oswald draws his sword, Edgar intervenes and, following a brief skirmish, kills the man he calls 'a serviceable villain', well-suited to serving his villainous mistress. **The letter that Goneril had written to Edmund is now in Edgar's hands. Edgar is horrified when he reads that Goneril wants Edmund to kill her husband ('You have many opportunities to cut him off'). The fact that she refers to 'our reciprocal vows' indicates that the unscrupulous, deceitful Edmund has won the hearts of both sisters and will use this to his advantage as he continues his relentless, ruthless pursuit of power.** Edgar struggles to come to terms with the depth of Goneril's evil: 'A plot upon her virtuous husband's life!'

At the close of this scene Gloucester envies the king his madness – he would prefer to be insane so that he would not be conscious of his own deep sorrow: 'Better I were distract, so should my thoughts be severed from my griefs'.

KEY POINTS

- Edgar deceives his father in order to restore his will to live.
- This scene brings the main plot and subplot together, with the insane Lear meeting the blind Gloucester.
- Lear displays considerable insight in his insanity – Edgar describes this phenomenon as 'reason in madness'.
- Goneril's callous, ruthless nature is reflected in the letter she sends Edmund, requesting him to kill Albany, her husband.
- Regan is equally evil, regretting that Gloucester was allowed to live, and ordering Oswald to kill him if he encounters him.
- The rivalry between the evil sisters over Edmund continues to grow in intensity.
- Edgar saves his father's life a second time when he kills his would-be assassin, the cowardly Oswald.
- While Gloucester is no longer suicidal, his torment is such that he envies Lear his insanity because, in his distracted state, he is unaware of his anguish.

ACT 4 Scene 7

This scene opens with Cordelia thanking Kent for his loyalty and devotion to Lear. She is sincerely thankful to Lear's most loyal subject for all that he has done for her father, despite Lear's mistreatment of him: 'O thou good Kent, how shall I live and work to match thy goodness?' Ever humble, Kent responds that to be acknowledged is to be 'o'er-paid'. This is a very moving scene, with Cordelia's forgiveness of her 'child-changed father' reinforcing our image of her as the very embodiment of love. In total contrast to the evil that pervaded the previous scene, this scene is full of positive emotions, with Cordelia not hesitating to forgive her father and doing everything possible to restore his sanity. She prays to the gods to 'cure this breach in his (Lear's) abused nature'. Like Edgar, Cordelia is a healing agent, whispering to the sleeping Lear: 'Restoration hang thy medicine on my lips; and let this kiss repair those violent harms that my two sisters have in thy reverence made!' She struggles to comprehend the depth of her sisters' cruelty. As she reflects on Lear being locked out to face the worst storm in living memory, she sadly remarks, 'Mine enemy's dog, though he had bit me, should have stood that night against my fire'.

When Lear awakens, he is confused, believing himself to be dead and Cordelia an angel: 'You do me wrong to take me out of the grave; thou art a soul in bliss; but I am bound upon a wheel of fire, that mine own tears do scald like molten lead.' The wheel of fire image suggests Lear's torment, while his tears are prompted by his feelings of guilt at his cruel mistreatment of Cordelia. As he gradually comes to his senses, he sees Cordelia, not as an angel, but as his loving daughter who is now asking for his blessing. Lear pleads with her not to mock him, describing himself as 'a very foolish fond old man' and acknowledging his mental difficulties: 'I fear I am not in my perfect mind'. In this lucid moment Lear shows how much he has grown on a personal level through his intense suffering. His feelings of guilt and shame are so strong that he declares himself willing to take his own life: 'If you have poison for me, I will drink it. I know you do not love me, for your sisters have, as I remember, done me wrong: You have some cause, they have not'. Cordelia's response shows her to be the epitome (embodiment) of tenderness and forgiveness: 'No cause, no cause'. As before, Cordelia does not express her feelings in any kind of effusive (gushing) manner, but there is no doubting the heartfelt sincerity of what she says to her aged and anguished father. Lear's new sense of personal awareness is again evident as he humbly asks for Cordelia's forgiveness: '. . . pray you now, forget and forgive: I am old and foolish'.

KEY POINTS

- In this very moving scene, Lear is reconciled with his one true daughter, Cordelia.
- Cordelia is portrayed as the personification of love, compassion and gentleness.
- Lear's lucid (clear-minded) moments show how much he has grown on a personal level through his deep personal suffering. In this scene he displays admirable self-knowledge and humility.

ACT 5 Scene 1

In this scene the critical battle between the forces of good and evil is imminent. Edmund is still not sure of Albany's support, describing him as being 'full of alteration and self-reproving'. Albany finds himself in a difficult situation – his sympathies lie with Lear and Cordelia, but his primary duty is to repel the French force that has landed at Dover and, in order to do this, he needs the military assistance of people he now despises. The rivalry between Goneril and Regan continues to intensify, threatening the unity of the English force. Regan asks Edmund directly if he loves her sister. His reply ('In honour'd love') in no way placates (appeases/calms) her. Regan is now consumed by jealousy: 'I shall never endure her: dear my lord, be not familiar with her'. Goneril is similarly obsessed by Edmund, declaring that she would sooner lose the battle than lose Edmund to Regan. However, her practical side quickly reasserts itself, as she demands unity in the face of the French, pointing out that all other matters can be addressed later.

Just before the battle commences, Edgar (still in disguise) arrives and gives Albany the letter from Goneril to Edmund which proves their treachery. He also tells Albany that, if he achieves victory, to sound the trumpet and he will produce a champion who will confirm the truth of the letter's contents.

Edmund's soliloquy at the close of this scene reinforces our image of him as a callous, immoral character. He delights in his deception and cynical manipulation of Goneril and Regan: 'To both these sisters have I sworn my love; each jealous of the other as the stung are of the adder'. He wonders which he shall take, knowing that 'neither can be enjoyed if both remain alive'. Edmund reflects on his need of Albany for the battle ahead, but wants him dead after the battle. While Goneril had earlier expressed her desire for Edmund to kill Albany, Edmund believes that it is Goneril who should arrange for her husband to be killed: 'Let her who would be rid of him arrange his speedy taking-off'. Edmund's total ruthlessness is further underlined by his decision to have both Cordelia and Lear executed after the battle, despite Albany having already stated his intention of sparing their lives. **While Edmund has nothing against either Lear or Cordelia on a personal level, anyone whom he perceives to be a potential threat in his quest for ultimate power is to be eliminated: '. . . for my state stands on me to defend, not to debate'.**

KEY POINTS

- Edmund's uncertainty regarding Albany's intentions points to the latter's dilemma – while his sympathies lie with Lear and Cordelia, his primary duty is to repel the French force that is now on English soil.
- The rivalry between Goneril and Regan in relation to Edmund has grown so intense and bitter that it now threatens the unity of the English force.
- Edgar gives Albany the letter proving Goneril's treachery, before going on to tell him that, after the battle, he can produce a champion who will defend the truth of the letter's contents.
- Edmund's ruthless ambition is reflected in his soliloquy at the close of this scene – he wants Albany, Cordelia and Lear to be killed because they are potential threats to his pursuit of power.

ACT 5 Scene 2

This brief scene is set on the battlefield. Edgar ensures that his father is safe and comfortable before leaving to join the battle. He returns almost immediately, with the grim news that Cordelia's forces have been defeated, and that Lear and Cordelia have been taken prisoner. While Gloucester is plunged into black despair ('No farther sir: a man may rot even here'), Edgar remains resilient, philosophically accepting life's varying fortunes: 'Men must endure their going hence, even as their coming hither: Ripeness is all . . .' In Edgar's view, death, like birth, is part of life, and what is most important is being prepared for and accepting of both.

ACT 5 Scene 3

With Lear and Cordelia now the prisoners of Edmund, their lives are clearly in great danger. Edmund has already stated his intention of killing them both in defiance of Albany's plan to pardon them. Cordelia remains as devoted as ever to Lear, telling him that she is sad only for him: 'For thee oppressed king am I cast down; myself could else out-frown false fortune's frown'. In his insanity, Lear looks forward to spending time in prison with Cordelia, where they will philosophise about the nature of life ('the mystery of things'). When Edmund orders that they be taken away, we again see the old fiery Lear: 'He that parts us shall bring a brand from heaven'. Without spelling out exactly what he wants done with them, Edmund leaves the captain who takes them away in no doubt as to what he expects of him: '. . . to be tender-minded does not become a sword'.

There appears to be some hope for Lear and Cordelia when Albany enters the scene, and asks that they be handed over to him. When Edmund replies that both have been imprisoned because of their potential ability to win popular support ('. . . to pluck the common bosom on his side'), he speaks to Albany as if he were his equal ('The question of Cordelia and her father requires a fitter time'). Angered by the content and tone of Edmund's remarks, Albany immediately asserts his authority over him: 'Sir, by your patience, I hold you but a subject of this war, not a brother'. When Goneril and Regan spring to Edmund's defence, they inevitably and immediately begin to quarrel. The jealousy between the two evil sisters reaches a dramatic climax in this final scene. When Regan publicly declares Edmund to be her 'lord and master', she has already been poisoned by Goneril. Albany now arrests both Edmund and Goneril ('this gilded serpent') on charges of treason, the proof for which is to be found in Goneril's letter to Edmund. Acting on the instructions of the disguised Edgar, Albany now asks that the trumpet be sounded. If no champion appears to defend the truth of his accusations, Albany declares that he will himself engage Edmund in trial by combat and throws down a glove. However, this does not prove necessary. After Albany orders the trumpet to sound, Edgar (still in disguise) enters.

Edgar now accuses Edmund of treachery: '. . . thou art a traitor, false to thy gods, thy brother, and thy father, conspirant against this high illustrious prince'. While the rules of knighthood allow Edmund to ignore a challenge from an unknown warrior, he immediately accepts the challenge: 'What safe and nicely I might well delay by rule of knighthood, I disdain and spurn: Back do I toss these treasons to thy head'. The fight is brief, with Edgar quickly inflicting a mortal blow on Edmund. When Goneril tells Edmund that he was not obliged 'to answer an unknown opposite', Albany contemptuously dismisses her: 'Shut your mouth, dame'. Albany then shows Edmund the letter Edgar had given him, confirming his and Goneril's treachery.

Edmund redeems himself to some extent in the final scene. He makes no attempt to deny the truth of the letter's contents: 'What you have charged me with, that have I done; and more, much more; the time will bring it out...' Edmund then forgives the man who has killed him, prompting a generous response from Edgar who now, in turn, forgives the brother who had brought such chaos and pain into his world: 'Let's exchange charity'. The manner in which events have developed reinforces Edgar's belief in the idea of divine justice: 'The gods are

34

just, and of our pleasant vices make instruments to plague us'. **Edmund accepts his fate in a philosophical manner: 'The wheel is come full circle.'** Edgar now gives a lengthy account of his life since he had to adopt a new identity, culminating in the news that Gloucester had died between 'two extremes of passion, joy and guilt' when Edgar revealed his true identity to him. **The high drama that characterises the closing scene continues with news of other dramatic incidents: Goneril is dead after committing suicide, as is Regan, who was poisoned by her sister. It is very ironic that these callous sisters died as a result of their shared love for Edmund, who derives some grim satisfaction from the fact that he was loved by two women: 'Yet Edmund was beloved: the one the other poisoned for my sake, and after slew herself'. Remarkably, it is Edmund who draws everyone's attention back to Lear and Cordelia, revealing a further hint of humanity before he dies: '. . . some good I mean to do, despite of mine own nature'.** Announcing that he has already signed Lear and Cordelia's death warrants, he asks that someone go to the castle where they are imprisoned with the utmost haste. Tragically, no sooner has Edgar departed for the castle than Lear arrives, carrying Cordelia's lifeless body in his arms. **Lear's suffering and sense of loss are so intense as to be almost beyond description.** He cannot comprehend how everyone else is not as devastated as he is: 'Howl! howl! howl! howl! O, you are men of stones . . .' We again see the old, fiery Lear as he rages against the world: 'A plague upon you, murderers, traitors all!' Despite his advanced age, Lear killed the man that hanged Cordelia. Interestingly, Lear finally recognises Kent ('Are

you not Kent?'), who goes on to explain that he was Caius, his servant who, from the start, had followed Lear's 'sad steps'. Kent aptly sums up the grim and desolate mood at the close of the play when he observes that 'all's cheerless, dark and deadly'.

When an officer enters with news of Edmund's death, Albany dismisses it as 'but a trifle here', before going on to describe how things would be in the kingdom under the new regime: 'All friends shall taste the wages of their virtue, and all foes the cup of their deservings'. By now the heartbroken Lear, unable to understand why 'a dog, a horse, a rat have life', and Cordelia 'no breath at all' is close to death himself. **As Lear slips into his final sleep, an attempt is made to revive him, but Kent immediately intervenes. Ever protective of his royal master, Kent points out that Lear has suffered enough: 'Vex not his ghost: O let him pass! He hates him that would upon the rack of this tough world stretch him out longer'.** The rack image (like the earlier 'wheel of fire' image) dramatically highlights the extent of Lear's torment.

In the closing lines of the play, Albany (assuming the role of kingmaker) addresses Kent and Edgar as 'friends of my soul', before stating that they both should rule in the kingdom from now on, 'and the gored state sustain'. However, Kent's primary duty is to Lear, and death is no barrier to his loyalty and devotion to his master: 'I have a journey, sir, shortly to go: my master calls me, I must not say no'. Kent plans to take his own life so that he can continue to serve Lear in the next life, leaving Albany and Edgar to restore the 'gored state' to health.

KEY POINTS

- The closing scene is filled with dramatic incidents, becoming increasingly grimmer with each new revelation.

- Lear and Cordelia are arrested. Edmund's intention is to have both executed because both have the ability to attract popular support and consequently may pose a threat to his political ambitions.

- When Edmund addresses Albany as if he were his equal, the latter puts him firmly in his place, pointing out that he is his 'subject', not his 'brother'.

- Albany arrests both Goneril and Edmund on charges of 'capital treason'.
- Edgar comes forward as Albany's champion to defend the authenticity (truthfulness) of Goneril's letter to Edmund (the document that proves their treason).
- After Edgar deals a fatal blow to Edmund, he reveals his true identity and the two are reconciled.
- Edmund redeems himself to some extent in the final scene by admitting to his crimes and by making a belated effort to do some good before he dies by revealing that he has signed Lear and Cordelia's death warrants.
- When Lear arrives, carrying his beloved Cordelia's lifeless body, his grief knows no bounds.
- Gloucester dies between two extremes of passion, joy and grief, after Edgar reveals his true identity to him.
- The love rivalry between Goneril and Regan over Edmund reaches a dramatic climax in this scene, with Goneril poisoning Regan, before dying by her own hand after her treachery has been revealed.
- Kent remains unwaveringly loyal to Lear, insisting that there be no attempt to revive him as he nears death because he has already suffered enough 'upon the rack of this tough world'. Kent's loyalty to Lear extends beyond the physical world – he intends to take his own life so that he may serve his master in the next world.
- It will fall to Albany and Edgar to restore the kingdom to a state of order and health.

Guidelines for Answering Exam Questions

Structure your Answer

1 A brief plan – this should be no more than key words or phrases.

2 An introduction – this should outline your general response to the question.

3 Aim for a points-based answer, avoiding excessive narrative.

4 Make one main point per paragraph.

5 Points should be discussed in a logical order.

6 The opening sentence in each paragraph (the paragraph sentence) should state the main point of the paragraph.

7 Maintain focus on, and refer back to, the terms of the question.

8 Support your points by close reference to, and quotation from, the text.

9 A brief conclusion.

Main Areas for Exam

1 The manner in which characters are portrayed.

2 The importance / role / dramatic function of particular characters.

3 Themes.

4 Key scenes.

5 Soliloquys.

6 Language, imagery and symbolism.

7 Your personal response to the play.

Exam Topics

1. *'Despite his serious flaws, the audience remains sympathetic towards Lear.'*

If the play is to work as a tragedy, we must retain a degree of sympathy for the protagonist (central character), King Lear through to the end of the play. While Lear is a deeply flawed character who is the architect of his own downfall, we ultimately see him as 'a man more sinned against than sinning'. While Lear clearly does wrong, the greater wrongs are done to him. He earns our sympathy because he is pained to the point of insanity by the unnatural behaviour of his 'pelican daughters' and elicits our admiration because he demonstrates a capacity to grow through his intense personal suffering. It is also significant that Shakespeare encourages us to see Lear in the same positive light as those characters in the play that we admire.

The dramatic opening scene brings Lear's serious and related flaws into sharp focus. We see the very harmful effects of his arrogance, his moral blindness, his gullibility and, particularly, his rashness. The love test dramatically underscores (underlines) Lear's foolishness: 'Which of you shall we say doth love us most?' His ego demands that his daughters flatter him and Goneril and Regan immediately try to out-do each other in their professions of love for their credulous father. Lear's treatment of both Cordelia and Kent is extremely harsh and unjust. Cordelia is disowned and disinherited simply for refusing to pander to Lear's ego ('Here I disclaim all my paternal care, propinquity and property of love'), while Kent is banished for bluntly telling Lear to reverse his 'hideous rashness' and for describing his treatment of Cordelia as 'evil'. **The Lear that we see in the opening scene is an utterly unappealing, unsympathetic character.**

While Lear is undeniably the architect of his own downfall, our initial disapproval of him ultimately develops into a profound sympathy when we see the intensity of his suffering. While

Lear's cruelty is impulsive and unthinking, Goneril and Regan's mistreatment of Lear is coldly pre-meditated. They conspire to strip Lear of his remaining power and dignity: 'Pray you sister, let us sit together'. Lear is profoundly shocked by the disrespect shown to him first by Goneril's servants, and then by Goneril herself ('Are you our daughter?'). He is pained by his sense of powerlessness: 'I am ashamed that thou hast power to shake my manhood thus'. We pity Lear as he senses his growing lack of control over himself ('O let me not be mad, not mad sweet heaven!'), others, and events in general. The stocking of Kent constitutes a deliberate, public show of disrespect towards Lear that shakes him to the very core of his being: 'They could not, would not do it: 'tis worse than murder to do upon respect such violent outrage'. Lear's pitiful running between sisters only sees him stripped of his remaining power and dignity when Goneril and Regan refuse to allow him to keep even a single knight: 'What need one?' We cannot but sympathise with Lear as he pleads with the gods not to let him break down completely in the face of Goneril and Regan's heartless behaviour: '. . . this heart shall break into a hundred thousand flaws, or ere I'll weep'. **The storm scene highlights the intensity of Lear's physical and mental suffering.** Callously locked out by Regan, the frail old man is exposed to the ferocity of the elements. The pain that drives Lear to insanity is caused by the ingratitude of his 'pelican daughters'. The old king is a particularly pathetic figure in the mock trial scene as he struggles to comprehend his daughters' unnatural behaviour: 'Is there any cause in nature that makes these hard hearts?' Like Edgar, the audience is deeply moved by Lear's anguish: 'My tears begin to take his part so much, they'll mar my counterfeiting'. Finally, it is impossible not to feel profoundly sympathetic towards Lear when he carries Cordelia's lifeless body onto the stage: 'Cordelia, Cordelia, stay a little'. The images of the wheel of fire and the rack effectively suggest the intensity of Lear's suffering. **By the closing scene, we feel that Lear has paid an inordinately high price for his personal failings.**

We also admire Lear for growing through suffering. His pain has a humanising, ennobling effect, and he consequently ends the play a better, wiser, more humble man. Lear gradually learns to see himself more clearly ('I am a very foolish, fond old man'), recognises his wrongdoing ('I did her wrong'), and is filled with guilt and shame at his mistreatment of Cordelia ('If you have poison for me I will drink it'). He ultimately acquires humility, asking for Cordelia's forgiveness ('Pray you now, forgive and forget') and comes to see others in a clear light, recognising that Goneril and Regan flattered him 'like a dog'. He acquires a social conscience, regretting his failure to look after the poor: 'O, I have ta'en too little care of this!' Remarkably, Lear even comes to preach the idea of social justice, arguing that wealth should be distributed more equitably: 'Expose thyself to feel what wretches feel that thou may shake the superflux to them and show the heavens more just'. We admire the manner in which Lear grows in wisdom. He becomes aware of corruption in high places, and of the absence of fairness in the administration of justice in the kingdom: 'Robes and furred gowns hide all. Plate sin with gold

and the strong lance of justice hurtless breaks; arm it in rags, a pigmy's straw doth break it'.

The remarkable loyalty of such characters as Kent, the Fool and Gloucester reminds us of an earlier, greater Lear. Kent returns in disguise to serve the king who banished him. His loyalty to Lear is total: 'My life I never held but as a pawn to wage against thine enemies'. Kent's loyalty to Lear is such that he is even prepared to follow him into the next world: 'I have a journey, sir, shortly to go. My master calls me, I must not say no'. The Fool remains with Lear throughout his descent into insanity and endures the worst storm in living memory alongside him. We also see Gloucester risking his life to help Lear. We realise that Lear must essentially be a good and noble character to inspire such unwavering loyalty and respect. We gradually come to see Lear in the same light as those characters who admire him.

In conclusion, Lear displays no redeeming features in the dramatic opening scene. In fact, his foolish and harsh behaviour inevitably alienates the audience. However, Shakespeare ensures that we ultimately sympathise with Lear by powerfully evoking his intense personal suffering. **We realise that Lear is the author of his own demise, but ultimately we see him more as victim than villain. We also come to admire Lear for his acquisition of wisdom, self-awareness and humility.**

---

2. 'Lear grows through a process of intense personal suffering, ending the play a better and wiser man.'

The personal growth of the central character is the dominant theme of the play, King Lear. When we meet Lear in the opening scene of the play, he is a deeply flawed and utterly unappealing character. He is arrogant, egocentric (self-centred), spiritually blind. and rash. However, Lear grows through suffering, gradually acquiring humility, self-knowledge and wisdom. **By the close of the play we feel both pity and admiration for the man who appeared to be**

nothing more than a cruel, foolish tyrant in the dramatic opening scene.

The opening scene dramatically highlights Lear's weaknesses. Lear is a foolish character – he divides his kingdom on the basis of a ridiculous love-test, believing that he can measure love in terms of words: 'Which of you shall we say doth love us most?' Goneril and Regan do not hesitate to exploit their ageing father's **gullible** nature. Lear is also extremely **rash**, disowning and disinheriting Cordelia because she refuses to flatter him: 'Here I disclaim all my paternal care, propinquity and property of blood . . .' He also banishes Kent for bluntly telling him that he is doing 'evil'. Through Goneril we learn that Lear has always been a **fiery** character ('The best and soundest of his time hath been but rash'). Accustomed to unquestioning obedience, Lear has grown **arrogant**. He is outraged by Kent's intervention: 'Come not between the dragon and his wrath'. The dragon image indicates that **Lear lacks self-knowledge**, suggesting that he sees himself as an all-powerful being, a 'dragon' whose anger must be feared. Regan remarks that Lear 'hath ever but slenderly known himself'. **Lear must acquire self-knowledge, before coming to understand others and life in general. He is spiritually blind at the start of the play, but through suffering gains true vision, ultimately coming to see himself and the wider world more clearly.**

Lear's personal growth is gradual and uneven. In contrast to Gloucester who gains insight (understanding) in a very sudden manner, Lear's path to self-knowledge and insight is a long, painful one. It must also be pointed out that even as Lear grows in wisdom, he occasionally shows signs of his earlier failings. At different times in the play, Lear displays the foolishness, arrogance, rashness and egocentricity (self-centredness) so dramatically in evidence in the opening scene. **However, Lear's transformation is all the more credible (believable) because it is not a simple process.**

Lear takes his first painful steps on the road to self-knowledge when he is stung by Goneril's 'marble-hearted' ingratitude. Once Goneril has her share of the kingdom, she has no need to flatter or humour Lear any longer. Encouraged by their mistress, Goneril's servants treat Lear with thinly-disguised contempt, while she herself expresses her impatience with his 'insolent retinue' (bad-mannered followers). **Lear is stunned to find himself treated, not as an all-powerful king, but as an irritating old man:** 'Are you our daughter?' Not only does he have difficulty recognising his daughter, he has difficulty recognising himself: 'Does any here know me? This is not Lear. . . . Who is it can tell me who I am?' **Lear's self-image is shaken by Goneril's display of filial ingratitude (which he describes as being 'sharper than a serpent's tooth') and he painfully acknowledges his own foolishness and lack of judgement: 'O Lear, Lear, Lear! Beat at this gate that let thy folly in and thy dear judgement out!'** Lear's anguish (mental/emotional suffering) is heightened by his awareness of his own powerlessness: 'I am ashamed that thou hast power to shake my manhood thus'. However, even though Lear has gained a degree of self-knowledge, he still displays the rashness that caused so much harm in the opening scene. Goneril is cursed in the strongest terms imaginable: 'Into her womb convey sterility . . . .'

The next step on the road to self-knowledge is taken when, speaking of Cordelia, Lear remarks to the Fool, 'I did her wrong'. It is ironic that as Lear begins to gain insight he simultaneously edges closer to insanity. Shocked by Goneril's ingratitude and pained by the knowledge that he gave her the power to humiliate him, Lear struggles to keep his sanity: 'O let me not be mad, not mad sweet heaven!' While the disintegration of his self-image lies at the root of Lear's loss of sanity, the onset (beginning) of madness is accelerated by his towering rages.

Lear is foolish to believe that Regan will treat him better than Goneril, but again learns through painful experience. When he arrives at Regan's castle, he is horrified to find his servant Kent in the stocks: 'They could not, would not do it; 'tis worse than murder to do upon respect such violent outrage'. Stung by this public insult, he senses the madness rising up within him: 'O how this mother (disease) swells up toward my heart!' Lear initially refuses to believe that Regan could be as ungrateful as Goneril: 'Thou shall never have my curse . . . thou better know'st the offices of nature, bond of childhood, effects of courtesy, dues of gratitude'. However, when Goneril arrives and takes Regan by the hand, it is clear that the two sisters are acting as one against Lear to strip him of his remaining power and dignity. Regan coldly reminds Lear of his powerlessness in a strikingly callous remark: 'I pray you father, being weak, seem so'. We see how much Lear still has to learn when he tries to measure love in terms of the number of knights each sister will allow him to have. He tells Goneril: 'Thy fifty yet doth double five-and-twenty, and thou art twice her love'. When his daughters refuse to allow him to keep even a single knight, Lear rants powerlessly, threatening them with 'the terrors of the earth'. **However, he continues to grow through suffering, showing signs of self-knowledge when he describes himself as 'a poor old man as full of grief as age'.** Sadly, he moves ever closer to insanity: 'O fool, I shall go mad!'

In the storm scene Lear's suffering is so intense that he finally loses his sanity. Kent tells us that 'all the power of his wits have given way to his impatience'. **The positive aspect to Lear's torment is that he paradoxically acquires 'reason in madness'.** He sees himself for what he is: 'A poor, infirm, weak and despised old man'. He shows an admirable concern for others, ushering the Fool into the hovel ahead of him ('I have one part in my heart that's sorry yet for thee'). He also acquires a social conscience, realising that he neglected the poor who do not even have adequate shelter from the storm: 'O, I have taken too little care of this'. Lear even preaches the idea of social justice, suggesting that wealth should be distributed more fairly: 'Expose thyself to feel what wretches feel that thou mayest shake the superflux to them and show the heavens more just'. We see further evidence of Lear's new-found wisdom when he sees Poor Tom as an example of the reality of humankind: 'A poor bare forked animal'.

It must be pointed out that even as Lear gradually grows and learns, he continues to display some of his old failings. This fact makes his personal transformation more realistic – he doesn't change suddenly or completely. On the heath Lear cries out for universal destruction because of his own intense suffering: 'And thou all-shaking thunder, strike flat the thick rotundity of the world'. This is a reminder of **Lear's egocentric (self-centred) nature.** He views everything in terms of his own

experience, concluding that Poor Tom could only have been reduced to his miserable state by his ungrateful daughters. When Kent points out that Poor Tom has no daughters, we again see **Lear's rash and fiery nature:** 'Death traitor! Nothing could have subdued nature to such a lowness but his unkind daughters'.

The pain of his daughters' filial ingratitude is so intense that Lear almost welcomes the storm as a distraction, reflecting that it 'will not give me leave to ponder on things would hurt me more'. On the heath, Lear occasionally becomes tranquil, but, when he calms down, he remembers how his daughters have mistreated him and another towering rage follows. **The mock trial highlights Lear's inner torment as he struggles to understand his daughters' 'hard hearts'. Lear continues to grow through his suffering, now acknowledging that Goneril and Regan flattered him 'like a dog'. However, the gradual, uneven nature of his personal development is again apparent when he arrogantly declares, 'I am the king himself . . . When I do stare, see how the subject quakes'.** Here we are reminded of the dragon image from the opening scene.

There are many examples of what Edgar describes as Lear's 'reason in madness'. Lear wisely tells the blind Gloucester that 'a man may see how this world goes with no eyes'. He comes to realise that the world is unjust and corrupt, observing that the rich can avoid justice, while the poor are always punished for any wrongdoing: 'Through tattered clothes small vices do appear: robes and furred gowns hide all'.

We get further evidence of Lear's personal development when his sense of 'burning shame' prevents him from rushing to Cordelia. We are reminded of the intensity of Lear's suffering when he finally meets his beloved daughter: 'I am bound upon a wheel of fire that mine own tears do scald like molten lead'. The dramatic nature of Lear's transformation is apparent when he describes himself as 'a very foolish, fond old man' and begs Cordelia's forgiveness ('. . . pray you now, forgive and forget'). He is so contrite (guilty) that he is even prepared to drink poison.

The closing scene brings unbearable anguish for Lear when he carries Cordelia's lifeless body onto the stage: 'Howl, howl, howl, howl! O, you are men of stones'. This dramatic scene reminds us that in some ways Lear remains unchanged. We again see his rashness in the immediate aftermath of Cordelia's murder: 'A plague upon you, murderers, traitors all'. **However, while Lear's personal transformation may not be total, it is certainly dramatic. We cannot but feel admiration for a man who acquires wisdom and humility through intense personal suffering. In the course of the play Lear is truly stretched 'upon the rack of this tough world', but ends the play a better and wiser man.**

3. 'King Lear – A Tragic Hero?'

King Lear is a true tragic hero. As the play opens he is a king with all the power and prestige that accompany this position. A tragic hero possesses a major flaw which brings about a catastrophe (disaster). Lear's tragic flaw is his rashness. Underlying this rashness are his arrogance, spiritual blindness and lack of judgement. The catastrophe brought about by Lear's flawed character causes immense suffering for Lear and for others. Lear descends from a position of absolute power to one where he owns nothing except the clothes on his back, while his kingdom is plunged into a state of chaos because of his tragic mistakes. As a tragic hero, Lear should retain our sympathy (to some degree, at least) and, as the play unfolds, we feel both pity and admiration for him. He grows through suffering, ultimately becoming a better and wiser man. What really casts Lear in the role of a tragic hero is the fact that wisdom and humility come too late for him to alter the disastrous sequence of events caused by his destructive rashness. The mood at the close of the play is particularly bleak as the audience is overwhelmed by a terrible sense of tragedy.

The play opens with Lear as a figure of immense power and authority. He is 'every inch a king'. He is almost a god-like figure as he leans over the map and proclaims how he will divide up the kingdom. His subjects are loyal and respectful. Kent addresses Lear in reverential tones ('Royal Lear whom I have ever honoured as my king, loved as my father . . .'), before going on to deliver a blunt warning to his master after he has disowned and disinherited Cordelia: 'Reserve thy state, and in thy best consideration, check this hideous rashness'. The autocratic (tyrannical) Lear sees himself as an all-powerful being as he warns Kent, 'Come not between the dragon and his wrath . . .'

However, for all his power, Lear is a flawed character. It is his human weaknesses that bring about his downfall and cause so much suffering for both himself and others. In this sense, he is the typical tragic hero. Lear is dangerously rash in his decision-making. He is arrogant and lacking in judgement and self-knowledge. Lear's rashness is the main cause of the catastrophe which affects both himself and his entire kingdom. He disowns Cordelia, his one true daughter: 'Here I disclaim all my paternal care, propinquity and property of blood . . .' In this one moment of terrible impetuosity, Lear sets in motion a train of disastrous events which lead to his own downfall and to the deaths of many of the participants in the opening scene. He unleashes evil forces which ultimately assume complete control of his kingdom. In cutting himself off from his one true daughter, Lear puts himself at the mercy of Goneril and Regan – a decision he lives to regret. By the close of the opening scene, the evil sisters are already conspiring (secretly plotting) against Lear: 'Pray you, let us hit together . . .' Lear's destructive rashness is also to be seen in his impulsive decision to banish Kent. Not only does Lear banish his most loyal servant for attempting to make him aware of his foolishness, he also threatens him with capital punishment (i.e. death).

Lear pays a high price for his human

weaknesses as he is driven to the point of insanity by Goneril and Regan's ingratitude and callousness (lack of feeling). While we realise that Lear is the architect of his own downfall, we still sympathise with him as he is rejected and belittled by his ungrateful daughters. Stung by Goneril's 'marble-hearted' ingratitude, Lear naively expects Regan to treat him better, only to realise that his two daughters are acting as one against him. Regan coldly reminds Lear of his powerlessness: 'I pray you father, being weak, seem so'. The two sisters strip Lear of his remaining power and dignity when they refuse to allow him to have even a single knight, coldly asking, 'What need one?' Locked out in the worst storm in living memory, Lear struggles in vain to retain his sanity. The pain of his daughters' filial ingratitude is such that he calls out for universal destruction: 'And thou all-shaking thunder, smite flat the thick rotundity of the world! Crack nature's moulds, all germens spill at once that make ingrateful man!' In the mock trial scene, Lear pathetically tries to understand his daughters' 'hard hearts'. **The images of the wheel of fire ('I am bound upon a wheel of fire that mine own tears do scald like molten lead') and the rack (used by Kent in the closing scene) underline the intensity of Lear's suffering.**

As Lear loses his sanity the forces of darkness, unleashed by his initial foolishness, take complete control of his world. Evil is depressingly dominant for much of the play because Lear gives it the opportunity to thrive. Edgar is reduced to the level of a mad beggar by Edmund's scheming, Gloucester is savagely tortured for going to assist Lear, while Goneril and Regan plumb new depths of evil in their rivalry over Edmund.

Like all great tragic heroes, Lear comes to acknowledge his own mistakes. He grows through suffering. He realises that he did Cordelia wrong and, towards the close of the play, begs her forgiveness ('Pray you now, forgive and forget'). He realises that Goneril and Regan flattered him 'like a dog'. He comes to see himself as 'a poor, infirm, weak, despised old man'. He also acquires a social conscience,

recognising that he neglected the poor when he was king ('O, I have taken too little care of this'). We see his compassion for others as he ushers the Fool into the hovel ahead of him ('In boy, go first'). He achieves a degree of wisdom, declaring that man is 'a poor bare forked animal'. He also comes to see that the system of justice is corrupt because 'robes and furred gowns hide all' (i.e. the rich avoid justice while the poor are always punished for any wrongdoing).

Lear is a classic tragic hero in that while he becomes a better and wiser man, his acquisition of self-knowledge comes too late for him to undo the harm that he has done. The hope offered by the counter-movement against evil is all-too-brief. The counter-action against the forces of evil begins almost as soon as Cordelia and Kent are unjustly banished by Lear. The two are in regular contact and Kent looks forward to co-operating with Cordelia in setting right the wrongs done to Lear ('seeking to give losses their remedies'). Gloucester also goes to Lear's assistance: '. . . the king, my old master, must be relieved.' Hope is heightened when Lear and Cordelia are reconciled. However, the defeat of Cordelia's forces extinguishes this hope and from this point Lear's suffering reaches new and heartbreaking levels of intensity. Cordelia is hanged after Edmund ordered her execution, and Lear's grief knows no bounds: 'Howl, howl, howl, howl! O, you are men of stones'. **The happiness that Lear had anticipated following his reconciliation with Cordelia is cruelly snatched from him:** 'Why should a dog, a horse, a rat, have life and thou no life at all?' This poignant scene brings the full extent of the tragedy into sharp focus. Lear dies, having truly been stretched 'upon the rack of this tough world'.

The ending of the play is particularly bleak. Lear and Cordelia are both dead. The death of Cordelia is particularly depressing because she is the epitome of virtue and the play's most innocent victim. Lear's kingdom has been profoundly disrupted by the forces of evil, and, in Kent's words, 'all's cheerless, dark and deadly'.

4. 'The sub-plot reflects and reinforces the key themes of the main plot.'

Plot and sub-plot run side by side, at times connecting and becoming interwoven. A cursory reading of the play indicates the striking similarities between plot and sub-plot. The sub-plot reflects and reinforces key ideas in the main plot, underlining the universal nature of such themes as moral blindness and redemption through suffering.

Both Gloucester and Lear are gullible, rash and morally blind. Just as Lear falls victim to the 'glib and oily' flattery of Goneril and Regan, Gloucester's credulous nature is easily exploited by Edmund. Both men are manipulated with consummate ease by children who prove to be callous and unnatural. Gloucester shares Lear's rashness, reacting impulsively to Edmund's revelation of Edgar's 'treachery'. Without ever affording Edgar the opportunity to defend his character and reputation, Gloucester immediately condemns him: 'Abhorred villain! Unnatural, detested, brutish villain! Worse than brutish!' Shortly afterwards, Gloucester reduces his loyal and loving son Edgar to the level of a hunted criminal, just as Lear had forced his one true daughter, Cordelia, into exile. 'Let him fly far: Not in this land shall he remain uncaught; and found – dispatch'. In the same scene, Gloucester disinherits Edgar, promising Edmund that he shall inherit his lands: '. . . of my land, loyal and natural boy, I'll work the means to make thee capable'. Morally blind, neither Gloucester nor Lear is capable of seeing themselves or others clearly in the early stages of the play.

While Gloucester and Lear share similar flaws, they are utterly contrasting personalities. While Lear is arrogant and domineering, Gloucester is passive and weak. His weakness of character is apparent when he makes no attempt to support Kent in highlighting the rash, foolish and unjust nature of Lear's actions in the dramatic opening scene. Initially manipulated by Edmund for his own evil ends, he is later manipulated by Edgar for the noble-minded purpose of ridding him of his suicidal despair. Edmund laughs at Gloucester's superstitious nature, describing as 'the excellent foppery of the world' the tendency to blame our disasters on 'the sun, the moon and the stars', when, in fact, they originate in 'our own behaviour'. Edgar exploits his father's gullible nature for a worthy purpose when he persuades him that he was led to jump from the cliffs at Dover by a demon in the form of a beggar, before convincing him that he is still alive through 'a miracle' and that the gods have 'preserved' his life. Having earlier believed that the gods wantonly killed men for their 'sport', Gloucester now prays to the 'ever-gentle gods' not to allow him to be tempted to die 'before you please'.

Notwithstanding their flaws, both Gloucester and Lear are both essentially noble characters. Gloucester protests against Kent being placed in the stocks, rightly pointing out to Cornwall that Lear will be angered by this act of blatant disrespect towards him: 'Let me beseech your Grace, not to do so . . . the king must take it ill that he is so slightly valued in his messenger'. While this protest has no impact on Cornwall's thinking, it serves to highlight Gloucester's sense of justice and fundamental decency. His finer qualities are again to be seen when he sympathises with the stocked Kent: 'I am sorry for thee, friend'. Gloucester's noble nature is also evident in his determination to go to Lear's assistance even at the risk of his own life: 'Though I die for it, as no less is threatened me, the king, my old master, must be relieved'.

Both Gloucester and Lear are victims of filial ingratitude. Goneril, Regan and Edmund show no respect for the natural bond that should closely bind child and parent (Edmund hypocritically claims to have told Edgar of 'how manifold and strong a bond the child was bound to the father'). However, both Gloucester and Lear are themselves initially guilty of blatantly disregarding these bonds in their unjust and harsh treatment of Edgar and Cordelia.

Both Gloucester and Lear undergo dramatic personal transformations in the course of the play, with both acquiring self-knowledge and

moral vision (qualities which are inextricably linked since one cannot see others and the world in general clearly until one sees oneself clearly) through suffering. Both are enlightened by their intense torment, ending the play better and wiser men. **Both gain insight in an ironic manner. In Edgar's words, Lear gains 'reason in madness', while Gloucester acquires moral vision at the very moment that he loses his physical sight:** 'Oh my follies! Then Edgar was abused; kind gods forgive me that, and prosper him!' The irony of simultaneously losing his physical sight and acquiring moral vision is not lost on Gloucester: 'I stumbled when I saw . . .' In striking contrast to Lear's gradual acquisition of insight, Gloucester's attainment of understanding is sudden and dramatic.

Both Gloucester and Lear show concern for others, even in their own suffering. Lear ushers the fool into the hovel ahead of him ('Poor fool and knave, I have one part of my heart that's sorry yet for thee'), while Gloucester expresses his concern for the old man who has been guiding him since he was thrown out at the gates of his own castle: 'Thy comforts can do me no good at all; thee they may hurt'.

Both Gloucester and Lear acquire a social conscience in the course of their personal growth, learning to care for the poor and the unfortunate. Observing the 'poor naked wretches' on the moor, Lear concludes that he took 'too little care of this' when he was king. He goes on to preach the gospel of social justice: 'Take physic pomp; expose thyself to feel what wretches feel that thou mayest shake

the superflux to them and show the heavens more just'. Gloucester similarly argues for a more equitable distribution of wealth so that 'distribution should undo excess and each man have enough'. Similar to Lear, Gloucester comes to see wealth as an obstacle to moral vision; he speaks of 'the superfluous and lust-dieted man... that will not see because he doth not feel'.

Gloucester and Lear are both rescued by the children they had treated so unjustly, with both Edgar and Cordelia ultimately giving consolation and hope to their respective tormented fathers. Edgar is Cordelia's counterpart in the sub-plot – both are noble-minded, loving and forgiving. Edgar and Cordelia are portrayed as healing agents, tending to and healing the fathers who have wronged them. Edgar sets out to rid Gloucester of his deep despair and suicidal tendencies ('Why I do trifle thus with his despair is done to cure it'), while Cordelia hopes that her love will 'repair those violent harms' done to Lear by Goneril and Regan ('Restoration hang thy medicine on my lips').

Both Lear and Gloucester pay the ultimate price for their own failings, with both experiencing the extremes of joy and grief before they die. Lear experiences the inexpressible joy of being reconciled with Cordelia, before being crushed by grief at her tragic death. Gloucester dies almost as Lear does. Edgar describes how his father reacted when he finally revealed his true identity to him: '. . . his flawed heart . . . twixt two extremes of passion, joy and grief, burst smilingly'.

---

5. 'Evil is vividly and frighteningly portrayed in the play.

A number of characters in the play display a frightening capacity for evil and for savage cruelty. When we consider that some of the greatest cruelties are inflicted on fathers by their own children and by children on their own fathers, we realise that the natural bonds that ordinarily bind families together can sometimes be broken in ways that are truly shocking.

Goneril is, from the beginning, transparently false. Insincerity drips from her words of flattery when she tells Lear, 'Sir, I love you more than words can wield the matter, dearer man eye-sight, space and liberty'. No sooner has she got her share of the kingdom than she starts to plot against Lear, conspiring with her sister against him: 'Pray you, let us hit together'. She encourages her servants to openly neglect Lear, ensuring that he clearly understands that he is not wanted: 'Put on what weary negligence you please'. Goneril sends a message to Regan, telling her to treat Lear as she has done: 'I'll write straight to my sister to hold my very course'. She insults Lear by telling him that he is old and doting: 'All's not offence that indiscretion finds and dotage terms so'. Along with Regan, she humiliates Lear by not allowing him to keep a single knight. Goneril wants immediate revenge on Gloucester when she discovers that he has been assisting Lear: 'Pluck out his eyes!' **Her cruelty is boundless as we see when she urges Edmund to kill her husband, Albany and when she herself poisons Regan** because she regards her sister as her rival for Edmund's affections.

Regan is as hypocritical as Goneril and, similar to her sister, has no qualms about using 'the glib and oily art' of flattery to ingratiate herself with (win the favour of) Lear before the kingdom is divided. We see her cruelty when she insists that Kent be kept in the stocks all day and 'all night too'. She is well aware that the stocking of Kent is a direct insult to Lear, with Gloucester reminding her that 'the king must take it ill that he is so slightly valued in his messenger'. Regan belittles Lear by refusing to see him when he first arrives at Gloucester's castle. In a particularly cruel put-down, she coldly reminds Lear of his powerlessness: 'I pray you father, being weak, seem so'. Regan is the epitome (embodiment/personification) of filial ingratitude. When Lear pathetically reminds her that he gave her 'all', she callously replies, 'And in good time you gave it'. Along with Goneril, she strips Lear of what is left of his power and dignity by denying him the right to have even a single knight: 'What need one?' She callously orders the doors of Gloucester's castle to be closed against Lear when he rushes out into the storm: 'O Sir, to wilful men the injuries that they themselves procure must be their schoolmasters'. **Like Goneril, Regan is cruel and vengeful, looking to punish Gloucester when it becomes known that he has helped Lear: 'Hang him instantly!' The depth of Regan's savagery is almost beyond belief.**

She demands that Gloucester's second eye be cut from his head: 'One side will mock another, the other too'. This scene is the most vivid and frightening depiction of evil. Not satisfied with physically torturing the unfortunate old man, she also torments him mentally. When Gloucester cries out for his son Edmund, Regan delights in telling him that it was Edmund who betrayed him: 'Thou call'st on him that hates thee: it was he who made the overtures of thy treason to us, who is too good to pity thee'. **Regan heartlessly throws the blind Gloucester out of his own castle, declaring that he can 'smell his way to Dover'.** Appalled by her cruelty, one of Regan's servants remarks, 'If she live long . . . women will all turn out monsters'. Regan later regrets not having killed Gloucester because his pitiable state is turning people against them, and promises to reward Oswald if he kills 'the blind traitor'. **Animal imagery underscores Goneril and Regan's inhuman cruelty** ('pelican daughters', 'tigers, not daughters', 'monsters of the deep' etc.).

Similar to Goneril and Regan, Edmund is capable of frightening evil and cruelty. What is particularly horrifying about the evil in the play is that its chief victims are elderly parents who suffer at the hands of ungrateful, unfeeling children. **Edmund coldly and ruthlessly exploits Gloucester's gullibility and Edgar's nobility in order to advance himself:** 'A credulous father and a brother noble whose nature is so far from doing wrong that he suspects none'. **Edmund betrays Gloucester to Cornwall** in the full knowledge that his father will be severely punished for assisting Lear. **He deceives both Goneril and Regan into believing that he loves them in order to achieve his own ends**, cynically delighting in his cleverness: 'To both these sisters have I sworn my love, each jealous of the other as the stung are of the adder'. **He plans to use Albany to help him defeat the French, before Goneril arranges her husband's 'speedy taking-off'** after the battle has been won. **Edmund orders the executions of both Lear and Cordelia** because he sees them as potential threats to his ambition to achieve absolute power.

Cornwall is a suitable husband for Regan in that he is equally cruel and vindictive. It is he who orders that Kent be placed in the stocks. He belittles Lear by refusing to meet him when he first arrives at Gloucester's castle. Most horrifyingly, he gouges out Gloucester's eyes in an act of monstrous savagery.

Oswald is a minor character, but is despicably cruel and evil. He treats Lear with visible disrespect, addressing him as 'my lady's master'. He is prepared to kill the blind, defenceless Gloucester in order to advance himself: 'That eyeless head of mine was first framed to raise my fortunes'.

In conclusion, while evil is present in every Shakespearian tragedy, it is depicted in a particularly frightening and vivid manner in *King Lear*.

6. 'The evil characters in the play are far more interesting than the good.'

The central characters in the play tend towards extremes of good or evil and consequently may seem one-dimensional and sometimes lacking in credibility. However, evil of its very nature is more interesting than good. While Cordelia and Edgar are hugely admirable characters who redeem their respective fathers and help to restore the natural order, they are not nearly as interesting as their evil counterparts. Goneril, Regan and Edmund fascinate us because of the sheer depth of their evil and cruelty.

Cordelia is a shining example of filial love and loyalty. She bears no grudge against Lear after he has unjustly disowned and disinherited her. Even after she departs for her new home in France, Cordelia continues to be informed (through Kent) of Lear's plight. Her love and concern for her father prompt her to lead a French expedition to rescue him: 'No blown ambition doth our arms incite, but love, dear love and our aged father's right'. Cordelia is utterly forgiving of her father, and in fact asks his blessing. She acts as a healing agent, comforting and consoling Lear in his darkest hour. As the personification of goodness, Cordelia cannot but be respected and admired. However, she is too perfect to excite our interest, being depicted as an almost saintly figure ('. . . she shook the holy water from her heavenly eyes'). Similar to Cordelia, Edgar is admirable, but not particularly interesting because he too is perhaps too good to be believable. He does not hesitate to forgive the father who wronged him. We see his loving, forgiving nature in his desire to cure Gloucester of his self-pity. Like Cordelia, Edgar acts as a healing agent, easing his father's suffering. We also see his nobility when he forgives Edmund.

Goneril is the most contemptible of the evil characters. While Regan is no less evil, it is Goneril who is the dominant sister. We see her sickening hypocrisy in the opening scene when she claims to love Lear 'more than words can wield the matter'. It is Goneril who suggests that she and Regan conspire together against Lear after he has handed over his kingdom to them: 'Pray you, let us hit together'. It is Goneril who initiates most of the evil schemes against Lear, humiliating him in a calculated, cold-blooded manner. She encourages her servants to openly neglect and disrespect him and strips him of his remaining power and dignity by denying him the right to have even a single knight. Her extraordinary cruelty can be seen in her vicious desire to avenge herself on Gloucester: 'Pluck out his eyes!' Goneril does not hesitate to undertake any act of evil, no matter how appalling. We see her complete lack of conscience when she plans the death of her own husband and poisons her sister. At no point does Goneril display even a hint of conscience. She is a truly hideous human being whose capacity for evil and cruelty both appals and fascinates. When her villainy has been revealed and all is lost, Goneril does not hesitate to take her own life.

Regan may not be as formidable a character

as Goneril, but she is no less evil, perpetrating some of the most shocking acts of cruelty in the play. Her treatment of Lear is utterly callous. It is hard to believe that any daughter could display such a complete lack of feeling towards her own father. When Lear pathetically points out that he gave his daughters 'all', Regan contemptuously replies, 'And in good time you gave it'. When Lear rushes out into the storm, **Regan orders that the gates of the castle be closed against him,** leaving her aged father to face the unforgiving elements. **Regan seems to have an insatiable appetite for savagery, and takes a perverse delight in physical torture.** It is she who extends Kent's time in the stocks ('Till noon! Till night my lord, and all night too') and demands that Gloucester's second eye be cut from his head ('One side will mock another, the other too'). The blind Gloucester is then left at the castle gates to 'smell his way to Dover'. **It is the almost unbelievable depth of Regan's savagery that fascinates the audience – it is difficult to believe that a woman in particular could be capable of such monstrous cruelty.**

Edmund is one of the most interesting characters in the play. Similar to both Goneril and Regan, Edmund is extraordinarily evil. **It is difficult to grasp the depth of the cruelty that these evil characters display towards their own fathers and siblings.** Edmund does not hesitate to betray Gloucester to Cornwall even though he knows that Gloucester will face torture and, possibly, death for assisting Lear.

While Edmund is an utterly amoral character, he fascinates us on a number of levels. We almost have a grudging admiration for his determination to defy society and rise above the lowly circumstances of his birth: 'Edmund the base shall top the legitimate -I grow, I prosper, now gods stand up for bastards!' Edmund is a sharp-witted villain who ruthlessly exploits Gloucester's gullibility and Edgar's nobility. He coldly sees people either as aids or obstacles to the achievement of his goals. **Edmund is a more credible character than Goneril or Regan because he is not as one-dimensional, displaying some redeeming features in the closing scene.** He exchanges forgiveness with Edgar and accepts that justice has been done: 'The wheel is come full circle'. **We admire his philosophical attitude and lack of self-pity. He also makes a belated effort to do some good by revealing that Lear and Cordelia are to be executed. The grim satisfaction that he takes in the thought of having been loved by two sisters is another indication of his humanity.** The irony that in death 'all three now marry in an instant' is not lost on Edmund, who remains sharp-witted to the end.

In conclusion, the evil characters are much more interesting than their moral opposites. The good characters are simply too perfect to be entirely believable. Furthermore, the evil characters fascinate us with the almost unbelievable depth of their cruelty.

---

7. *'The Importance of Kent'*

From the opening scene, Kent wins the admiration of the audience – he is loyal, courageous and shrewd. Kent is a very important character in the play, performing a number of key dramatic functions.

Kent is the only character to highlight the gravity of Lear's foolishness in the dramatic opening scene: '. . . be Kent unmannerly when Lear is mad . . . Think'st thou that duty shall have dread to speak when power to flattery bows?'

When everyone else is silenced by Lear's fury, Kent considers it his duty to confront the king and attempt to make him aware of the great mistake he is making when he disowns Cordelia. He urges Lear to 'see better', bluntly telling him, 'I tell thee thou dost evil'. Kent clearly perceives that Lear's ill-judged behaviour is more than mere folly, it is 'hideous rashness' and 'evil'.

Kent unwittingly helps to bring the quarrel between Lear and his evil daughters into the

open. Kent's undisguised contempt for Oswald and his bluntness when subsequently questioned by Cornwall results in his being placed in the stocks. Kent points out that, since he is the king's messenger, this degrading punishment represents an open insult to Lear. Unsurprisingly, when Lear arrives he is shocked and enraged to find Kent in the stocks: '. . . 'tis worse than murder to do upon respect such violent outrage'. From this point on the battle-lines between good and evil are clearly drawn.

One of Kent's most important dramatic functions is to maintain the link between Lear and Cordelia. Kent has kept Cordelia informed of Lear's plight and shares her determination to set right the wrongs done to the king: '. . . and shall find time from this enormous state seeking to give losses their remedies'. After Cordelia lands in England, Kent sends a messenger to Dover to inform her of Lear's 'unnatural and bemadding sorrow'. Kent keeps Cordelia in the minds of the audience during her absence.

Kent updates the audience on important military and political developments. Through Kent we learn of the growing division between Albany and Cornwall: 'There is division, although as yet the face of it be covered . . . 'twixt Albany and Cornwall'. Through Kent we learn that the forces of good are assembling to rescue Lear: 'From France there comes a power into this scattered kingdom'.

Kent regularly comments on and clarifies Lear's mental state for the audience: 'His wits begin to unsettle', 'All the power of his wits have given way to his impatience', '. . . . his wits are gone', ' . . . sometime in his better tune remembers what we are come about'. Kent also explains why Lear is reluctant to meet Cordelia: '. . . burning shame detains him from Cordelia'. **Kent is important for what he represents. He is the epitome of fidelity (loyalty). His allegiance to Lear is absolute and unwavering.** Kent's love for Lear is the guiding force of his life. It is no exaggeration to state that Kent lives for Lear: 'My life I never held but as a pawn to wage against thine enemies'. It is this loyalty which prompts Kent to risk Lear's wrath by intervening when he sees the dramatic nature of the king's rashness. Despite being unjustly banished, Kent's loyalty to Lear never diminishes and he returns in disguise to serve him in any capacity he can: 'Now banished Kent, if thou canst serve where thou dost stand condemned, so may it come, thy master whom thou lovest shall find thee full of labours'. Kent is infuriated by Oswald's blatant disrespect for Lear and defends his master's honour by tripping up the unmannerly servant and pushing him out. Kent watches over Lear as the storm rages on the heath, guiding him to the shelter of a hovel. When Lear asks him, 'Wilt break my heart?' Kent's response reflects his deep affection for and absolute loyalty to his master: 'I had rather break mine own'. Even when Lear loses his sanity, Kent never fails to address him respectfully: 'Good my Lord . . .', 'Sir . . .' When the bewildered Lear seems to recognise him at the close of the play ('Are you not Kent?'), Kent explains that he has followed his master's 'sad steps' from the beginning of his troubles. Kent shows great understanding of and sympathy towards his king in his final agony. While others hope to revive the dying Lear, Kent knows that Lear has suffered enough and that it would not be right to further prolong his agony: 'Vex not his ghost: O let him pass! He hates him that would upon the rack of this tough world stretch him out longer'. Kent's unswerving loyalty to Lear is such that, when the king dies, he is determined, in the noble manner of an ancient Roman, to be at his side in the next world also. It is for this reason that he rejects Albany's offer of joining with himself and Edgar in ruling the kingdom: 'I have a journey, sir, shortly to go. My master calls me, I must not say no'. **Kent's selfless loyalty is inspiring, while his fundamental goodness helps to counterbalance the evil in the play.**

Kent's loyalty to Lear reminds us that Lear was not always the rash and foolish figure we see in the opening scene. His extraordinary fidelity to the king strongly suggests to us that there was an earlier, greater Lear who inspired such loyalty in the wise and noble Kent.

8. 'The transformation of Albany'

Albany's dramatic transformation from ineffectual, dominated husband to strong, assertive leader is one of the most uplifting aspects of the play. His transformation is as total as it is dramatic. Little wonder that, in Act 4, Scene 2, a bewildered Oswald says of Albany: '. . . never man so changed'. By the close of the play, Albany has developed into a figure of real substance and authority and plays an important role in the restoration of peace and order.

When the audience first encounters Albany, he leaves us decidedly unimpressed. He seems to live in the shadow of his forceful, domineering wife, Goneril. He doesn't utter a word of concern about Lear's glaring mistreatment of Cordelia in the opening scene. Albany does make an attempt to take issue with his wife over her harsh treatment of Lear ('I cannot be so partial, Goneril, to the great love I bear you'.), but his feeble protest is contemptuously dismissed by his arrogant wife: 'Pray you, content'. Goneril regards Albany with undisguised disdain, scorning his 'milky gentleness' and 'want of wisdom'. Goneril perceives Lear's one hundred knights to be a potential threat to her power, and demands that the old king reduce his retinue. However, she neither consults nor informs Albany about this matter. Albany appears to be genuinely bewildered by Lear's fury: 'My lord, I am guiltless as I am ignorant of what hath moved you'. He seems to be a well-meaning, but weak character, incapable of acting (or even thinking) independently of his imperious (dictatorial) wife.

While we are unsure how it happened, Albany undergoes a truly dramatic personal transformation. He is presented in a far more positive light in the later stages of the play and gradually wins our respect and admiration. Albany finds himself in a difficult position when the French force lands. While his sympathies lie with Lear and Cordelia (who leads the French force), he has an inescapable duty to repel a French army on English territory. Oswald is clearly taken aback by the extent of Albany's transformation: '. . . never man so changed. I told

him of the army that was landed; he smiled at it . . . What most he should dislike seems pleasant to him; what like, offensive'. Goneril completely misinterprets Albany's reluctance to engage the French force when she attributes this hesitancy to 'the cowish terror of his spirit'. Goneril, at this point, appears to be utterly unaware that her once 'mild-mannered' husband has undergone a change of truly dramatic proportions. However, Albany leaves her in no doubt but that she is now dealing with a very changed man when he bluntly tells his evil wife what he thinks of her: 'O Goneril, you are not worth the dust which the rude wind blows in your face'. He is convinced that his wife's unnatural treatment of Lear will ultimately be her undoing: 'She that herself will sliver and disbranch from her material sap perforce must wither and come to deadly use'. Albany now regards Goneril with total revulsion as he tells her that 'filths savour but themselves'.

A firm believer in the notion of divine justice, Albany is convinced that 'the heavens' will 'tame these vile offences'. He regards Cornwall's death as divine justice at work: 'This shows you are above you justicers that these our nether crimes so speedily can venge'. In this scene we see Albany as a man capable of anger and action. His passionate hatred of Goneril is such that he could physically tear her asunder ('tear thy flesh and bones'). Albany's earlier timidity is nowhere evident in this scene; instead we see a newly assertive, forceful leader possessed of and motivated by strong moral principles. At the close of this scene, Albany clearly aligns himself with the forces of good and promises to avenge the outrage of Gloucester's eyes.

In the final Act of the play, Albany emerges as a major force, playing a significant role in the restoration of peace and order to the kingdom. Edmund criticises Albany for being 'self-reproving'(self-critical) and we can see in this criticism Albany's regrets that he has not taken action sooner against the injustice and cruelty visited on both Lear and Gloucester. While reluctant to take up arms against Cordelia,

Albany knows that intervention by a foreign force must be opposed. However, we learn from Edmund that Albany intends showing mercy to both Lear and Cordelia ('As for the mercy which he intends to Lear and Cordelia . . .'). Albany acknowledges the justice of the revolt of many of his own people, who have, he says, been 'forced to cry out' by the harshness of the regime ('the rigour of our state') ruling in place of Lear.

The last scene of the play helps us to appreciate more fully the full strength of Albany's character. Pragmatism demanded that he ally himself with Goneril, Regan and Edmund against the French invasion. However, when the external threat has been dealt with, Albany takes charge, impressing us with his dignity and authority. His strength of character is obvious in his refusal to tolerate Edmund's arrogance: 'I hold you as a subject of this war, not as a brother'. He arrests Edmund and Goneril ('this gilded serpent') for 'capital treason'. Albany emerges as a man of action willing, if necessary, to fight Edmund himself in trial by combat (he is the first to throw down his glove to Edmund). When Goneril states that, according to the rules of knighthood, Edmund is not obliged to accept a challenge from a person of lesser rank (the unknown warrior who challenges Edmund is the disguised Edgar), Albany puts her firmly in her place: 'Shut your mouth, dame . . .' Albany is also sufficiently perceptive to realise that Goneril may attempt to commit suicide ('Go

after her: she's desperate; govern her'.) He also recognises the nobility of the disguised Edgar: '. . . thy very gait did prophesy a royal nobleness.'

Albany displays many of the qualities required of a good and strong leader. He is compassionate and sensitive. He is deeply moved by Edgar's account of Gloucester's suffering and death ('I am almost ready to dissolve hearing of this') and by the intensity of Lear's grief at Cordelia's death ('Fall and cease'). **However, he only shows sympathy towards those deserving of it. He barely reacts to news of his wife's death, seeing Goneril's demise as divine justice:** 'This judgement of the heavens, that makes us tremble, touches us not with pity'. Tragically, while preoccupied with all that is happening around him, Albany seems to forget Cordelia and Lear and the fact that they must now be in a position of great danger. When Edmund confesses to having ordered their executions, Albany makes a belated and ultimately vain attempt to save them, telling Edgar to 'Run, run, O, run!' He subsequently dismisses news of Edmund's death as 'but a trifle here'. **At the close of the play, Albany promises that justice will be done in the kingdom:** 'All friends shall taste the wages of their virtue, and all foes the cup of their deservings'. **Along with Edgar, Albany will play an important role in restoring the health of 'the gored state' and in reinstating the natural order.**

9. *'The theme of madness is central to the play.'*

Madness is one of the central themes of the play. Madness, in its various forms, is a theme that relates to Lear, Edgar and the Fool. While we sympathise with Lear when he is pained to the point of insanity by the ingratitude and callousness of his 'pelican daughters', there is a positive aspect to Lear's madness, as there is to Gloucester's blindness. In his madness Lear acquires a peculiar type of wisdom – a wisdom that is encapsulated in Edgar's paradoxical expression: 'reason in madness.' When Lear acquires 'reason in madness', he is able to see

himself, others and society in general more clearly than ever before. The Fool was also regarded as mad, but his idiotic antics conceal a sharp wit. While the Fool may or may not be entirely sane, he is certainly wise and commonsensical. The final character to whom this theme relates is of course Edgar, who is forced by his brother's treachery to adopt the disguise of a mad Bedlam beggar in order to avoid arrest. Act 3, Scene 6 brings all three of these 'madmen' together as Lear imagines himself putting his ungrateful daughters on trial. In this memorable scene we observe Lear's genuine insanity, Edgar's feigned madness and the Fool's half-foolish jests.

Lear's madness has its origins in Goneril and Regan's unnatural ingratitude. When Lear is first rebuked and attacked by Goneril, the shock to his system is immense. His self-image is dramatically undermined: 'This is not Lear . . . Who is it that can tell me who I am?' The realisation of the injustice he did to Cordelia ('I did her wrong') combined with the pain of Goneril's 'monster ingratitude' cause Lear to fear for his sanity: 'O let me not be mad, not mad, sweet heaven!' The sight of Kent in the stocks (''tis worse than murder to do upon respect such violent outrage'), and Cornwall's refusal to meet him are further insults to Lear's royal dignity. Lear now struggles to resist the insanity rising within him: 'O how this mother swells up toward my heart! *Hysterica passio* down, thou climbing sorrow, thy element's below!' Regan's contemptuous ejection of him ('. . . being weak, seem so') is the next great shock to his system. **While Lear is very much the architect of his own downfall, we cannot but feel pity for a powerless old man who can only rave helplessly against his daughters' filial ingratitude.** When he declares 'O Fool, I shall go mad', it is clear that he is losing the battle to retain the balance of his mind. **Lear's towering rages accelerate the onset of madness.**

The storm on the heath reflects the storm in Lear's mind. Yet even as his 'wits begin to turn', Lear shows signs of growing through suffering. He begins to acquire insight and humility, seeing himself now as 'a poor, infirm, weak and despised old man'. The mentally unstable king displays a new concern for others when he ushers the Fool into the hovel in front of him: 'In boy, go first'. Even though he is now on the verge of insanity, he becomes aware of his failings as a king. He realises that he neglected the poor and now preaches the doctrine of social justice: 'O I have taken too little care of this! . . . Expose thyself to feel what wretches feel, that thou may shake the superflux to them and show the heavens more just'. Lear's belief that Poor Tom's misery is attributable to 'his unkind daughters' prompts the concerned Fool to suggest that 'This cold night will turn us all to fools or madmen'. As Lear tears off his clothes in an attempt to identify with 'unaccommodated man', it is clear that he has lost the balance of his mind. Kent simply says: 'All the power of his wits have given way to his impatience'. The 'trial scene' sees Lear's insanity reach a peak. In this bizarre scene he struggles to understand his daughters' callousness as he wonders, 'is there any cause in nature that makes these hard hearts?'

Like Edgar ('My tears begin to take his part so much, they'll mar my counterfeiting'), the audience is deeply moved by Lear's intense suffering. Yet Lear continues to grow through his mental torment. Further evidence of Lear's personal growth comes when Kent informs us that 'burning shame' prevents Lear from going to Cordelia. Lear gradually acquires moral vision. He now realises that Goneril and Regan flattered him 'like a dog'. He wisely tells the blind Gloucester that 'A man may see how this world goes with no eyes'. He becomes aware of corruption in high places and of social inequalities: 'through tattered clothes small vices do appear. Robes and furred gowns hide all'. Little wonder that Edgar should speak of Lear's 'reason in madness'.

The ennobling, humanising effects of Lear's mental suffering are most strikingly apparent when he meets Cordelia. Now lucid (clear-minded), Lear displays self-knowledge and humility, describing himself as 'a very foolish, fond old man'. His sense of guilt in relation to Cordelia is so overwhelming that he would willingly drink poison if that would somehow prove the depth of his shame and regret. Lear's personal redemption is complete when he is reconciled with Cordelia. When he is arrested, the increasingly philosophical king only wishes for himself and Cordelia to be together so that they can ponder the meaning of life ('the mystery of things'). **While we cannot but sympathise with Lear in his intense suffering, his madness has a positive dimension. Lear's acquisition of 'reason in madness' enables him to see himself, others and the world in general more clearly.**

While the Fool was generally regarded as a madman, he clearly possesses a sharp wit. His primary dramatic function is to make Lear more aware of his foolishness. **The Fool is able to speak his mind to Lear precisely because he is regarded as a madman.** Lear describes him as 'a bitter fool' because he speaks the bitter truth, while Goneril refers to him as Lear's 'all-licensed Fool' because his apparent madness allows him to say whatever he likes. As Kent shrewdly observes, the Fool is no ordinary comic buffoon: 'This is not altogether Fool, my Lord'.

The Fool continually reminds Lear of his foolishness: 'Thou hadst little wit in thy bald crown when thou gavest thy golden one away', '. . . thou madest thy daughters thy mother', 'thou shouldst not have been old till thou hadst been wise'. The Fool disguises many of his philosophical utterances with nonsense songs: 'Fathers that wear rags/Do make their children blind'. He is the voice of Lear's conscience, the nagging inner voice that relentlessly reminds him of his wrongdoing. He is also sufficiently perceptive to realise the consequences of his master's intense suffering on the heath: 'This cold night will turn us all to fools and madmen'. Once the Fool has prompted Lear to reflect on his folly, his dramatic function is fulfilled, and he takes no further part in the action.

Edgar adopts the disguise of a mad Bedlam beggar for purposes of survival. His brother's falseness and his father's rashness have reduced him to the level of a hunted fugitive and, with all of the ports closely guarded, Edgar is forced adopt the persona of a madman: 'I will preserve myself; and am bethought to take the basest and most poorest shape'. Edgar's assumed madness has a definite purpose: self-preservation. While Edgar is able to keep up the pretence of being mad for a long time, he is so deeply moved by his father's suffering that he nearly dispenses with his act: 'My tears begin to take his part so much, they'll mar my counterfeiting'. **Edgar's 'madness' also has a very positive aspect in that it enables him to stay alive, go on to redeem his father and play his part in restoring the natural order.** He assumes the role of a madman in order to protect his own life, but dispenses with his disguise as soon as his country needs him.

Of the trio of 'madmen' who find themselves together on the heath (Lear, the Fool and Poor Tom), only Edgar is entirely sane. His feigned madness is a contrast to Lear's real madness and helps to relieve the dramatic tension. When Lear declares that Poor Tom's misery is attributable to his 'unkind daughters', it is clear that he has finally lost the balance of his mind. Obsessed with the ingratitude of his own daughters, Lear cannot see that Edgar does not have any daughters. **The exchanges between the real madman (Lear), the official madman (the Fool), and the pretended madman (Edgar) make for one of the most memorable scenes in the play.** Now at the height of his madness, Lear finds in Edgar a true image of the basic humanity he wants to share: 'unaccommodated man is no more but such a poor, bare, forked animal as thou art'.

At one level the mock trial scene is bizarrely comic as the mad Lear, the blanketed Edgar and the Fool preside over the mock trial of Goneril and Regan. **However, the mock trial serves a significant thematic purpose:** the fact that Lear appoints a fool and an apparent madman to pass judgement on his daughters suggests that he has now grown in wisdom to the point where he perceives that sanity and reason have nothing to do with justice as it is administered in his kingdom.

In conclusion, the play presents us with three very different kinds of 'madness'. While Lear's madness is a human response to the pain of his daughters' filial ingratitude, Edgar's 'madness' is a matter of choice. **However, in both cases madness, real or feigned, is the result of the natural bonds that should bind families together being broken.** It is the ingratitude and treachery of those closest to them that reduces both Lear and Edgar to the level of madmen. **As an 'official' madman, the Fool fulfils a traditional role in the royal court,** entertaining the king with his witty observations and clever rhymes. **However, the Fool's unofficial role**

as **Lear's conscience is more important** as, under the guise of madness, he points out Lear's mistakes to him, helping him to grow in wisdom and become more self-aware.

10. *'The play explores the meaning of love.'*

King Lear is notable as much for its exploration of love as it is for its portrayal of evil. From the impressive sincerity of France's love for Cordelia in the opening scene through to the healing, redemptive love of Cordelia and Edgar for Lear and Gloucester respectively in the latter stages of the drama, love is a central theme of the play.

Having witnessed and been repelled by the false love of Goneril and Regan, the audience is greatly impressed with the genuine nature of France's love for Cordelia. After being disowned and disinherited by Lear, Cordelia understandably fears for her reputation, requesting Lear to make it known that she has not lost his favour because of any dishonourable action on her part. However, it is immediately apparent that France is aware of the strangeness of Lear's behaviour towards Cordelia when he asks the king how the daughter 'who even now was your best object, the argument of your praise, balm of your age' could in a moment commit an act 'so monstrous' to completely fall from favour. He is incredulous when he learns that Cordelia has lost everything simply because of her unwillingness to flatter Lear. In contrast to the romantic Paris who believes that Cordelia 'is herself a dowry', the mercenary-minded Burgundy is unwilling to marry Cordelia without the portion of the kingdom promised him. Paris openly expresses his love for her at this point: 'Fairest Cordelia, thou art most rich, being poor; most choice, forsaken; and most loved, despised!' **Paris' love for Cordelia highlights the fact that true love is never influenced by material considerations: 'Love is not love when it is mingled with regards that stand aloof from the entire point'.**

Kent's love for Lear is one of the most positive and uplifting aspects of the play. It is no overstatement to say that Kent lives for Lear: 'Royal Lear, whom I have ever honoured as my king, loved as my father, as my master followed, as my great patron thought on in my prayers . . .' Kent's love for Lear means that he sees it as his inescapable duty to make the king aware of any mistakes he is making that may ultimately cause him suffering. He describes Lear's decision to disown and disinherit Cordelia as 'hideous rashness'. After Kent is banished and threatened with death, he still returns in disguise to serve Lear as a humble servant: 'Now banished Kent, if thou canst serve where thou dost stand condemned, so may it come, thy master, whom thou lov'st, shall find thee full of labours'. Kent remains with Lear throughout his painful journey to self-awareness and wisdom. He never fails to defend Lear's honour, ending up in the stocks after beating the despicable Oswald for disrespecting Lear. It is Kent who leads Lear to the shelter of a hovel in the dramatic storm scene and who ensures that Cordelia remains informed about Lear's plight. In the closing scene, Kent is deeply pained by Lear's heartbreak at the death of his beloved Cordelia, insisting that no attempt be made to revive him if he loses consciousness: 'O let him pass! He hates him that would upon the rack of this tough world stretch him out longer'. Kent's love for and loyalty to Lear does not end with the latter's death. He refuses the offer to join Albany and Edgar in ruling the kingdom because of his enduring devotion to Lear: 'I have a journey, sir, shortly to go; my master calls me, I must not say no'. **Kent's love for Lear reminds us that unwavering loyalty is a key feature of real love.**

Cordelia's love for Lear is another of the play's most inspiring features. In total contrast to her sisters' hollow declarations of love for Lear, Cordelia's love for her father is genuine and deep. Once she becomes aware of Lear's plight, she leads an expedition to England to rescue him. Cordelia's motivation for this military intervention has nothing to do with political ambition, and everything to do with her loving concern for her father: 'No blown ambition doth our arms incite, but love, dear love and our aged father's right'. The scene where she meets Lear is deeply moving. She struggles to come to terms with the appalling cruelty inflicted on her father, telling Kent that she would have kept her enemy's dog close to her fire on the night that Lear was forced to endure a particularly violent storm on the moor. Cordelia is seen as the very embodiment of love and forgiveness as she tenderly addresses Lear: 'O my dear father! Restoration, hang thy medicine on my lips, and let this kiss repair those violent harms that my sisters have in thy reverence made!' Remarkably, Cordelia even asks Lear's blessing: 'O! Look upon me sir, and hold your hands in benediction o'er me'. **Cordelia's love for Lear indicates that a capacity for forgiveness is an integral aspect of love, while also highlighting the redemptive power of love.**

Edgar's enduring love for Gloucester is another of the play's most heartening (uplifting) features. Notwithstanding the fact that he has been reduced to the level of a hunted criminal by Gloucester's rashness and has been forced to adopt the disguise of a mad Bedlam beggar in order to survive, Edmund, like Cordelia, bears no feelings of resentment towards his father. Seeing his father's dark despair and desire to end his life, Edgar engages in a kindly deception, tricking the credulous (gullible) and disorientated Gloucester into believing that he has fallen from the steep cliffs of Dover and that the gods have saved his life: 'Thy life's a miracle.' Edgar's loving action rids Gloucester of his suicidal tendencies, with the latter now proclaiming: '. . . henceforth I'll bear affliction till it do cry out itself "Enough, enough", and die'. **Edgar's love for Gloucester reinforces the idea that love is always kind and forgiving and can be redemptive.**

Unsurprisingly, the relationships involving Goneril and Regan tell us a great deal about what love should not involve. Their transparent flattery of Lear immediately suggests the insincerity of their declarations of 'love' for their father. Their attempts to ingratiate themselves with him are far removed from genuine expressions of love since they are motivated solely by the desire for self-advancement.

All of these relationships help us to better understand the nature and meaning of love. We see that love is not influenced by material considerations and that love based on loyalty and a willingness to forgive has the power to redeem characters who, like Lear and Gloucester, have lost their way in life through their spiritual blindness.

---

11. 'Describe a dramatic scene in the play.'

Act 3, Scene 7 is one of the most dramatic scenes in the play, indeed in any Shakespearian drama. This is the scene in which Gloucester's eyes are gouged out in an act of monstrous cruelty.

Gloucester bravely goes to Lear's assistance when he learns of the plot upon his life. Gloucester does not realise that he has been betrayed by his son Edmund in whom he confided this dramatic news. We know that Cornwall has sworn to Edmund that he will have his revenge on Gloucester for this act of 'treachery' and fear for Gloucester. The irony whereby the audience knows more than the character adds to the dramatic nature of this scene.

This scene opens dramatically with Cornwall ordering Gloucester's arrest and Goneril ('Hang him instantly!') and Regan ('Pluck out his eyes!') trying to outdo each other in their vengeful bloodlust. When Cornwall tells Edmund to leave because 'the revenges we are bound to take upon your treacherous father are not fit for your beholding', our fears for Gloucester intensify. When Gloucester arrives, he is immediately bound. We sympathise with Gloucester who, sensing that these evil characters mean to harm him, pathetically reminds them that he is their host. However, since the evil sisters show scant regard for the natural bond that should link parent and child, they are unlikely to display any respect for the natural bond that should link a host and his guests. Goneril, Regan and Cornwall are intent on revenge and will abuse Gloucester's hospitality in the most dramatic and horrifying way imaginable. Regan starts the cruel process of revenge when she shows her disrespect for Gloucester by plucking his beard.

The tension mounts as Gloucester is bound and interrogated about his involvement in the French landing and his knowledge of Lear's situation. Gloucester shows admirable courage and loyalty to Lear in philosophically accepting his predicament: 'I am tied to the stake, and I must stand the course'. When Regan asks Gloucester why he sent Lear to Dover, his response is charged with irony: 'Because I would not see thy cruel nails pluck out his poor old eyes; nor thy cruel sister in his anointed flesh stick bearish fangs'. Like all of the other noble characters in the play, Gloucester believes in the idea of divine justice, defiantly telling his captors: '. . . but I shall see the winged vengeance overtake such children'. However, the evil characters will first have their revenge on him.

There follows one of the most horrifying moments in any Shakespearian drama as Cornwall, in an act of unimaginable savagery, gouges out one of Gloucester's eyes. However, even this act of barbarity does not satisfy Regan who, clearly feeling that no punishment is adequate for a man who has helped her father, demands that Gloucester's second eye be cut from his head: 'One side will mock another; the other too'.

More drama and physical action follows when, in an instinctive act of humanity, one of Cornwall's servants intervenes on behalf of Gloucester. In the sword fight that ensues, Cornwall is mortally wounded and the noble servant stabbed from behind by Regan. **Cornwall's wound does not prevent him from completing his vicious blinding of Gloucester:** 'Out vile jelly! Where is thy lustre now?'

Gloucester endures further suffering when, in his agony and blindness, he calls out for his son Edmund. Regan, not satisfied with Gloucester's physical torture, delights in tormenting him mentally by revealing that it was Edmund who betrayed him: 'Thou call'st on him that hates thee, it was he who made the overtures of thy treasons to us . . .'

Gloucester now experiences a sudden, dramatic moment of self-awareness: 'O my follies! Then Edgar was abused. Kind gods, forgive me that and prosper him'. While Lear acquires insight in a slow, gradual manner, Gloucester gains understanding in an instant. **The irony in Gloucester gaining spiritual vision at the very moment that he is made physically blind adds to the dramatic qualities of this scene.**

Almost unbelievably, Gloucester has to endure even more misery when Regan orders that he be thrown out of his own castle: 'Go thrust him out at the gates, and let him smell his way to Dover'. This is yet another dramatic example of the evil sisters' seemingly insatiable appetite for cruelty.

This scene dramatically highlights the depths of inhumanity and savagery of which people are capable. The fact that two female characters are involved and delight in physical torture adds to the barbarity of Gloucester's blinding. This scene is also important because it sees the death of the first of the evil characters. Like Gloucester, Albany subscribes to the notion of divine justice. When he learns of Cornwall's death, he sees it as an example of the gods punishing evil-doers: 'This shows you are above you justicers that these our nether crimes so speedily can venge'.

12. 'Imagery and Symbolism in the play'

Certain images recur throughout *King Lear*. These patterns of imagery convey key themes, portray characters and help to create the distinctive atmosphere of the play.

Animal Imagery

There are numerous references to animals in the course of the play. Animal images suggest the unnatural cruelty of Goneril and Regan and underline their lack of humanity. Lear angrily describes Goneril as a 'detested kite' and speaks of her 'monster ingratitude'. Speaking to Regan of the pain of Goneril's ingratitude, Lear (pointing to his heart) tells her, 'O Regan, she hath tied sharp-toothed unkindness like a vulture, here'. He later refers to his two 'pelican daughters'. Albany is horrified by Goneril and Regan's bestial cruelty, describing them as 'tigers, not daughters'. He declares that if such unnatural cruelty goes unchecked, the human world may become like that of the wild beasts: '. . . humanity must perforce prey on itself like monsters of the deep'. Kent speaks of Lear's 'dog-hearted daughters'. Serpent imagery suggests Goneril and Regan's falseness: in the closing scene, Albany orders the arrest of 'the gilded serpent' that is Goneril. Kent uses animal imagery to highlight the insidiously destructive evil of 'smiling rogues' like Oswald who undermine the natural bonds that link families: '. . . like rats oft bite the holy cords a-twain which are too intrinse to unloose'. Animal imagery suggests a society based on the law of the jungle where only the strongest and the most ruthless survive and where there is little or no room for humanity or compassion.

Images of Suffering and Violence

King Lear is a play characterised by intense suffering. This suffering is physical, mental and spiritual in nature. The pain of his daughters' ingratitude is such that Lear declares that his heart 'shall break into a hundred thousand flaws'. Two key images underscore the intensity of Lear's anguish. Speaking to Cordelia, Lear imagines himself as a tortured soul: 'I am bound upon a wheel of fire that mine own tears do scald like molten lead'. At the close of the play, Kent insists that his royal master be allowed to die since death will release him from the agonies of life: 'O let him pass! He hates him that would upon the rack of this tough world stretch him out longer'.

The violent behaviour of human beings is often linked with that of animals. Speaking to Goneril, Regan and Cornwall Gloucester explains his loyalty to Lear in the following terms: 'Because I would not see thy cruel nails pluck out his poor old eyes, nor thy fierce sister in his anointed flesh stick bearish fangs'. The blinding of Gloucester is an act of savage cruelty. Bound to a chair and disrespectfully plucked by the beard, Gloucester accepts that he is 'tied to the stake' and 'must stand the course'. He has both eyes gouged out ('One side will mock the other, the other too', says the inhuman Regan) and is thrown out of his own castle to 'smell his way to Dover'. The image of the blinded Gloucester stumbling in his world of darkness is particularly powerful, dramatically underscoring the savage cruelty of the evil characters.

Clothing Imagery: Appearance and Reality

Clothing imagery suggests the contrast between appearance and reality that lies at the heart of this play and indeed all Shakespearian tragedies. Clothing is a symbol of wealth and social status and is associated with the dishonesty of those in positions of power. As Lear grows in wisdom, he declares, 'Through tattered clothes small vices do appear, robes and furred gowns hide all. Plate sin with gold and the strong lance of justice hurtless breaks: arm it in rags, a pigmy's straw doth pierce it'. Lear has learned much by the time he makes this pronouncement. He had initially confused appearance with reality, accepting his daughters' declarations of love at face value.

Edgar's nakedness (Gloucester refers to him as 'this naked soul') contrasts with the 'furred gowns' of the nobility and suggests his honesty. Edgar has nothing to hide behind. Lear tears off his clothes in order to be like Edgar:

'. . . unaccommodated man is no more but such a poor, bare, forked animal as thou art. Off, off, you lendings! Come, unbutton here'. Lear is closest to self-knowledge when he dispenses with the clothing symbolic of wealth, high social status and deception. He runs about in the storm 'unbonneted' and 'bareheaded', reducing himself to the level of the poorest of his subjects, and sharing in their deprivation and suffering.

Storm Imagery

The storm on the moor suggests that nature is in sympathy with Lear's suffering. The storm is symbolic both of the storm in Lear's mind and of the disorder and turbulence in society that follows the shattering of the natural bonds that bind families and wider society together: 'Blow winds and crack your cheeks! Rage! Blow! You cataracts and hurricanes spout . . .' In his intense suffering, Lear cries out for universal destruction: 'Strike flat the thick rotundity of the world! Crack nature's moulds. All germens spill at once, that make ingrateful man!' The unnatural intensity of the storm may also symbolise the unnatural cruelty of Goneril and Regan. Kent describes the storm as the worst in living memory: 'Since I was a man, such sheets of fire, such bursts of horrid thunder, such groans of roaring wind and rain, I never remember to have heard'.

13. 'King Lear is a very gloomy play.'

The play is, in many respects, a very dark drama. Evil is dominant for much of the play. Lear and Gloucester suffer intensely and indeed all of the central characters suffer to some degree as a result of the disruption of the natural order. The ending is especially dark with the death of Cordelia and Lear's heartbreak. **However, the play has a number of positive aspects that serve to relieve the gloom.** Both Lear and Gloucester grow through suffering, and both characters are redeemed (rescued) by loving children. Also, good ultimately triumphs over evil.

The ease with which the evil characters deceive others, and the fact that evil seems to thrive for much of the play creates a sense of gloom. Goneril and Regan employ the 'glib and oily art' of flattery to easily fool their doting father into giving them their share of the kingdom: 'I love you more than words can wield the matter . . .' Edmund similarly manipulates the gullible and rash Gloucester with consummate (expert) ease, convincing him that the loyal and loving Edgar is plotting against him. He also takes advantage of his brother's trusting nature: 'A credulous father and a brother noble, whose nature is so far from doing harms that he suspects none: on whose foolish honesty my practices ride easily'.

The scheming of the evil characters reduces Lear to a madman, deprives Gloucester of his sight and forces Edgar to play the part of a Bedlam beggar. The defeat of the French force led by Cordelia intensifies (heightens / increases) the sense of gloom.

The extreme suffering of Lear and Gloucester is another gloomy aspect of the play. Both Lear and Gloucester suffer intensely as a result of filial ingratitude. Goneril and Regan's unnatural behaviour causes Lear such extreme spiritual agony that he eventually loses his sanity, while Gloucester suffers intense physical pain as well as mental anguish as a consequence of Edmund's betrayal of him. Lear is stripped of all dignity by his 'pelican daughters'. Goneril's servants treat Lear with visible contempt while Regan places his messenger in the stocks, and refuses to see him. The final humiliation comes when the two evil sisters deny Lear even a single knight. It is impossible not to feel sympathy for 'a poor old man as full of grief as age' who can do no more than rant helplessly when he finally sees Goneril and Regan for the 'unnatural hags' that they are. Lear realises too late his utter folly (foolishness) in handing over his royal authority to ungrateful daughters who now have the power to humiliate him. The image of Lear 'bound upon a wheel of fire' underlines the intensity of his suffering, as does Kent's description of Lear being stretched 'upon the rack of this tough world'. Gloucester's intense suffering also adds to the overall sense of gloom. The brutal gouging out of Gloucester's eyes is one of the most horrifying and repulsive moments in Shakespearian literature. His extreme physical pain is matched by his mental anguish when Regan delights in telling him that it was Edmund who betrayed him,

The ending of the play is very grim. The death of Cordelia is particularly tragic since she is seen as the embodiment of goodness and love. Lear's unspeakable grief as he leans over the dead body of Cordelia is deeply moving: 'Why should a dog, a horse, a rat have life, and thou no breath at all?' Like Kent, we are affected by Lear's pitiful death. The death of Gloucester, who dies ''twixt two extremes of passion, joy and grief', further contributes to the sense of despondency that envelops the close of the play.

However, it would be an overstatement to describe King Lear as 'overwhelmingly gloomy' because the play is not without its positive, uplifting aspects. While Lear and Gloucester both suffer intensely, they grow and learn through suffering, ending the play as better, wiser men. Both men ultimately acquire self-knowledge and moral vision. Lear comes to see himself as 'a very foolish fond old man'. He eventually sees Goneril and Regan for the 'unnatural hags' that they are, and humbly begs Cordelia's forgiveness: 'You must bear with me; pray you now, forget and forgive: I am old and foolish'. Lear also acquires a social conscience, regretting his neglect of the 'poor naked wretches' he sees on the heath and preaching the doctrine of social justice: 'Expose thyself to what wretches feel, that thou mayst shake the superflux to them and show the heavens more just'. He also comes to see the falseness and corruption of political life: 'Robes and furred gowns hide all'. **Gloucester similarly grows through suffering. Ironically he gains moral vision at the moment he loses his physical sight.** He finally realises that he misjudged Edgar: 'O my follies! Then Edgar was abused. Kind Gods forgive me that and

prosper him!' Like Lear, he also displays a new concern for the poor: 'So distribution should undo excess, and each man have enough'.

Cordelia and Edgar are shining examples of filial love and forgiveness, redeeming their respective fathers despite the great wrongs done to them. Cordelia's intervention in English affairs is motivated solely by an admirable concern for her father, Lear: 'No blown ambition doth our arms incite, but love, dear love and our aged father's right'. She acts as a healing agent: 'Restoration hang thy medicine on my lips and let this kiss repair those violent harms that my two sisters have in thy reverence made!' Cordelia bears no grudge against her father, insisting that she has 'no cause' to resent him, and even seeks his blessing. Edgar's kindly deception of his father cures Gloucester of his despair. Convinced that he has fallen from the Cliffs of Dover, and that the gods have saved his life ('Thy life's a miracle!'), Gloucester regains the will to live. **Edgar's positive philosophy also helps to lift the gloom: 'The worst returns to laughter'.**

Kent and the Fool are inspiring examples of loyalty, remaining with and supporting Lear through his darkest hours. Kent even returns in disguise to serve the man who had earlier banished him: 'Now banished Kent, if thou canst serve where thou dost stand condemned, so may it come, thy master, whom thou lovest shall find thee full of labours'. Kent literally lives for Lear: 'My life I never held but as a pawn to wage against thy enemies'. At the close of the play the ever loyal Kent prepares to follow his master into the next world: 'I have a journey, sir, shortly to go: My master calls me, I must not say no'. The Fool never abandons Lear, remaining with him even in the eye of the fiercest storm in living memory: 'But I will tarry, the Fool will stay'.

Albany's emergence as a strong character and force for good is another positive aspect of the play. In the early stages of this drama, Albany appears to be a weak, ineffectual character, living in the shadow of his domineering wife. However, as the play unfolds, Albany develops into a stronger, more assertive character who finally tells Goneril what he really thinks of her: 'O Goneril, you are not worth the dust which the rude wind blows in your face'. He warns her that she will pay the price for her 'vile offences' and is so angry with her that he declares he would like to tear her limb from limb. No longer the 'milk-liver'd' man scorned by his wife, Albany is now capable of anger and action and promises to avenge the outrage of Gloucester's eyes. While he is compelled to do battle with the French force, he plans to be merciful towards both Lear and Cordelia. At the close of the play he plays an important part in bringing peace and order again to the realm. He is personally courageous and is prepared to engage Edmund in trial by combat, until Edgar emerges to champion his cause. He condemns Goneril and Edmund's treachery, and has no sympathy whatsoever for them when they die. He promises to reward friends and punish enemies: 'All friends shall taste the wages of their virtue, and all foes the cup of their deservings'. **Albany's development into a leader of real substance offers hope for the future.**

The humanity and glimmer of conscience that Edmund reveals in the final scene also helps to lift the gloom that shrouds the close of the play. He is moved by Edgar's account of Gloucester's death, and makes a belated effort to undo some of the evil he had intended by revealing that he has signed Lear and Cordelia's death warrants: 'Some good I mean to do despite mine own nature'. Here we see that even the villainous Edmund is not entirely devoid of humanity.

Most importantly, good ultimately triumphs over evil. All of the evil characters die at the close of the play. While the evil characters initially prosper, evil is ultimately seen to be self-destructive: Goneril poisons Regan so that she can have Edmund for herself and takes her own life when her treachery is revealed, while Edmund's evil earns its own reward when he is killed by the brother he wronged.

In conclusion, by the close of the play all the characters, good and bad, have suffered as a result of the disruption of the natural order. However, suffering brings wisdom to both Lear and Gloucester and the natural order is restored in the closing scene. Albany and Edgar will restore the kingdom to health. **Although evil is defeated at a high price, good ultimately triumphs. The triumph of good over evil leaves us feeling optimistic for a brighter future. While this play is undeniably dark, it is certainly not overwhelmingly gloomy.**

---

14. 'Why study the play?'

King Lear, like all of Shakespeare's tragedies, remains relevant to a modern-day audience. The play makes for compelling viewing because the plot is full of often surprising twists and turns and is rich in dramatic incident. The play abounds with truly dramatic scenes: the opening scene where the rash and arrogant Lear banishes the two people who love him the most and gives his two evil daughters power and authority over him; Act 3, Scene 7 where the unspeakably cruel blinding of Gloucester takes place; the storm scene where the anguished Lear cries out for universal destruction; and the heartbreakingly sad and deeply moving final scene. Everyone loves a good story, and the tale of King Lear and his daughters is precisely that.

The play presents us with themes that are enduringly relevant. Firstly, it is based on the fascinating and age-old struggle between good and evil. Evil is vividly and frighteningly portrayed in the play. Goneril and Regan display unnatural depths of cruelty, treating Lear with visible contempt after he foolishly hands the kingdom over to them. When Lear protests against the placing of his messenger in the stocks, Regan's response is dripping with contempt for her now powerless father: 'I pray you father, being weak, seem so'. Goneril and Regan heartlessly strip Lear of his remaining power and dignity, refusing to allow him to keep even a single knight ('What need one?'). Edmund is one of Shakespeare's most opportunistic and ruthless villains. Devoid of any sense of morality, Edmund believes in the law of the jungle: 'Thou, Nature, art my goddess . . .' He does not hesitate to betray his own father after he goes to Lear's assistance, even though he knows that Gloucester will face dire punishment when he returns. Evil initially prospers, but is ultimately defeated by the forces of good. In this sense the play is very reassuring: it asserts the inevitable triumph of justice, with the forces of evil ultimately preying upon and destroying each other. The play powerfully demonstrates the self-destructive nature of evil.

King Lear **offers us a range of insights into the parent-child relationship, a theme of obvious universal relevance.** We see how families and wider society are thrown into turmoil when the natural bonds that link family members are broken. In this play, both Lear and Gloucester are the first to shatter the parent-child bond when their rashness causes them to misjudge and subsequently mistreat Cordelia and Edgar respectively. Both Lear and Gloucester suffer extreme torment when they are in turn mistreated by their ungrateful and unfeeling children – Lear is driven to the point of insanity by the filial ingratitude of Goneril and Regan, while Gloucester suffers both mentally and physically after Edmund betrays him.

The play highlights the human capacity for personal growth. Both Lear and Gloucester grow through intense personal suffering, ending the play as better, wiser men. Both men ultimately come to see themselves, others and society in general more clearly. There is a memorably ironic quality to the manner in which both men attain self-knowledge and wisdom. Lear acquires what Edgar describes as 'reason in madness', while Gloucester gains moral vision at the very moment that he loses his physical vision ('I stumbled when I saw').

We are also provided with inspiring examples of the redeeming power of love. Lear and Gloucester are saved by Cordelia and Edgar respectively, loyal and loving childrern who bear no grudge against the fathers who had treated them so unjustly. Cordelia insists that she has 'no cause' to resent Lear in any way. Her only desire is to ease the pain that her evil sisters have caused Lear: 'O my dear father! Restoration, hang thy medicine on my lips, and let this kiss repair those violent harms that my two sisters have in thy reverence made'. Edgar similarly redeems Gloucester when he cures him of his despair by deceiving him into believing that he has fallen from the Cliffs of Dover and that the gods have saved him: 'Thy life's a miracle!'

The play also presents us with uplifting examples of nobility and loyalty in the persons of Kent and the Fool respectively. Kent devotes his entire life to Lear's service. Even though he is a nobleman, Kent returns in disguise to serve Lear in any way he can after he has been banished from the realm by the rash king: 'Now, banished Kent, if thou canst serve where thou dost stand condemned, so may it come, thy master, whom thou lov'st, shall find thee full of labours'. Kent's loyalty to Lear is total and unwavering; even death is not regarded as a barrier to his extraordinary fidelity to his master. Even though Albany asks him to join Edgar and himself in ruling the kingdom, Kent refuses the offer because, in the manner of an ancient Roman, he is determined to follow his master into the next world: 'I have a journey, sir, shortly to go; my master calls me, I must not say no'. The Fool similarly follows Lear through his painful journey towards self-awareness. Like Kent, the Fool does not hesitate to highlight Lear's foolish behaviour; indeed he sees it as his primary duty to relentlessly remind Lear of all that he has done wrong ('. . . thou hadst little wit in thy bald crown when thou gavest thy golden one away', '. . . thou madest thy daughters thy mothers'). The Fool's remarkable loyalty to Lear is best seen when he remains with him on the wild moor throughout the worst storm in living memory. It is here that we see the Fool's loving concern for Lear: 'Good nuncle, in and ask thy daughters' blessing. Here's a night pities neither wise man nor fool'.

The fact that the sub-plot reflects and reinforces key themes in the main plot underlines the universality of these themes.

The Characters

LEAR

While Lear initially appears to be nothing more than an arrogant, autocratic tyrant, we gradually realise that he is essentially a noble, but tragically flawed character. We sympathise with Lear in his suffering and admire his acquisition of humility, insight (vision) and self-knowledge, **However, our sympathy for Lear must not blind us to the reality that he is very much the architect of his own downfall.** Lear's description of himself as a man 'more sinn'd against than sinning' is essentially correct. We naturally sympathise with a 'fond, foolish old man' who is deliberately and callously humiliated by his 'pelican daughters' and pained to the point of insanity by their ingratitude. However, it is Lear's tragically-flawed character and his initial disruption of the natural order (brought about by his selfish abdication from power and his unnatural treatment of the loyal and loving Cordelia), that sets an ultimately tragic train of events in motion.

From the opening scene, we are aware of a number of weaknesses in Lear's character. Lear is concerned only for himself; he is selfish and egocentric. His self-centred attitude is strikingly evident in his desire to enjoy the trappings of power, without any of the responsibilities: 'Only we shall retain the name, and all the additions to a king; the sway revenue, execution of the rest, beloved sons be yours'. **Lear is also extremely arrogant,** reacting angrily to Kent's efforts to make him aware of his own wrongdoing in relation to Cordelia. Lear's self-image underscores his arrogance. He sees himself as a fearsome 'dragon' whose 'wrath' is to be avoided. Lear is gullible and susceptible to flattery, as the 'love test' shows. **Lear is fiery and rash** – he disinherits and disowns Cordelia because she refuses to pander to his ego and banishes Kent because he urges him to 'check this hideous rashness'. The rashness, which Lear displays in the opening scene, is no isolated moral lapse - it is again evident in the violent language used to curse Goneril: 'into her womb convey sterility; dry up in her the organs of increase . . .'

Lear lacks self-knowledge and moral vision. In Regan's words, Lear 'hath ever but slenderly known himself'. Lear must acquire self-knowledge before coming to understand others and the world in general. It is only through suffering that Lear acquires humility and insight. **Lear's spiritual or moral growth is gradual and painful.** While he ironically acquires 'reason in madness', his personal development is uneven. Even as he acquires self-understanding, Lear at different times displays the naivety, arrogance, rashness and egocentricity (self-centred nature) so dramatically in evidence in the opening scene.

When Goneril treats her father with open disrespect, the effect on Lear is profound. When Lear was king, he had no conception of himself as a man, rather ridiculously seeing himself as a terrifying dragon-like figure. When he gives away his power and authority, he is treated not as an all-powerful king but as an irritating old man. As a result, his self-image is severely shaken: 'Who is it that can tell me who I am?' Stung by what he sees as Goneril's 'marble-hearted' ingratitude Lear takes his first painful steps on the road to self-knowledge: 'O Lear, Lear, Lear! Beat at the gate that led thy folly in and thy dear judgement out!' The realisation that he is powerless to respond to Goneril adds to his frustration and anguish. Lear's acknowledgement that his treatment of Cordelia was wrong marks another step in his personal growth. He tells the Fool: 'I did her wrong'. It is ironic that as Lear begins to acquire insight, he simultaneously edges closer to insanity: 'O, let me not be mad, not mad, sweet heaven! Keep me in temper: I would not be mad'. It is the disintegration of his self-image that lies at the root of Lear's loss of sanity. The actual onset of madness is accelerated by his towering rages.

Lear is further humiliated when his servant Kent is placed in the stocks. He reacts with disbelief to this deliberate act of blatant disrespect: 'They durst not do it; they could not, would not do't; 'tis worse than murder to do upon respect such violent outrage'. Lear senses how close he is to insanity: 'O, how this mother swells up toward my heart!' We are reminded of Lear's continuing spiritual blindness when he is unable or unwilling to see that Goneril and Regan are fundamentally alike. Naively, he tells Regan: 'Thou shalt never have my curse . . . thou better knows't the offices of nature, bond of childhood, effects of courtesy, dues of gratitude'. Goneril and Regan's treatment of their father is particularly reprehensible because of its deliberate, pre-meditated nature. Lear realises that his daughters are acting as one against him when Regan takes Goneril by the hand. We cannot but sympathise with a powerless old man who pathetically points out, 'I gave you all'.

While Lear grows through suffering, his acquisition of self-knowledge is a gradual process. Lear foolishly continues to believe that he can measure love. In the opening scene, he believed that he could measure love on the basis of words; now he believes that he can measure love in terms of the number of knights he is to be allowed: 'Thy fifty yet doth double five-and-twenty, and thou art twice her love'. Having given up all of his power and authority, his daughters now strip him of his dignity: 'What need one?' Lear's sanity is profoundly shaken: 'O fool, I shall go mad!' Lear's 'heart-struck injuries' result in what Kent aptly describes as 'bemadding sorrow'.

The storm scene represents the climax of the play; it is a scene full of drama and irony. Stripped of his authority, dignity, even his very clothes, Lear acquires 'reason in madness'. He sees himself for what he is: 'A poor, infirm, weak and despised old man'. He shows his humanity in his concern for the Fool and realises that, as king, he neglected the poor. Lear's newly-discovered social conscience prompts him to preach the idea of social justice, as he suggests that wealth should be distributed more fairly: 'Expose thyself to what wretches feel that thou mayest shake the superflux to them and show the heavens more just'.

Lear's towering rages accelerate and finally precipitate (bring about) the onset of madness. On the heath, Lear feels his wits 'begin to turn'. By the end of the storm scene, Kent observes that 'all the power of his wits have given way to his impatience'. While he promises to be 'the pattern of all patience', tranquillity inevitably leads to reflection, recollection, and another 'high rage'. In this sense, Lear's behaviour on the moor assumes a cyclical pattern.

In the storm scene we see many examples of Lear's acquisition of 'reason in madness'. He wisely tells the blind Gloucester that 'A man may see how this world goes with no eyes'. He realises that appearances can be deceptive: 'Robes and furr'd gowns hide all'. The clothing image suggests how clothes (symbolising wealth and material possessions) can blind people to their own and to others' shortcomings. Lear himself is closest to nature and to self-knowledge when he is naked on the moors in the eye of the storm. He becomes aware of the unjust, corrupt nature of the world in which he lives: 'Plate sin with gold and the strong lance of justice hurtless breaks: arm it in rags, a pigmy's straw doth pierce it'. In other words, he realises that wealthy people are never punished for their wrongdoing.

A further indication of Lear's personal growth is the 'burning shame' that he feels in relation to Cordelia. The extent of Lear's anguish and torment is clear in his initial reaction to seeing Cordelia; he imagines himself 'bound upon a wheel of fire that mine own tears do scald like molten lead'. Lear now sees himself for what he is: 'a very foolish, fond old man'. He realises that he is not in his 'perfect mind' but knows that Cordelia has 'cause' not to love him: 'If you have poison for me, I will drink it'. Lear has acquired humility and self-understanding and now seeks forgiveness: 'You must bear with me; pray you now; forget and forgive: I am old and foolish'.

Lear's enduring rashness is evident in the immediate aftermath of Cordelia's death when he curses all of those around him: 'A plague upon you, murderers, traitors all'. Lear's personal growth is uneven in the sense that even as he grows, certain ingrained weaknesses persist. However, we cannot but be deeply moved by Lear's intense grief at Cordelia's death: 'Howl, howl, howl, howl! O, you are men of stones!' While we are fully cognisant (aware) of Lear's responsibility for Cordelia's death (it was he who set the entire train of tragic events in motion in the opening scene), we cannot but sympathise with an old man who ends the play a better and wiser character having been truly stretched on the rack of life.

KEY ADJECTIVES

Initially:	Ultimately:
• rash, impetuous, impulsive	• rash (his most ingrained weakness through to the close of the play)
• arrogant	
• foolish	• humble
• gullible, naive, credulous	• wise, perceptive (to a degree)
• unjust, harsh	• compassionate, caring

GLOUCESTER

Like Lear, Gloucester is initially gullible, rash and morally blind. In the same way that Lear falls victim to the 'glib and oily' flattery of Goneril and Regan, Gloucester's credulous nature is easily exploited by Edmund. **Gloucester, like Lear, is rash in his reactions,** impulsively condemning Edgar without any objective evidence of his guilt: 'Abhorred villain! Unnatural, detested brutish villain!' The manner in which Gloucester disinherits Edgar is strikingly similar to Lear's treatment of Cordelia, being similarly rash and unjust. Without ever giving Edgar an opportunity to defend his reputation and honour, Gloucester makes a fugitive of his loyal son before going on to impetuously declare that Edmund will be his heir : '. . . of my land loyal and natural boy, I'll work the means to make thee capable'.

Gloucester is a decidedly weak though good-natured man, making no effort to support Kent in challenging Lear's dangerously foolish decision-making in the opening scene. He strikes us as an ineffectual character who is easily manipulated – initially by Edmund for his own evil ends and later by Edgar for the compassionate purpose of ridding him of his despair. Edmund laughs at Gloucester's superstitious nature, describing as 'the excellent foppery of the world' the tendency to blame our disasters on 'the sun, the moon and the stars'. Gloucester's superstitious nature is to be seen in his belief that the gods dictate the course of human life: 'As flies to wanton boys are we to the gods; they kill us for their sport'. Edgar exploits his father's superstitious nature for a noble purpose when he tricks him into believing that he has jumped from the cliff at Dover, before convincing him that the gods have spared his life ('Thy life's a miracle'), thereby renewing Gloucester's desire to live and accept whatever life presents him with.

Gloucester is a flawed but essentially noble and decent character. He protests against Kent being placed in the stocks, pointing out to Cornwall that Lear will be angered by this act of blatant disrespect towards him: 'Let me beseech your grace not to do so . . . the king must take it ill that he is so slightly valued in his messenger'. Gloucester's gentle protest is ignored, but reflects his sense of justice. His noble nature is also evident in his determination to help Lear even at the risk of his own life: 'Though I die for it, as no less is threatened me, the king my old master must be relieved'.

Gloucester displays a stoical (philosophical

acceptance of life's varying fortunes) **side to his character when he is tortured by Cornwall:** 'I am tied to the stake, and I must stand the course'.

Similar to Lear, Gloucester acquires self-knowledge and moral vision through intense suffering. Both are enlightened by their sufferings and both gain insight in an ironic fashion. While Lear acquires 'reason in madness', Gloucester acquires inner or spiritual vision at the moment he is made physically blind: 'O my follies! Then Edgar was abused, kind gods, forgive me that, and prosper him!' Gloucester acknowledges the irony of simultaneously losing his physical sight and acquiring moral vision when he remarks, 'I stumbled when I saw . . .' While Lear's personal growth is a protracted (drawn out) process, Gloucester's acquisition of insight is sudden and dramatic.

Gloucester learns to care for others. Lear's

concern on the moor for the Fool is reflected in Gloucester's concern for the old man who guides him after he has been blinded: '. . . good friend, be gone; thy comforts can do me no good at all; thee, they may harm'. Both learn to care for the poor and unfortunate and come to subscribe to the idea of social justice. Gloucester declares that 'distribution should undo excess and each man have enough'. He learns that wealth can contribute to spiritual blindness, speaking of 'the superfluous and lust-dieted man . . . that will not see because he doth not feel'.

Gloucester pays the ultimate price for his failings. Like Lear, Gloucester experiences both joy and grief before his death. Edgar describes how his father reacted when he finally revealed his true identity to him: 'his flawed heart . . . 'twixt two extremes of passion, joy and grief, burst smilingly'.

KEY ADJECTIVES

Initially:
- gullible, credulous, naive
- superstitious
- rash, impetuous, impulsive
- unjust, harsh

Ultimately:
- wiser
- philosophical
- caring, compassionate

CORDELIA

While her appearances are rare and her contributions limited, Cordelia's character remains etched indelibly (forever imprinted) on our memories. Cordelia plays a central role in the drama. Had she gone along with Lear's whims and pandered to his ego, the whole tragedy might have been avoided. However, if Cordelia had flattered her father, she would not have been true to herself and to those aspects of her character which earn our admiration. Like Edgar, she is a shining example of filial love and loyalty. Her genuine affection and capacity for forgiveness stand in stark contrast to the false love and vengeful natures of her sisters.

In the dramatic opening scene, Cordelia's

courage and integrity are immediately evident. Even though she risks losing her inheritance, she refuses to employ the 'glib and oily art' of flattery so effectively used by her sisters. Cordelia's motto is to 'love and be silent'. Her love for her father is genuine: 'I am sure my love's more richer than my tongue'. She prefaces her declaration of love for her father by stating, 'I cannot leave my heart into my mouth', reflecting her inability to engage in the ingratiating art of flattery. In refusing to flatter her father, Cordelia makes a brave and principled stand against both Lear's foolish pride and her sisters' sickening hypocrisy. While Cordelia's declaration of love for Lear ('I love your majesty according to my bond; nor more nor less') suggests cold indifference rather than genuine affection, her love for her father is real. Her declaration of love is characterised by economy of language and – more importantly – sincerity of feeling. Cordelia believes that actions say a great deal more than words: '. . . what I well intend, I'll do't before I speak'. While we admire her courage and spirit, it is her stubborn refusal to humour a foolish, sentimental old man by participating in his childish 'love test' which brings about the catastrophe.

Cordelia's strong character is again evident when she confronts her father in front of the whole assembly and asks Lear to 'make known' **that she has not fallen from favour because of some 'unchaste action or dishonour'd step'.** Cordelia displays great composure throughout this opening scene; she remains firmly in control of her emotions and, though treated very unjustly, never expresses anger or resentment.

Cordelia is shrewd and sharp-witted, seeing her sisters for what they are: 'I know you what you are'. She believes that their true natures will become apparent in time: 'Time shall unfold what plaited cunning hides'. **Her loving and forgiving nature** is evident in her concern for her father now that he is dependent on Goneril and Regan: 'I would prefer him to a better place'.

Cordelia's royalty of nature is reflected in the manner in which she responds to the news of Lear's suffering: she is described as being 'a queen over her passion'. She responds to Kent's letter (informing her of her father's plight) with 'patience and sorrow' rather than anger. Cordelia is deeply moved by Lear's suffering but, as in the opening scene, does not allow her emotions to overwhelm her. She is regarded as an almost saintly figure:'. . . she shook the holy water from her heavenly eyes'.

Her generous and forgiving nature is reflected in her desire to restore Lear's 'bereaved sense'. She would willingly give all of her material wealth to anyone who could restore her father to health: 'he that helps him take all my outward

worth'. She is perceptive and recognises that Lear's 'ungovern'd rage' not only exacerbates his mental condition but threatens to 'dissolve' his life. The depth of her love for her father is evident when she explains the motivation behind the French intervention: 'No blown ambition doth our arms incite, but love, dear love and our aged father's right'.

Cordelia displays her leadership qualities when she leads the French expedition to rescue Lear. After landing in Dover a messenger arrives to inform her that the British forces are marching towards them. However, Cordelia is already aware of this development and has ensured that her forces are ready: ''Tis known before; our preparation stands in expectation of them'.

Cordelia is seen as a healing agent who comforts and consoles her suffering father: 'Restoration hang thy medicine on my lips; and let this kiss repair those violent harms that my two sisters have in thy reverence made!' Her innate (natural) goodness is such that she finds it difficult to comprehend the depth of her sisters' cruelty: 'Mine enemy's dog, though he had bit me, should have stood that night against my fire'. She bears no ill-will towards her father. Cordelia tells Lear that she has 'no cause' to be angry. Her forgiving, warm nature brings out the good qualities in Lear. He is a much humbler man now and readily admits to his faults. Cordelia's strength of character and concern for her father are evident when she and Lear are taken prisoner by Edmund: 'For thee, oppress'd king, am I cast down, myself could else out-frown false fortune's frown'. Like Edgar, Cordelia, is ever sensitive to the sufferings of others but refuses to indulge in self-pity.

If Goneril and Regan are the embodiments of evil, Cordelia is the personification of goodness. Aside from a stubborn streak, she epitomises all that is best in human nature. Her virtue is a necessary counterweight to the evil represented by her sisters. She is a model of filial love and loyalty and her death is the darkest moment in the play.

KEY ADJECTIVES

- good, virtuous
- honest, sincere, candid
- stubborn, obstinate (slightly)
- brave, courageous
- shrewd, perceptive, astute
- calm, composed
- capable
- loving, tender, affectionate
- forgiving, compassionate

EDGAR

Edgar undergoes significant personal development in the course of the play. While he may initially be regarded as a credulous, malleable (easily influenced) character, he ultimately emerges as an impressively capable figure and a force for good. Like Lear, Gloucester and Albany, Edgar grows as a character, learning from his own painful experience and from witnessing the suffering of others at first hand. In the course of his personal development, Edgar always retains his nobility of mind. Like Cordelia, Edgar is a shining example of goodness and a model of filial love and loyalty. Like her, he too is wronged by his father but bears no resentment towards him. Both Edgar and Cordelia act as healing agents, easing the suffering of their respective fathers.

While Edgar initially strikes us as a gullible, rather lightweight character who is easily manipulated by his more cunning brother, it should be remembered that it is his fundamentally noble nature which prevents him from suspecting that it is Edmund who is the 'villain' who has blackened his reputation.

As the play unfolds, Edgar displays great inner strength and endurance. He is optimistic, stoical and resourceful. He never succumbs to despair or self-pity, even when he is forced 'to take the basest and most poorest shape'. In assuming the guise of a mad beggar, Edgar demonstrates his resourcefulness. He makes light of his own suffering. When he witnesses Lear's anguish, he dismisses his own pain: 'How light and portable my pain seems now when that which makes me bend makes the king bow'.

Edgar is extremely sensitive to the suffering of others. He is deeply moved by the intensity of Lear's pain: 'My tears begin to take his part so much, they'll mar my counterfeiting'. He is so affected by the heartbreaking sight of the blinded Gloucester that he finds it difficult to keep up his pretence (act) as Poor Tom ('I cannot daub it further').

Edgar's noble and forgiving nature is evident in his desire to cure Gloucester of his self-pity: 'Why I do trifle thus with his despair is done to cure it'. The pretence of leading Gloucester to the edge of the cliffs at Dover is an innocent deception, which is designed to restore his father's will to live. While Gloucester is initially angry to find that he is still alive, Edgar convinces him that his life is a 'miracle' and that 'the clearest gods, who make them honours of men's impossibilities' have preserved him. While Edmund had earlier exploited Gloucester's gullibility for his own evil ends, Edgar exploits his father's credulous nature for a noble purpose. Edgar's plan is successful, and from this point Gloucester is determined to accept whatever the gods have in store for him: 'Henceforth I'll bear affliction till it do cry out itself "Enough, enough" and die'. Gloucester, who had earlier compared the gods to 'wanton boys' who kill flies (men) for 'their sport', now prays to the 'ever-gentle gods' that his 'worser spirit' will never again tempt him to end his life.

Edgar is a man of action. When the cowardly Oswald raises his sword against Gloucester's 'eyeless head', Edgar confronts this 'serviceable villain' and kills him. Edgar later accuses Edmund in a direct manner and challenges him to deny the truth of his accusations: '. . . thou art a traitor/False to thy gods, thy brother and thy father,/Conspirant 'gainst this high, illustrious prince'. Before his brother dies, Edgar nobly and generously exchanges forgiveness with him.

Throughout the play Edgar never accepts that life will not improve, regardless of how low an ebb his fortunes may be at: 'The worst returns to laughter', '. . . .the worst is not so long as we can say "This is the worst"'. Edgar's cheerful confidence comes not only from his optimistic temperament, but from his unshakeable faith in the 'clearest gods'. He has a deep and unwavering faith in the ultimate triumph of good over evil. He regards Edmund's death as divine justice as work: 'The gods are just, and of our pleasant vices make instruments to plague us'.

In an age when the natural bonds that should bind families together are often shattered without a thought, Edgar, like Cordelia stands out as a model of filial love and loyalty. His **admirable stoicism** (acceptance of life's varying fortunes) is reflected in the advice which he offers to Gloucester: 'Men must endure their going hence, even as their coming hither: Ripeness is all'. At his lowest point, when he is forced to play the part of a mad Bedlam beggar ('the lowest and most dejected thing of fortune'), Edgar remains **resilient and optimistic**. He helps not only to ease his father's suffering but to restore the natural order. **After an unpromising beginning, Edgar develops into a character of real substance who, by the close of the drama, is set to play a central role in ensuring the recovery and future welfare of the state.**

KEY ADJECTIVES

- noble, honourable, virtuous
- credulous, gullible (initially)
- resilient, strong, tough, stoical
- resourceful, capable
- optimistic, cheerful, positive
- brave, courageous
- forgiving, compassionate
- loyal, devoted
- loving

KENT

From the opening scene Kent wins the admiration of the audience – he is loyal, courageous, blunt and perceptive. Kent continues to demonstrate these traits throughout the play.

Kent's loyalty to Lear is absolute and unwavering. Kent's love for Lear is the guiding force of his life; it is no exaggeration to say that Kent lives for Lear: 'My life I never held but as a pawn to wage against thine enemies'. Kent's love and respect for Lear are evident in the manner in which he addresses his king: 'Royal Lear, whom I have ever honoured as my king, loved as my father, as my master followed, as my great patron thought on in my prayers'. However, Kent's love for and devotion to Lear do not blind him to Lear's faults, on the contrary, it is these very

qualities that compel him to confront the king and highlight the gravity of his wrongdoing: '. . . be Kent unmannerly when Lear is mad . . . Reverse thy doom and in thy best consideration check this hideous rashness'. When all others are intimidated by Lear's fury and remain silent in the face of his blatantly unjust treatment of Cordelia, Kent counsels him to 'see better', before bluntly telling him: 'I'll tell thee thou dost evil'. Kent is perceptive and sees people for what they are. He expresses his respect and concern for Cordelia ('The gods to their dear shelter, take thee, maid'). He sees through Goneril and Regan's flattery and doubts if their actions will match their words: 'And your large speeches may your deeds approve/That good effects may spring from words of love'.

Despite Lear's harsh mistreatment of him,

Kent's loyalty to his master never wavers.
Even after being banished and threatened with
death, he is determined to return in disguise and
serve Lear in some capacity: 'Now, banish'd
Kent,/If thou canst serve where thou dost stand
condemn'd, so may it come, thy master, whom
thou lovest shall find thee full of labours'. Kent
is infuriated by Oswald's blatant lack of respect
for Lear, and does not let it pass unpunished,
immediately tripping Oswald up and pushing
him out. There is no element of tact or diplomacy
in Kent's make-up; on the contrary, he can be
quite a fiery character.

**It is Kent's undisguised contempt for
Oswald and his subsequent blunt responses
to Cornwall that result in him being placed
in the stocks.** Kent is aware that Oswald has
come as Goneril's messenger 'with letters
against the king'. He subjects this 'cowardly
rascal' to a tongue-lashing before drawing his
sword and beating him, accusing him of taking
'the puppet's part' against the royalty of his
mistress' (Goneril) father. When questioned by
Cornwall, Kent is typically direct: '. . . anger
hath a privilege'. He later tells Cornwall, 'I am
no flatterer'. Cornwall orders that this 'stubborn
ancient knave' be placed in the stocks. Kent
points out that since he is the king's messenger,
this degrading punishment is in fact an insult
to Lear: 'You shall do small respect, show too
bold malice against the grace and person of
my master, stocking his messenger'. Lear is
incensed to find Kent in the stocks ('. . . 'tis
worse than murder to do upon respect such
violent outrage') and in the dramatic scene
which follows comes to realise the full extent of
his foolishness. This episode brings the quarrel
between Lear and his daughters into the open,
with the battle-lines between good and evil now
clear to be seen.

**Significantly, Kent's soliloquy at the end
of this scene reveals that he has succeeded
in getting news of Lear's predicament to
Cordelia.** Kent resolves to co-operate with
Cordelia in her efforts to set right the wrongs
done in the kingdom: 'seeking to give losses
their remedies'. In helping to re-establish links
between Lear and Cordelia, Kent performs one

of his most important dramatic functions. In Act
3, Scene 1 Kent asks the gentleman to hurry
to Dover to report on Lear's 'unnatural and
bemadding sorrow'. While this gentleman does
not know Kent, the latter proudly asserts that
he is 'a gentleman of blood and breeding' and
as such that he speaks the truth. Kent gives the
gentleman a ring which Cordelia will recognise.
Through Kent's later conversation with the
gentleman we learn of Cordelia's response to
the news of Lear's suffering. Her reaction to the
news contained in Kent's letters is characterised
by 'patience and sorrow'. Kent helps to keep
Cordelia in the minds of the audience when she
is not on stage.

**Kent updates the audience on important
political and military developments.** He
informs us of the growing division between
Albany and Cornwall: 'There is division,
although as yet the face of it be covered with
mutual cunning, 'twixt Albany and Cornwall'.
Through Kent we learn that the forces of good
are now assembling and are on their way to
rescue Lear: '. . . from France there comes a
power into this scattered Kingdom'.

**Kent regularly comments on and clarifies
Lear's mental state for the audience:** 'His
wits begin to unsettle'; 'All the power of his
wits have given way to his impatience'; '. . . his
wits are gone'; '. . . sometime in his better tune
remembers what we are come about'. Kent also
explains why Lear is reluctant to meet Cordelia:
'. . . burning shame detains him from Cordelia'.
**Kent remains with and watches over Lear
as the storm rages on the heath, guiding his
master towards the shelter of a hovel.** Lear
asks him, 'Wilt break my heart?' Kent's response
reflects his deep affection and absolute fidelity
(loyalty) to his master: 'I had rather break mine
own'. Again that loyalty does not prevent Kent
from speaking the truth to Lear. When Lear,
with typical egocentricity, blames Poor Tom's
miserable condition on his daughters, Kent tells
him: 'He hath no daughters, sir'. Recognising
that Lear's angry outbursts exacerbate (worsen)
his mental condition, the concerned Kent urges
Lear to be patient: 'Sir, where is the patience
now that you so oft have boasted to retain?' Even

when Lear loses his sanity, Kent never fails to address him respectfully: 'Good my lord . . .'; 'Sir . . .'

Kent is an admirably philosophical character who believes that life is governed by the stars: 'it is the stars, the stars above us, that govern our conditions'. He believes that the wheel of fortune always turns full circle. After he has been placed in the stocks, Kent looks forward to better times ahead: 'Fortune, good night: smile once more, turn thy wheel'.

Kent's affection for and total loyalty to his master are strikingly evident in the closing stages of the play. Cordelia thanks Kent for his loyalty to Lear: 'O thou good Kent, how shall I live and work to match thy goodness?' Kent's own heart is close to breaking point when he witnesses Lear's overwhelming grief at Cordelia's death: 'Break, heart; I prithee, break!' Kent has followed his master's 'sad steps' through all his sorrow and suffering and shows great compassion for his king in his final agony. While others hope to revive the dying Lear, Kent knows that Lear has suffered enough and that it would be cruel to prolong his agony further: 'Vex not his ghost: O, let him pass! He hates him that would upon the rack of this tough world stretch him out longer'. Kent's loyalty to Lear is not limited to the physical world; his devotion to his master is such that he wishes to join him in death: 'I have a journey, sir, shortly to go, my master calls me, I must not say no'. Kent's unwavering loyalty to Lear reminds us that we are witnessing the downfall of a once-great man. Through Kent's eyes we see an earlier, greater Lear – a man whose finer qualities inspired such selfless devotion in the noble Kent.

KEY ADJECTIVES

- loyal, devoted
- loving (towards Lear)
- shrewd, perceptive, astute
- blunt, direct
- courageous, fearless
- philosophical

THE FOOL

The Fool is no ordinary court jester introduced into the play for the sole purpose of providing a little levity and relieving the tension of the drama. It would probably be incorrect to regard him as an entirely sane man pretending to be mad (the evidence of the play suggests that he was well-suited to playing the role of court jester), yet he possesses penetrating insight and sound common sense. **In relentlessly reminding Lear of his foolishness, the Fool helps his old master to achieve self-knowledge.** The Fool displays remarkable loyalty, remaining with Lear throughout his descent into insanity. He also shows a real and sincere concern for Lear's welfare.

Lear describes his jester as 'a bitter fool' because he tells Lear the bitter truth at all times: 'Thou hadst little wit in thy bald crown when thou gavest thy golden one away'. The fool recognises that the truth is not always well-received: 'Truth's a dog must to kennel,' but nonetheless never refrains from giving full rein to his caustic (sarcastic/barbed) wit in reminding Lear of the errors of his ways. When Lear asks him: 'Dost thou call me fool, boy?' The Fool's response is typically sharp: 'All thy other titles thou hast given away; that thou wast born with'. The Fool reminds Lear that he has given Goneril and Regan power and authority over him:

'. . . thou madest thy daughters thy mother'. Emphasising that Lear has left himself at the mercy of his daughters, the Fool tells him that even a snail has a house and would not 'leave his horns without a case'. Determined to make his master aware of his mistakes and shortcomings, the Fool never spares Lear's feelings: 'Thou shouldst not have been old till thou hadst been wise'. The Fool disguises many of his highly philosophical reflections with nonsense songs: 'Fathers that wear rags do make their children blind'. There is a sharp edge to the Fool's wit and his seemingly meaningless songs often contain an element of truth. Goneril describes the Fool as 'all-licensed' because he seems to be allowed to say whatever he likes. The Fool can speak his mind precisely because he is regarded as an idiot. Kent acknowledges the Fool's sharp wit: 'This is not altogether fool, my Lord'.

The Fool's most striking quality is his loyalty to Lear. In one of his songs, he informs Lear that while his knights have already gone, he will stay: 'But I will tarry; the fool will stay'. As Lear faces the fury of the storm tormented by his daughters'

filial ingratitude, the Fool is still with him, doing his best to keep up the spirits of the king in his blackest hour. The Fool has a real and sincere concern for Lear's welfare. He is worried about the destructive effects of the storm on Lear's mind, as well as the obvious physical hardship which it brings: 'Good nuncle, in, and ask thy daughter's blessing: here's a night pities neither wise men nor fools'. Throughout the play, the Fool continually reminds Lear of the foolishness of his abdication. However, he makes no attempt to impart any moral lessons during the storm, fearing the effects of the violent tempest on Lear's mind: 'This cold night will turn us all to fools and madmen'.

The Fool's purpose is to prompt Lear to reflect on those foolish actions which gave rise to the tragedy. He is Lear's conscience, his inner voice that relentlessly reminds him of his foolishness. The Fool helps and supports Lear on his painful spiritual journey to self-knowledge. **Once Lear has acquired self-knowledge, the Fool's dramatic role is fulfilled and we neither see nor hear of him beyond the storm scene.**

KEY ADJECTIVES

- loyal, devoted
- courageous
- insightful, wise

- blunt, direct
- caring (towards Lear)

GONERIL

Goneril is the most abhorrent of the evil characters. Her sister is equally evil, but Goneril is stronger and more repulsive than Regan and dominates this sibling relationship. There are no moral depths that Goneril will not plumb in her utterly ruthless pursuit of her ambitions.

In the opening scene we clearly see her hypocrisy when she claims to love her father, 'more than words can wield the matter'. She is cunning and unscrupulous in the way she uses flattery to achieve her ends. She tells Regan what she really thinks of Lear, criticising his 'poor judgement' and 'unruly waywardness'.

Having seen Cordelia suffer because of Lear's rashness, Goneril is determined to ensure that she never suffers because of his fiery nature. She conspires with Regan to further undermine (weaken) Lear's position: 'Pray you, let's hit together'. It is Goneril who insists that they take action against Lear without delay: 'We must do something and in the heat' (without delay).

Goneril's utter contempt for Lear is obvious when she refers to him as an 'idle old man that still would manage those authorities that he hath given away'. When she witnesses Lear's behaviour in her castle, she disdainfully concludes that, 'Old fools are babes again'.

Goneril encourages Oswald and her other servants to neglect and openly disrespect Lear: 'Put on what weary negligence you please'. Along with Regan, she is determined to take away all that remains of Lear's kingly dignity. She complains about Lear's 'insolent retinue' (bad-mannered knights) before going on to dismiss half of them in an instant. Lear had naively expected his daughters to treat him like a king, but this blatant insult to his status opens his eyes to his daughter's true nature. Lear curses Goneril in the strongest terms imaginable, but she is unmoved by his vitriolic attack. While both Goneril and Regan deliberately humiliate Lear, it is Goneril who initiates most of the schemes to undermine Lear's status. She writes to Regan, urging her to treat Lear as she has done ('hold my very course'). When the enraged Lear leaves her home to go to Regan's, Goneril follows shortly afterwards to ensure that Regan acts on her instructions. She is the more enterprising and domineering of the two evil sisters.

As the play unfolds, we see the growing gap between Goneril and her husband. She regards Albany with contempt, and is disparaging (insulting) in what she regards as his 'milky gentleness' and 'cowish terror'. Goneril is attracted to Edmund, an ambitious, ruthless man of action, perhaps seeing in him a kindred spirit. This attraction appears to be the only indication of her humanity.

Goneril's extraordinary cruelty is dramatically displayed in her desire to avenge herself on Gloucester: 'Pluck out his eyes!' She has no reservations about any action, however evil. Most strikingly, she displays no qualms of conscience about planning her husband's death. Edgar is horrified to discover this 'plot upon her virtuous husband's life'. In her letter to Edmund, Goneril writes that he will have 'many opportunities' to 'cut him [Albany] off'. Goneril's ruthlessness is further reflected in her poisoning of Regan. She also adds her name to Edmund's on the death warrant for Lear and Cordelia. Her calculated humiliation of Lear only hints at the depths of evil demonstrated later in the play.

Unsurprisingly, Goneril is a strong, capable leader. While she initially claims that she would sooner lose the battle against the French than lose Edmund to Regan, her more practical side quickly asserts itself as she perceives the necessity of unity in the face of the enemy: 'Combine together 'gainst the enemy; for these domestic and particular broils are not the question here'.

Ruthless, vengeful and utterly devoid of humanity, she is a truly monstrous character. She possesses no redeeming traits and may be regarded as the embodiment of evil. Hesitation is not part of Goneril's make-up and her unhesitating suicide is entirely in keeping with her character.

A series of images suggest that Goneril is devoid (without) of humanity. She is a 'detested kite', a 'sea-monster', 'a devil', 'a fiend', a 'gilded serpent', 'a vulture'. For Lear, the pain of her filial ingratitude is 'sharper than a serpent's tooth'. These images suggest her formidable, but despicable, character.

KEY ADJECTIVES

- evil, malevolent, malicious
- amoral (no morals)
- false, deceptive, hypocritical
- ambitious
- despicable, contemptible, vile, detestable
- ruthless, inhuman, callous, cruel
- domineering, autocratic
- strong, capable, practical

REGAN

Like Goneril, Regan is innately evil and capable of savage cruelty. These evil sisters are fundamentally alike in that their actions are never influenced either by conscience or by normal human feelings. However, as early as the end of the opening scene, we see that Regan tends to be dominated by Goneril, who is the more domineering, more active sister.

Regan's hypocrisy is evident in the opening scene. There is irony in Regan's suggestion that she is made of 'the self metal' as her sister, because both are equally false and evil. Her response to Lear's love test is to claim that Goneril's expression of love 'comes too short' – an early sign of rivalry that destroys their relationship later in the play. Regan's treatment of Lear is callous. She emphasises Lear's advanced age ('O, sir you are old, nature in you stands on the very verge of her confine') and his powerlessness ('I pray you, father, being weak, seem so'). Nowhere is her filial ingratitude more obvious than in her contemptuous response to Lear's pathetic attempt to remind his unnatural daughters of his generosity towards them ('I gave you all . . .'): 'And in good time you gave it'. Her utter lack of feeling for her father is strikingly evident when she shuts the doors of her castle against him: 'O, sir, to wilful men the injuries that they themselves procure must be their schoolmasters'. Lear is left to face what Kent later describes as the worst storm in living memory. Stunned by the depth of this cruelty, Cordelia later remarks that she would have kept her enemy's dog by her fire on the night of that most violent of storms. Regan, in contrast, displays not a trace of filial love or loyalty towards her father, whom she contemptuously refers to as 'the lunatic king'. It is little wonder that in the mock trial scene the insane Lear asks, 'Is there any cause in nature that makes these hard hearts?'

We see Regan's vindictiveness when she countermands her husband's order and lengthens Kent's punishment in the stocks.

No sooner has Cornwall ordered that Kent is to remain in the stocks 'till noon', than Regan immediately orders that he is to remain there 'all night too'. That she is no less evil than Goneril is particularly clear from the role she plays in the mutilation of Gloucester. She initially demands that he be hanged 'instantly'. When Gloucester still possesses one eye, she cruelly says: 'One eye will mock another, the other too'. The servant who goes to Gloucester's assistance is stabbed in the back by Regan, and she takes a cruel delight in informing Gloucester that it was Edmund who betrayed him: '. . . it was he that made the overture of thy treasons to us, who is too good to pity thee'. She callously tells Gloucester to 'smell his way to Dover'. Regan's ruthlessness is again evident when she later remarks that 'it was great ignorance Gloucester's eyes being out to let him live'. She promises to reward Oswald if he kills Gloucester: 'Preferment falls on him that cuts him off'.

Regan's rivalry with and jealousy of Goneril is such that she is willing to open a private letter from her sister to Edmund. Regan's passion for Edmund ultimately leads to her handing her title, her soldiers and her prisoners over to him and calling the world to witness that she has made him her 'lord and master'. It is ironic that Goneril and Regan, who were so utterly unfeeling towards their aged father, should be destroyed by the depth of their feeling for a man who cares nothing for either of them: 'Which of them shall I take? Both? One? Or neither?'

While Goneril and Regan are united in evil and display a number of similar characteristics, they are not entirely alike. Regan is weaker in character than Goneril, tending initially to live in her sister's shadow. Goneril and Regan eventually turn out to be each other's greatest enemy as their partnership is destroyed by their intense jealousy of each other over Edmund. Their actions reveal how low human beings can sink when they are utterly insensitive to the feelings of others, while the fate of these malevolent sisters shows us that evil is ultimately self-destructive.

KEY ADJECTIVES

- evil, malevolent, malicious
- ruthless, callous, unfeeling, unscrupulous
- false, deceptive, hypocritical
- amoral
- contemptible, despicable

EDMUND

Like Goneril and Regan, Edmund is extraordinarily evil. He is utterly unprincipled and totally amoral (has no moral principles). He is motivated entirely by self-interest and has no feelings for anybody else, regarding others either as aids or obstacles to the achievement of his ambitions. He betrays his own father and turns his brother's life upside down. He orders the deaths of Lear and Cordelia and deceives two sisters, turning them into mortal enemies. However, while neither Goneril nor Regan possess any redeeming features, Edgar is in some respects an attractive villain.

Edmund's illegitimacy is no excuse for his evilness and villainy but it does, to an extent, influence our feelings towards him. It is understandable that Edmund is bitter. Having the misfortune to be born outside of wedlock, he will not, in the normal course of events, inherit anything from his father. His first soliloquy (Act 1, Scene 3) earns him a degree of sympathy and even admiration because he is so determined to rise above the circumstances of his birth and 'fashion' his own future. Edmund is a proud, clever villain who cannot accept society's view of him as 'base' (low) when he knows that he has a 'mind as generous and shape as true as honest madam's issue'. He shows resolve in his assertion that he will 'top the legitimate' and defiance as he challenges the gods to 'stand up for bastards'. He displays a single-minded will to succeed and believes that he has the power to shape his own destiny.

Edmund is a sharp-witted villain with the capacity to perceive (the ability to see) the strengths and weaknesses of others and to plan his schemes accordingly. He is also entirely unscrupulous in the pursuit of his ambition to possess his father's lands and ultimately, the crown. He forges a letter to supplant (replace) his brother Edgar as heir to the earldom. He ruthlessly exploits his father's credulous (gullible) nature and his brother's noble-mindedness: 'A credulous father and a brother noble whose nature is so far from doing harms that he suspects none'. Edmund cunningly wounds himself to impress the gullible Gloucester with his apparent loyalty. He is a ruthless opportunist who turns every situation to his own advantage. When Gloucester confides in him regarding the letter which tells of the French landing and informs him of his intention to help Lear, Edmund immediately decides to betray him: 'This courtesy, forbid thee, shall the duke instantly know; and of that letter too'.

Edmund's hypocrisy is evident when, speaking with Gloucester, he describes Goneril and Regan's treatment of Lear as 'savage and unnatural'. He betrays his own father in the certain knowledge that Gloucester will be severely punished for his 'treason'. Edmund's hypocrisy is again evident in his apparent reluctance to inform Cornwall of Gloucester's intentions: 'O heavens! that this treason were not, or not I the detector.' In reality, he is entirely unmoved by his callous (unfeeling) action, believing that 'the younger rises when the old doth fall.' Goneril and Regan are exploited in a similar fashion to advance Edmund's selfish goals. In Act 5 Edmund reflects nonchalantly (casually) on his double-dealing in relation to the two sisters: 'To both these sisters have I sworn my love; each jealous of the other, as the stung are of the adder'. Albany is to be used to help win the battle before 'her who would be rid of him' (Goneril) devises 'his speedy taking'. Lear and Cordelia are to be killed, not for personal reasons, but because they represent a political threat. Edmund believes that both have the power 'to pluck the common bosom on their side', i.e. to win popular support. Intelligent and charming, hypocritical and ruthless, Edmund is utterly insensitive to the human suffering which results from his single-minded desire to defy society and achieve wealth, status and power.

Edmund displays some redeeming features in the final scene. When he is unsuccessful in his ambitious designs, he accepts his failure without showing personal animosity (hatred). **He exchanges forgiveness with Edgar and accepts that divine justice has been done:** 'The wheel is come full circle'. He also displays a touch of humanity and a glimmer of conscience. Edgar's description of Gloucester's suffering and death prompts Edmund to respond: 'This speech of yours hath moved me and shall perchance do good . . .' As he nears death, Edmund attempts to do 'some good . . . despite of mine own nature' by revealing that he has ordered the deaths of Lear and Cordelia. The grim pleasure which he takes in the thought of having been loved by two sisters is another indication of his humanity: 'Yet Edmund was beloved: The one the other poison'd for my sake and after slew herself'. The irony that all three are, in a sense, married in death ('all three now marry in an instant') is not lost on him. While Edmund's attitude towards and treatment of others throughout the play is reprehensible, his final words and actions hint at his humanity and prevent him from being viewed as a complete monster. Edmund is a more believable and more interesting character than Goneril and Regan because he is not wholly evil.

KEY ADJECTIVES

- ambitious, determined
- false, deceptive, hypocritical, two-faced
- clever, resourceful, quick-witted
- ruthless, unscrupulous
- humane (to some extent at the very end of the play)

OSWALD

Oswald is a truly contemptible character. Encouraged by his mistress, Goneril, Oswald treats Lear with blatant disrespect. When Lear asks him: 'Who am I, sir?' Oswald contemptuously replies: 'My lady's father'. Oswald's cowardice is displayed when, confronted by the angry Kent, he shouts for help. He subsequently lies to Cornwall, suggesting that he had 'spared' Kent because of his advanced age. Oswald is to be despised for drawing his sword against the 'eyeless head' of Gloucester in order to advance himself ('to raise my own fortunes'). He runs from Kent, but is willing to kill a blind old man. **He is a servile character** (fawning, excessively respectful), ever anxious to ingratiate himself with (please) his superiors. His only redeeming trait (positive quality) is his absolute loyalty to his mistress Goneril; indeed, with his dying breath he asks Edgar to give the letters which he carries to Edmund. Edgar accurately describes Oswald as 'a serviceable villain as duteous to the vices of thy mistress as badness would desire'.

KEY ADJECTIVES

- disrespectful, discourteous, insolent
- cowardly
- servile, obsequious, fawning

CORNWALL

Cornwall seems to be a suitable husband for Regan in that he is equally cruel and vengeful. He appears to be dominated by his wife. When Regan suggests that 'wilful men' must learn from 'the injuries that they themselves procure' and closes her doors against Lear, Cornwall's response is, 'My Regan counsels well'. After Cornwall orders that Kent is to remain in the stocks 'till noon', Regan insists on a more severe punishment: '. . . and all night too'. Cornwall is rather gullible in that he too is impressed with Edmund's apparent loyalty to his father early in the play: 'For you, Edmund, whose virtue and obedience doth this instant so much commend itself, you shall be ours'. Cornwall's vengeful nature is to be seen in his anticipation of Gloucester's return from his attempt to assist Lear: 'I will have my revenge ere I depart his house'. We see his brutality and cruelty when he gouges out Gloucester's eyes: 'Out, vile jelly! Where is thy lustre now?' Although his character is only sketched (not developed fully), he displays no redeeming features.

KEY ADJECTIVES

- evil, malevolent
- gullible, credulous
- cruel, vengeful

Comparative Study

Texts

- *The Plough and the Stars*
- *Children of Men*
- *The Great Gatsby*

Summary of the 3 Texts

The Plough and the Stars by Seán O'Casey

The events in the play take place first of all in Dublin during November 1915 during the build-up to the 1916 Rising and then during the Rising itself. Much of the action takes plays in a tenement building in Dublin's inner city. During the play, the poverty-stricken residents of the tenement building find their relationships and their lives in jeopardy as a result of the political violence taking place in Dublin. Jack and Nora Clitheroe, a young married couple, find their lives torn apart due to the violence erupting on the streets of Dublin. Jack's determination to be part of the action and give orders to his comrades in the Irish Citizen Army puts him in direct opposition to his wife's desire to create domestic harmony in their home. Other residents – such as Fluther Good, Uncle Peter and The Covey – reveal their true levels of bravery and their real commitment to political ideals throughout the play. Bessie Burgess, a Protestant unionist living in the tenement, has a pivotal role as a trouble-maker and a life-saver during the play. Mrs Gogan, a widow who lives in the building with her young baby and dying teenage daughter, Mollser, benefits from Bessie's kindness but ultimately ends up with more tragedy in her life. O'Casey relentlessly forces the audience to confront the reality of poverty and the danger of stirring up violence for what prove to be ultimately hollow political and social ideals.

Children of Men, directed by Alfonso Cuarón

This film is set in the near future of 2027. A mysterious plague of infertility means the human race is dying out. The world is filled with war and chaos. Britain is one of the few stable nations. Refugees from war-torn countries are making their way to it in their thousands. As a result Britain has become a police state in which government forces hunt refugees and force them into camps. Theo Faron becomes involved in an attempt to help Kee, a refugee, flee Britain. His ex-wife Julian is the leader of a militant political group, the Fishes. As the film unfolds, it transpires that Kee is pregnant and that members of the Fishes, having already killed Julian, plan to use Kee's baby as a political tool during the coming revolution. Theo and Kee manage to escape the Fishes with the help of some other friends along the way: Jasper, an ex-political cartoonist turned drug dealer; Miriam, a former midwife; and Marichka, a Romanian woman at the camp where Theo and Kee end up hiding whilst waiting for a boat, the *Tomorrow*, that will deliver Kee to a group of scientists called The Human Project who are working on a way to restore fertility. Other characters, such as Syd, a camp guard, initially help Theo and Kee but ultimately turn on them when their own interests are not met.

The Great Gatsby by F. Scott Fitzgerald

This novel is set on Long Island, New York, and tells the story of an eccentric millionaire, Jay Gatsby. The story is narrated by Nick Carraway, a neighbour of Gatsby's who becomes intrigued by the legendary parties held next door in Gatsby's mansion. Nick's cousin, Daisy, and her husband, Tom Buchanan, also live on Long Island. One night at a dinner party in their house, Nick meets and begins a romantic relationship with a professional golfer named Jordan Baker. Nick soon learns that Gatsby is in love with Daisy, who also lives on Long Island. Gatsby and Daisy were a couple before the war but she met Tom Buchanan and married him while Gatsby was in Europe during World War I. Through Nick, Gatsby engineers a 'chance' meeting with Daisy. They embark on an affair until Tom realises what is happening and becomes infuriated. Tom is also having an affair. His mistress, Myrtle, lives between Long Island and New York City. Despite his own infidelity, Tom is furious at the idea of Gatsby stealing his wife from him. He forces a group, including Nick, Daisy and Gatsby, to drive into New York City. There, he confronts Gatsby and Daisy. Daisy decides to return to Long Island with Gatsby but on the way home she knocks down and kills Myrtle. Myrtle's husband, George, initially blames Tom for her death but Tom tells him it was Gatsby's car that killed Myrtle. George turns up at Gatsby's mansion the next day and shoots Gatsby dead before killing himself. Nick organises a funeral for Gatsby and is shocked at how few people attend. Disillusioned by the insincerity of the people surrounding him in Long Island, Nick quits his job and moves back to the Midwest, where he was born and reared.

A. Cultural Context

The Plough and the Stars

The cultural context of any work of literature introduces us to the world that forms a backdrop to the entire narrative. This 'world' of the text is a distinctive shaping force in terms of what happens to the characters in the course of the plot. It also allows readers to understand the circumstances under which individuals make certain choices and the influences that affect their lives and destinies.

Politics

The Plough and the Stars by Seán O'Casey is set in the city of Dublin in the build-up to and during the 1916 Rising. This civil revolt was led by a commandant of the Irish Volunteers, Pádraig Pearse and by a commandant of the Irish Citizen Army, James Connolly. **Although many saw this revolt as heroic and idealistic, many others, including O'Casey, saw it as a complete waste of life and a cause of immense suffering for ordinary people. O'Casey viewed the rebellion as the root cause of many subsequent acts of terror and of the horrific civil war which followed the signing of the Anglo Irish Treaty in 1922.**

The political situation is a common topic of discussion among the inhabitants of the tenement building in Dublin in which much of the play is set. In Act I, Fluther Good, Uncle Peter and The Covey – three residents of the tenement – argue bitterly about their conflicting political beliefs. The Covey is a self-proclaimed socialist who questions the value of nationalism and objects to the labour flag being used for politics: 'They're bringing nice disgrace on that banner now' he tells Jack Clitheroe. He insists that 'It's a flag that should only be used, when we're buildin' th' barricades to fight for a Worker's Republic'. Fluther is a nationalist who brags about his political beliefs – 'the blood was boilin' in me veins!'– but does not take part in any military action. Uncle Peter belongs to

a group known as the 'Foresters', but his main interest is in dressing up in the group's fancy uniform and attending meetings at the Wolfe Tone memorial in Bodenstown. **The hollow political and social ideals of these characters become the subject of O'Casey's mockery throughout the play and provide much comic relief.**

The romantic, heroic ideal of war is, however, presented more seriously by the Voice of the Man in Act II. The 'Voice' is an unnamed character who can be heard giving a rousing speech outside a public house, extorting people to rise up violently against British rule. Referring to the bloodshed of World War I, he proclaims it is an inspiration for a civil uprising against British colonial rule in Ireland: 'We rejoice in this terrible war. The old heart of the earth needed to be warmed with the red blood of the battlefields'. It is rhetoric such as this which sends men like Jack Clitheroe to their deaths. **The imagery used later adds to the horror of the suffering which war brings: Nora Clitheroe, one of the main characters in the play, describes 'somethin' huddled up in a horrible tangled heap . . . his face was jammed against th' stones, an' his arm was twisted round his back . . . an' every twist of his body was a cry against th' terrible thing that had happened to him'.** Nora is totally opposed to war, begging her husband Jack to have nothing to do with the uprising and revealing the fear which even the fighting men experience. She claims that the men are only fighting out of fear that they might be called cowards if they didn't.

Jack Clitheroe's attraction to the Irish Citizen Army is possibly related to the fact that it gives him an opportunity to command. His 'vanity' impels him to desert his wife in the name of political idealism because 'Ireland is greater than a wife'. Later, his fear that Nora will embarrass him when she tries to drag him away from his comrades leads him to reject her. This rejection leads to her mental breakdown and a miscarriage. Ultimately it paves the way for the death of Bessie Burgess, another tenement resident and a staunch loyalist who is strongly opposed to the Rising.

Bessie Burgess shows herself to be more politically aware than many of the other characters. Being a Protestant loyalist, she is extremely critical of the rebels and insults them at every opportunity: 'Yous are all nicely shanghaied [tricked into an action] now!' She regards the empty incitements to civil uprising as 'fairy tales that had no beginnin', but, please God,'ll have a bloody quick endin'. She views the nationalists as traitors: 'Stabbin' in the back th' men that are dyin' in th' threnches for them'. Her prediction that the rebellion will come to a bad end is prophetic in its accuracy.

The cultural context of *The Plough and the Stars* shows us O'Casey's concern with the politics of the time. He presents widely differing attitudes to the rebellion, showing not only those who see it as a chance to strike a blow for freedom but also those who see the chaos as an opportunity to loot. Every character in the play is affected to some extent by the political upheaval which makes it a crucial feature of the cultural context and an essential element of our understanding of the play.

Social pressures

Political chaos is not the only social issue that has a negative impact on the lives of the characters. **The appalling poverty suffered by the tenement dwellers is another important element in our understanding of the cultural context.** The poverty in Dublin's tenements in 1916 was actually what we would nowadays describe as destitution. Although Nora attempts to affect some semblance of gentility, she is actually no better off than her neighbours. Her description of the tenements as 'Vaults that are hidin' th' dead, instead of homes that are shelterin' the livin'' seems an accurate appraisal of what O'Casey says is a 'fine old house struggling for its life against the assaults of time'. The natural inclination of any human being when faced with the degradation of poverty is to attempt escape. According to Mrs Gogan, Nora is 'screwin' every penny she can' out of her lodgers – Peter and The Covey – in order to keep up appearances.

Nora engages in flights of fancy, convinced that if she works and tries hard enough, she can escape from the tenements and create a better life for her husband and their expected child. One could claim that she is addicted to this 'dream' and is not only unwilling but also incapable of surrendering to the forces which threaten to rob her of it. She goes to extraordinary lengths to prevent Jack from engaging in the rebellion, tearing up his letter of commission and even risking her life at the barricades in her effort to save him, and in doing so, save her vision of a brighter future.

The poverty of the surroundings and the sense that the poor are despised by those of higher social status may very well be reasons why young men like Jack Clitheroe engaged in the rebellion. Perhaps it offered them an opportunity to feel that they were more than just 'slum lice'. Efforts to escape reality often take the form of addictions, so it is perhaps unsurprising that Jack is addicted to the image of himself as a hero, leading his men into combat for the noble cause of freedom. In the same way that Nora cannot accept her husband loves his image more than he loves her, so Jack cannot tolerate anything which might lower him in the estimation of his comrades. We see this clearly in a key moment when he roughly pushes her away as she pleads with him to return to her. O'Casey makes it clear in the stage directions that he does so for 'fear her action would give him future shame'. His callous almost brutal rejection of her is motivated by his addiction to his self-image and hunger for the respect of others: 'What possessed you to make a show of yourself, like that? … What way d'ye think I'll feel when I'm told my wife was bawlin' for me at th' barricades?'

The addiction to alcohol is yet another method of escape not only from poverty and degradation, but also from the reality of illness and death. One of the most heroic characters, Fluther, grapples with his need for drink as described from the very first stage direction: 'fond of his 'oil' but determined to conquer the habit before he dies'. So important is alcohol to Fluther that he risks his life to 'save' a half-gallon jar of whisky during a riot and shoot-out in the streets. At one stage Fluther attempts to give up the drink: 'It's three days now since I touched a dhrop, an' I feel a new man already' but as soon as he contemplates becoming ill or dying, he sees no escape but to return to his old ways: 'I feel as dizzy as bedamned! I hope I didn't give up th' beer too suddenly'. Bessie Burgess and Mrs Gogan also take refuge in drink to help them endure the ugly circumstances of their lives. We see this most clearly in the scene in the pub where they both engage in an alcohol-fuelled verbal exchange. Bessie urges Mrs Gogan to 'stupefy your foolishness be gettin' dhrunk', only to be accused by Mrs Gogan of being one of those 'persons' who 'think more of a ball of malt than they do of th' blessed saints'. Fluther comments that Bessie is 'always dangerous an' derogatory when she's well oiled'. There is no doubt that heavy drinking is very much a part of how people escaped the challenging realities of life in the tenements; the realities of social upheaval, poverty, illness and death.

Religion/spirituality

Despite frequent references to God and religion, the actual impact of religion on the lives of people is hard to assess. Bessie Burgess strongly defends her right to sing Protestant hymns although she knows that most of her neighbours are Roman Catholic. She obviously knows that not all of her neighbours practise their religion, 'I attend me place o' worship anyhow . . . Not like some o' them that go to neither church, chapel nor meetin' house'. Her drunken hymn singing can be regarded as a form of self-assertion most of the time. Bessie does, however, draw real strength from her faith. In Act III, as she is setting out for a doctor for Nora she says, 'Oh God, be Thou my help in time o' throuble', and at the end of the play she sings hymns to comfort Nora. It is not so surprising that Bessie dies praying and singing a hymn, not to torment others this time,

but because her faith is the only support she has had throughout her life and is now her only hope when facing death. People also use religion as a way to postpone meaningful action. The coward Peter, for instance, cannot act out his threats to The Covey so he always hides behind an irate prayer for patience. He pretends his decision not to loot is based on moral principles.

Although they use the language of religion in their everyday speech, Fluther, Mrs Gogan and Bessie have no moral scruples about looting during the rebellion. Religion is not a dominant force in their lives although it may offer some consolation in times of sorrow or death. The dying Lieutenant Langon calls out for a priest and Captain Brennan, in his account of Jack Clitheroe's death says that he 'said a prayer for th' dyin', an' twined his rosary beads around his fingers'.

Religion is also used for political reasons. The Covey is extremely sarcastic regarding the influence of the Church over the working classes. **We also hear the Voice of the Man invoke religious images and symbols to encourage men to become 'martyrs' in a political cause.** 'Bloodshed' is referred to as 'a sanctifying thing' and 'Such august homage was never offered to God as this: the homage of millions of lives given gladly for love of country'. **The response of the listeners to this rhetoric is very powerful and shows that religion plays a prominent role in the cultural context of the play.**

Roles of men and women

The roles of men and women are clearly defined in *The Plough and the Stars*. None of the women are involved in any way with the rebellion and neither are they swayed by the rhetoric of the Voice of the Man. O'Casey depicts women as being strong-willed, determined fighters; they are much more capable of heroic acts than men. Their role is of the utmost importance in understanding the playwright's intentions.

Mrs Gogan, although a gossip, is a lively, spirited woman who manages to retain a sense of humour despite the deaths of her husband and child and the tremendous poverty she has to endure. She has an inbuilt survivor's spirit, which is a form of heroism in itself. It is she who takes over the care of Nora after Bessie is shot dead.

Nora Clitheroe seems to be a strong character at the start of the play. She burns Jack's letter and keeps his promotion a secret from him. She also effectively controls The Covey and Peter. However, as the play unfolds we see that Nora depends far too much on Jack and crumbles when she loses him. There is no denying, however, her extraordinary courage in going to the barricades to bring Jack home. She sees through the empty rhetoric and false courage of the fighting men and is aware that vanity is a prime motivation for Jack. 'That's what's movin' you: because they've made an officer of you, you'll make a glorious cause of what you're doin'. Nora recognises the fear in the eyes of the rebels and refuses to believe that any woman would sacrifice a husband or son to a political cause. **Nora's main function is to show the effects of the Rising on ordinary men and women. Therefore her part in the play highlights the philosophy of O'Casey who had very little time for the empty rhetoric or jingoism used by the men in the play.** Unfortunately, Nora cannot deal with the reality of her situation and descends into insanity and despair.

Bessie Burgess presents a rough exterior initially, fighting with her neighbours, getting drunk and taunting the rebels with her singing of 'Rule Brittania'. Her pronouncements are almost a parody of the Voice of the Man, as she cries out that 'judgements are prepared for scorners an' sthripes for th' backs o' fools'. Yet it is Bessie who has the humanity to offer food to the dying Mollser, goes to find a doctor for Nora and risks her own life to save her neighbour from being shot. **Although she is by no means a saint, she comes nearest to being the only truly heroic character in the play.**

Even the young Mollser demonstrates the strength of women. Her fear of death is honest and admitted: 'I do be terrible afraid I'll die sometime when be meself'. This acknowledgement is in stark contrast to the bragging claims of the willingness to die spoken by the male revolutionaries. Even though we do not witness Mollser's death, we can assume that her acceptance of its reality conferred a dignity on her passing. This cannot be said about the dying Langon or, presumably, Jack Clitheroe. Their deaths for a romantic, political ideal are accompanied by the fear and terror Nora witnessed at the barricades.

The men in the play are not presented as being as strong as the women. The boasting and posturing of Fluther and Peter becomes farcical when we see them proclaim their nationalism while taking advantage of an opportunity to go looting. They both retreat to Bessie's room when the real fighting breaks out. Clitheroe is presented as a man of vanity rather than ideals. Nora tells him 'Your vanity'll be the ruin of you an' me yet . . .' Clitheroe, Brennan and Langon show how a political creed can dehumanise individuals and become more important than human relationships. 'Ireland is greater than a mother . . . Ireland is greater than a wife.' Later in the play, Captain Brennan deserts Clitheroe, leaving him to die in a burning building. His account of his services to the dying man are not verified by any witness and may be no more than a façade. **There is no doubt that O'Casey is saying that simple acts of unselfish courage are more praiseworthy than the military actions of the rebels.**

It is not only the male rebels who are negatively presented in the play. The Covey preaches Marxism and refers to others as 'comrades'. However, his socialism is as shallow as the vanity of Clitheroe's nationalism. He is a hostile, pretentious and argumentative presence.

Fluther is the only male character who, despite his earlier posturing, exhibits some degree of courage and humanity. Nora gives him all the credit for bringing her home safely after shooting breaks out on the streets. Mrs Gogan also owes him a debt of gratitude for arranging the burial of Mollser, 'I'll never forget what you done for me, Fluther, goin' around at th' risk of your life settlin' everythin' with th' undhertaker an' th' cemetery people. When all me own were afraid to put their noses out, you plunged like a good one . . .' **These courageous and compassionate actions by Fluther redeem to some extent the negative portrayals of other men.**

There is an irony in the roles of men and women in the play. We see this when Jack Clitheroe sings to Nora in Act I but by Act IV, he has left her and Bessie sings to comfort her instead. The men in the tenement take refuge in the room of Bessie Burgess, reversing the normal stereotype of men being the protectors of women. **Although women emerge as the stronger sex overall, the play celebrates the courage and endurance of ordinary men and women rather than the political speechmakers and those who promote war.**

Social class

Differences in social class are evident at certain points in the play. The majority of the characters in *The Plough and the Stars* are working class, impoverished people who struggle to survive. However, there are a few notable exceptions whose presence throws light on the class differences that existed at the time. The character known as the Voice of the Man who addresses the rally in Act II is clearly from a different social class than the other characters in the play. This is most obvious in the quality of his speech. The voice (which is probably meant to be that of Pádraig Pearse) is full of fine rhetoric, excellent syntax and correct pronunciation. The vocabulary and turns of phrase are undoubtedly those of one of the educated middle-class. **The impact of the rhetoric on the listeners is not only related to the ideals being promoted in the speech but also to the fact that the speaker gains a certain authority by virtue of his superior background and speech.** Fluther expresses the feelings of many when he tells how he 'listened to th' speeches pattherin' on the people's head' and urges Peter out of the bar to listen to more by saying, 'Come on man, this is too good to be missed'. **The people of the tenements speak with strong Dublin accents, malapropisms (incorrect use of words) and occasional slang.** The uneducated background of the speakers is evident in the way they drop the endings of certain words – comin', goin' – and insert a 'h' sound into words like 'scatther', 'plundher' etc. They also use incorrect grammar when they say 'yous' for the plural of you and phrases like 'I'll never forget what you done for me . . .' **Although the speech of the tenement dwellers lacks sophistication or elegance, it is nevertheless extremely rich with striking, descriptive imagery. O'Casey not only reveals social class in the dialect but also in the lyrical beauty of their use of language.**

Nora's efforts to improve her social status by keeping her home clean and nicely decorated is frowned upon by Mrs Gogan and Bessie Burgess. Mrs Gogan asserts that Nora is developing 'notions of upperosity' and regards the hygiene practices imposed on The Covey and Peter as being 'penal servitude'. Bessie also reacts to Nora's efforts to improve herself when she asks Jack Clitheroe to explain his wife's behaviour, 'Why is she always thryin' to speak proud things, an' lookin' like a mighty one in th' congregation o' th' people'. Perhaps her neighbours' resentment of Nora is due to the fact that her efforts act as a bitter reminder to them of their own degraded conditions.

The contrast in social classes in 1916 is graphically presented when a fashionably dressed woman from Rathmines approaches the tenement dwellers shortly after the fighting commences. She asks the men to 'come some of the way' with her and see that she gets home safely. O'Casey humorously depicts the woman's attitude that her situation is more 'awful' because she 'cawn't get a car or a tram'. The upper class accent, along with the claim that she is 'different to others', underscores the very different worlds inhabited by different social groups. She clearly believes that the men should risk their own safety to assist her, given that she hails from 'Wrathmines'. Peter has no problem putting her in her place when he bluntly asks, 'D'ye think I'm goin' to risk me life, throttin' in front of you?' Even her attitude to the rebellion marks a difference in class – 'I was foolish enough to visit a friend, thinking the howl thing was a joke . . .' **This entire incident serves to highlight the vision of the poorer city dwellers as being something of a dispensable sub-class in the eyes of the inhabitants of the wealthier suburbs.**

KEY POINTS

- The political background of World War I and the 1916 Rising forms a backdrop to the entire play. Every character is affected to some extent by the political upheaval, making it a crucial feature of the context and an essential element in our understanding of the playwright's intention.

- The need to escape the realities of appalling poverty, illness and death suffered by the tenement dwellers is another crucial element in our understanding of the cultural context. Addictions to alcohol, to imagined futures and to the notion of heroism are apparent throughout the play. Some of the rebels may have been motivated to engage in the rebellion as an escape from the degradation of being powerless and poor.

- Despite frequent references to God and religion, the actual impact of religion on the lives of people is hard to assess. It seems to offer comfort and strength in suffering but can be manipulated for political motives. Religion is also seen as a divisive aspect of life in the tenement building.

- The roles of men and women are clearly defined in *The Plough and the Stars*. None of the women are involved in any way with the rebellion and neither are they swayed by the rhetoric of the Voice of the Man. O'Casey depicts women as being strong-willed, determined fighters; they are much more capable of heroic acts than men.

- Fluther is the only male character who, despite his earlier posturing, exhibits some degree of courage and humanity when he assists Nora and looks after the funeral arrangements for Mollser. He does this at great personal risk to his own safety.

- Differences in social class are evident at certain points in the play. The majority of the characters in *The Plough and the Stars* are working class, impoverished people who struggle to survive. However, there are a few notable exceptions whose presence throws light on the class differences that existed at the time.

Children of Men

Politics

Although set in a fictional Britain in 2027 (a little over a century after O'Casey's play), there are significant overlaps in the political landscape between *The Plough and the Stars* and the film *Children of Men*. The film is built around a mysterious plague of infertility, rendering the whole human race unable to have children for eighteen years. **This results in a profound sense of powerlessness and despair. Britian's way of dealing with this unrest is similar in some ways to the historical British response to Ireland's frustration with its own powerlessness in the early twentieth century.** The government hardens in the face of revolt, and becomes authoritarian and xenophobic (prejudice against or dislike of people from other countries). Throughout the film there are drab ads and billboards filled with stern warnings, e.g. '*Avoiding fertility tests is a crime*'. All foreigners are now deemed to be 'illegal immigrants' and are being rounded up by the security forces to be deported. On-board screens on buses tell their passengers to report all illegal immigrants for immediate deportation.

The response from the streets is a series of graffiti messages. Some offer rays of hope for a secret scientific community who are working on a cure for the plague: 'The Human Project lives!' Other messages are wryly defeatist: 'The last one to die please turn out the lights'. There are a few scenes of fields with cattle being burned in great charred heaps. This adds to the sense of oppression, as the cull looks as though it has been ordered by the authorities. The competing pressures of authoritarian measures, a hopeless and dying population and rampant xenophobia lead to the creation of a freedom fighter/terrorist organisation called the Fishes. They support immigrant rights and accuse the government of setting off bombs and blaming The Fishes in order to drum up support against the group. It is never made clear if this claim is true or not, but the Fishes are certainly serious enough about their mission to launch 'the uprising' by the film's end. In a brief scene in the last seconds of the film, we see jet fighters flying over Bexhill and massive explosions light up the sky. **It is strongly implied that the Fishes' uprising (or at least their violent version of it) has met with the same fate as O'Casey's nationalists at the end of The Plough and the Stars.**

Social pressures

Whereas O'Casey focuses on the environment of a specific Dublin neighbourhood (a single tenement and nearby pub), director Alfonso Cuarón takes us on a wide-ranging tour of his nightmare Britain. There are many forms of poverty and despair on display. From the opening scene of the film, the colour palette itself seems to be composed almost entirely of variations of grey. Waste bags line the footpath. Crude motorised rickshaws spew black clouds into the air. It is evident that this is a world where either no one cares about the environment anymore or they lack the knowledge of how to avoid this pollution. Either cause, apathy or ignorance, could be seen as a form of mental impoverishment.

Despair and addiction are often found together. People who feel they have no hope in life tend to seek out substances or activities that distract them or temporarily kill the pain. In O'Casey's Dublin, this is, as we have seen, a tendency to engage in fantasy, self-delusion and, most obviously, drinking alcohol. In Children of Men, Theo drinks very heavily very often. The opening scene establishes him as a man who cannot even go to work in the morning without adding spirits to his black coffee. He also smokes heavily, and ends up sharing cigarettes with a variety of characters he meets throughout the film. **But unlike the escape that alcohol offers in The Plough and the Stars, the significant route of escape in the film from the point of view of plot is marijuana.** Jasper, Theo's friend and an ex-political cartoonist, grows masses of marijuana in his house. This is relevant to the film's cultural context for a few reasons. The first is that Jasper remarks ironically that even though the government hands out suicide drugs to the general populace, marijuana is still illegal. This establishes Jaspar and Theo as ironists and as people with low regard for the letter of the law. They see that an oppressive government will always want to control people. In the film, that control extends to how people deal with extreme stress. Offering a quiet death in this world is presented as more legitimate than taking a drug that (though not without risks to one's physical and mental health) might promote critical thinking about that world. In this regard, Jasper, as a drug dealer, is doing something similar to when he was a political cartoonist: trying to get people to see the world in a skewed but funny way. **The effect is not unlike that of the comedy O'Casey creates around the heavy drinking of the tenement dwellers. We laugh at their cutting jibes, while being reminded of their hopeless desperation and need to escape from reality.**

Jasper's drugs are valuable in such a despairing world. He deals with a devoted customer, Syd, who works in the local refugee camp at Bexhill. **In the same way as characters are 'labelled' or categorised according to their political views in The Plough and the Stars, Jasper** calls Syd a 'fascist pig' and when we meet him, we realise this is not a joke. In a camp which does not permit public access, guards like Syd can live like Nazis. Using Syd as their contact into the camp, Theo, Kee and Miriam are exposed to a view of a world far darker and more needful of literal escape attempts than the desolate one they left outside. The images of refugees (predominantly men of Middle-Eastern background) are disturbing. Cuarón has deliberately lit and shot these scenes to imitate the photos that were leaked to world media from the US prison Abu Ghraib in Iraq in 2003. The photos showed a series of torture and humiliation techniques used to dehumanise the Iraqi prisoners, including placing black hoods on them and making them stand in 'crucifix' positions while they were electrocuted. Guard dogs were allowed to snap very near to the prisoners' bodies. Many were forced to stand naked while soldiers photographed and jeered at them. Much of this is re-created in the Bexhill camp. We see clearly that this is a commentary on the moral poverty that occurs when people with power think no one is watching. Much of the action in this closing section of the film is focused on escape. Faced with Marichka's lack of English, Theo is reduced to drawing a crude picture of a boat on a wall, begging her to help them get away from the insurrection that is breaking out around them. A science vessel called the *Tomorrow* that meets them in the end of the film is also a form of escape. **Science and reason itself, it seems to imply, may help us all escape our history of warring tribes and belief systems. No such escape is offered in O'Casey's play. There is no boat and no exit.**

Other scenes set in the Bexhill camp show more echoes of recent images haunting the Western imagination: a procession of Islamic fighters, many brandishing machine guns and bearing their dead, fill the streets; mothers wailing and screaming in grief. These scenes precede a massive aerial bombing from British fighter jets, again re-creating the tensions in the Middle East that threaten to destabilise our real world for years to come. **These scenes set the film up as a commentary on war and xenophobia in**

general. **The despair they create, independent of the horror of the infertility plague, echoes the destruction and horror in O'Casey's tenements when political factions and extreme power imbalances clash at the expense of the poor and dispossessed.**

Religion/spirituality

O'Casey shows us **a veneer of religious faith** as practised by most of his characters. Only Bessie Burgess seems deeply invested in her religion, genuinely invoking prayer as she bleeds to death at the end of the play. This suggests that, for O'Casey, there are layers of engagement in religion, from simple group identity (like the nationalist/Catholic faction and the loyalist/Protestant faction) to sincere spiritual experience. **These layers are even more tiered and diverse in *Children of Men*.**

On the superficial level, we are shown penitents from religious cults gathering on the streets to claim blame for the plague, calling it 'God's punishment'. It is implied there are many of these types of cults. Theo tells Jasper that he recently lost a girlfriend to one, the 'Renouncers'. Jasper confuses two groups: 'Renouncers, are those the ones that kneel down for a month or so for salvation?' Theo replies 'Nah, they're the Repenters. The Renouncers flagellate themselves for the forgiveness of humanity'. Jasper's response is as dismissive as it is funny: 'Dating ain't what it used to be, is it amigo?' Jasper's scepticism reminds us of The Covey's dismissive attitude to religion in O'Casey's play: 'science shows you that th' head of your god is an empty one'. **In both texts the role of religious belief is connected to desperation and a search for divine intervention in times of danger.** Bessie Burgess is typical of the religious attitudes of her time. She prays fervently as she ventures out into the gunfire to fetch a doctor for Nora and again when she realises that her death is imminent. **In both texts, religious belief is a support which some people turn to in despair and their only hope when facing death.**

Unlike the generally traditional Christian

beliefs which we see in *The Plough and the Stars*, *Children of Men* presents us with alternative, confusing beliefs. The film pokes gentle fun at the beliefs of Miriam, the mid-wife appointed to accompany Kee throughout much of the action. Miriam showcases an awkward mindset of garbled new-age beliefs, largely cobbled together from Taoism and reiki, but also featuring belief in UFOs. She's charitably described as 'earnest' by Theo as she artlessly practices a tai chi form in Jasper's yard. This seems to be a comment on what happens to desperate people who reject traditional religion in favour of making their own. Miriam's religious/spiritual/supernatural beliefs are largely presented as harmless, but they disgust Theo, who has made a point of telling himself that nothing in life matters except simple pleasures like drinking and gambling on the greyhounds. Theo's active rejection of religious belief is explained to Miriam by Jasper in a scene where they are relaxing around a shared joint. Jasper tells the story of how Theo and Julian met. 'Everything is a mythical cosmic battle between faith and chance', Jasper explains. He says that Theo met Julian at a political rally by chance, but the fact that they were there in the first place was a result of faith. When their son, Dylan, died in a flu pandemic, 'Theo's faith lost out to chance'. Again, one is reminded of The Covey who asserts that '...we're all only human bein's. Scientifically speakin', it's all a question of the accidental gatherin' together of mollycewels an' atoms'. Miriam's weak response to Jasper, that everything 'happens for a reason', is just as deluded as Mrs Gogan's belief that 'Mollser, in th' happy place she's gone to, won't forget to whisper, now an' again, th' name o' Fluther'. It is almost as if life would be unbearable without the comforts which religious belief offers. Later, when Jasper is being executed by the Fishes, Theo watches from a distance, and demands Miriam tell him the 'reason' for that death.

Because Theo is presented as a strong character and Miriam as a brave but naïve one, this may initially trick the audience into seeing things from Theo's sceptical and secular perspective.

But unlike *The Plough and the Stars*, the film functions as a spiritual allegory, and more particularly as a Christian one. The title itself, from P.D. James' original novel, alludes to Psalm 90 from the Bible: 'Thou turnest man to destruction, and sayest Return, ye children of men'. This means that people without eternal life (or faith) are nothing more than the dust and chaos of the material universe. Theo unwittingly adopts the role of St Joseph in a Holy Family scenario as he helps Kee deliver her child in a manger-like room in a refugee camp, dogs howling in the background. (Note coincidentally, the US release date for the film was Christmas Day).

All of these elements suggest that the film, like some aspects of O'Casey's play, is staging a conflict between secular humanistic values and those of traditional religion.

Roles of men and women

It may be a stretch to claim that *The Plough and the Stars* is a perfect example of a feminist play. A critical reader could argue that Mollser is a stereotype of the helpless invalid – her main role is to be sad and frail and then die – and Nora's descent into abject hysteria is a well-worn device from late nineteenth and early twentieth-century novels and dramas. But certainly O'Casey's sympathies are mainly with the women. Although a drunken trouble-maker, Bessie proves herself brave and selfless in the end. Nora can see through male bravado and has the sanest priorities (a happy home life) before she goes mad. Even timid Mollser has the wit to roll her eyes at the faction fighting of the day and ask if anyone has a 'titther o' sense'.

Because *Children of Men* is about a crisis of biological reproduction, the roles of men and women are drawn into the sharpest contrast possible. There are three main female characters in the film: Julian, a leader of the Fishes; Kee, an African immigrant and the world's only expectant mother; and Miriam, Kee's mid-wife. Julian does not get much screen time, but her role is vital. She first appears having commanded her group to kidnap Theo. Her cool demeanour as she tries to alternately frighten and bribe Theo into helping the group establishes her as a detached, intellectual but deeply committed activist. **Like Nora Clitheroe, she can see her partner's inner workings with crystal clarity**. She accuses him of hiding in his grief while she gets on with the business of what needs to get done. As they ride in a bus, he says he could never understand how she got over the loss of their son so easily. 'No one could get over it,' she replies. 'I *lived* with it... You don't have a monopoly on suffering.'

She's a complex character, alternating between cool taskmaster and passionate ex-lover. Her game of mouth ping-pong is also oddly intimate. She has tried this with 'hundreds' of other partners, but Theo is the only one who has ever managed to return her volley. This implies a few things. The first is that the ball game is a stand-in for intimacy, and Julian is a sexually liberated person who has left monogamy and family life behind her as useful values or goals. But it also illustrates that she appreciates how rare it is to find someone whose chemistry is compatible with her own. In other words, she seems at once capable of warmth and intimacy, and yet remains aloof and calculating, as one would expect the leader of a radical activist group to be. Julian is Kee's only contact with the Human Project, (a group of scientists trying to find a way to restore fertility) which implies she is more trustworthy than the other Fishes. This is confirmed in the film when the group's second-in-command, Luke, has his henchman Patric murder Julian so they can frighten Kee into staying with them and raising the child as one of the Fishes. **In some respects, Julian and Theo's relationship is a gender reversal of Nora and Jack's marriage, with Julian focusing on making any sacrifice for her political goals, and Theo being left to his private grief over the loss of their child**. Julian's death (along with Jasper's) devastates Theo. At her rushed funeral in the woods, Theo slips away, but he cannot even light a cigarette without breaking down. We infer that Julian is one of the only people he ever really trusted, loved or respected.

As noted in the previous section on religion/spirituality, Miriam is almost a comic character. Her uneasy collection of new-age beliefs (cobbled together randomly from sources like eastern mysticism and curiosity about UFOs) makes her seem overly-impressionable. But in a deserted children's school, she gives some background about her previous role as a hospital mid-wife, witnessing the sudden drop-off in pregnancies. She acts as a bridge between the last days of fertility and a possible fertile future. As she narrates her history, calmly but poignantly, it is implied that this is a sensible woman who has simply been devastated – as everyone has – by the change which has come over the world; her unusual beliefs are an earnest response to a bizarre universe. She wants the world to have some sort of order, and she seeks it by any means possible. By the film's end, her claim that 'everything happens for a reason' may be more true than even she realises, because the series of improbable events that she witnesses result in humankind's only hope being born and ferried to safety.

Like Bessie Burgess tending to Nora, Miriam is intensely loyal and refuses to leave Kee's side for an instant, no matter how great the danger. In one of the most tense scenes, Miriam draws down the rage of a seething camp guard in order to distract him and his dog from Kee, whose waters have broken. We see Miriam dragged away to an uncertain fate, and we suddenly recognise that she is one of the bravest and most self-sacrificing characters in the film. **In this regard, she has much in common with Bessie who, although unintentionally, nevertheless sacrifices herself to save another.**

Kee, the world's mother-saviour, is initially presented as hostile. She spits out her first line of dialogue at Theo: 'What the fuck you looking at?' We later learn why she is so defensive, but the first impression is one of hardness and toughness. Later she reveals a sense of humour, claiming she is a virgin and then laughing at how far from the truth that is. She also tests out absurd names for the baby like 'Froley' and 'Bazooka'. **In her ability to laugh under stress,** but not back down from a fight, her character is reminiscent of O'Casey's Mrs Gogan, who deals unflinchingly with the stark facts of her poverty and single-parenthood.

Unlike the main male characters in *The Plough and the Stars*, Theo and Jasper are presented as honourable men with a clear-eyed sense of priorities and duty. Jasper is devoted to his wife, who, though not a traditional character, is represented as someone of incredible integrity and courage. From a shot of newspaper clippings, we learn that she is an award-winning political journalist who has been tortured by the authoritarian government and now lives in a state of semi-comatose trauma. Although she doesn't perform any actions during the film, Jasper and Theo's obvious respect and love for her reflects the film's larger insight: the world is better when men and women work together and respect each other. Such a harmony of male and female relationships is almost totally absent in *The Plough and the Stars*, where Mrs Gogan is attacked by Bessie for fraternising with men, Rosie the prostitute is insulted by The Covey and Nora is rejected by her husband in favour of his war.

In *Children of Men* two male characters, Luke and Patric, are similar to the men who sign up to fight for the Easter Rising. Theirs is a cause so pressing that they believe any means are justified to achieve this end, including kidnapping and murdering innocent people. Luke is presented as more thoughtful – a leader who has been driven to extreme lengths by his sense of duty to his mission. Nevertheless, he is a brutal force that drives much of the suffering in the film. Patric, his lieutenant, is more of a thug who clearly relishes his role as a tough guy with a licence to kill. Unlike the combatants in O'Casey's play, Patric never seems to display any fear or conflicted attitudes to combat that might humanise him. He is a radical infused with a pure zeal for glory or death whose attitude reminds us more of the Voice of the Man in *The Plough and the Stars*. Theo enjoys taking Patric down a peg from his heroic role by telling him his breath stinks. This simple insult

confuses and annoys Patric, suggesting perhaps that here is a young man who takes himself too seriously.

Social class

With the exception of the poetic Voice of the Man and the parody of the upper-class lady from 'Wrathmines' who thinks the fighting is 'awful', O'Casey's play largely focuses on a contained social strata: working-class Dubliners. Even so, one sees how people like to draw distinctions between themselves and others based on intelligence, taste etc. Some examples include when The Covey sneers at anyone unfamiliar with Jenersky's thesis, when Mrs Gogan complains about Nora's 'notions of upperosity' and when Bessie dismisses the Catholics around her as 'slum lice'. We see the same tensions around social status in *Children of Men*. Although the film is set in a world where traditional roles and society in general are collapsing, anxiety about one's place in the scheme of things remains. Looking out at the white, English-born Miriam attempting to practise a form of Tai Chi, Kee asks Theo if her mid-wife 'looks posh'. Theo, a shabby alcoholic, cultivates an upper-class sophistication throughout the film. When first introduced to Kee and barked at, he comically replies: 'Apparently the pleasure is all mine…' The streets are filled with penitents renouncing their earthly goods; bus and train stations are equipped with large cages for rounding up foreigners for inspection. These 'fugees' are an underclass – a problem considered beyond help or repair. They suffer an enhanced version of the same dehumanisation of the consumption-riddled tenements in O'Casey's Dublin. In one of the film's final scenes, the shoot-out in the crumbling building, Luke says between bursts of gunfire that there can be no peace when they 'take away your dignity'. This quest for dignity even in the face of death can be seen in men like Jack Clitheroe who risks his life and his marriage.

In the film's most marked social class contrast, Theo travels to meet Nigel, an art conservationist. Nigel exudes a regal manner, welcoming Theo with open arms while a damaged Michelangelo's *David* idles in the background. As the men dine, they are waited on by servants bringing fine wines and multiple dishes. Nigel's austere son ignores everything around him, immersed in a complex video game. Behind Theo is Picasso's painting *Guernica*, a high art depiction of a world tearing itself apart. Nigel seems as serene about all the suffering as it is possible to get – his only focus is on keeping aesthetic treasures safe. Referring to a disaster in Spain, he says 'The thing in Madrid was a real blow to art.' Theo has to reply: 'And to people'.

Theo asks how Nigel can summon up the effort to protect the world's artistic treasures when no one will be around to enjoy them. In one of the most damning lines, which sums up his attitude to human suffering, Nigel replies 'You know what it is, Theo. I just don't think about it.' **Like the woman from Rathmines in *The Plough and the Stars* who thinks the rebellion is a 'joke', the wealthy in the film are seen as a mix of aloof and deluded, sticking their heads in the sand to avoid the face of the nightmare that is rising up all around them.**

KEY POINTS

- The political background of World War One and the 1916 Rising are the backdrop to *The Plough and the Stars*. Every character in the play is drawn into the political upheaval whether they want to be or not. An infertility plague is the main backdrop in the film *Children of Men*, but this plague destabilises the world politically and gives rise to an oppressive British government and an immigrant 'uprising' similar to the nationalist uprising in O'Casey's play.

- The need of the Dublin tenement residents to escape the realities of appalling poverty, illness and death is a crucial element in our understanding of the cultural context of this play. Addictions to alcohol, as well as the imagined dignity of an heroic role, are apparent throughout the play. Members of the Fishes in *Children of Men* are also motivated to engage in their rebellion as an escape from the degradation of being powerless and poor, as well as feeling like they have no future in any country.

- Despite frequent references to God and religion in the play, the actual impact of religion on the lives of people is as negative as it is positive. Religion is a divisive aspect of life in the tenement building. In *Children of Men*, overt religiosity is presented as an act of desperation in the face of the mysterious plague. However, the film functions as an ambiguous parable about the power of hope (spiritual or secular) to lead people from apathy or despair to love and selflessness.

- The roles of men and women are clearly defined in *The Plough and the Stars*. O'Casey depicts women as being strong-willed, determined fighters who are less susceptible to idealistic posing. Fluther is the only male character who, despite his earlier posturing, exhibits some degree of courage and humanity. In *Children of Men*, men and women cooperate. Both sexes display immense capacity for courage and selflessness, as well as cold detachment in the name of a cause (e.g. Julian, Luke and Patric).

- The majority of the characters in *The Plough and the Stars* are working-class people who struggle to survive. *Children of Men* presents class difference as an absurdity in a world that is dying.

The Great Gatsby

Politics

In both *The Plough and the Stars* and *Children*

of Men the faction fighting (fighting within a large organisation/country) is overt and brutal. Both texts depict groups of people pushed by extreme circumstances (i.e.

colonisation, poverty, plague) into violent conflict. **The Great Gatsby reverses this trend by revealing what evils luxury and comfort may breed in people.** The novel is set in the summer of 1922, which is notable for at least three reasons:

1. **A lack of interest in the horrors of war (past or yet to come) radically distinguishes Fitzgerald's novel from O'Casey's play and Cuarón's film.** In terms of war, *The Great Gatsby* is set a few years after World War I (1914-18) ended. Nick and Gatsby are veterans of World War I, and this plays a role in how they come to respect each other and feel they have something in common. In this regard, Nick and Gatsby's fairly positive attitude to the war is radically different to the horror of combat that is conveyed in O'Casey's play and Cuarón's film. One of the first things Nick tells the reader is that 'I enjoyed the counter-raid so thoroughly that I came back restless'. Gatsby is proud of his rank as major. He actually carries medals of honour around with him. He seems most fond of his commendation from 'Little Montenegro' and its 'warm little heart'. Most soldiers who fought in World War I returned home to find it difficult to get a job. **One is reminded here of Bessie Burgess's son, who is marching home from World War I with a 'shattered arm', towards a future of slum poverty and the loss of his mother. Nick and Gatsby face no such horrors.** They were deeply anxious to collect their war payment from the government, which claimed it was too costly to completely reimburse the soldiers for their service. The book seems to gloss over the difficulties of the typical war veteran. Gatsby's only regret about being a soldier seems to be that it took him away from Daisy. He has since flourished as a businessman, while Nick has begun a career in stock market bonds. **Nothing could be further from the future which awaits the tenement rebels in O'Casey's play.**

2. **Another significant difference between *The Great Gatsby* and the other texts is its frivolous, comfortable and seemingly non-political social setting. This is the reverse of** the combative uprisings in O'Casey's play and Cuarón's film.** Although Fitzgerald could not have known at the time he published it (1925), his novel precedes the Great Depression (1929 until the mid-1930s). However, his decision to make Nick a 'bond man' may have been more than a coincidence. Stocks and bonds fluctuate (i.e. bob up and down) in value based on public confidence in them. The fantastical world of Gatsby and his partygoers is known as the Roaring 20s – a boisterous period characterised by rapidly changing lifestyles, financial excesses and the fast pace of technological progress. It is built entirely on perception. If something seems 'great' then that is good enough for them. And just like stock market crashes, Gatsby plummets in 'value' when almost no one attends his funeral. From our own cultural context (as we recover from a global recession), this renders the frivolity and carelessness of Fitzgerald's protagonists all the more poignant as a symbol of a manic ruling class lost in the belief that everything is only going to get better forever.

3. Bad politics is often paired with pseudo-science or crank philosophy. **We see a version of this when the posturing The Covey sneers at anyone who hasn't read Jenersky's thesis, or through the variety of people with absurd beliefs in *Children of Men*, e.g. Miriam and Jasper's fascination with UFOs. The rise of pseudo-science is often a warning sign that a country is losing its grip on reality. Fitzgerald's book strikingly anticipates the hateful pseudo-science and politics of fascism that will fuel Hitler's rise to power and set off World War II.** Tom Buchanan is presented as a model fascist: he's physically imposing and has 'a cruel body'. He is also financially powerful, speaks only in absolutes and seems incapable of kindness: 'Now, don't think my opinion on these matters is final…just because I'm stronger and more of a man than you are'. But Fitzgerald implies that behind the veneer of certainty, Tom is intellectually weak. When he first appears, Tom explains that 'civilisation's going to pieces' and he has become 'a terrible pessimist'. He demands to know whether Nick has read a book

called *The Rise of the Colored Empires* and declares it is 'all scientific stuff'. He labours on to convince his wife and visitor that 'we're Nordics' and that 'we've produced all the things that go to make civilisation – oh, science and art, and all that. Do you see?' Tom is concerned that they need to 'watch out or these other races will have control of things'. Nick is disgusted not so much by Tom's overt racism as by the attempts to speak about ideas at all: 'There was something pathetic in his concentration...' Any attempt at thinking philosophically or scientifically reveals how helpless people like Tom are. Not only does Tom fail to see how these ideas are 'stale' as Nick does, but he cannot even convey them properly. Of course, these 'stale' ideas (built around racism and xenophobia) are the very life blood of the fascist movement that will come to prominence just a few years later in Europe.

Resentment of the 'Other' is drawn very vividly in the Catholic/Protestant tensions in O'Casey's tenements and in the British anxiety about 'fugees' in *Children of Men*, but there is a subtle trace of it in Fitzgerald's prose. Ironically, although Nick sees Tom's fascist concerns as 'pathetic', Nick's own narration reads as extremely problematic in parts. At one point, he and Gatsby drive past two Negro 'bucks', which reads as an animal term. 'I laughed aloud as the yolks of their eyeballs rolled toward us in haughty rivalry.' Depicting the largeness of their eyes in this manner reads like an antiquated racist cartoon. Even more notable is Fitzgerald's rendering of the character, Wolfsheim. He is 'a small, flat-nosed Jew' with 'tiny eyes'. In keeping with the notion that Jews selfishly control world events, Gatsby informs Nick that Wolfsheim is the man who 'fixed the World's Series back in 1919'. He hasn't been caught because he's 'a smart man'. Nick thinks himself naïve not to have realised that one person can rig something so vast. This plays into the many conspiracy theories in the book, not only about Gatsby's personal history, but also Tom's fear of losing civilisation itself to a mysterious racial 'other'.

Social pressures

O'Casey's tenement dwellers are trapped in poverty. Many of them respond by drinking heavily. Fluther risks his life to get his hands on whisky during a looting spree in *The Plough and the Stars*. Jasper's experimental marijuana seems to help residents of Cuarón's childless world deal with the absurdity of their situation by laughing. In a strange reversal, Fitzgerald's characters break the law and get dangerously drunk not because they are *deprived* of anything, but because they are so pampered they suffer from profound boredom. The pressure for these elites is to entertain and be entertained. It seems there is nothing worse in Gatsby's world than to be a 'bore'. The vast parties he throws present his guests with spectacle after spectacle and favour after favour. But the whole enterprise is fuelled by the bootlegged alcohol that has paid for the mansion in the first place. (Prohibition 1920-1933 banned all production and sale of alcohol in America. Gatsby has a series of explanations for how he earned his wealth, but bootlegging – illegally selling alcohol – is the main factor). It is implied that the quiet desperation of the leisure class leads them to seek out intense intoxication and partying. **Nick notes that, by contrast, Gatsby doesn't drink. Perhaps this is due to his gift for supernatural levels of hope for a brilliant future. It is notable also that O'Casey's Bessie Burgess, perhaps the most aggressive and provocative drinker in the play, is a model of sobriety when she has a noble task to do, such as caring for Nora. In *Children of Men*, Theo has been discreetly swigging from a bottle since the opening scene, but he uses his precious alcohol to sanitise his hands instead of drinking it when it comes time to help Kee deliver her baby.** In one of the great ironies of Fitzgerald's novel, we are told Daisy doesn't drink. Nick muses that it is 'a great advantage not to drink among hard-drinking people. You can hold your tongue...' and time any sexual escapade when 'everybody is so blind that they don't see or care'. And yet it is Daisy who causes the fatal chain of events when she drives while drunk back from New

York and kills Myrtle Wilson. Her drinking in this episode is caused directly by the conflict between the social pressure to remain with her husband and her romantic inclination to throw her repressed life away and elope with Gatsby. She initiates the pleasure trip to New York with the question: 'What'll we do with ourselves this afternoon?' and then adds 'and the day after that, and the next thirty years?' The struggle of the wealthy in the book is against the 'senselessness' of their comfort, trying to mould it into meaningful form.

Religion/spirituality

Religion acts as a social divider in *The Plough and the Stars* with characters like the Voice of the Man using Christian imagery to recruit men to martyr themselves for Ireland. In *Children of Men* the overt religiosity of the various penitential sects is presented as poignant or absurd, but the film can be seen as a spiritual allegory of a sceptical man's journey from despair to hope. By contrast, *The Great Gatsby* is deeply secular in almost every aspect. The only overtly religious figure in the novel is George Wilson, and he commits murder and suicide. The absence of religion, or a compelling spiritual practice in any of the characters, reflects the cultural context of the novel. With the exception of Nick, who thinks himself scrupulously honest, no one seems to have any real moral compass. Nothing is sacred to anyone, except possibly Gatsby's dream of Daisy. And even Daisy herself falls painfully short of Gatsby's glowing ideal, proving to be a false idol. However, absences can be as powerful as presences. Amid the drunken frolics of the super-wealthy, the novel inserts the 'persistent stare' of a judgemental Old Testament God. A billboard showing just the eyes of 'Doctor T.J. Eckleburg' sits on the road between Long Island and New York City. Nick describes the eyes, wearing an enormous pair of glasses, as having a 'persistent stare'. They look out of 'no face' and need spectacles 'which pass over a non-existent nose'. The novel is set during the age of modernism, which is a period of simultaneous optimism and pessimism. The optimism stems from a sense that humankind can use science and reason to solve nearly every problem of living. The despair of modernism comes from the anxiety that 'God is dead', and there are no absolute values any more. Life is simply what you can get away with. Many modernist authors and artists came to reject the idea of a 'single window' from which to view reality. There are no final truths and no easy answers about guilt. George Wilson does not have the luxury of decadent parties to explore his sexual, artistic or intellectual self. All he sees are the old certainties (such as monogamy) slipping away from him. When his wife is killed by a drunken, dishonest member of the elite, the absence of a traditional God is too much to bear:

'God knows what you've been doing... you can't fool God!...God sees everything.' **All three texts show us moments of kindness, courage, and honour in some of their main characters. But each text remains ambiguous about the role of faith in their fictional worlds.**

Roles of men and women

In *The Plough and the Stars* we see men and women at their most ideologically divided. No female character is seriously invested in the uprising. Some women, like Bessie Burgess and Nora, actively despise the conflict, albeit for different reasons. By contrast, the men are drawn to ideologies like moths to a flame, with Peter, Fluther and Jack Clitheroe mesmerised by nationalist sentiment and The Covey constantly reducing all struggle to Marxist philosophy. O'Casey's women seem to be pragmatists, living in the urgent-now. The men are posers and dreamers, living more in a what-may-be fantasy land. In *Children of Men* the relationship between men and women is simultaneously more fraught and yet more mature. Although the film's plight stems from the fact that men and women cannot successfully mate and produce children, the relationship between the main male and female characters is far from

sterile. **Jasper is devoted to his traumatised wife, and Theo and Julian still harbour intense love and respect for each other. The film celebrates the love that can exist between people – male or female – whose actions are dictated only by the strength of their feelings for the other person and not out of any hope of reproducing.** *The Great Gatsby*, **true to form, does two opposing things at once in this regard.** It presents men and women of the Jazz Age as happily partying together and enjoying a lot of drink and free-wheeling affairs. This might read like liberation, but the sub-text is that there are as many characters (male and female) who are devastated by all this new-found 'liberty' as characters who are charmed by it. Daisy is disgusted by Tom's lover phoning the house, for instance, but feels it is too old-fashioned to oppose it. At one point she even seems to resent the pressure on her to be so progressive: 'Sophisticated – God, I'm sophisticated!' In one of the bleakest and damning lines in the book on how women only seem free in this dazzling world of wealth and parties, Daisy speaks about learning she had a daughter: 'I'm glad it's a girl. And I hope she'll be a fool – that's the best thing a girl can be in this world, a beautiful little fool'. It is a measure of how much Daisy resents her position in life, and how much she secretly suffers, that she could say this about her own daughter. Her ironic critique of her society is clear: if a woman accepts the role of pretty decoration in a man's life, she won't have any problems. The tragic accident stems, in part, from her bungled attempt to assert control over her own life.

The two other main female characters are Daisy's friend Jordan, and Myrtle Wilson, her rival for her husband's affections. Myrtle too is angry about her station in life, and again blames her husband. However, Tom breaks her nose in a drunken row and she doesn't leave him. She also challenges Wilson to 'beat me!...Throw me down and beat me, you dirty little coward'. Since Myrtle is having an affair with the 'cruel body' of Tom Buchanan, she seems attracted to power, a quality she lacks. **There are no female characters this self-hating or depressed in either O'Casey's play or Cuarón's film.**

The only confident female character is Jordan Baker. Reading her characterisation now, it is hard to appreciate how progressive it would have been at the time of publication. For instance, the history of women's voting rights in America is long and complicated, but females could not vote nationwide until 1920, just two years before the novel is set. It was also only a recent phenomenon that women could go out without a chaperone, smoke in public with men or wear less constrictive clothing. In this regard, the 'flapper' and pro-golfer Jordan would seem almost futuristic to some readers of the time. The character's name is a mixture of two car companies from the era. The Baker Motor Vehicle company made electric cars, something that sounds futuristic even today. The Jordan Motor Car company produced vehicles that were famed more for their stylish looks and clever ads than their quality as vehicles. They were typically aimed at the new market of female drivers. This seems to inform Fitzgerald's take on Jordan as an attractive, clever but unreliable woman. Nick notes that she's a 'rotten driver'. He confides that even though Jordan is a sportswoman (a masculine pursuit associated with high-minded fairness) she's a cheat. Jordan is fashionable and fun rather than someone Nick loves or respects. The inherent sexism of the era sweeps breezily through Nick's forgiveness of Jordan's womanly failings: 'Dishonesty in a woman is a thing you never blame deeply'. Daisy, Myrtle and Jordan all live in a hell of low expectations.

Gatsby is gallant to a fault. He has achieved a hollow 'greatness' by using Daisy as a muse, converting her from a person into a symbol: 'He knew when he kissed this girl, and forever wed his unutterable visions to her perishable breath, his mind would never romp again like the mind of God'. **In its own subtle way, this worship of an ideal woman is as much a de-humanisation as the 'slum lice' in O'Casey's play or the 'fugees' in** *Children of Men*. **By contrast, Kee manages to be perceived by her society as a symbol of fertility (and therefore species survival) while maintaining** her unique humanity. Although O'Casey lets his characters lapse into parodies of male and female stereotypes, he refuses to let any become romantic or spiritual symbols. They start and remain as flawed human men and women.

Social class

O'Casey's play is set steadfastly in the realm of the Dublin working class. Cuarón's film ranges over different classes from oppressed refugees to elite members of the ruling class. Fitzgerald's novel has four major settings, and each one represents a different sphere with different possibilities: East and West Egg, the valley of ashes and New York City.

The 'white palaces' of East Egg in Long Island represent 'old money' or the elite clans who have never known financial struggle. Tom and Daisy are members of this leisure class and do not work (unless you count Tom's 'work' at managing a string of polo ponies). Nick comes from the wealthy Carraway clan, but he intends to make his own way. In this regard he is an outsider of sorts, renting 'a small eyesore' on West Egg, next door to Gatsby's mansion. His neighbour represents the nouveau riche, or 'new money': someone who has swept into the wealthy world from some lower status, either through talent, luck or sheer daring. Because Gatsby has no pedigree (no one knows he is really Jimmy Gatz from dirt-poor rural North Dakota), there is a parlour game developing around guessing who he is and how he earned his fortune. Gatsby's guests project murderous fantasies onto this 'blow-in', adding to his legend and making his parties even more essential entertainments for the bored rich. Nick notes the irony that just as curiosity about Gatsby was at its highest, the lights in his house 'failed to go on one Saturday night' and suddenly 'his career as Trimalchio was over'. Fitzgerald even considered calling the novel *Trimalchio in West Egg*. The name Trimalchio was a character in a Roman novel dating back to the first century. In this novel, Trimalchio was a freed slave. As a host, Trimalchio lavishes his guests with bizarre treats like live birds trapped inside fake eggs, a possible mirroring of the elites trapped in their own West/East Egg worlds. Trimalchio even reveals plans for his enormous tomb, and his drunken guests all act out his funeral for his amusement. This is ironic in Fitzgerald's hands as no one attends Gatsby's funeral once they learn he is not one of them and they can no longer use him for their amusement. Trimalchio is a symbol of the worst excesses of the new rich and their desire to win love and respect through grotesque displays of luxury. The concept of a freed slave is also interesting when contemplating the oppressive forced jollity of Fitzgerald's Egg residents. Is Gatsby a free man? He cannot seem to win true acceptance by the elites he courts, nor can he ever win the idealised Daisy he has built up in his head. Tom and Daisy are trapped in a deeply unhappy marriage. Jordan cannot enjoy intimacy because, according to Nick, she is a fraud at heart. **There are many forms of slavery on show here, just as there are cages of small-mindedness as well as poverty revealed in O'Casey's play. These can be as real as the literal cages for immigrants in Cuarón's film.**

The next setting in the novel is the valley of ashes. Very little time is spent here, but it is vividly described. Set 'about half way' between the worldliness of New York City and the escapist heaven of West Egg lies the netherworld. It is described as a place where 'ashes grow like wheat' in 'grotesque gardens'. With a 'transcendent effort' the ashes even form men. With the exception of the various servants in the novel, this is the only glimpse the reader gets of the working class. **The 'spasms of bleak dust' remind one of the 'well fallen' dust in Bessie Burgess's living quarters or the opening polluted scenes of Cuarón's London.** The novel chooses not to stay in the valley of ashes, because no one does. Even the 'motor road hastily joins the railroad' (routes to a brighter world) 'to shrink away from' this desolate place. The poor here are depicted as people who cannot move. They are like ghosts in comparison to the jubilant rich who populate the novel. And yet it is here that Tom chooses his lover, as if what he really sought was to be someone's saviour. Here, Myrtle Wilson is killed by Daisy, and here Mr Wilson loses his mind looking into the eyes of 'god'. If most of the novel is a series of detailed character sketches, the valley of ashes is a strange shift into impressionist landscape. People aren't fully human here, and this is how Fitzgerald is implying the rich see the poor. It is significant that in the novel even the poor refuse to see themselves as poor, but merely as temporarily embarrassed high society. Explaining how she came to live in the valley of ashes with her husband, Myrtle paints a picture of a very strict and stark social ladder. She blames Wilson for misleading her about what rung he stood on it: 'I thought he knew something about breeding, but he wasn't fit to lick my shoe.'

The final sphere in the novel's universe, New York City, is presented as a place of infinite possibility, a place you enter 'with fenders spread like wings', where 'even Gatsby could happen, without any particular wonder'. Nick briefly becomes a romantic when he paints the scene: 'The city seen from the Queensboro Bridge is always the city seen for the first time, in its first wild promise of all the mystery and the beauty in the world'. Even though he is introduced to Wolfsheim and the criminal underworld here and witnesses Tom beating Myrtle in their apartment, New York is seen through Nick's eyes as a place so radical and free that all sins are forgiven here. The more staid social sphere of Long Island seems to earn his implied disdain. **While there are glimpses of the wealthy and powerful in O'Casey's play (the Voice of the Man and the woman from Rathmines) and the aesthete Nigel in *Children of Men* is clearly from an elite background, there is no setting in those works that brims with hope and glory like New York City does during the Jazz Age for Fitzgerald.** For him, true wealth seems to equate with possibility, and that seems to be a quality that escapes both the destitute and the super-rich, unless they know how to dream.

KEY POINTS

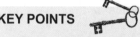

- The political background of World War One and the 1916 Rising are the backdrop to *The Plough and the Stars.* Every character in the play is drawn into the political upheaval whether they want to be or not. An infertility plague in the near future of 2027 is the main backdrop in the film *Children of Men*, but this plague destabilises the world politically and gives rise to an oppressive British government and an immigrant 'uprising' similar to the nationalist uprising in O'Casey's play. *The Great Gatsby* is set after World War One, but combat is presented as a glorious time when young men proved their heroism. Prohibition is also an opportunity (during peace time) to prove one's courage and entrepreneurship.
- The Dublin tenement residents' appalling poverty is another crucial element in our understanding of the cultural context of this play. Addictions to alcohol, as well as the imagined dignity of an heroic role, are apparent throughout the play. Members of the Fishes in *Children of Men* are also motivated to engage in the rebellion as an escape from the degradation of being powerless and poor, as well as feeling like they have no future in any country. By contrast, the main characters in *The Great Gatsby* suffer from boredom and a lack of direction. Their wealth and the constant leisure it gives them becomes a kind of oppression – hence the intense focus on partying.
- Religion is tied to politics and is mostly divisive in O'Casey's tenement building. In *Children of Men*, overt religiosity is presented as an act of desperation in the face of the mysterious plague. However, the film functions as a parable about the power of hope (spiritual or secular) to lead people from apathy or despair to love and selflessness. In *The Great Gatsby*, the absence of a coherent religious or moral framework in the free-wheeling Jazz Age generates the tragic action.

- The roles of men and women are clearly defined in *The Plough and the Stars*. O'Casey depicts women as being strong-willed, determined fighters who are less susceptible to idealistic posing. Fluther is the only male character who, despite his earlier posturing, exhibits some degree of courage and humanity. In *Children of Men*, men and women cooperate. Both sexes display immense capacity for courage and selflessness, as well as cold detachment in the name of a cause (e.g. Julian, Luke and Patric). Fitzgerald's novel is progressive in how it depicts women to be as daring and corrupt as men. The three main female characters are trapped in different ways in a hell of low expectations for their sex. The three main male characters see themselves as full of masculine virtue (Nick claims he is honest, Tom is strong, and Gatsby is resourceful and brave) but not one of them reports the hit-and-run or prevents the tragedy.

- The majority of the characters in *The Plough and the Stars* are working-class people who struggle to survive. *Children of Men* presents class difference as an absurdity in a world that is dying. *The Great Gatsby* depicts an intricate web of social spheres but is mostly focused on the bored rich and their reckless efforts to amuse themselves.

Sample Answer

A. CULTURAL CONTEXT

'Understanding the cultural context of a text allows you to see how values and attitudes are shaped.'

A. Show how this statement applies to ONE of the texts on your comparative course. (30)

B. Compare the way in which values and attitudes are shaped in TWO other texts on your comparative course. (40)

A.

A text's characters are defined by their actions, but those actions never happen in a vacuum. Typically, a character is revealed through their reactions to the social landscape – the cultural context – they act within and against. This social 'world' of the text is a distinctive shaping force in terms of what happens to the characters in the course of the plot. It allows readers to understand the circumstances under which values and attitudes are shaped.

The texts I have chosen for my comparative study are the play *The Plough and the Stars* by Sean O'Casey, the film *Children of Men* directed by Alfonso Cuarón, and the novel *The Great Gatsby* by F. Scott Fitzgerald. For the purposes of this answer, I want to focus first on the cultural context that informs Fitzgerald's novel, and specifically how a clash of modern and old-fashioned values and attitudes shape the actions of Tom and Daisy Buchanan.

Set during the Jazz Age (the summer of 1922), the novel is superficially about a time that values celebration and frivolity in the wake of World War I. Gatsby's ostentatious parties function as a microcosm for the crumbling of old social dictates about public decorum: for instance, we see attitudes to female modesty start to relax as women dress casually and enjoy new freedoms like smoking, drinking and flirting with (married) men.

Introduced early in the novel, Daisy and Tom Buchanan suffer from a conflict between old and modern values and attitudes to what is acceptable behaviour for a married couple. Their home is one of the 'white palaces' of opulent East Egg. They seem godlike in their ability to lounge around all day, tended to by a mostly invisible staff of servants. Their worst challenge appears to be boredom. Tom is both physically and financially robust – he is a commanding presence but has a 'cruel body.' By contrast, one of the first words to describe Daisy is that she is a 'girl' with 'an absurd, charming little laugh'. From the outset, this couple represents an elite power couple: as a polo and football player, Tom is masculine strength personified, and Daisy, from her name to her laugh, is delicate feminine charm. In one of the strange ironies of the novel, the difficulty that besets Tom and Daisy is that they fill these pre-fabricated roles too well. He is so 'manly' that he seems incapable of even a moment's kindness. Daisy is almost a caricature of the submissive upper-class wife. When Tom's lover calls the house during Nick's first visit, Daisy's response is to laugh it off 'with tense gaiety' and keep playing the gracious hostess. The conflicting old-fashioned attitude that she should maintain her marriage (even put up a front that everything is fine) and the modern value of maintaining her dignity by rejecting her domineering and unfaithful husband is the basic crisis that Daisy faces. These are people who live trapped in a web of gossip. Daisy never spells out her thinking, but she seems to believe that if she leaves her husband it will be a scandal, and if she stays she is a doormat. Unable to fully commit or decisively leave, Daisy chooses neither. Instead she opts to have a secret affair with Gatsby. This is probably because it allows her to try on a pose of independence without risking any definitive choice. The affair initiates the tragic action of the novel but also reflects the general anxiety about the weakening of traditional values (like monogamy) in the modern era.

Another example of a strange attitude or conflicted value system is seen by how the Buchanan's treat their young daughter, Pammy. The girl barely appears in the book. We infer that she spends most of her time cared for by a nurse. This cool attitude to family intimacy shows how repressed people like the Buchanans are. In the rare moment we see Daisy with her daughter, we're told it is because 'mother wanted to show you off'. The attraction of the upper-class toward appearance over substance is the same driving force behind Gatsby's own 'greatness'. His parties are legendary, so therefore Gatsby himself must also be legendary. There is plenty to eat and drink, so America must be in great shape.

Tom's lack of substantial values is introduced early in the novel. He tells Nick that he has become 'a terrible pessimist about things.' He launches into a ham-fisted synopsis of a racist book he has read, weakly repeating that it is 'all scientific stuff'.

In contrast to Tom, Nick is intelligent and well-read. He notes there is 'something pathetic' in Tom's effort to mount an intellectual argument. Here we see, again almost from the outset of the novel, that Tom is as much a victim of his life of ease and entitlement as Daisy is. He has not needed to enrich his mind enough to see through 'stale' and morally bankrupt ideas, and Daisy has not needed to develop her own sense of dignity or self-possession. Everything has been handed to them, so they are helpless.

Daisy's private attitude to being a rich man's wife in a picture-perfect home is revealed when she exclaims: 'Sophisticated – God, I'm sophisticated!' She is too self-aware to be happy and too cowed by convention to be free. Revealing her secret suffering in the value system of a paternalistic and sexist society, Daisy recalls learning she had given birth to a daughter and thinking: 'I'm glad it's a girl. And I hope she'll be a fool – that's the best thing a girl can be in this world, a beautiful little fool'. There is so much anger and disappointment here. For Daisy, sexism and perfectionism are toxic values she cannot bring herself to reject. She acts out by having an affair. When that is uncovered by Tom, she drives home drunk. A lifetime of avoiding or delegating responsibility to someone else gets played out when Daisy kills Myrtle Wilson with her car and flees the scene. In this moment she is still playing the 'girl' role pre-set for her by her old money high-society world. Her attitude is that someone else will come and clean up her mess because someone always does.

B.

In marked contrast to *The Great Gatsby*, the values and attitudes on display in *The Plough and the Stars* and *Children of Men* are often shaped in response to the violent uprisings and depressed social settings that feature in both texts. Even before the fighting begins in O'Casey's play, the environment of the Dublin tenement is one of oppressive poverty. This creates tension between the various neighbours. An air of paranoia hangs over everything. Mrs Gogan, for instance, accuses Nora of having 'notions of upperosity' because she tries to emulate a more middle-class existence, spending time tending to home décor and subjecting The Covey and Uncle Peter to the 'penal servitude' of rigorous hygiene regimens. The attitude here is that anyone trying to act above their station is implicitly criticising their neighbours. This status anxiety is expressed openly by the immigrant Kee in *Children of Men* when she asks if her English-born midwife Miriam seems 'posh'. Bessie Burgess, being a Protestant and loyalist, makes status anxiety much more explicit when she calls the Catholic tenement dwellers 'slum lice'. Even though she is an alcoholic living in destitution, her son is fighting for King George V and this makes her feel she is above the poverty that surrounds her. Singing *Rule Britannia* is her way of wrapping herself in a regality her home does not reflect. The attempt by insecure and suffering people to attach themselves to the idea of a powerful empire is also dealt with in *Children of Men*. News propaganda claims 'Only Britain Soldiers On' and guards dehumanise refugees, saying they are scum who make them sick, despite the fact that Britain is sliding into rampant pollution, decay, depression and overt cruelty.

In O'Casey's play, we also see complex political attitudes beyond nationalism and religious division emerging before the fighting begins. The Covey dismisses any fight that is not a struggle for the universal working class. Despite his affectation as a Marxist revolutionary (he calls people 'comrade' a lot and pretentiously references 'Jenersky's thesis' every chance he gets), The Covey's actual values seem bankrupt. Most of his energy is spent irritating Uncle Peter for no other reason except that he can. In an exchange with an actual worker, Rosie the sex worker, instead of expressing real solidarity with her and her plight, he pompously informs her he won't be taking instructions from a 'prostitute'. His moral and intellectual superiority is again shown to be an empty pose when the looting begins and The Covey is one of the first out the door to 'save' the surplus capital lying about defenseless in the shops. In the film, Luke and his hyper-violent lieutenant Patric are men of action (like Jack Clitheroe and his company), but Luke's claim to be fighting for 'dignity' is just as questionable as The Covey's stabs at dignity, as the Fishes torture and assassinate defenseless people in pursuit of their goal.

O'Casey reserves his most withering critique for the values and attitudes shared by war-infatuated men. Quoting almost verbatim from the speeches of Pádraig Pearse he shows, in the guise of the Voice of the Man, how efficient war propaganda can be when it fuses with the notion of religious martyrdom. The 'tall dark figure' is never seen but his voice is eloquent, an obviously well-educated middle-class mind. Taking a Christian value like self-sacrifice and mutating it to violent ends, the Voice calls on Irishmen to 'rejoice in this terrible war. The old heart of the earth needed to be warmed with the red blood of the battlefields'. Jack Clitheroe and his fellow combatants are intoxicated by this rich rhetoric. They throw over their natural allegiances to their families in favour of an abstraction: 'Ireland is greater than a mother... than a wife'. The naïve fervour of these attitudes leads to a tragic failed uprising, to many innocent deaths and eventually to a 'terrible' civil war that is nothing to rejoice in. In a virtual reversal of this, *Children of Men* effects a miracle – a baby is born – and soldiers temporarily cease fire, kneeling to bless themselves, while refugees stop huddling in terror to touch the baby and gaze at it. A religiously-charged symbol – the holy family – creates a moment of peace rather than acting as a cynical recruitment tool.

The cultural context of *Children of Men* is bleaker than *The Plough and the Stars*: the whole human world is slowly extinguishing. The British government's authoritarian response includes Abu Ghraib-style internment camps for non-British 'fugees'. (This brutal overreach undermines their moral superiority, as does the British response to the Irish rebellion when a frustrated soldier asks why the Irish refuse to 'foight fair!') In the film, the British government prioritises order over all other values. It even distributes a suicide pill to the public to promote quiet private deaths over large-scale protests. The Fishes engage in terrorist tactics and plan an uprising as doomed as the Dublin revolutionaries. Like Jack Clitheroe and his comrades, the Fishes' attitude seems to be that any means justify the end of disrupting an oppressive government's iron rule. Over the course of the film we see the Fishes kidnap, threaten and murder to pursue their goals. By contrast, Theo is initially presented as a model of political disengagement. In the very first scene he narrowly escapes being killed in a bomb blast. His response to this event is the same as his attitude to the collapse of civilisation: one of cultivated apathy. In O'Casey's play, characters sneer at the cherished values of others, e.g. The Covey dismissing nationalism or Bessie deriding the uprising. But no one is as apathetic about everything as Theo is. He maintains a low-key government job he doesn't care much about, drinks alcohol steadily throughout the day and seems uninterested in revolt or the plight of the oppressed. He sneers at the death of 'Baby Diego', the youngest man in the world, and uses it as an excuse to get off work and visit his (possibly only) friend Jasper. Out in the woods, he can get stoned, laugh at the mounting absurdities of his world such as the religious cults and briefly forget his grief over his dead son. Later we learn that Theo used to be a political activist. His apathy is really a mask for dealing with the pain of losing all hope for the future. Apathy can look calm and detached, even stoic, but is often a way of hiding feelings of powerlessness. The other way to mask powerlessness is bluster, the preferred attitude for characters like Uncle Peter in the play. Nothing sums up his impotence better than how he was 'burnin' to dhraw me sword, an' wave it an' wave it over me' in a magical display of strength.

By contrast to Peter's impotence and Theo's apathy, Julian is presented as someone who is genuinely stoic in her attitude. As a leader of the Fishes, her value system promotes active engagement in fighting injustice (unlike the purely theoretical arguments of The Covey). Accusing Theo of dwelling in private grief, Julian risks her life to see that Kee is ferried to safety away from the clutches of her own organisation. In this regard, Julian is much more aware and savvy than Jack Clitheroe and his citizen-soldiers. Julian knows that her colleagues cannot be trusted. She keeps her cards close to her chest. She is not mesmerised by a rhetorical spell like O'Casey's men are. She is not working for an abstraction, but instead fearlessly trying to secure the survival of the first baby born in eighteen years. In this regard, Julian embodies the best qualities of the rebel fighters in O'Casey's play (who fight against an injustice) but avoids their posturing. She focuses on immediate and real needs, as Bessie Burgess does when Nora breaks down in the face of her husband's ideological obsession.

Children of Men and *The Plough and the Stars* depict bleak societies plagued by fear and resentment. The characters in both texts operate under immense stress from their political and social contexts. But O'Casey shows us how social chaos on a large scale can bring down even the bravest and kindest of people like Bessie. Conversely, even in a hellscape like Cuarón's, the values of courage and selflessness emerge when people rally to protect Kee and baby Dylan, demonstrating that where there is hope for the future, virtue can trump apathy and hate.

B. General Vision and Viewpoint

The Plough and the Stars

The general vision or viewpoint of a text relates to the authorial/directorial outlook on life. Is the world essentially kind or cruel? Meaningful or meaningless? A place for hope or despair? Does the artist look at their world in an earnest, straightforward way or ironically and with detachment? Can these different attitudes mix so we get a richer, more complex and more compelling worldview than simple optimism or pessimism? This viewpoint inevitably influences our perspective on the text and on the world in which it is set. The vision of an author can be conveyed through his/her attitude towards significant events in the political or social background of a society, through key characters and relationships and also through language and imagery. Often, the dominant viewpoint of a text can be reflected in a key moment.

O'Casey's viewpoint concerning the power of politics and group identities to divide a society and bring about destruction and desolation is essentially negative. The play is set in 1916 in the Dublin tenements when people were rebelling against Ireland's status as a British colony and against poverty and deprivation. A people without a voice easily adopt patriotic slogans and catchwords which can lead to destructive consequences for those influenced by the rhetoric of others. The hero-worship of dead patriots and the linking of politics with religion had the potential at that time to make impoverished people believe that they also could become martyrs in the cause of an Irish Republic. In Act II, the Voice of the Man, an unnamed character who delivers passionate speeches on the glory of bloodshed during war to his listeners, declares that war is 'the Angel of God'. Suffering, bloodshed and death are seen as 'a cleansing and sanctifying thing'. The death of Jack Clitheroe, a key character in the play, is depicted as being a 'gleam of glory' and Nora, his widow, is expected to experience 'a joy when she realises that she has had a hero

for a husband'. This empty rhetoric is in marked contrast to the reality of the situation.

Jack Clitheroe sees himself and his fellow nationalists in the Citizen Army (an organisation set up to prepare to fight for Ireland's independence from Britain) as being true freedom fighters who take inspiration from the sacrifices being made in World War I, which is taking place in Europe at the same time. He, Langon and Brennan (fellow Citizen Army members) openly state their willingness to die, if necessary, to set Ireland free from British rule. They perceive themselves to be patriots and soldiers but their slogans and fine words reverberate with hollowness, 'Ireland is greater than a mother...greater than a wife'. They claim to welcome and embrace 'Imprisonment...wounds...death' for Ireland but their apparent loyalty is depicted as being not only misguided but really a proclamation of their own intense vanity. Nora, in Act I, angrily expresses this when she asks Jack 'Is General Connolly an' th' Citizen Army goin' to be your only care? Is your home only goin' to be a place to rest in? Am I goin' to be only somethin' to provide merry-making at night for you? Your vanity'll be the ruin of you an' me yet'. Although many may claim that O'Casey's view is very negative towards men like Jack Clitheroe, who were genuine in wanting to make the sacrifices that they made, the reality is that many people suffered death and desolation as a result of the actions of the men of 1916. It was a symbolic act as no military tactician could have honestly believed this skirmish would result in a victory against the British Empire. Many innocent men, women and children who did not volunteer to take part in this doomed act died or were severely injured. This capacity of a tiny group of idealists to claim they speak for everyone and to risk the lives of others as well as their own for a symbolic gesture horrifies O'Casey.

In direct contrast to the nationalists in the play, Bessie Burgess, a resident of the

tenement building in which the Clitheroes live, is a staunch loyalist who believes that those involved in the uprising are traitors. Her son, whom she sees as a true hero, is serving with the Dublin Fusiliers in World War I in France. She angrily attacks those who have not joined the British Army to fight in the World War, 'There's th' men marchin' out into the dhread dimness o' danger, while th' lice is crawlin' about feedin' on the fatness o' th' land'. Bessie's singing of 'Rule Britannia' is meant to inflame the men whom she declares are 'all nicely shanghaied [tricked into an action] now' when the rebellion is brutally quashed. There is something profoundly sad in the fact that Bessie will not be able to 'Keep the home fires burning' for her only son, as she loses her life later in the play.

The Covey, Jack's cousin who lives with the couple, is also extremely hostile to the Citizen Army but for different reasons to those of Bessie. He believes that the men should be fighting for an international workers' revolution rather than political freedom, 'There's only one freedom for the workin' man'. He creates conflict by arguing with Fluther and Peter, other tenement residents, about the links between religion and politics. He is deeply critical of the use of the flag of the Plough and the Stars by nationalists, an act which he considers a betrayal of the working classes whom the flag is meant to represent: 'it's a Labour flag an' was never meant for politics' he tells Jack. He refers to the nationalists as 'th' mugs' who have to 'renew their political baptismal vows' in order to be loyal to their Republican ideals. He claims that 'There's no such thing as an Irishman, or an Englishman, or a German or a Turk; we're all only human bein's'. This attitude of The Covey causes uproar with Fluther who describes his neighbour as 'a word-weavin' little ignorant yahoo of a red flag socialist'.

From the above examples and from many other moments in the play, it is clear that O'Casey has a profoundly negative attitude towards the power of political divisions to destroy a community. We see the illogical pointlessness of the struggle at the end when Bessie Burgess is shot by the British soldiers

whom she was so loudly praising earlier. Many of the nationalists have also been killed and wounded without achieving the freedom of their ideals. Mollser, a teenage girl dying of tuberculosis in the tenement, sums up the attitude of the playwright himself when she asks Nora, 'Is there anybody goin', Mrs Clitheroe, with a titther o' sense?'

O'Casey, while admiring to some extent the courage of the men who fought and died in 1916, is clearly disillusioned by nationalism. He is outraged by the deflection of the labour cause and socialist ideals into nationalistic politics. He is both critical and condemnatory, using the full range of rhetoric, colloquialisms, irony and caricature to highlight the tragic forces at play and the futility and waste of life and effort. The general vision and viewpoint of his play is thus essentially dark and pessimistic.

O'Casey's ironic view of posturing and cowardice is revealed in the course of the play and adds to the pervading negativity. Several of the men in the play are depicted as weak and inadequate. Some characters engage in absurd posturing. This is particularly true of The Covey and Peter, Nora's uncle. The Covey proclaims himself to be a socialist and enjoys displaying his knowledge and understanding of 'Jenersky's Thesis'. There is no doubt that he has a point in his objections to nationalism and its effect on the community. However, he is not as humane as he claims to be as can be seen when he attacks Rosie Redmond, another neighbour, and belittles her by calling her a prostitute. It's clear he is more interested in the idea of solidarity with his working-class brothers and sisters than the practice of it. Later, he is more than willing to engage in looting, hurrying Fluther on with the words, 'Come on then, or there won't be anything left to save'. Peter also engages in self-delusion, proudly dressing himself in his Foresters' uniform, even though the society's only function seems to be an annual march to Wolfe Tone's grave. Fluther boasts that he has not missed a 'pilgrimage to Bodenstown' in 25 years and never failed to 'pluck a leaf off Tone's grave'. Although Peter claims during the patriotic speech in Act II that he is 'burnin' to draw me sword, an' wave, an' wave it over me', his heroism is merely a façade. The only reason he does not go looting with the others is because he is afraid of being shot. Defeated by his own cowardice, he sanctimoniously condemns the looters, 'Makin' a shame an' a sin o' the cause that good men are fightin' for'. With his gaudy uniform of the Foresters and his loud declarations of valour, Peter represents very little that is truly admirable. His appalling self-centredness is shown when, hearing the sound of rifle shots, he tries to shut the door against Bessie and Mrs Gogan before they can get to safety. Bessie sums him up well when she describes him as 'a little sermonising, little yella-faced, little consequential, little pudgy, little bum…'. Despite the humour of the dialogue and characterisation, there is no doubt that the playwright is highlighting the hypocrisy and shallowness of certain characters who profess the highest ideals.

There's a tension here, because O'Casey seems to be saying that these people are so badly trapped by poverty that they cannot escape their roles in life. Yet there is also an implicit condemnation of their pettiness and their hypocrisy. This is a profound problem: does the crushing weight of poverty create (emotional, intellectual, political) cripples or do people stay trapped because they keep playing the role of cripple? If you say they have no choice but to act the way they do and that everything is out of their hands because they are poor, uneducated and so on, then you deprive them of free will and essential humanity. If you say that their situation is largely due to their own faults (laziness, dishonesty, stupidity) this is an equally heartless and over-simplified assessment. **O'Casey never gives us the key out of this trap, but he will not let us sit in easy judgement of these people, nor will he let us relax by making them simple victims of large impersonal forces.**

The extent to which comedy is used serves to intensify and exacerbate the tragic vision which lies at the heart of the play. Sean O'Casey described the play as being 'A Tragedy in Four Acts', despite the presence of many comic elements. In Act I, the snooping,

nosy nature of Mrs Gogan and her comments on Nora's new hat, which she furtively tries on, initially create a light-hearted, humorous atmosphere. Further humour is introduced by Fluther and Uncle Peter. Both men are comic creations. Fluther, who is attempting to give up drinking alcohol, constantly misuses the word 'derogatory' assuring Mrs Gogan that there 'is nothing derogatory wrong with me' when she comments on his cough. However, Mrs Gogan's anecdote about the woman who died of a 'tickle in her throat', gives rise to a comical panic attack in Fluther who instantly believes that his cough is getting worse and that he is beginning to feel dizzy: 'I hope that I didn't give up th' beer too soon'. Peter, with his face 'shaped like a lozenge' adds an extra element of farce with his childish obsession concerning his Forester's uniform which, according to Mrs Gogan, makes him look 'like somethin' you'd pick off a Christmas tree'. However, although the audience may succumb to laughter at the clownish antics and the comic dialogue, a more fitting response to the general vision of the play would be anger at the political beliefs and at the effects of poverty which destroyed people like the Clitheroes, Bessie and Mollser.

The poignant loss of the happiness that Jack and Nora once experienced in their marriage adds a further negative tone to the play. Mrs Gogan seems to have insight into the nature of their relationship when she says of Jack that 'the mystery of havin' a woman's a mystery no longer ' and that Nora is like a 'clockin' hen if he [Jack] leaves her sight for a minute'. Mrs Gogan is a comical character but these remarks flag the importance of the Clitheroes' relationship to the central tragedy. The opening act reveals that the source of this conflict is related to Jack's membership of the revolutionary Citizen Army. When General Connolly sends Captain Brennan with battle orders to Jack Clitheroe he is engaging in the destruction of the domestic order that Nora strives so hard to maintain. After a touching love scene between husband and wife, in which Jack sings Nora a love song, calamity strikes. An officer arrives with orders for Jack to actively engage in combat. Nora's desperate plea to her husband to 'Pretend we're not in... don't break our happiness', falls on deaf ears as Jack, enraged that she has deceived him by hiding a letter which appointed him as a commandant in the Citizen Army, storms out of the room, declaring that he will be home very late and that she needn't wait up for him. Nora's bitter response – 'I don't care if you never come back' – sums up the despair she feels when her husband makes his political ambition and vanity more important than his marriage. This disintegration of what was once a loving relationship casts a gloom over this section of the play. Although he has effectively abandoned her, Nora's love for Jack is unshakeable. It is beyond her comprehension that any woman would willingly sacrifice her husband to a political ideal: 'If they say it, they're lyin', against God, Nature an' against themselves'. Her cursing of the rebels and her broken-hearted cry that war has 'dhriven' away th' little happiness life had to spare for me' is profoundly upsetting and true. Later, when Jack briefly returns, only to desert her again, she cries pathetically 'Oh Jack, I gave you everything you asked of me'. Nora then descends quickly into insanity under the pressure of her loss and suffers a miscarriage. Bessie Burgess, filled now with compassion for Nora's sad state, remarks that 'her eyes have a hauntin' way of lookin' in instead of lookin' out'. Indeed, O'Casey's general vision and viewpoint is summed up by Bessie when she exclaims: 'Blessing o' God on us, isn't this pitiful'.

Despite the predominantly pessimistic vision there are moments when O'Casey celebrates the human spirit. Bessie not only supports Nora when Jack deserts her, she also risks her own life by going for a doctor when Nora has her miscarriage. This courage is all the more impressive when one remembers the conflict between them earlier, when she flew at Nora 'like a tiger' and attempted to 'guzzle' her. Bessie also displays a tremendous compassion and humanity in her kindness towards Mollser. Mrs Gogan appreciates Bessie's generosity to her daughter. She thanks Bessie for 'all your gentle hurryin's to me little Mollser . . . never

passin' her without liftin' up her heart with a delicate word o' kindness'. We learn that Bessie offered food to Mollser at a time when food was in very short supply and to do so would be a genuine personal sacrifice. Fluther Good also reveals a courageous and compassionate nature when he risks his own life bringing Nora back from the barricades. These acts of humanity and courage affirm the audience's belief that human beings can rise above self-interest and become heroic in spite of the human failings which they inevitably possess.

A significant event that shows the dominant vision of the play occurs in the final act. Bessie's sterling quality (i.e. of the highest quality), which is celebrated by O'Casey in his portrayal of women in the play, adds to the horror and shock of her death. She is shot by British soldiers as she is trying to protect the hysterical Nora from dangerously approaching the window during a gun battle. O'Casey builds up the tension skilfully. First we hear a burst of rifle fire and rapid shots from a machine gun. The distraught Nora, crying for her husband and her miscarried baby, wakens the sleeping Bessie, who rushes forward to protect her from a window that she has opened. Frantically Bessie drags Nora, pleading with her, 'Come away, come away woman, from that window!' The strength she used forces her to stagger against the window herself. The stage directions tell us that 'Bessie jerks her body convulsively; stands stiffly for a moment, a look of agonised astonishment on her face . . .'. Her screams of fear and pain make a tremendous impact on the audience who, in disbelief, realise that she is critically injured, 'I'm shot, I'm shot, I'm shot! . . . Th' life's pourin' out o' me'. Her death is one of the darkest and most moving moments in the play; she cries out as she is dying: 'Jesus Christ, me sight's goin'! It's all dark, dark! Nora, hold me hand!' This event, which effectively marks the end of the play, leaves no doubt that O'Casey's general vision and viewpoint is profoundly pessimistic. Hopes and ideals have been extinguished and lives have been destroyed in so many diverse ways throughout the entire play.

KEY POINTS

- O'Casey's viewpoint concerning the power of politics to divide a society and bring about destruction and desolation is essentially negative.
- The playwright's ironic view of posturing and cowardice is revealed through the characterisation. Many of the men in the play are depicted as weak and inadequate. They engage in hollow rhetoric and self-delusion.
- O'Casey refuses to let us sit in easy judgement of these people, nor will he let us relax by making them simple victims of large impersonal forces.
- The extent to which comedy is used serves to intensify and exacerbate the tragic vision which lies at the heart of the play.
- The poignant loss of the happiness which Jack and Nora once experienced in marriage adds a further negative tone to the play.
- Despite the predominantly pessimistic vision there are moments when O'Casey celebrates the human spirit. This is most evident in the unexpected heroism and humanity of Bessie and Fluther.
- The deaths of Mollser, Nora's baby and Bessie Burgess, which effectively brings the play to a close, emphasise the darkness of the overall vision.

Children of Men

If the pervasive air of death caused by extreme poverty and war in O'Casey's play seems dark, the film *Children of Men*, directed by Alfonso Cuarón, manages to be even more bleak. Set in a fictional Britain in 2027, the world has been ravaged by a mysterious plague of infertility. With no more children being born, much of humanity has succumbed to despair or degenerated into violence. **Britain claims to have maintained some order in the face of humankind's seeming extinction, but only through a totalitarian government that abuses its desperate immigrants to keep the country running. Like Dublin in 1916, this is an understandably fractured society.** It is broken up into various obsessive religious sects, terrorist political groups and wild gangs living in the countryside. The government even offers a suicide pill called Quietus to people who cannot bear the sadness of seeing the world die out. A piece of street graffiti captures the despair in a polite request: 'Last one to die please turn out the lights'.

Unlike O'Casey's technique in *The Plough and the Stars*, Cuarón opens the action at the lowest emotional point possible for the society in *Children of Men*. A wall of stricken faces in a café watch the TV news announcement that 'Baby Diego', at 18 years old the youngest person in the world, has just been killed by a fan for not signing an autograph. It is a cruel absurdity: their symbol of youth has been murdered for no reason at all. Theo watches numbly before slipping out of the café to fill his coffee with alcohol. He narrowly avoids his own sudden death when the place explodes from a bomb blast, filling the street with glass, terror, and even more grief. The blast also damages Theo's ear. In fact, he starts to lose his hearing in that ear from this point onwards. The street itself is a degraded version of a typical English city scene: some buses and cars still run, but we can see the regression into more basic forms of transport as rickshaws move through the thin crowds, and refuse bags clog the footpath. Everything is rendered in a muted and washed-out colour palette. In just a few seconds of screen time and almost no dialogue, the director has established a world that (despite the bomb blasts) is ending not with a bang, but a whimper.

In many respects, Cuarón's strategy is the opposite of O'Casey's. *The Plough and the Stars* opens with a sprawling, relaxed view of the Dublin tenements and showcases the inhabitants' wit and liveliness as much as their bickering and competing values. We warm to them and laugh with (or at) them first. This makes their devastation later in the play all the more heart-wrenching. **Conversely, *Children of Men* opens in such a hopeless and hollow place that there is nowhere to go but up.** O'Casey's opening shows you a tough world, but it gets you to drop your guard by using humour first. Then it emotionally wrenches the audience at the end as we see hubris (Jack Clitheroe's military pride, for instance), cowardice, confusion and naiveté (Nora's dreams of domestic bliss, or the rebels' dreams of a glorious stand) destroy the lives of each of his characters. ***Children of Men*, on the other hand, opens by hitting you emotionally as hard and fast as it can from the outset.** Only when its action relents at the peaceful conclusion, with Theo, Kee and her baby floating in their boat, do we feel a sense of hope: they live in a world where there is a tomorrow. **That may sound vague, but because we have seen the hell that descends when all hope is lost, as it seems to be in *The Plough and the Stars*, we know that Cuarón is saying that as long as hope is alive, anything is possible.**

The film, like O'Casey's play, is not without humour, but it often takes a more ironic form. For example, Theo's best (and possibly only) friend is Jasper, a political cartoonist who loves bad jokes. Some of these are juvenile, like his habit of asking people to 'pull my finger' signalling that he is about to break wind. But there is a darker form of 'bad joke' called 'gallows humour'. That refers to laughter that arises when someone has given up hope and knows death is inevitable. During one of Theo's visits to his friend's house – a beautifully designed place hidden in a wood about to reclaim the landscape – Jasper shares some marijuana. He wryly

notes that the government hands out suicide pills but still, absurdly, keeps recreational drugs illegal. Then he starts his joke. The opening line mentions the Human Project, a semi-mythical secret organisation trying to solve the infertility problem. Theo angrily interrupts him to dismiss the Human Project as a fantasy. Even if it is real, there is no hope for humankind. There wasn't any hope even before the infertility plague, Theo snaps.

'I'm still tryin' to tell a joke, man,' Jasper replies. Then he continues:

'Ok, the Human Project gives this great, big dinner for all the scientists and sages in the world. They're tossing around theories about the ultimate mystery: why are all the women infertile? Why can't we make babies anymore? So, some say it's genetic experiments, gamma rays, pollution, same ol', same ol'. So, anyway, in the corner, this Englishman's sitting, he hasn't said a word, he's just tuckin' into his dinner. So, they decide to ask him, they say, "Well, why do you think we can't make babies anymore?" And he looks up at 'em, he's chewin' on this great big wing and he says "I haven't the faintest idea," he said, "but this stork is quite tasty isn't he?"'

It is a ludicrously bad joke, playing on the simplistic child's myth that storks deliver babies. The two men enjoy it immensely nevertheless. Perhaps it is the joke's cosmic absurdity, or the faint implication that the British are somehow to blame. It may simply be the result of the drugs they are smoking to numb their sense of loss, but somehow the scene is strangely life-affirming. It implies that as long as people are laughing, joking, and still able to creatively pull faces at death, they are still potently human.

In a similar manner to *The Plough and the Stars*, the humour subtly bonds us to the characters. Later, when the Fishes are interrogating Jasper to find out where Theo and Kee have fled, he refuses to tell them. Facing down the barrel of a gun, he asks them to pull his finger. After they shoot it off, he drops to the ground, and offers his other hand: 'Pull my finger'. Again, even though the scene is cold (lit with a sombre morning sun) it shows us that people can use even the most juvenile gestures to stand up to violent powers. Nothing breaks the cartoonist, even as he is executed. **This is a radical reversal of O'Casey's critique, voiced mainly through his female characters, that the Easter Rising is an immature act perpetrated by men who wear masks of courage but are inadequate to such an impossible task. Where the play shows us immaturity as a weakness, Cuarón's film shows the layers of courage and character that can hide behind a childlike mask.**

Of course, none of this shields us from another competing message embedded in the scene: that there is no limit to the cruelty that humans can inflict on one another when they feel they are on a vital mission, or fighting for a 'just' cause.

Almost all the tragic action in the play is perpetuated by men trying to do what they think is right. The rebels sacrifice themselves (and unwittingly many innocent bystanders) by rejecting what they see as an unbearable colonial oppression. The British 'Tommies' in the final scene see themselves as decent men who want a 'fair fight' and who wish to restore law and order. There are no monsters or villains, only flawed humans. **Likewise, in *Children of Men* there are many factions grappling for what they see as essential goals.** The government's nightmarish treatment of immigrants and refugees is terrifying, but they see it as the last effort at a possible law-abiding society on Earth. The Fishes are brutal terrorists, but they see their tactics as a way to draw attention to the plight of the oppressed. Their ruthless pursuit of Kee and her baby makes a kind of awful sense in Cuarón's dying world: whoever holds the first baby in 18 years holds the future and all the bargaining chips. Everything else is absurd.

Absurdity is a hard word to define, but it generally means the state of things when there is no way of knowing what is important and what isn't. In *The Plough and the Stars*, for instance, it makes psychological sense that the very poor might loot the shops when they get a chance, but O'Casey presents their glee at destroying their

own neighbourhood as being so at odds with their stated values of religious observance and/or nationalist pride that it is absurd. How can people care about fancy hats when their world is burning around them? But people can hope that their poverty will end, or that faction fighting might resolve itself. *Children of Men*, **on the other hand, presents us with a world that cannot escape its own absurdity.** What is the point of doing anything in particular if humanity is ending? Theo goes to visit his contact at the Ministry for Art and Culture to organise transit visas for himself and Kee to escape the country. Cuarón uses this visit to show us a catalogue of absurdities. The government car that ferries Theo through the dour crowds is a status symbol, but what is status in a world crumbling apart? All wealth seems silly in the face of inevitable extinction. From the backseat, Theo takes in views of large groups of penitent sinners claiming that infertility is God's punishment. They blame themselves and everyone else. Past them, we see the pomp and circumstance of the royal guard on display through the park near Buckingham Palace. What does this display of strength mean now? Finally, when Theo meets Nigel, his government contact, we find him living in a vast apartment surrounded by cultural treasures: Michelangelo's David, Picasso's Guernica etc. They drink fine wine calmly. When Theo asks how Nigel spends all this time and energy looking after art that will be worthless in one generation, Nigel answers with a weak smile and gestures out to his grand view over London: 'Do you know what it is, Theo. I just don't think about it.' Outside, floating in the sky is a giant pig balloon.

A flying pig is a symbol of absurdity itself, but more specifically, because of the factory smokestacks in view, this scene is an allusion to the Pink Floyd album *Animals* (1977). That album is in turn an allusion to the novel *Animal Farm* by George Orwell, where the various animals learn at the end that their 'liberty' is an illusion, and they have been betrayed by believing that they could trust their leaders, the pigs, who only care about working the animals to the bone and making themselves richer. By

109

showing us the huddled sinners praying and blaming themselves, the military marching to protest their strength and the luxury car that takes Theo on his journey through it all, Cuarón seems to be asking what is it that separates us from animals? **O'Casey's answer dismisses the 'big answers' like politics and religion, as these are mostly presented as absurd forces in the play. Instead, O'Casey suggests it is the small grace notes of simple human compassion, often played out on a small scale in little acts of neighbourliness that constitute true human life.** In *Children of Men* Nigel has apparently made his own answer: art and fine culture is what separates us from the animals. But this is still an answer that suffers from a hollowness. What is art if no one is there to love it? Faced with this, Nigel chooses simply to not think about it at all. This is the choice many of us make every day when we see unjust violence, unchecked greed and bizarre accumulations of wealth for some while others starve. We just don't think about it. This is one of the calmest and yet, subtly, the most depressing scenes in the film which captures the general vision and viewpoint of the director.

Faced with the absurdity of the human condition, characters in both texts turn to religion as a means of escape or to provide comfort. Religions are typically attempts to find the sacred in life, in suffering or in death.

Certainly there are a lot of references to religion in *The Plough and the Stars*. Most characters, with the pointed exception of the self-proclaimed Marxist-Socialist The Covey, appeal to the heavens throughout the play. Fluther threatens violence when he thinks the story of Genesis is being challenged. Peter constantly makes pious appeals for patience, but seems to have none himself. Bessie wears her Protestantism like a shield or badge of honour to set her apart from the Catholic neighbours. There is even a mock-sanctimonious question of whether it is acceptable to play cards in a place of worship, to which Fluther, acting the theologian, decides: 'Ah, I don't think we'd be doin' anything derogatory be playin' cards in

a Protestant church'. O'Casey is not mocking sacredness here, but rather the debased and absurd factions it breaks itself into in the hands of some people. A hundred years on, we see clearly that The Covey's socialist revolution never happened, the poor worker did not rise up and religious division is worse than ever across the globe. **Similarly, in the parallel universe of *Children of Men*, no one has an answer to their absurd world** with no storks but plenty of flying pigs, and the result is rampant religiosity and mythic belief. Even the Human Project, a scientific enterprise, has taken on mythic levels of faith from the dejected populace. Do they exist? Will they save us? Here we see how science itself can take on a religious fervour in the eyes of desperate people.

One major way we can see the artist's attitude to life in general is how they depict children and family life in their work. The general vision of both texts is influenced by how family is perceived. The family does not fare well in O'Casey's play. Not only does the young Mollser succumb (as many did) to consumption, but Nora's child does not even get a chance at life. Jack, the father, is absent, off fighting for an abstraction – an Irish Republic – while his baby is born dead in a war-zone. If life is not sacred, O'Casey seems to be saying, nothing is. **This is in marked contrast to the well-spoken Voice of the Man who encourages bloodletting and death as a way of making a country's soil fertile again:** 'The old heart of the earth needed to be warmed with the red wine of the battlefields... And we must be ready to pour out the same red wine in the same glorious sacrifice, for without shedding of blood there is no redemption'. This call to killing is a perversion of the red wine imagery of Christ's sacrifice. **The ending of the play is essentially dark with very little to suggest that a new dawn may be about to break and that a new generation may bring about a positive change.**

Children of Men **ends on a radically different version of the family.** Theo and Julian's partnership dissolved when their own child died. Julian consequently wholly commits herself to her fight for justice and dies for it, like Jack Clitheroe, leaving Theo to his political apathy and grief. But there is another form of family that emerges between Theo and Kee. In a film that has filled nearly every frame with vivid detail, the closing scene is almost featureless. Kee and her miracle baby are being hauled out on the waters by their protector, Theo, in a humble rowboat. The world of violence and fear has been swallowed up by a vast fog. The only sound is a bell and the only light a small bulb shining from a buoy. This tiny device is the only reference point locating the boat in space, like the star over the manger in Bethlehem. **Theo has been shot and is bleeding, but unlike the furious terror of Bessie, who just before saying her last prayer curses the woman she tried to** **keep safe, Theo seems very much at peace.** He instructs Kee on how to hold and burp the baby and learns that she will name her daughter after his son, Dylan. As soon as he knows his legacy will live on in the name of humanity's last hope, Theo begins to fade. Just then Kee sights the large scientific vessel, the *Tomorrow*, emerging from the fog. It's unclear if Theo will survive, but that seems unimportant even to him. Perhaps this is a snapshot of how life always is, trying to unroot itself from a furious and absurd past, floating about, frail and improbable, hoping to survive. Cuarón's film may have a bleak look to it, and there are many hellish moments that play out, but the message seems to be that where there is life there is hope, and that is something sacred.

KEY POINTS:

- O'Casey's depiction of political folly and its capacity to destroy on every level, from the family to large-scale society, is essentially negative. Cuarón's tale of a world collapsing into despair and vicious in-fighting is even starker, but it ends with an affirmation of hope.

- The playwright's ironic view of posturing and cowardice is revealed through the weakness and inadequacy of his characters. The men in particular engage in hollow rhetoric and self-delusion. By contrast, Cuarón's main characters reveal depths of courage and commitment when they are roused by a goal that transcends religion or politics. Although the setting is even bleaker than O'Casey's devastated Dublin, the ultimate vision in *Children of Men* is of humanity's potential for compassion.

- The oppressive poverty of the Dublin City tenements is a tragic force that drives individuals to desperate lengths. They risk their lives for fantasies such as military glory or looting the shops for fine clothing. In *Children of Men*, the source of the plague is unknown, but like O'Casey's poverty it reduces people to faction fighting. Unlike in the play, there is a 'miracle baby' and not a stillbirth: new life and not just death.

- O'Casey uses comedy extensively to exacerbate his tragic vision. Cuarón uses comic moments briefly for levity, to bond us to characters and to reveal surprising sources of bravery, e.g. Jasper's 'pull-my-finger' response to torture and death.

- Despite his predominantly pessimistic vision there are moments when O'Casey celebrates the human spirit. This is most evident in the unexpected heroism and humanity of Bessie and Fluther. Cuarón shows us heroic impulses too in the selfless actions of Miriam, Jasper, Theo and Marichka.

- The disintegration of Jack and Nora's marriage, the miscarriage and Bessie's death confirm the play's vision as a tragic one despite all the lively and comical exchanges that precede these events. Kee and baby Dylan's survival promises the greatest possible hope: the continuation of our species.

The Great Gatsby

On the surface, F. Scott Fitzgerald's novel is set in a world as different from O'Casey's slums and Cuarón's apocalyptic future as it is possible to get. The first two texts are bullet-riddled hellscapes with red glaring skies, while the otherworldly wealth of New York's Long Island, made manifest in the outrageous opulence of Jay Gatsby's house parties, is set in a balmy heaven. The worst physical complaints people seem to suffer from in the (fictional) West and East Egg are hangovers in the summer warmth. But under this veneer of luxury, Fitzgerald shows us some of the darkest characterisation of the three texts.

The novel is set in the 'Roaring 20s', a carefree (or careless) period of dancing and drinking between the world wars and before the Great Depression in America. **O'Casey's play and Cuarón's film are set during crisis points, where the characters are being tested by a broken society pressured to boiling point. Political divisions have given way to faction fighting and murder. By contrast, Fitzgerald's portrait of the elite East Coast upper-class is calm, cool and detached. Consider the narrator Nick Carraway's voice from the opening pages:**

'Whenever you feel like criticising any one,' [my father] told me, 'just remember that all the people in this world haven't had the advantages that you've had.'

This sounds like a call for non-judgemental acceptance of other people's flaws. **The unwitting reader might think that Nick (and by extension Fitzgerald) will be less angry or disgusted a social critic than O'Casey, or less horrified at man's capacity for cruelty than Cuarón.** But Nick doesn't take his father's advice at face value. He turns the words over in his mind: 'He didn't say any more, but we've always been unusually communicative in a reserved way, and I understood that he meant a great deal more than that.' Nick goes on to say that because he has tried to remain open-minded about people's flaws, he has been afflicted by

the company of 'veteran bores' and 'abnormal' minds, and he has been 'privy to the secret griefs of wild unknown men'. Being exposed to so many confessions and insights into the human mind, Nick comes to a more nuanced stance about the world:

'Reserving judgments is a matter of infinite hope. I am still a little afraid of missing something if I forget that, as my father snobbishly suggested, and I snobbishly repeat, a sense of the fundamental decencies is parcelled out unequally at birth.'

There are layers to this view of the world. The first is the notion that there are things called 'fundamental decencies'. Nick never tells us what these are, as if assuming that his reader is as instinctively moral and good-natured as he claims himself to be. Whatever these fundamental virtues are, they are not evenly 'parcelled out' to everyone. Because Nick regards himself as being smart and self-aware, he notes that this worldview he has inherited from his father (along with his name and social position) is elitist; by holding it, he too is elitist, or snobbish. Put in other words: some people are nobler than others, and I am noble enough to know that not judging others is an elitist sentiment. Before we are ever introduced to any of the main characters or action, Nick starts the novel already in a double-bind: good people care about fairness but the ability to be fair is not given to everyone equally. Privilege, it would seem, is a problem one cannot avoid, even in the moral realm. We live in an unequal world – this is a negative – but we can cultivate an open mind, which is a matter of 'infinite hope'. **From the outset, Fitzgerald's worldview (about the haves and have-nots) is intricate and subtle, avoiding moral extremes of pessimism and optimism. It could be argued that this is a 'reserved' stance only possible in times of relative peace and prosperity. In O'Casey's play or Cuarón's film, people are too poor, dispirited or terrified to be this self-reflective.**

The very next paragraph contains many clues to the complexity of Fitzgerald's overall vision. There are ironies and paradoxes here, as if Nick is at odds with what his worldview or value system really is. For instance, he says: 'after boasting this way of my tolerance, I come to the admission that it has a limit'. His 'boasting' is actually a confession of a flaw. He flatters himself that he is tolerant of moral flaws and their causes, but ultimately he 'has a limit'. After what he has learned from his insights into Gatsby's life, he wants the world to behave itself and stop giving him special lessons about the human condition. Strikingly, his first description of Gatsby is with a paradox (i.e. a seeming contradiction): 'Gatsby, who represented everything for which I have an unaffected scorn... there was something gorgeous about him'. Gatsby represents everything Nick thinks he has 'scorn' for. It is not clear what Nick is scorning – perhaps it is the vulgar and wasteful displays of the sprawling summer parties or Gatsby's obsessive pursuit of an impossible dream. But behind all of this, Nick clearly admires Gatsby because he has an 'extra-ordinary gift for hope, a romantic readiness such as I have never found in any other person and which it is not likely I shall ever find again.' In a further irony, Nick has lost all hope that he will ever find someone as hopeful as Gatsby again. **And even though his friend dies in the course of the novel, this doesn't reflect on the moral nature of the character.** According to Nick, Gatsby 'turned out all right in the end'. **An early death is not what determines tragedy in this worldview, but rather the quality of people's 'conduct'.** There is something here about Gatsby's genius for hope or 'romantic readiness' for dreaming himself into a new reality that attracts a 'foul dust' to him in much the same way that Nick claims his non-judgemental manner attracts, to use his highly-judgemental phrase, the 'abnormal mind'.

Because of the intricate web of ironies on display in the opening pages, we should be careful not to confuse Nick's jaded and conflicted worldview with Fitzgerald's own. As we will see below, Nick's own behaviour doesn't always match up with his proposed high moral view of himself.

O'Casey's view of human nature, at least under the pressure of extreme poverty

and war, is essentially negative. Cuarón's hellscape offers a glimmer of hope, but only under the extraordinary circumstances of a miracle birth. Fitzgerald offers an ironist's view of romantic hope, at once championing it and damning it for being naïve. This double-take is captured by Nick's claim: 'I was within and without, simultaneously enchanted and repelled by the inexhaustible variety of life'.

O'Casey showcases his characters' posturing initially for comedic ends, but eventually the humour dissolves as we see the final effects of ambition, hypocrisy and cowardice are tragic. Jack's need for military glory and Nora's hysteria when she loses her chance at domestic bliss make them stand out as a doomed romance. **They are damned by holding onto the wrong dreams or holding on too tightly for too long. This is pure tragedy. Conversely, *Children of Men* reverses this pattern.** Since the death of his child, and losing Julian to the Uprising's cause, Theo tries to set himself up as anti-heroic. He does things for money or to amuse himself. This hard-bitten surface is to protect himself from any more disappointment. It feels safer to play a cynic, one who doesn't believe in any sentimental goal or ideal. He even sneers at the death of 'Baby' Diego and uses it to get off work. But the wonder of the miracle birth re-awakens an idealism and sense of self-sacrifice not only in him but in everyone else who sees the child. The gypsy woman, Marichka, who barely knows Theo or Kee, risks her life to defend the baby. The soldiers who are storming a rebel stronghold stop fighting, with some dropping to their knees to bless themselves before the child. **Here, idealism takes on an almost supernatural awe and serves as the only frail light in the darkness of Cuarón's world. In a strange coincidence, the tiny red light of the buoy floating at the close of *Children of Men* – something which suggests but does not promise salvation – has a mirror symbol in *The Great Gatsby*.**

The first time Nick sees Jay Gatsby it is at night and from a distance as Gatsby is touring his own immense estate. Nick assumes that Gatsby has 'come out to determine what share was his of our local heavens'. But then he notices Gatsby is reaching 'in a curious way' toward a ghostly pale green light at the end of a distant dock. 'I could have sworn he was trembling.' Just as suddenly, Gatsby vanishes, leaving Nick 'alone again in the unquiet darkness'. This first sighting does a few things. **It establishes Gatsby's romantic character; he is reaching beyond the physical world toward a spectral goal – the pale green light is near where Daisy lives. The light has become to him a symbol of the eternal just-out-of-reach promise of some unspeakable satisfaction.** His sudden disappearance, leaving Nick 'alone' in the 'unquiet night' shows just how much Nick (and possibly also Fitzgerald) is enchanted by man's capacity to dream beyond his physical needs, even when he seems to have everything. An unanswered question posed by the scene is whether a world without dreamers like Gatsby is nothing but an unquiet night (dark and pointless), or whether life is 'unquiet' precisely because of the obsessions and relentless desires of such unreasonable dreamers. Much later, when Gatsby seems poised to claim Daisy as his, the moment suddenly becomes poignant and not triumphant: 'He knew when he kissed this girl, and forever wed his unutterable visions to her perishable breath, his mind would never romp again like the mind of God'. **Dreamers can achieve the impossible, Fitzgerald seems to be saying, but they die a little once their wish materialises. This is a bittersweet view of life.**

O'Casey's landscape of suffocating poverty includes not only financial but also intellectual and moral poverty, albeit with flashes of true human kindness, generosity and courage. Cuarón, by contrast, adds a severe global, biological poverty to increase the moral strain on his characters. His characters meet this strain with incredible acts of selflessness: Theo fights through a mortal wound to row Kee to safety, Jasper dies to protect Kee from the Fishes and the midwife Miriam distracts a prison guard away from Kee and ends up hooded and possibly tortured in a nightmare version of a refugee camp. These acts are lights in a dark world. **Fitzgerald, by contrast, shows us the**

shade of moral poverty by situating it in the most gleaming wealth imaginable. Jordan Baker, Nick's casual girlfriend, we are told is a pro-golfer but also 'incurably dishonest'. She moves her ball during the semi-final round of a game and leaves the top down on a borrowed car during a rainstorm and then lies about it. These might seem petty faults, but what's worse is the insidious sexism Nick brings to her station as a woman: 'Dishonesty in a woman is a thing you never blame deeply'. Not only is Jordan an instinctive liar, but she is expected to be. **While the line is delivered casually, it carries elements of the paranoia and low expectations O'Casey's tenement neighbours have of each other or nearly everyone has of everyone else in Cuarón's England.**

Comedy in *The Plough and the Stars* is used to disarm us for the devastation that will ensue. It is mostly character driven and even lapses into caricature at times, but it often reveals moral flaws. Comic moments are much rarer in *Children of Men* but serve to bond us to the main characters. As we have seen in the case of Jasper, even a juvenile joke can reveal deep reserves of courage and compassion. In *The Great Gatsby*, humour has been largely replaced by wit. Consider this counter-intuitive (not agreeing with what seems right) claim by Nick's friend Jordan: '…I like large parties. They're so intimate. At small parties there isn't any privacy.' This kind of cleverness attracts Nick, and he engages with it himself. Early on, he contemplates his time in Yale writing 'solemn and obvious editorials' and decides once again to become that 'most limited of all specialists, the "well-rounded man".' He adds to this paradox the ironic line: 'life is much more successfully looked at from a single window, after all'. Reading such lines is a puzzle. If we take it at face value, it means that the literary life allows one to judge others from a comfortable remove, and this is a very rewarding way to live. Assuming Nick (and Fitzgerald) does not endorse such a simple claim, we have to figure out how sincere he is when he champions literature's ability to help one see into the heart of one's neighbour. This ironic detachment pervades the text, making it simultaneously amusing and discomforting. There are some funny descriptions, such as Nick's claim that Jordan holds herself with such practiced poise that she seems to be balancing an invisible object on the end of her nose. There are also ludicrous portraits of people drinking themselves silly, posturing as artists or intellectuals at parties or making urbane (polished, very polite) small talk, but there are no jokes as such. It's a tale told by a man so refined that he rarely laughs out loud. The absence of genuine humour, either in the narrator or any of the people he describes, subtly but effectively renders this world bleak in its own way.

In O'Casey's play the Clitheroes' marriage is under stress from many factors, among them poverty, the cramped conditions of having to share space with so many other characters and the incompatible dreams of military glory and domestic calm. It ends with a symbolic stillbirth, both of a child and a nation state. **O'Casey presents the group of tenement dwellers as a kind of large 'family', capable of care for each other in moments but one so divided against itself that the fighting and distrust outweigh the love. In *Children of Men*, Julian and Theo drift apart after the loss of their son, but a set of deep bonds emerge between Theo, Jasper, Miriam and Kee in service of the new baby, and they endure any sacrifice in the service of the child. Conversely, Daisy and Tom live like deities, with maids and servants tending to their every whim, but they are miserable in their domestic roles.** Tom openly cheats on his wife, getting phone calls from his mistress at his house. Daisy gets 'possessed by intense life' when she re-ignites her romance with Gatsby. Tom and Daisy have a three-year-old girl, Pammy. The first time she is mentioned (without being named) by Daisy, she is interrupted by Tom demanding to know what Nick does for money. The second time Pammy features in the text is for a single page. She is shyly brought in by a nurse because her 'mother wanted to show you off'. Daisy calls her 'bles-sed pre-cious' and an 'absolute dream' and proclaims that the child has her face and not Tom's. Then the girl is promptly

whisked away by the nurse and we never see or hear from her again. She doesn't seem to factor in any way into her parents' decisions to cheat on each other, or drive drunk or anything else. Pammy is merely a pretty decoration of married life. **This character who barely appears is one of the saddest elements of the book and acts as a subtle but damning commentary on how removed people like Tom and Daisy are from a warm human reality.**

One of the most significant events in the novel, which affects the general vision of the entire text, is the accidental manslaughter of Tom's lover Myrtle by his wife, who is driving while drunk. Daisy commits a serious crime by fleeing the scene, and everyone's instinct is to lie. Even Nick, who tells us 'I am one of the few honest people that I have ever known', doesn't go to the police. Everyone evades responsibility except for Gatsby who is prepared to take the blame because he believes Daisy loves him. Because of this group dishonesty, a deluded Mr Wilson decides to avenge himself by murdering the man he believes to be both his wife's secret lover and killer. **Tragedy comes from both the personal faults of the characters and the vast impersonal forces of poverty and political hatred in O'Casey's play. Cuarón's film spirals from utter despair to profound hope. However, in Fitzgerald's novel much of the suffering comes directly and solely from the apathy, carelessness and dishonesty of people who have all the power and freedom in the world.** Nick never seems to blame himself for his indirect role in the murder-suicide. His disdain is reserved purely for the Buchanans, and even then it is cool and detached. However, he does invest himself in organising Gatsby's funeral. He seems more disturbed by how poorly attended it is than by Gatsby's death itself. This 'acceptance' of death is moving in the case of Jasper and when Theo lies wounded in the rowboat. It is also sad but understandable in the case of the all-too-common loss of the consumption victim Mollser in O'Casey's tenements. But as Nick and Gatsby were friends and healthy young men living privileged lives, it's striking to see Nick's reaction. He treats his friend's death as if it were an idea rather than an event, an occasion to reflect on the greater lesson learned rather than feel pain.

Besides Pammy, there is one more significant character who barely appears in *The Great Gatsby* but who nevertheless gives powerful clues as to Fitzgerald's worldview. This character literally pertains to vision. In the valley of ashes, a pocket of oppressive poverty in the novel, there is a large billboard ad for an optician: Dr. Eckleburg. The disembodied eyes have a 'persistent stare'. When Mr Wilson goes mad with grief after the loss of his wife, he starts to chant of the eyes: 'God knows what you've been doing… you can't fool God!...God sees everything'. Granted, Wilson has gone mad, and Nick presents the billboard with a worldly dismissal. Some 'wild wag of an oculist' put it there to 'fatten his practice', but Fitzgerald is implying more. In an era where modernity is collapsing old religious beliefs and traditional social mores and opening the world to a scientific understanding never seen before, Fitzgerald returns to his concern with judgement. We can have our excuses, we can lie, posture behind great parties, we can move the ball from where it lies on the golf course, but we cannot escape who we are and what we do. **O'Casey's slum-dwellers are too tormented to reflect on this lesson, and too powerless to change their station in life. Cuarón's main characters manage to exchange their nightmare world for a shaky chance at salvation through a mixture of courage, cunning, faith and luck. But Fitzgerald's novel ends with a gentle shaking of its head in a kind of divine judgement on its people.** Despite all their advantages of breeding and wealth, they cannot see. They think they are reaching into an 'orgiastic future' (wild, depraved) but it 'recedes before us'. The bittersweet tragedy of Fitzgerald's worldview is that all our strivings (successful or not) come from a fundamental confusion that we can willfully reach into a glorious future, but we are really reaching into the past, into old desires, pursuing ghosts. For Fitzgerald, pairing 'greatness' with wisdom is an impossible task; his dreamers are perversely hopeful because they are so confused. Hence the famous closing line, which sums up the dreamer's romantic imagination: 'So we beat on, boats against the current, borne back ceaselessly into the past'.

KEY POINTS

- O'Casey's depiction of political folly and its capacity to destroy on every level from the family to large-scale society is essentially negative. Cuarón's tale of a world collapsing into despair and vicious in-fighting is even starker, but it ends with an affirmation of hope. Fitzgerald's world of East Coast elites is ironic and bittersweet, showing us a world that is not so much cruel as vain, deluded and dangerously careless.

- The playwright's ironic view of posturing and cowardice is revealed through the weakness and inadequacy of his characters. The men in particular engage in hollow rhetoric and self-delusion. By contrast, Cuarón's main characters reveal depths of courage and commitment when they are roused by a goal that transcends religion or politics. Although the setting is even bleaker than O'Casey's devastated Dublin, the ultimate vision in *Children of Men* is of humanity's potential for compassion. In the case of Nick's view of Gatsby, it varies between disdain, admiration and forgiveness. There are no monsters in any of the texts, but Fitzgerald's characters have the fewest excuses for their callous selfishness.

- The oppressive poverty of the Dublin City tenements is a tragic force that drives individuals to risk their lives for fantasies such as military glory or looting the shops for fine clothing, but they have no real future. In *Children of Men*, the plague, like O'Casey's poverty, reduces people to faction fighting. Unlike in the play, there is a 'miracle baby' and not a stillbirth: new life and not just death. There is a chance at a future. In *The Great Gatsby*, the irony is that Fitzgerald's dreamers think they are reaching into a glorious future, but are actually trapped by past obsessions.

- O'Casey uses comedy extensively to exacerbate his tragic vision. Cuarón uses comic moments briefly for levity, to bond us to characters and to reveal surprising sources of bravery, e.g. Jasper's 'pull-my-finger' response to torture and death. In the novel, Nick wields knowing wit rather than broad humour. The effect is amusing but substitutes cool cleverness for warmth.

- Despite his predominantly pessimistic vision there are moments when O'Casey celebrates the human spirit. This is most evident in the unexpected heroism and humanity of Bessie and Fluther. Cuarón shows us that as long as there is hope, virtue is still possible. Fitzgerald celebrates the romantic imagination and its gift for hope, but ultimately he sees such dreamers as vain and in blind pursuit of ghosts.

- The disintegration of Jack and Nora's marriage, the stillbirth of their baby and Bessie's death confirm the play's vision as a tragic one despite all the lively and comical exchanges that precede these events. In *Children of Men*, Kee and baby Dylan's survival promises the greatest possible hope: the continuation of our species. Fitzgerald ends with a bittersweet paradox: our attempt to build the future is really an unwitting pursuit of the past. We may achieve our goals, but often dreams realised are dreams killed.

Sample Answer

B. General Vision and Viewpoint

'Significant events in texts and the impact they have on readers often help to clarify the general vision and viewpoint of those texts.'

With reference to three texts on your comparative course, compare the ways in which at least one significant event in each text, and its impact on you, helped to clarify the general vision and viewpoint of these texts.

The general vision or viewpoint of any text relates to the authorial/directorial outlook on life. It basically answers the question of what kind of world the text is set in. Significant events in each of the texts that I studied helped to clarify differing attitudes to life and humanity which enriched each narrative and provoked me to question my own views of what constitutes a meaningful existence. The texts I studied are *The Plough and the Stars* by Seán O'Casey; *Children of Men*, directed by Alfonso Cuarón and *The Great Gatsby* by F. Scott Fitzgerald.

I had never seen or read Seán O'Casey's *The Plough and the Stars* before reading it for my comparative study. Knowing that it was supposedly a tragedy set in Dublin in 1916, I was surprised by the humour which permeates the opening of the play. The banter between the main characters is often harsh but also weirdly playful, for example The Covey's constant goading of the easily irritated Peter or the humorous way Fluther keeps using (and mis-using) the word 'derogatory'. As I read through the first two acts, I thought maybe the playwright was being ironic by calling the play a 'Tragedy'. However, the impact of certain key moments helped to clarify the playwright's vision and viewpoint. In the midst of the humour and witty repartee, certain serious themes emerge. The lack of privacy in the tenement is highlighted by Nora wanting to put a lock on her door and being attacked by her neighbour, Bessie Burgess, for doing so. Mrs Gogan's resentment at her neighbour's 'notions of upperosity' and her nosy inspection of Nora's home and private life highlight the personal tensions which exist when people are forced into close contact through overcrowding and poverty. These are all hints of a darker vision which becomes clearer as the play evolves. O'Casey's characters help to clarify the viewpoint and make an impact in a different way than Cuarón's or Fitzgerald's do. Cuarón's characters put up a gruff exterior, but we see from how they act when they are under intense pressure (for instance, when they break into a prison rather than out of it) that they are more resourceful, selfless and brave than most of O'Casey's victims of the Easter Rising. This significant breaking into the prison prepares us somewhat for a more positive outcome in the film. Fitzgerald's characters, unlike those in the other texts, are for the most part haughty, conceited people who see themselves as socially superior. Fitzgerald describes this attitude as 'supercilious' more than once. They act as if frustration is for lesser people, but their lives seem to be wall-to-wall frustration and boredom. A very significant event is Daisy's drunk-driving accident, which is caused by her having an affair because she feels unloved. As a result of the affair's exposure, she becomes flustered about having to choose between her bully of a husband and an obsessive boyfriend. Her hit-and-run episode reflects her life and the lives of her peers: distracted, complacent and selfish.

Another surprise from reading *The Plough and the Stars* comes late in the play but makes even more of an impact. The action gradually takes a dark turn, but O'Casey keeps the humour up even through what should be serious scenes such as the looting spree in Act III in which everyone takes part. We see Peter's cowardice when he's too scared to join in the looting of the local shops, 'Supposin' I happened to be potted?' Then he tries to turn his fear into a virtue by locking the door on The Covey, who is laden down with stolen food, and chiding him for 'makin' a shame an' a sin o' th'cause'. It's almost pantomime. But when the rebel soldiers Brennan, Langon and Jack Clitheroe appear and Langon is severely wounded, this is a brutal reminder that O'Casey doesn't find the world of his 1916 Dublin tenements funny at all. Suddenly fear and desperation are everywhere, and no one knows how to escape. Several significant moments clarify O'Casey's vision and had a profound impact on me. When I saw Nora pleading and begging Jack not to return to the fighting and Jack's torment at his divided loyalties to country and family, I realised with a shock that O'Casey had tricked me into thinking everything would be fine and then pulled the rug out from under me. My own general vision and worldview has always been that life is more or less good and our society is fair. While everyone has their share of frustrations and disappointments, things are more likely to work out than not if you work hard and play by the rules. But anyone who has lived through the kind of poverty O'Casey has or seen the vicious reality of warfare up close doesn't necessarily believe, like the optimistic Fluther, that 'nothin' derogatory'll happen…'. Far from it, O'Casey finishes the play with one fatal blow after another. We learn that Jack is dead as a result of falling for the Voice's empty rhetoric about spilling the 'red wine' of blood for Ireland, Mollser is dead from the sickness that is a direct result of overcrowding the poor into tenements and Nora's baby has been stillborn. O'Casey's comment seems to be that the baby is like the result of fantasies of 'liberation' that are not rooted in some kind of realistic plan: they have no future. The final end that any hope might come out of the play is when Bessie, in a display of courage and kindness, tries to save an hysterical Nora by pushing her away from the window. Two shots ring out destroying Bessie's life and telling us that this is what can happen to the brave and the kind. The world is not fair and may even be cruel, or worse, insane. The stage directions call for 'agonized astonishment' on Bessie's face, but the astonishment is ours too. What kind of world do we live in? Can I really be so sure I live in such a different one from the mad, frustrated and deeply unjust universe O'Casey is showing me?

An even more insane and unjust world is explored in Alfonso Cuarón's *Children of Men*. Set in 2027, the world is suffering from a plague of infertility – no one has been born for eighteen years. The cause of the problem is never explained. For me, this makes the situation feel even more unfair or arbitrary. If it is a punishment from God, as many of the new and strange religious sects argue that it is, then there is no way of knowing what humanity did wrong, or if there is any way to put it right. The most significant event in the film is the revelation that there is a young woman, an African immigrant named Kee, who has become pregnant. The film never gives any answers as to how this has happened. I get the impression that Cuarón is saying that that is how life really is; we never understand the reasons for the biggest, most important things that occur, good or bad.

In that respect, I see a big overlap between O'Casey's play and Cuarón's film. They both show us a world that is fundamentally unknowable or uncontrollable. Both worlds are dark and full of pain and cruelty. Both worlds are populated by deeply scared, frustrated and divided groups. But the major difference between the texts is how they end. O'Casey shows us an uprising that is 'stillborn' like Nora's baby. Nora goes insane, Jack is killed, Mollser dies and Bessie's injured son is on his way home from the war unaware of the fate of his mother. Despite the moments of kindness, humour, and courage that emerge throughout the play, the ending says that this meaningless suffering is how life plays out all too often for the poor and disenfranchised people of the world. It makes an impact by leaving me with a hollow feeling, wanting to argue against such a bleak vision but finding myself unable to whenever I watch the news, and see terrorist attacks and military reprisals happening all over the globe. Violence begets violence, and it is hard to see any end to it in my lifetime.

Cuarón certainly doesn't have a rosy counter-argument, but unlike O'Casey he shows us a glimmer of hope. I think the most significant event in *Children of Men* is Kee's delivery from the shelled building the day after she has her miracle baby. The Fishes, a group of dissident immigrant-rights activists who plan to lead their own 'uprising', have kidnapped her and the world's only child to support their cause. While she is trapped in a ruined building, caught in a firefight between Fishes and the British government, her baby starts to cry. The soldiers who are storming the ruin suddenly stop shouting and shooting. A silence falls over everything. All we hear are the baby and the angelic voices in the soundtrack as Kee descends the stairs. All the witnesses – grim soldiers and harrowed immigrants – visibly soften. For just a moment, the hardness of the world melts: some people kneel and bless themselves; others gently reach out to touch the child's foot. This significant key moment makes a forceful impact, revealing the vision of the director with crystal clarity. The brilliance of this science-fiction conceit is that it shows you really vividly how life is the only thing that matters. The power squabbles of the totalitarian government and the Fishes make sense until the baby appears. Then suddenly these strangers seem ridiculous. The briefness and profundity of the peace (the soldiers and rebels resume fighting almost instantly) draw attention to how rare moments of sanity and hope are in this future world. But this is no distant fantasy world. In fact, it reminds me of a video I saw of a hospital being bombed in Aleppo, Syria. In the blast, the city's last pediatrician was killed. It's such a poignant image: in that moment there are no more doctors alive in that place whose job it is to help people into the world. It's like there are parts of the world that are suffering so much they try to make themselves disappear. Cuarón's world is trying to do that, with factions killing each other as fast as they can, even when they think there is no one to replace all the dead. But because Kee and her baby make it out to the sea and are set to be collected by the science vessel the *Tomorrow*, Cuarón offers us a vague hope in two things: as long as there is new life and reason (here in the guise of science), there is a glimmer of hope for mankind.

On the surface, no fictional world could be more different from the hellscapes that O'Casey and Cuarón offer us than the vision of sun, fun and frolics of West and

East Egg in F. Scott Fitzgerald's *The Great Gatsby*. Again, like *The Plough and the Stars*, I wasn't familiar with this work until I studied it for my comparative study, and again it surprised me. In some ways, I think this is the hardest text to say 'here is what the author feels about the world'. For a start, everything is told through a narrator, Nick Carraway, so it isn't easy to know how much to trust that his view is Fitzgerald's own. But since he is showing us the world, and all the characters in it, Nick's viewpoint must reflect Fitzgerald's to some extent. Nick is intelligent, witty, well-educated and really self-aware. In other words, he is as different from O'Casey's frustrated tenement dwellers and Cuarón's despairing warring factions as he could be. From the very first page, he sets the reader up for a very subtle, nuanced picture of how life can be viewed. 'Reserving judgments is a matter of infinite hope,' he tells us, but then doubles back on this by saying that the ability to reserve such judgement is something his father has 'snobbishly suggested, and I snobbishly repeat'. He adds that 'a sense of the fundamental decencies is parcelled out unequally at birth.' So the novel opens with the idea that life is unfair, and all things, even moral virtues like open-mindedness, are not justly distributed to all people. This is a strange kind of darkness. Unlike the oppressive suffering in the play and film, the novel's negativity requires that you think about what is being implied before you even understand how dark it really is. Otherwise Nick's opening could just sound chatty and self-deprecating.

Overall, the tone of the book is ironic and bittersweet. Nearly everything Nick says has some edge to it. You need to think about it rather than just take it at face value. At one stage he plans to renew his literary inclinations and claims that 'life is much more successfully looked at from a single window, after all'. I think he simultaneously means this earnestly *and* insincerely. He is disgusted at the idea that someone could be so vain as to believe they were seeing anything as it really is if they were only to look at it with one set of eyes, from one perspective. But that's the situation we are all stuck in as humans, isn't it? No matter how smart or privileged we are, we are always limited to a single perspective in the end. This doesn't seem to be an anxiety in the other texts; they both paint humankind's political and social follies as enduring problems, but no one in *The Plough and the Stars* or *Children of Men* seems to think about things or endlessly question their own motivations or others as much as Nick does. It's a sort of intellectual frustration that prevents him from ever being simply happy. But if Nick is never entirely satisfied, he never seems to really suffer much either. Even as he is being dragged around New York by people whose company he does not entirely want, he says 'I was within and without, simultaneously enchanted and repelled by the inexhaustible variety of life'. Perhaps we could say that O'Casey shows us a comedic hell, Cuarón gives us a bleak glimpse of a heavenly miracle, but Fitzgerald paints us a cool detached purgatory. Even when it looks like Gatsby is about to win his ultimate prize, the love of Daisy Buchanan, Nick decides that Gatsby's 'mind would never romp again like the mind of God'.

The most significant event in the novel which not only makes an impact on the reader but clarifies the entire viewpoint of the author is the drunk-driving incident. Daisy accidentally kills Myrtle Wilson (her husband's lover) and then flees the scene. Despite all the talk of reserving judgement, the book takes a decisive turn here to present her, and her kind, the wealthy elites speeding carelessly through their lives, as morally bankrupt people who care about no one and nothing more than themselves. Nick claims that 'I am one of the few honest people that I have ever known', but for all his condemnation of Daisy and Tom for covering up the crime, he never reports it to the police. Such an act of honesty might have prevented Mr Wilson from wrongfully blaming and killing Gatsby. Even if no one is there in this weird purgatorial world to lay down a definitive judgement, Wilson shows the deep need people who suffer have for there to be justice. As Wilson goes mad, he points to the optician billboard, which sports a disembodied 'persistent stare', and exclaims: 'God knows what you've been doing… you can't fool God!…God sees everything'. Maybe there is no god. Maybe there is no punishment here. It's never clear if it is fate or chance that brings Daisy and Myrtle together in a fatal collision of speed and drunkenness. But Fitzgerald shows us that somehow cold judgement (or a need for it) looms over the scene.

Thinking back over the three texts, I see that all three of them have their own bleakness. There are moments of levity in all of them, and glimpses of real virtue are on display in each. Cuarón's is the bleakest world but offers the greatest hope in the end. O'Casey spirals from funny antics and petty frustrations to the deepest despair at our inability to ever work our way out of the worst problems: poverty and hatred. I am not rich or American, but if my life aligns with any of the works, it probably lies closest to the one Fitzgerald paints, one where people are generally optimistic about the future, if a bit complacent about what they are doing in the present. If I take any lesson from these three visions of the world and how it may be, I suppose I should aim to take responsibility for what I do, even if the circumstances around my actions may not be 'fair' and even if no 'persistent stare' is watching.

C. Literary Genre

The Plough and the Stars

Literary genre refers to how an author tells his or her story. Plays, films, novels and short stories all differ from each other as regards the specific techniques employed by the authors/directors and an understanding of these techniques is important for any appreciation of a text.

Significance of title

The title of any text has an important function in stimulating reader/audience interest and in indicating a central issue or focus. *The Plough and the Stars* refers to the flag originally used by the Irish Citizen Army, a socialist, Republican movement. James Connolly, a co-founder of the movement, said that the flag symbolised a free Ireland in control of its own destiny. The flag depicted a plough surrounded by stars. O'Casey's play was written as a specific reaction against a play that Connolly had written and first staged in March 1916. Connolly's play was called *Under Which Flag?*, a title which posed a question as to which kind of banner Irish men and women ought to support: that is, whether to join Britain's wartime battle for the freedom of small nations (i.e. World War I), or whether instead to take the chance of striking out for an independent Ireland. At the end of Connolly's play the audience learns that the latter answer is the correct one. This simplistic moral infuriated O'Casey. The title of *The Plough and the Stars*, therefore, acts as a response to Connolly's question by referring to the flag of the Labour movement. Perhaps, O'Casey suggests, Irishmen could rally behind these colours, but by the end of the play this emblem proves inadequate. **Fighting for any cause is portrayed as empty and dehumanising with political idealism drawing men away from life and from love.**

Type of text

Although *The Plough and the Stars* is described as being a tragedy by the playwright, it is difficult to identify any one character as being a tragic hero or heroine. Some might consider that the revolutionaries who die fighting for freedom are heroes. Jack Clitheroe is described as a hero by the General who instructs Captain Brennan to tell Nora that 'Commandant Clitheroe's death was a gleam of glory'. Brennan himself adds that 'Mrs Clitheroe's grief will be a joy when she realises that she has had a hero for a husband'. However, it is very difficult for the audience to accept Jack as a true tragic hero given the weakness of his character. One senses that he is more motivated by vanity and a desire to command than by any real dedication to a political ideal. Mrs Gogan tells us that Jack 'Wasn't goin' to be in anything where he couldn't be conspishuous'. His desire to strut around in a Sam Browne belt looking for admiration seems more like the behaviour of a poseur than that of a hero. The other revolutionaries are also portrayed as men who imagine themselves as heroes without really understanding what war is all about.

The female characters whom we might consider as tragic heroines are Nora Clitheroe and Bessie Burgess but as with the male characters, there are reasons why it is hard to classify them as such. The intense possessiveness of Nora could be regarded as a tragic flaw which eventually leads to her own mental anguish and collapse when Jack leaves her to fight in the rebellion. Tragedy, however, demands that the tragic hero or heroine brings their disaster upon themselves by some action. Rather than causing Jack's death, Nora merely suffers the consequences of her husband's actions, so she cannot be considered a tragic heroine in any real sense. Bessie Burgess's death certainly is 'tragic' in the modern sense of the term but she cannot be considered a tragic heroine because she did not die as a result of any tragic flaw or action on her own part. She died accidentally while trying to drag Nora away from an open window. Her dying words leave no doubt that she had no intention of sacrificing her life. She calls Nora a 'bitch' and cries out: 'This is what's afther comin' on me for nursin' you day an' night . . . I was a fool, a fool, a fool!'

From a close examination of every character in the play, it becomes obvious that *The Plough and the Stars* is therefore not a tragedy in the classical sense. None of the characters gain tragic wisdom or insight from their suffering.

It is probably more accurate to classify the play as a tragi-comedy which combines elements of both tragedy and comedy without belonging fully to either genre. It is tragic because of the many deaths which occur and also because we see the devastating effects of war and poverty on the lives of ordinary human beings who struggle to survive in the most challenging of circumstances. Several forms of the comedy genre are contained in the play. Slapstick or clownish comedy can be observed in several scenes: Peter chases after The Covey with a sword; there are humorous quarrels between Bessie and Mrs Gogan and between Fluther and The Covey; the looting; there is an argument over a pram etc. Verbal comedy abounds through the use of repetition of phrases by Fluther, who consistently misuses the word 'derogatory' when expressing his opinions. A similar repetition can be seen in the long-winded title of a book by Jenersky, a political writer, which The Covey quotes to impress his listeners. Mispronunciation of words like 'conspishuous', 'wurum', 'mollycewels' etc. also create humour as do the long, lyrical speeches given by Bessie and Mrs Gogan in Act II.

Irony contributes to the comedy when Bessie and Mrs Gogan aggressively defend their good names in Act II but have no problem joining forces when it comes to looting later on in the play. Likewise, the bragging of Peter and The Covey concerning their notions of honour and idealism are shown to be hollow and almost farcical when they are later revealed as cowards, both physically and morally. O'Casey uses the quarrels between these characters in Act II as a type of satirical (mocking) parody of the Rising where ordinary individuals wage their own personal battles while the Voice of the Man

can be heard outside extolling the virtue of war. The fact that the whole scene takes place in a pub adds to the satirical effect.

Use of contrast

In addition to the contrasting tragic and comic elements, O'Casey makes effective use of many other contrasts or juxtapositions to highlight serious issues in his play. Fluther's simple Catholicism is contrasted with The Covey's Marxism; Nora and The Covey's opposition to militarism contrasts with Peter's love of military uniforms and processions; Bessie's loyalism and Protestantism contrasts with the republican Catholicism of Mrs Gogan, Jack Clitheroe and Captain Brennan; The Covey's academic socialist theories are contrasted with Rosie's practical attitudes to personal survival. A major juxtaposition (placing things side-by-side for contrast) is the speech made by the Voice of the Man, which is opposed to the reality we observe in the pub scene in Act II. Here, O'Casey moves rapidly from the outside Voice to the indoor ordinary people in such a way that the view advanced by the Voice as a sacred truth is shown as being false. O'Casey does not tell us that the Voice is speaking empty rhetoric but that implication is clear.

Plot structure

The play does not follow the conventional narrative format where a situation evolves as complications arise, builds to a climax and reaches a conclusion after a key, climactic scene. There is actually no single plot in this play, even though the Clitheroe couple seem to provide the main narrative thread. The play is structured around the development of a theme concerning the clash of opposing ideals – the social cause of the Labour movement against the delusions of romantic Republican patriotism. It is not that O'Casey wishes to attack the latter so much as that he wants to show that the wrong war was being fought. The real war, in the playwright's opinion,

should have been that waged against poverty, disease and deprivation. Act I is remarkable for its shapelessness, lack of significant incident and the wide variety of themes introduced. As the play develops through the next three acts, the audience's attention is focused on different characters at different times: Nora, Bessie, Fluther and the interactions between Peter and The Covey. Although Bessie's death is often considered to be the climax of the play, it does not function as such because it does not create any type of resolution. Rather than contriving a conventional form, O'Casey chose to allow events to develop as they would in real life. Exits, entrances and actions appear to be uncontrived – a technique known as 'naturalism'.

Tension is used effectively at critical moments in the play. In Act I tension builds as Nora and Jack argue about Jack's membership of the Citizen Army. When Jack complains that Nora was '. . . always at me to give up th' Citizen Army, an' I gave it up; surely that ought to satisfy you', Nora angrily retorts 'Ay, you gave it up – because you got the sulks when they didn't make a Captain of you. It wasn't for my sake Jack'. This tension is slightly relieved by a romantic interlude but builds again steadily when Captain Brennan arrives to summon Jack to a meeting and the whole story of Nora's deception concerning the letter of commission is exposed. Jack's rough handling of his wife and her bitter comment that she doesn't care if he never returns from the meeting create tension in the audience and foreshadow another tense scene in Act IV when Jack and Nora engage in a similar exchange. The tension between Nora's desire to keep her husband by her side and Jack's fear that 'all the risks' he is taking will be turned into 'a laugh' is exacerbated by the fact that Lieutenant Langon is badly injured and Captain Brennan is taunting Jack because Nora refuses to let go of him. The scene reaches a climax with Jack roughly flinging his wife to the ground.

The tension in the scene where Bessie Burgess is shot is skilfully managed by the playwright. The audience is presented with the demented Nora, who has miscarried her child and is, as yet, unaware that Jack has been killed. The voices chanting 'Ambulance...lance! Ambu... lance! Red Cro...ss, Red Cro...ss' in a distant street are reminders of the bloodshed outside and are intermingled with Nora's gentle singing of a love song which is suddenly shattered with a burst of rifle fire. Bessie's efforts to pull Nora away from the open window reach a horrifying climax when Bessie stumbles and falls, two rifle shots ring out and Bessie realises that she has been shot. The convulsive jerking of her body, her futile cries for help and her pleading with Nora to fetch help mark what is probably the highest point of dramatic tension in the entire play.

Use of dialogue

Dialogue plays a crucial role in any play as it has the ability to anchor the narrative in a particular time and place. O'Casey succeeds in representing authentically the language and dialect of the tenement people in the early decades of the twentieth century. Their speech is vibrant, colloquial and wonderfully colourful. An example of this in Act II is when Bessie Burgess exclaims, 'There's a storm of anger tossin' in me heart, thinkin' of all th' poor Tommies, an' with them me own son, dhrenched in water an' soaked in blood, gropin' their way to a shatterin' death, in a shower o' shells!' There is a lyrical quality in this speech that indicates the depth of the speaker's emotion and compassionate attitude to those who suffer. Although she can be aggressive and argumentative, particularly when she is drunk, many of the things Bessie says indicate her true humanity and good nature.

Mrs Gogan's imaginatively embellished images create humour but also indicate a character who is morbidly obsessed with death. When she sees the ostrich plume on Peter's Foresters' uniform she links it to men hanging at the end of ropes, 'When yous are goin' along, an' I see them wavin' an' noddin' an' waggin', I seem to be lookin' at each of yous hangin' at the end of a rope, your eyes bulgin' and your legs twistin' an' jerkin', gaspin' an' gaspin' for air while yous are thryin' to die for Ireland'. The vivid, graphic details used by Mrs Gogan when she is discussing anything to do with death or dying reveals her as a character who has been deeply affected by the deaths of others close to her and by the impending death of her daughter Mollser. Her obsession with this subject is possibly the only way she can actually deal with it.

The socialist jargon used by The Covey is another example of language being used to define a type of character. He enjoys using words and phrases such as 'comrade' and 'th' emancipation of th' workers'. But his socialism is merely a façade or type of mask which he wears to conceal his real self-centredness and cowardice. These features of his character emerge later in the play.

The use of violent dialogue occurs frequently in the play and generally reflects the depth of feeling characters have on subjects ranging from politics to religion and social issues. Peter uses the language associated with 'fire and brimstone' sermons to describe his hopes for those who insist on tormenting him, 'I'll leave you to th' day when th' all-pitiful, all-merciful, all-lovin' God'll be handin' you to th' angels to be rievin' an' roastin' you, tearin' an' tormentin' you, burnin' and blastin' you!' The alliteration adds considerably to the venom of this comment, revealing Peter as a peevish and childish individual. Excellent examples of the use of violent language occur particularly in Act II where the tenement dwellers wage a war of words on a variety of subjects.

The Voice of the Man is extremely different in terms of the vocabulary and the phrases used from that of the other characters. The Voice incites the rebels: 'We must accustom ourselves to the thought of arms, we must accustom ourselves to the sight of arms, we must accustom ourselves to the use of arms . . . ' This language is rhetorical in nature with carefully balanced phrases, triadic patterns (groups of three) and repetition. However, there

is an underlying violence in this language which is actually more threatening than that voiced by the uneducated people from the tenements who are usually merely venting frustration.

Stage directions

Stage directions (the descriptive text that appears within brackets) are an essential narrative technique in a dramatic text. They speak for the playwright when he is not there, providing details about how he has imagined the environment and atmosphere and describing critical physical aspects of the characters and settings. For example, the elaborate description of the tenement building at the start of the play not only indicates the setting but provides an insight into the efforts of Nora to provide a comfortable home in what is essentially a building which has been the object of 'savage assaults' by its tenants. The presence of Peter's military uniform hints at the military ideals which form so much of the play's meaning. Character is implied in the physical descriptions of characters. For example, Fluther's flashes of violent temper are excellently captured in the description of him as being 'harshly featured, under the left eye is a scar, and his nose is bent from a smashing blow received in a fistic battle long ago'. O'Casey's stage directions are also critical in dictating the intended tempo and rhythm of the piece, particularly in scenes of high suspense or tension such as the death of Bessie Burgess. One could say that they help tell the complete story that is in the playwright's mind.

Character creation

Character creation is a technique at which O'Casey excels and one which is fundamental to all narrative texts. As already stated, the language used by the characters and the descriptions of these characters in stage directions give the audience great insight into their personalities and motives. We learn about them through what they say, what is said about them by others and how they act.

Mrs Gogan provides an insight into the character of Nora in her comments to Fluther in the first scene. Before we even see her in person, we learn that Nora has 'notions of upperosity' and that her relationship with her husband is strained. Her obsessive nature is apparent in her efforts to control not only Jack but The Covey and Uncle Peter. When we actually see and hear Nora, these observations by her neighbour are shown to be quite accurate. Her words, as she attempts to separate her sparring lodgers reveal her personal determination and dominant motivation, 'Are you always goin' to be tearin' down th' little bit of respectability that a body's thryin' to build up? Am I always goin' to be havin' to nurse yous into th' hardy habit o' thryin' to keep up a little bit of appearance'.

Perhaps the finest example of O'Casey's skill in creating character is seen in his creation of Bessie Burgess. She is distinguished from the other characters by her religion, her politics and by the fact that she has a son fighting in a different war. O'Casey highlights her tremendous courage when he shows her hanging out a Union Jack and singing songs like 'Rule Brittania' to enrage her rebel neighbours. Although courageous and oftentimes aggressive, Bessie has a softer, more compassionate side which is hinted at in her subtle acts of kindness to Mollser and becomes more explicit in her compassionate care of Nora towards the end of the play. Bessie is not, however, a sentimental presentation of a heart of gold in a rough exterior. She curses Nora after she herself is shot, calling her a 'bitch'. By creating such a complex individual, O'Casey gives an additional sense of realism to the play.

Most of O'Casey's characters do not bring about changes in events. They are presented as being peripheral to what is going on around them. Although some – like Clitheroe, Langon and Brennan – do engage in the rebellion, they do not bring about any social or political change. What we see is the impact of poverty and low social status as well as the power of rhetoric to influence the uneducated. The characterisation is built around the differing efforts of individuals to cope with such forces.

Imagery and symbolism

Imagery and symbolism help to convey much of the play's meaning. Simple items like Nora's new hat and her efforts to furnish her rooms serve to symbolise her hopes of a better life beyond that of tenement living. The insertion of a lock on the door indicates the lack of privacy endured by the tenants generally and symbolises the need for an escape from the surrounding chaos of the building where children play on stairs and neighbours can enter another's room at will.

However, in the overall context of the play's meaning, these symbols are minor compared to those O'Casey employs to express his personal indignation. **The scene set in the pub while a political rally takes place outside is a key moment in *The Plough and the Stars*.** We see and hear the shadowy outline of the Voice like a ghost from the past imposing itself on the living as the workers are inflamed and incited to action by this speech. The pub scene symbolises the obscuring of reality. While Pádraig Pearse (symbolised by the Voice) praises the heroism of bloodshed, the intoxication this causes among those in the pub leads to a series of brawls.

A prominent presence in this scene is that of the prostitute Rosie Redmond who needs to sell her sexual favours in order to survive. The symbolism of this would have been unmistakable to O'Casey's audience, since the Anglo-Irish literary revival of the time often depicted Ireland or Irish nationalism as a woman (for instance in WB Yeats' play *Cathleen Ní Houlihan*). The revolutionaries consider Ireland to be greater than any wife or mother.

In Act IV, the men playing cards on the lid of Mollser's coffin create a metaphor for how the working people have become helpless pawns in the power struggles of political idealists. By failing to fight for their own interests (i.e. an end to the poverty they endured and their lack of access to education) they have lost even more. O'Casey's characters are thus seen as the victims, rather than the protagonists of the 1916 Rising.

KEY POINTS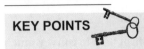

- The title of the text has an important function in stimulating audience interest and indicating a central issue or focus. The title here is drawn from the flag used by the Labour movement which O'Casey regards as being misused for a different political agenda.

- Although *The Plough and the Stars* is described as being a tragedy by the playwright, it is very difficult to identify any one character as being a tragic hero or heroine. It is not a tragedy in the classical sense as no wisdom or growth in awareness occurs. It could be more accurately described as a tragi-comedy, combining elements of both forms.

- Several forms of the comedy genre are contained in the play: slapstick, verbal comedy, comic repetitions, comic irony, parody and satirical parody.

- In addition to the contrasting tragic and comic elements, O'Casey makes effective use of many other contrasts or juxtapositions to highlight serious issues in his play.

- The play does not follow the conventional narrative format where a situation evolves as complications arise, builds to a climax and reaches a conclusion after a key, climactic scene. It is structured around the theme of opposing ideologies.

- Tension is used effectively at critical moments in the play.

- Dialogue plays a crucial role in any play. O'Casey succeeds in authentically representing the language and dialect of the characters.

- Stage directions (the descriptive text that appears within brackets in the text of the play) are an essential narrative technique in this text.

- Character creation is a technique at which O'Casey excels and one which is fundamental to all narrative texts.

- Imagery and symbolism help to convey much of the play's meaning.

Children of Men

Significance of title

In common with *The Plough and the Stars* the title of *Children of Men* has an important function in indicating the central focus of the film. Whereas *The Plough and the Stars* can be seen as an ironic response to an earlier play (James Connolly's *Under Which Flag?*), the title of the film *Children of Men* is a reference to *Psalm 90:3*, which reads in the King James Bible: 'You [God] turn men to destruction and say, Return, you children of men'. The context of this quote is the tribe of Israel lost in the wilderness. The biblical author reflects on how man is a dying animal. All his comforts are dying comforts – individual lives are desperately short. It also implies that people without faith (children of men rather than God) return to dust rather than living on. The significance of this biblical allusion to Cuarón's film is complex. If we recognise the Psalm, then the title prepares us for something of epic scope or importance: the struggle of man to survive in a 'wilderness'. Other ironies emerge upon reflection. For instance, the awareness of the brevity and relative unimportance of a single human life is given particular importance in the film as people contemplate being the final generation before extinction. Paradoxically, the birth of baby Dylan (and the awe that ensues) shows us how vastly important each individual life is. The title also stages a conflict between a loss of faith or hope (people becoming mere children of men) versus the profound liberation that comes from seeing that we are all a part of something bigger than ourselves. **As with O'Casey's title, Cuarón's is deeply symbolic and does a lot of conceptual heavy lifting in only three words.**

Type of text

O'Casey's play is a tragi-comedy that abandons traditional plot structure in favour of a meandering and multi-layered storyline following an ensemble cast of characters, i.e. every character is of roughly equal importance. Several parallel stories emerge, such as the disintegration of Jack and Nora's marriage, the consumptive death of Mollser and the alcoholic struggle and death of Bessie Burgess, along with the tensions between Fluther, Peter and The Covey. *Children of Men* is very different. Amongst other things, it is a tightly-plotted action film, meaning every scene must advance the tension of a singular story and/or deepen our sympathy for the main characters. It also tends toward the traditional Hollywood action film in that the plot centres on a charismatic leading man who (though helped by others) saves the day largely through competency and courage.

Although there are significant differences between O'Casey's play and Cuarón's film, both texts are interesting fusions of genres. *The Plough and the Stars* mixes tragedy, comedy, slapstick and historically accurate details from the uprising. **It attempts to recreate the environment of an actual event but with fictional and highly-stylised characters to draw out the surreal quality of history.** *Children of Men* **practically reverses this technique by depicting a surreal fictional event (a mysterious plague of infertility), but it uses naturalistic performances to sell it as real.** The film avoids almost all of the genres employed in O'Casey's play but is inventive in its own combination of different genres and techniques. *Children of Men* could be read as dystopian (nightmarish future) science fiction. However, unlike most science fiction, there is not much evidence of futuristic technology. Far from it, aside from some onboard displays on buses and cars, most devices look dated and crumbling. Also unusually for a science-fiction film set in the future, the film seems to be located more in a nightmare version of our present. What renders it science fiction is that it is based on an event that occurs in the natural world and which the film implies will be dealt with by technological means (i.e. the science vessel the *Tomorrow*). What complicates this is the implied possibility of divine intervention (not an element of science fiction). **This ambiguity between whether what we are seeing is**

worldly disaster or divine lesson is totally absent in O'Casey's play, which presents only human folly interspersed with glimmers of compelling but ultimately inadequate human virtue.

Unlike *The Plough and the Stars* which functions as a critique of an actual historical event, *Children of Men* could be read as a modern allegory about the soul's journey (embodied by the character Theo) from doubt and despair to hope and love. As the film's main protagonist, Theo initially seems to be a distinctly modern type: the anti-hero. Anti-heroes are typically flawed. They become involved in the action of the plot reluctantly or engage in adventure for morally questionable reasons. The concept of the anti-hero is not to be confused with characters like Jack Clitheroe who try to be heroes from the outset but lack the sympathy of the viewer because they prize glory above all else. If there are anti-heroes in the play, they are the unassuming Fluther and the alcoholic and belligerent Bessie who unwittingly reveal heroic traits under their failings. In Theo's case, he initially accepts his mission to ferry Kee to safety because he wants the Fishes' money. He cares little for Kee or anyone else. However, as the plot progresses, we see Theo evolve into a traditional hero, someone who selflessly puts the well-being of others (or even all of society) before his own needs.

Use of comedy

In contrast to *The Plough and the Stars* there is almost no use of comedy in *Children of Men*. The few scenes with jokes tend toward black comedy, or gallows humour, such as when Jasper tells the story about the oblivious Englishman eating a stork while wondering aloud why there are no more babies. Other examples of black humour emerge in the form of Syd, the sadistic camp guard who revels in his fascist power like a pantomime villain as if he knows he is playing his last role so he may as well enjoy it. He even instructs his 'prisoners' to pretend to be 'fugees' by putting on a pantomime mask

of suffering: 'fugee face... sad face. [seeing their real misery] That's good!' Humour can be used to humanise characters even as it mocks them in *The Plough and the Stars*: Fluther's hypochondria takes him from a single cough to the fear of death and then hoping he didn't 'give up th' beer too suddenly'. It is a place where people are dying of TB regularly, after all, so we laugh *with* as much as laugh *at*. By contrast, in Syd's case the impulse to laugh at reveals the depths of coldness people in power can wield. Syd could be seen as a stand-in for many guards and soldiers throughout history who have chuckled in the face of those they have tormented. This mockery of his prisoners (who unbeknownst to Syd include the hidden baby saviour of humankind) may be an ironic allusion to the numerous occasions when sadistic Roman guards mock Jesus precisely for claiming he was a saviour. Syd likes to laugh, but we do not laugh with him because he is a monster who abuses his power. By contrast, Corporal Stoddart at the end of the play is a soldier and a caricature of a British Tommy ('I do loike a snoice mince poy!') but he is warm and jovial. There are no monsters in the play. Humour plays a role in banishing the tendency to see any side as evil. Syd's laughter in the face of real suffering has the opposite effect of showing that evil can live among us.

Setting and staging can play a role in establishing whether the world we are viewing is ironic, comedic or deadly serious. O'Casey's stage directions are vivid and straightforward: 'there is an unmistakable air of poverty'. By contrast, Cuarón's bleak landscapes are filled with ironic grace notes. He weaves in several allusions that walk the fine line between irony and comedy. For instance, there is anti-government graffiti that looks strikingly like Banksy's political cartoon work, including wry but polite demands to 'please turn out the light' if you are the last person to die. Another example is the allusion to Pink Floyd's *Animals* album that we see from Nigel's art conservatory window: a giant pink pig flying over a drab factory. The pop-culture friendly soundtrack is full of ironic song choices like *Arbeit Macht Frei* by Pete Doherty and *Running the World* by Jarvis Cocker. **Through his choice of songs on the soundtrack and the pop culture references throughout the film, Cuarón shows that he likes to give the viewer opportunities to spot their own culture being used in a way not previously envisaged by the audience. O'Casey paints a more straightforward realist landscape of suffering and squalor, with no visual or musical game play.**

Use of contrast

The *Plough and the Stars* generates much of its tension from the pairing of ideological opposites: Bessie the Loyalist (or Covey the Socialist) vs the Nationalists, Jack the radical vs Nora the homemaker etc. No position is presented as being entirely wrong or right. This allows O'Casey to present a complex and nuanced human reality. It also allows for multiple strands of what the play is 'about'. *Children of Men* **is more focused on a singular plot, but we still see many ideological tensions emerging through contrasting pairs, again with no one being completely right or wrong.** For example, Theo and Julian are an ex-couple who still love each other but represent extreme ideological opposites. Theo is a cynic and Julian is an idealist and radical. Luke and Patric are presented as brothers in arms, but where Luke represents the thoughtful man who becomes brutal under extreme circumstances, Patric seems to relish his role as a bully and a killer. Miriam's belief in UFOs is paired with Jasper's, as against what we assume Theo thinks of the matter. Similarly, the film is full of allusions to penitential religious sects who punish themselves for the sins of humanity. Jasper and Theo joke about such groups. However, since the film never answers the question of whether the plague is natural or supernatural, the viewer finds these tensions about who is right or wrong, sane or insane, hard to resolve. **Like O'Casey's play, the ideological tensions (faith vs secularism, violence vs peace, authoritarianism vs anarchy etc.) remain long after the curtain** falls or the closing credits roll.

Plot structure

As we saw above, O'Casey's play avoids traditional plot structure in order to emphasise **multiple points of view** and to deny the possibility of a neat or clear-cut closure to the action. It leaves the viewer with questions rather than answers: what *is* the central struggle? How can one respond to such problems. What is the right thing to do? *Children of Men*, **however, uses a more traditional plot structure: the central protagonists and antagonists are clearly drawn. Theo has an unambiguous mission to protect Kee and the baby and ferry them to the *Tomorrow*.** The film's first half or so allows for a leisurely exploration of this dystopian landscape. Pacing of the plot is an important element in how much a viewer is invited to question the world of the text, consider the competing values on show etc. Plot and character are tied to one another, as plot reveals character (what choices they make in the presence or absence of crises) and character drives plot (brave people take on adventures, cowards betray their friends etc.). Typically, lots of moments of high-stakes tension result in a response to the text where we have no time to question the protagonists' values. **O'Casey lets the opening of his play reveal almost no plot points, so we have time to observe his characters and get to like and distrust them in roughly even measure. On the other hand,** *Children of Men* **subjects Theo to dramatic events from the opening scene, but his nonchalance in the face of such action makes us question what is important in this world where human life itself, even as it becomes rarer and rarer, seems less and less valuable.** The slow pace of the opening third of the film allows Theo to initially wander into Jasper's wooded retreat to get aimlessly stoned and later visit an aristocratic friend for a meal and to ask a favour. **The slow tempo lets the texture of the world come into richer focus, much as O'Casey's lengthy stage directions do.** Taking the time to calmly follow Theo in a luxury car past an absurd display of religious devotion and military parades does a fine job of implying the question: what is worth valuing? What is central to a good life? As the film picks up pace and the stakes rise as the Fishes are revealed to be murderers, the ambiguity of such philosophical questions falls away in favour of our hopes and fears for the survival of the protagonists. **Although the closing scene is still thoughtful and loaded with questions and ambiguity (will Theo, baby Dylan and the human race survive?), this form of plot leads to a more satisfying and hopeful conclusion. This contrasts with O'Casey's style of plot, which seems designed to unsettle the audience and provoke a questioning of political and social ideologies.**

Use of dialogue – How it assists characterisation

O'Casey's dialogue manages to combine the social realism of working-class Dublin with a heightened or stylised quality that lets us know that the characters are also 'types' (The Covey is the pretentious fake-socialist, Peter is the fake-pious 'forester' living in the past, Jack is the posing revolutionary etc.) As always, accents play a major role in establishing social class and nationality. **In *Children of Men* the dialogue is more naturalistic with less verbal play. However, class, nationality and other social cues are still on full display.** Theo, being the most fully realised of all the characters, expresses the greatest variety of verbal expression, perhaps implying how divided he is against himself. At times he appears droll and upper class, as when he is introduced to Kee who spits, 'What the fuck you looking at?!' and Theo blithely responds, 'Apparently the pleasure is all mine'. Other times he is self-deprecatory, as when Julian defends him by saying 'You should have seen him in the old days when he was a real activist'. Theo responds: 'You were the activist. I just wanted to get laid'. At other times, he comes across as vulgar and angry, using coarse language when describing Baby Diego or undermining people by bluntly claiming they have something in their teeth or their breath

stinks. The effect is to create a character that is smart, savvy and complex but not especially warm or initially likeable. This is the behaviour of a reluctant survivor – someone who does not believe things can improve and that the worst is yet to come. **In this regard Theo's barbed but witty language is reminiscent of much of the cut and thrust of O'Casey's banter. The main difference is that the dialogue tends to place Theo in a position of (assumed) superiority to those he is speaking to, whereas O'Casey's tenement dwellers can never seem to get any leverage over one another, insulting and undermining each other to little effect.**

Miriam and Jasper seem superficially similar, sharing an interest in UFOs and using much of the same hippy/counter-culture language. **Like O'Casey's types, Jasper veers sometimes into caricature, in this case a hippy from a bygone revolutionary era: 'I'm still tryin' to tell a joke here, man'.** He and Miriam exchange a series of equal terms for Jasper's pairing of 'faith and chance'. She suggests yin and yang and Shiva and Shakti. Jasper suggests 'Lennon and McCartney!' These references establish both of them as non-violent dreamers and people with a playful nature. **This playful, cooperative quality is largely missing from the humorous but frustrated exchanges in O'Casey's play.**

Unlike in *The Plough and the Stars*, the characters in *Children of Men* are depicted as effectively driving the action forward through their choices. Although they are victims of the infertility plague, they are not passive but rather extremely active protagonists and antagonists.

Camera replaces stage direction

One major difference between a stage play and a film is that a play can be performed differently every time it is produced, whereas a film is a set text that doesn't change over time. Having said that, O'Casey's extremely detailed stage directions, which include elaborate descriptions of actors' faces and physiques as well as how the settings should be realised, leave little room for variation in interpretation. There is a very specific ambiance which O'Casey wants to generate. In film, the camera direction decides for the viewer what they are looking at when they aren't focusing on the actors delivering dialogue and significant actions. **Cuarón, like O'Casey, has a very detailed sense of the world he is representing.** Each scene in the film is loaded with information about the social and political landscape, and it is introduced seemingly casually. The long cages located at train stops, for instance, or the steady stream of state propaganda that appears on TVs, in buses and on billboards is depicted as a simple fact of life that people barely react to. The ubiquitous but low-key demands, orders and reminders of one's duty create an atmosphere that is at once oppressive and perfunctory – a jaded acceptance. Even though the film opens with an explosion, the overall muted colour palette and steady shots imply a human world that is quietly fading out while a patient nature waits to take the world back. This is most clearly expressed in the scene of the deserted school. In one of the quietest moments in the film, we see Cuarón's poetic sensibilities at play in the staging and shooting alone. A lone deer trots through the halls where children should be learning. Kee sits alone on a swing, framed by a window with a teardrop-shaped break in the pane of glass. Weeds engulf the space. The use of subdued and restrained scenes like this one distinguish the film from other 'apocalyptic' genre offerings. They create a tone of poignancy over fear or a desire to see massive scenes of destruction and death. **Both the play and film enjoy a measured pacing and detailed but subdued poetic rendering of scenes. This allows for a pervasive sadness to weave itself throughout both texts.**

Imagery and symbolism

As with O'Casey's play, *Children of Men* **manages to deploy powerful imagery and symbolism within a realistic setting.** Much of the play's images are subtle but clear, such as the lock on the door, the card game on the coffin

lid or Rosie as a prostituted Ireland. **Cuarón's work similarly uses details that, on their own, could be dismissed as simple realistic touches, but in the context of the film as a whole, they take on more significance.** Several aspects of symbolism and imagery have been touched on previously in these notes, but one not yet discussed in detail is the film's use of animals. As the humans die out, animals start to reclaim the world. People keep young pets to remind them of youth itself; at a farmhouse, kittens seem drawn magically to Theo, as if they see him as a protector. The farm dogs too approach him like their master. One of the more overt (some might say heavy-handed) scenes at the farm is when Kee chooses to reveal her pregnancy in a shed full of cows being milked. Here she suddenly becomes a fertility symbol surrounded by milk and motherhood. She worries about the cows, however. They are being used by men, and Kee is worried with good reason that she too is in danger of being used, reduced to a pawn in a larger power grab between the warring factions in the film. Turning characters into symbols can run the risk of reducing them too, but Kee seems to self-consciously fight against playing a fertility goddess or earth mother by speaking bluntly, joking with her helpers, coming up with terrible names for her child and swearing that she cannot push the baby out during labour. **As with the realist touches that O'Casey brings to his characters' exchanges, Cuarón's gritty details help to bring levity or worldliness to scenes that otherwise might feel overloaded with symbolic weight.** During the birth, for instance, the sound of dogs barking in the distance grows louder. This creates the sense that this may be a Christmas manger scene, with animals sharing the miraculous event with the human world. Or it may simply be animals responding to the intense animal struggle, the labour endured, to give birth to a child. **Again, as with O'Casey's play, the film works as a realistic plot with imagery that can either be read as coincidental or enjoyed as symbolic to add another layer of significance and meaning to the unfolding events.**

KEY POINTS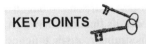

- Titles in both texts are used for symbolic or ironic purposes. *The Plough and the Stars* refers to a Labour movement flag that is being misused for a different political agenda. Cuarón's title is from *Psalms*, and raises the question of whether we are nothing but lost and dying animals or part of a divine mystery.

- Each text belongs to a different literary genre. *The Plough and the Stars* is best described as a tragi-comedy, combining elements of both tragedy and comedy. *Children of Men*, by contrast, has elements of dystopian (or apocalyptic) science fiction. It also functions as an ambiguous modern allegory about the tensions between spiritual and secular views of the world.

- Humour is used differently in both texts. O'Casey's play exhibits slapstick, verbal comedy, comic repetitions, comic irony and satirical parody. The film, on the other hand, uses black humour (e.g. the stork joke, Syd's mockery) to illustrate how some people deal with suffering. It also engages in playful pop-culture references.

- Contrast is effectively used in both texts. In addition to the contrasting tragic and comic elements, O'Casey contrasts various value systems (e.g. domestic vs military; socialism vs nationalism). *Children of Men* contrasts a natural vs supernatural view of reality. It also juxtaposes idealism against cynicism, anarchy vs authoritarianism and the violent courage of the Fishes against the pacifist courage of Jasper, Miriam and Theo.

- Rather than a conventional narrative, the play is structured around the theme of opposing ideologies and refuses to resolve any tensions or offer closure. The film exhibits a more traditional plot (clear mission with sympathetic protagonists) and ends with an ambiguous but hopeful conclusion.

- Dialogue plays an essential role in each of the texts. O'Casey's dialogue manages to combine the social realism of working-class Dublin with a heightened or stylised quality. In *Children of Men* the dialogue is more naturalistic with less verbal play. However, class, nationality and other social cues are still on full display.

- Through stage direction for the play and camera direction for the film, both texts create detailed but subdued poetic rendering of scenes.

- O'Casey's characters are vividly drawn but ultimately are trapped in ineffectual cycles of frustrated action. Cuarón's characters are similarly trapped in a dire situation but seem more capable of working toward a possible solution.

- The imagery in both the play and film can be enjoyed as naturalistic detail or interpreted as a heightened symbolic dimension of the texts' created worlds.

The Great Gatsby

Significance of title

There is an irony that haunts all three titles: *The Plough and the Stars* refers to a workers' flag being used in a nationalist rather than socialist movement, so it is one of many things in the play that is in the wrong place at the wrong time. *Children of Men*, referencing *Psalms*, is ambiguous about whether it describes a world of dying human animals or something more uplifting. **Fitzgerald's novel is perhaps the most explicitly ironic of all the titles.** We as readers never fully know how 'great' Gatsby is, either in the eyes of Nick the narrator or Fitzgerald himself. On the one hand, Nick states from the outset – but without going into details – that Gatsby 'represented everything for which I have an unaffected scorn'. But on the other hand, Nick claims there was 'something gorgeous about him, some heightened sensitivity to the promises of life'. From the very beginning, Gatsby is an enigma. He is a criminal and an adulterer who regularly hosts the most garish and vulgar displays of wealth imaginable. He is also brave, resourceful, romantic, dedicated and enjoys 'an extraordinary gift for hope' that deeply inspires Nick. What are we to make of this 'greatness'? What does it say about a society that produces such a man? **It is worth noting that while the play and film allude to larger movements or texts (socialism and the Bible) outside of themselves, *The Great Gatsby* refers only to its own protagonist. It is as if the novel's title recreates the egotism of the world it will be focusing on. The titles of all three texts invite the audience to question what these works are taking as their subject matter and imply that each text enjoys a certain degree of ironic awareness.**

Type of text

On the surface, each text is very different from the others in terms of form and subject matter. O'Casey's play is a tragi-comedy that largely rejects traditional plot structure to depict a variety of social and political tensions; Cuarón's film fuses apocalyptic science fiction with modern allegory; Fitzgerald's novel gives us a glimpse into the world of the spoiled rich of mid-twentieth century America. **But what the texts have in common is that they are all, to some extent, cautionary tales.** O'Casey's play warns of the dire consequences of letting people become so oppressed (either through poverty or colonialism) that they will become alienated enough to let empty philosophy or rhetoric sway them into danger. The play offers little consolation. Cuarón's film presents us with an even larger and more mysterious problem: a global plague. It focuses on how cruel and desperate people can become when they lose hope. It offers consolation, but only with the aid of a miraculous birth. **Both the play and film are set in bleak worlds with damaged characters trying to survive as best they can. In sharp distinction,** Fitzgerald's novel is set in a superficially comfortable world of ease and opportunity. Although the citizens of Long Island suffer from boredom and envy (so this is not a utopia), theirs is the suffering of the socially privileged.

One major formal difference of the novel from the play and film is that its story is told through a narrator. Because this is a modernist novel, the text can experiment with how reliable a narrator can be. When we watch *The Plough and the Stars* or *Children of Men*, no matter how strange the action may get, we can take as a given it is happening right there and then. Everything in *The Great Gatsby*, however, is narrated by Nick as he looks back on his summer of 1922. For instance, he gets so drunk at Tom's love nest in Manhattan that he admits he cannot be trusted to convey events clearly, as 'everything that happened has a dim, hazy cast over it'. He ends that second chapter with a series of disjointed and confusing fragments of recollection. This recreates not so much events, as the experience of an imperfect mind witnessing or recollecting things from a distance. This 'distance' is key to *The Great Gatsby* specifically. The main characters seem emotionally distanced not only from each other but from themselves. But a different kind of distancing is key to modernist texts in general. They approach life with a toolkit of distancing techniques (unreliable narrators, for instance), reminding us that all art is made by flawed and biased humans and as such cannot be simplistically trusted. **This modern sceptical attitude to any final or absolute truth is a hallmark of much twentieth/twenty-first century narrative art. It is evident in the play and film too. Not one of the tenement dwellers or anyone they interact with seems to grasp the full mechanism of their oppression or how to fix it. In *Children of Men*, Theo struggles with whether life is meaningless chance or meaningful revelation of a greater divine will. The film never answers the question. *The Great Gatsby* makes almost everything an enigma. We have to ask ourselves questions as to who Jay Gatsby/Jimmy Gatz really is, whether he is actually 'great' and whether we can trust the man telling us the tale in the first place.**

Use of comedy

Comedy in *The Plough and the Stars* is used to disarm us for the devastation that will ensue. It is mostly character driven and even lapses into caricature at times, but it often reveals moral flaws. Comic moments are much rarer in *Children of Men* but serve to bond us to the main characters. As we have seen in the case of Jasper, even a juvenile joke can reveal deep reserves of courage and compassion. We also see black humour emerge in the character of Syd. In *The Great Gatsby*, humour also exists and is mainly of a verbally witty nature. Consider this apparently contradictory claim by Nick's friend Jordan: 'I like large parties. They're so intimate. At small parties there isn't any privacy'. This kind of cleverness attracts Nick, and he engages with it himself. Early on, he contemplates his time in Yale writing 'solemn and obvious editorials' and decides once again to become that 'most limited of all specialists, the "well-rounded man".' He adds to this paradox the ironic line: 'life is much more successfully

looked at from a single window, after all'. Reading such lines is a puzzle, and this is typical of modernist works. If we take Nick at face value, he means that the literary life allows one to judge others from a comfortable distance, and this is a very rewarding way to live. Assuming he (or Fitzgerald) does not endorse such a simple claim, we have to figure out how sincere Nick is when he champions literature's ability to help one see into the heart of one's neighbour. This ironic detachment pervades the text, making it simultaneously amusing and discomforting. There are some funny descriptions, such as Nick's claim that Jordan holds herself with such practiced poise that she seems to be balancing an invisible object on the end of her nose. There are ludicrous portraits of people drinking themselves silly, posturing as artists or intellectuals at parties or making urbane small talk, but there are no jokes as such. It's a tale told by a man so refined that he rarely laughs out loud. **Comedy or humour is thus an integral feature of each text, but is used in a different way by O'Casey, Cuarón and Fitzgerald.**

Use of contrast

All three texts use contrast to great effect. This is often based on differences in social class. In *The Plough and the Stars*, the lady from Rathmines is introduced almost like an alien into the setting of the 1916 Rising. Her role is to show how lightly she takes the world of political struggle (she thought the 'howl thing was a joke') and the sense of entitlement she feels to expect working-class people to risk their lives to save hers. In *Children of Men*, Theo's aristocratic friend Nigel dismisses all concerns beyond art: 'I just don't think about it', while below him on the streets cults flagellate (whip) themselves for the sins of man, and soldiers round up random immigrants for internment. **There are several contrasts in *The Great Gatsby*,** e.g. the exciting (and possibly criminal) world of New York City vs the staid opulence of the Buchanans' mansion, or Nick's 'small eyesore' next to Gatsby's pleasure palace. But the most striking and important contrast in setting is the valley of ashes as against anything else in the book. The poverty here is so great that Nick almost fails to see it as part of the world, rendering it in language more befitting an apocalyptic vision: 'a fantastic farm where ashes grow like wheat'… 'grotesque gardens'… 'ash-grey men swarm up with leaden spades and stir up an impenetrable cloud, which screens their obscure operations from your sight'. The effect derives much of its power from just how alien Nick perceives these 'others' to be from himself and his neighbours. **The valley of ashes in the novel is almost an inversion of the effect O'Casey creates, as he sets his entire play in such an obscure valley of poverty. The only upper-class characters seem to be brief visitors: the wealthy lost woman and the shadowy and manipulative Voice of the Man. *Children of Men* moves through a wide variety of spaces and features a range of social classes and value systems all working at odds with one another.**

Plot structure

Of the three texts, *Children of Men* has the most traditional plot structure: much of the action takes place over a short period of time, the protagonists are clearly identified and sympathetic and the tension builds to a climax that resolves into (tentative) relief. The play and the novel are more modernist, in that they reject traditional plot in favour of more sprawling timelines: *The Plough and the Stars* begins in November 1915 and then leaps to Easter 1916; *The Great Gatsby* meanders through the summer of 1922. Neither O'Casey nor Fitzgerald offer any real closure in their work. Certainly there is no clear hero to the play, and no character ends up wiser or better off by curtain-fall. The novel pulls off an interesting trick in that it tells a disjointed and nuanced tale about a man, Gatsby, who himself seems to be entertaining a simplistic fairytale narrative in his head. First, he achieves great wealth, largely through illicit means. Then he establishes himself as a major player in the monied world of his beloved Daisy. Finally, he plans to win her over with a display of

bravado and flamboyance. Gatsby is presented as a great dreamer, but he is so naive that it never occurs to him that happily-ever-after endings cannot actually exist. We learn he was a fan as a young man of the heroic *Hopalong Cassidy* books, where the brave cowboy is simply *good* and saves the day every time. This paradoxical failure of imagination in Gatsby creates much of the thin plot, as almost everything that does happen in the book is a result of a naïve but determined fantasist trying to cram a complex world into a simple tale; he just wants to win the girl and ride off into the sunset. **This blindspot of uncompromising idealists such as Jack Clitheroe and Luke drives the major plot element of the failed (or failing) uprisings in O'Casey's play and Cuarón's film also.**

Use of dialogue – how it assists characterisation

All three texts use specific dialogue techniques to create memorable characters. Whereas O'Casey's dialogue reflects a stylised but realistic portrayal of working-class Dublin, and Cuarón's protagonists tend to be savvy, worldly and intelligent, if a little rough around the edges, Fitzgerald's characters mostly speak in the affected manner of people who lead sheltered lives. Nick opens the novel referring to his father's 'reserved way' of communicating. That repressed manner seemingly is reflected in how most of the characters behave in the novel. Nick suggests that 'personality is an unbroken series of successful gestures' and so each of the main characters initially appear to be just that – gestures. Tom's speaking voice is described as a 'gruff husky tenor' with a 'touch of paternal contempt in it'. But what is more significant is that the first quote attributed to him is not something he literally says. Instead, it is Nick's translation of Tom's bodily gestures rather than the actual words which he speaks: 'Now, don't think that my opinion on these matters is final,' he seemed to say, 'just because I'm stronger and more of a man than you'.

The difference between the words being spoken and the meaning or the gesture behind them is another **distancing technique** used in the novel. The first actual quote from Tom is on the same page: 'I've got a nice place here,' but Nick notes that his eyes were 'flashing about restlessly'. Here, Fitzgerald uses the dialogue to undermine the speaker's real gesture or personality. Tom cannot value what he has, be it his property or his wife.

Dialogue and the way Nick frames it is used to establish Daisy as another complex and conflicted character. The first thing she does when we meet her is produce 'an absurd, charming little laugh' which serves to depict her as being childish. The first words out of her mouth are stuttered: 'I'm p-paralyzed with happiness'. The stutter conveys nervousness, and the paralysis she mentions seems to be a problem in her life far greater than simply having too much happiness on her hands.

Jordan Baker likewise has hints of her character revealed the moment she opens her mouth. Her first word is a dynamic and focused, 'Absolutely!' But true to form, even she is in two minds about what she says or means. Nick adds that 'it [her forceful 'Absolutely!'] surprised her as much as it did me'.

When Gatsby speaks he seems perfectly at ease. However, he does not introduce himself, implying that he assumes everyone knows who he is. On a deeper level, this may also mean there is a lack of clarity about who exactly he is. No one ever seems to really grasp him throughout the book.

All three texts – play, film and novel – use naturalistic dialogue to great effect, but Fitzgerald does the most economic job of foreshadowing the tensions and contradictions that beset his characters from the very first words they speak, or do not speak but imply.

Format

Plays can create a world using set direction, actor casting and behaviour and other devices besides dialogue. Films, however, have even more options ranging from soundtracks and special effects to editing techniques and multiple camera angles. The world of a novel, by contrast, is conjured entirely from words. *The Great Gatsby* has two layers of speech, namely Nick's first-person narration of everything that happens, and his reporting of what other people say and how they say it. As we saw previously in this section, O'Casey establishes an engaging and dramatic contrast by juxtaposing his drab and depressing interiors against character dialogue that is often feisty, obscene and vivacious. *Children of Men* creates a jaded colour palette, with many of the scenes shot at dawn, at dusk, at night or in thick fog to enhance a dark look to the world. **Both the play and the film unfold their action more or less as we watch it.** There are no flashbacks or breakaways to parallel action. O'Casey locks us in the tenement or the pub and forces us to hear the world change outside the window. We cannot look out the window, and there is nothing anyone can do to stop it. Similarly, in *Children of Men*, we are thrust into the street from the opening scene. The bomb blast goes off right in front of us. A series of action scenes (the forest mob attack on the car, the escape from the farmhouse, the shelling of the building) are similarly immersive (i.e. the action seems to surround the audience so that they feel as if they are almost in the scenes themselves). *The Great Gatsby* is a tale told from a detached distance. Although Nick is in the room for some of the key scenes, such as Gatsby's reunion with Daisy or when Tom and Gatsby confront each other in New York, still Nick acts as a buffer to the action in a way that could not happen in a film or play, or even a novel with an omniscient narrator. The most dramatic events, Myrtle's death and Gatsby's murder, are muted by being relayed after the fact. This has the effect of making the novel less about the shock of the events as they happen, and more about how Nick interprets the meaning of the events. Just as with dialogue, there is what is said (or what happens) and then the deeper layer of what it all really means.

In many respects, the novel subtly rejects traditional plot because it is rejecting the idea that the 'orgiastic future' (wild, depraved) that Gatsby believes in even exists. The most important motivations for our behaviour stem from our past, not our future. **The closing paragraphs of the book are not about what might happen next, unlike the foggy but forward-looking close of** *Children of Men*, **but a reflection on what has happened and why. The despairing final scene of** *The Plough and the Stars* **is full of red glare from the rifle and machine-gun fire, demanding answers even as it furiously rejects any possible excuses for the chaos that has descended.** But Nick, as a reflective and philosophical narrator, ends the novel by looking up at a cool, moonlit sky and hazarding a theory. Gatsby's greatness, like the New World itself, is an enigma whose value is in its 'aesthetic contemplation'. Nick has come 'face to face for the last time in history with something commensurate to his capacity for wonder'.

All three texts weave a poetic spell through their settings, be it O'Casey's hellish red glare through the window, Cuarón's purgatorial (i.e. a state of suffering by souls who are waiting to enter heaven) fog and buoy or Fitzgerald's (through Nick's) poignant image of Long Island at night. As the novel only has words to create its world, it is worth noting that the technique that stands out most in the final line is, ironically, an auditory one: the poetic repetition of 'b' sounds creating tension and then giving way to a release: 'So we beat on, boats against the current, borne back ceaselessly into the past'.

Imagery and symbolism

All three texts combine realism and symbolism. *The Plough and the Stars* is an historically accurate depiction of poverty and political turmoil, but the use of symbolic images (e.g. playing a game of cards on a coffin lid)

marks the play as resolutely modern and even experimental for its time. The symbolism tells us these are the players and these are the stakes but refuses to give any answers, or even any priority, to the various tensions (political, economic, domestic) that seethe on stage. Similarly, *Children of Men* continues the modern tendency to reject final answers and play with uncertainty. The imagery, along with the choral aspects of John Tavener's soundtrack, are highly reminiscent of Christianity, but the film walks a fine line of ambiguity between whether we are witnessing a divine intervention, or if this is a secular world destroying itself with violence and trying to save itself with luck and science. *The Great Gatsby*, **like the play and the film, is set in a world both lushly embodied in realist detail but also infused with a rich poetic symbolism.** Whereas religiosity is openly depicted (and often shown as problematic) in the play and film, the traditionally religious is absent from Fitzgerald's novel. Any 'sacred' imagery is reserved for Nick imagining Gatsby's attitude to Daisy, represented in images like the green light at the end of the dock. Even so, when it looks like Gatsby is about to win his ultimate prize, the love of his dream girl, Nick decides that Gatsby's 'mind would never romp again like the mind of God'. Images like the disembodied pair of 'God's eyes' in the form of a giant pair of eyes on an optician's billboard is another playful modernist ambiguity. Modernism takes as a given that all grand narratives about absolute goodness or truth (like God) are dead. And yet people still feel the need for certainties. **What all three of these texts have in common despite their overt differences in style, genre, and medium, is that they draw the reader into a modern world – a world of multiple valid viewpoints, and one with more questions than answers.**

KEY POINTS

- The titles of each of the texts act as symbolic or ironic pointers to the central concerns of each narrative. O'Casey's title refers to a Labour movement flag that is being misused for a different political agenda. Cuarón's title is from *Psalms*, and raises the question of whether we are nothing but lost and dying animals or part of a divine mystery. Fitzgerald's title refers to an individual character and conveys an ambiguity about whether the 'greatness' is ironic or not.

- Each of the texts is different in form and subject matter. *The Plough and the Stars* is best described as a tragi-comedy, combining elements of both forms. *Children of Men* has elements of dystopian (or apocalyptic) science fiction but also functions as an ambiguous modern allegory about the tensions between spiritual and secular views of the world. *The Great Gatsby* is a modernist novel; it has a sceptical view on absolute narratives and a slightly unreliable but self-aware narrator.

- Humour is used differently in each of the texts and has a different impact on the narratives. The play exhibits slapstick, verbal comedy, comic repetitions, comic irony and satirical parody. The film uses black humour (e.g. the stork joke, Syd's mockery) to illustrate how some people deal with suffering. It also engages in playful pop-culture references. The novel employs intellectual modes of humour, namely witticisms and droll paradoxes.

- Contrast is an extremely effective technique in each of the texts and serves to highlight crucial differences. In addition to the contrasting tragic and comic elements, *The Plough and the Stars* clashes various value systems (e.g. domestic vs military; socialism vs. nationalism). *Children of Men* contrasts a natural vs supernatural view of reality. It also juxtaposes idealism against cynicism, anarchy vs authoritarianism, and the violent courage of the Fishes against the pacifist courage of Jasper, Miriam and Theo. *The Great Gatsby* contrasts extremes of wealth with the crushing poverty of the valley of ashes. Also, Gatsby's criminal connections and courage are contrasted against the morally bankrupt but straitlaced world of the old-money rich.

- Each text is structured in a different way. Rather than a conventional narrative, the play is structured around the theme of opposing ideologies and refuses to resolve any tensions or offer closure. The film exhibits a more traditional plot (clear mission with sympathetic protagonists) and ends with an ambiguous but hopeful conclusion. By contrast, the novel's action is told entirely in reflection. Although there are moments of tension, the focus is on contemplating the aesthetic treasures of that summer and interrogating its events for significance.

- The effective use of dialogue is apparent in each text. O'Casey's dialogue manages to combine the social realism of working-class Dublin with a heightened or stylised quality. In *Children of Men* the dialogue is more naturalistic with less verbal play. However, class, nationality and other social cues are still on full display. In the novel, dialogue is naturalistic and spare but often works at odds with Nick's interpretation of what the speakers really mean or want.

- Through stage direction for the play and camera direction and soundtrack for the film, both texts create detailed but subdued poetic rendering of scenes. Fitzgerald, through Nick, creates a lush verbal world of description, not only of sights and sounds, but also of emotion and intellectual apprehension.

- O'Casey's characters are vividly drawn, but they are ultimately trapped in ineffectual cycles of frustrated action. Cuarón's characters are similarly trapped in a dire situation but seem more capable of working toward a possible solution. Fitzgerald's characters are trapped by a kind of blindness that prohibits them from seeing that they are indeed trapped by their own unrecognised frustrations and anxieties.

- The imagery in the play, film and novel can be enjoyed as naturalistic detail or interpreted as a heightened symbolic dimension of the texts' created worlds.

Sample Answer

C. Literary Genre

'Compelling storytelling can be achieved in a variety of ways.'

(a) Identify two literary techniques found in **ONE** text you have studied. Discuss the extent to which these techniques contributed to compelling storytelling in this text.

(b) Identify one literary technique, common to **TWO OTHER** texts on your comparative course. Compare the extent to which this technique contributed to compelling storytelling in these texts.

(a) At first glance, the phrase 'compelling storytelling' might imply a plot that is so exciting that the reader/viewer is on the edge of their seat to find out what happens next. But the three texts and their literary techniques that I want to examine here do more than just tell exciting stories with plenty of action. The first part of my answer will focus on F. Scott Fitzgerald's novel *The Great Gatsby* and its use of irony and a subjective narrator. The second part of my answer will examine symbolism in Seán O'Casey's play *The Plough and the Stars* and Alfonso Cuarón's film *Children of Men*.

Fitzgerald's novel was written in and set during the Jazz Age – a high point for modernism. Its use of irony is compelling in many ways. For instance, Nick sets up ironic distance between how characters speak and how they really see themselves when he introduces his characters of Tom, Daisy and Jordan. Tom's first line of dialogue boasts about his house: 'I've got a nice place here'. But Nick notes Tom's 'eyes flashing about restlessly'. Similarly, Jordan comes across as someone who says one thing but means another. The first word out of her mouth is a decisive-sounding 'Absolutely!' but Nick's description of how she says it undermines her superficial certainty: 'it surprised her as much as it did me'.

Daisy embodies a different kind of irony when she first appears. She announces to Nick in a stutter that she is 'p-paralyzed with happiness'. The stutter conveys nervousness, which intrigues the reader. But it is not until re-reading the book that we realise the dramatic irony at play here: Daisy is right about being paralysed, but not by happiness. She is trapped in a gilded cage, disliking her husband but not being strong enough to leave him. Such notes of foreshadowing are compelling for people like me, who spend time re-reading the novel and examining the depth of the characters rather than simply scanning the book for what happens.

This ironic detachment that characters display – to themselves and to each other – renders them compelling because I see these people as complex, even profoundly conflicted, and therefore more interesting than simplistic characters.

A further irony of the novel is Gatsby himself, who is presented as unique among the sophisticates of Long Island. Where they are jaded, he is a great dreamer; he is fantastically ambitious and never wavers from his goals. But he is totally out of touch with reality. Unlike the novel he is starring in, Gatsby seems capable of entertaining only very simple stories about himself and how life may play out. His father reveals at one point that Gatsby's self-improvement plan was written inside an escapist *Hopalong Cassidy* novel. This might be an ironic commentary on how America worships the rough man of action over the one of reflection, but it also seems to imply that Gatsby lives with his head in the clouds and does not have enough critical or emotional distance from his simple fantasies of gaining massive wealth and winning the girl.

One of the most compelling ironies of the narrative is one that haunts modernism in general: the sense that God is dead but evil somehow remains. The optician's billboard that hosts the fading and disembodied eyes of 'god' is at once both ironic and deeply sincere. The billboard is both an attempt to drum up business and a claim that science holds the answer to poor sight. Is there nothing but commerce and money to give value to things? The reader is invited to dismiss poor Wilson when he goes mad and claims that you cannot fool God. After all, no one goes to jail for their part in the hit-and-run crime the novel builds to, and no one confesses a real sense of remorse. If there is any retribution at all, it is reserved for Gatsby, who wasn't driving. We are invited to wonder: is his death ironic? Or is Gatsby being punished for some other crime: threatening the sobriety of his community, perhaps. Or having the nerve to dream simplistic dreams. The puzzle that Fitzgerald has set for me compels me to ponder it even now, long after I have finished reading the book.

This question of irony connects to the second literary technique I want to consider: a radically subjective narrator. Nick is insightful and poetic but unreliable. For instance, toward the end of the second chapter he gets so drunk he blacks out and leaves the reader only with fragments of memory. This unreliability makes Fitzgerald's narrative more compelling because we must pay attention and read between the lines more. Nick claims he is the most honest person he knows, but he never reports a serious crime. He opens the book by saying he doesn't like to pass judgement, but goes on to be highly judgemental of everyone he meets.

Because the story is told from the viewpoint of Nick, it is personal in tone but also somewhat distanced from the action itself. Using the technique of a flashback, Nick reflects on events, evaluates them and strives to deduct lessons about life from what he has observed. One could argue that recollected action from an intellectual and detached observer is less urgent in its impact on the reader. Perhaps one could argue that an omniscient narrator or even the recounting of events from the perspective of Gatsby or Daisy would provide more vivid detail – especially in such moments as the description of the car crash. However, in my opinion, the thoughtful, poetic reflections of Nick made the novel more compelling and encouraged me to look beyond the action to a more thoughtful analysis of the central themes. When Nick ends the narrative by surveying the night sky, he notes that the 'inessential houses began to melt away' until he can see the 'fresh green breast of the new world'. You get the impression that Nick (and maybe Fitzgerald) believes that specific realistic details, like Gatsby's massive parties, can obscure bigger truths. Having a slightly remote observer recall the plot for us lets us see a wider landscape. Nick leaves us with the closing ironic image of backward-rowing lovers of the 'future'. This paradox, that the 'orgiastic future' that powers the American Dream is fuelled by chasing ghosts from the past, is striking to me.

(b) Symbolism, like irony, is another aspect of storytelling that adds to the compelling nature of the story-telling. O'Casey's play and Cuarón's film both offer great examples of how symbolism can be woven into a text to make us think harder about what is really being said – or asked – in the work. Consider the set directions that open Act IV of *The Plough and the Stars*. They are so detailed and paint such a naturalistic picture of the place and time that a careless reader could miss the subtle poeticism. Bessie Burgess's living room has the look of 'compressed confinement', suggesting that she too is compressed or forced to cram her human complexity into a caricature of alcoholism and loyalist sentiment. Even the title of the play takes on a new light when we read that one of her window panes has been 'starred by a bullet'. So now the 'stars' under which people work could be seen as bullet holes! The dust has 'well fallen' and perhaps this implies we are looking into a crypt of some kind. O'Casey seems to suggest that these people are in a living death due to their poverty.

Later, some looted, luxury items symbolise a way of life which is outside the experience of the poor and serve to draw attention to the degradation of life in the tenements.

O'Casey layers another symbol into the final act of the play by setting the men up in a card game near a coffin. On one level, there's nothing symbolic about the coffin because there is an actual dead person in it showing us that war and poverty tend to result in actual rather than symbolic events. But the proximity of the card game is striking. Fluther looks out the window and wonders if 'half o' th' city must be burnin'' and tells The Covey to give the cards 'a good shuffling'. Shuffling is supposed to make a game fair, but these people cannot get to reshuffle their positions in life. Perhaps O'Casey is implying that a real socialist revolution (a non-violent one) might have reshuffled the deck of life for the poorest people, but instead there is just a dead girl in a box who spent her life dying in a box. This symbolism makes the story more compelling and creates a powerful impact when one considers the play in its entirety. It certainly hit me harder when I thought back on it, than when I saw it for the first time. It is still like a delayed shock, a message I keep unpacking.

Children of Men works most effectively, like *The Plough and the Stars*, through symbolic details that haunt you when you think back over what you have seen. Like O'Casey's play, Cuarón's film presents scenes to the viewer straightforwardly, as if saying 'this is simply how it is' so the poeticism may not be apparent. It even seems hidden. O'Casey's symbols are woven so seamlessly into his work that you could dismiss that they are symbols or you can embrace them. So too with Theo, Kee and her baby struggling through a war zone in an effort to reach a boat. These could be people simply trying to survive, or they could be a representation of the Holy Family in the twenty-first century. The film remains ambiguous about whether or not this is a secular world where the plague is just bad luck and the baby is just good luck, or if this is a spiritual world with divine intervention at play. Because of this fundamental ambiguity, the religious symbolism could be seen as coincidence or alternatively implying something magical about reality itself. That unknowable quality makes the story more compelling to me because it is a puzzle that refuses to let the final pieces fall into place. I keep turning it around in my mind, and asking myself: well, what do I believe?

There is a danger to symbolism. In *The Plough and the Stars*, the Voice of the Man uses symbolism to lure young men into a futile dogfight with the British Empire by fusing war propaganda with religious imagery: 'without the shedding of blood there is no redemption!' A different kind of danger is glimpsed in *Children of Men* when we see Kee naked and pregnant in the milking shed. Here, this African immigrant becomes a fertility symbol. My concern here is that as soon as someone becomes a symbol, they stop being a person. This is a problem in both texts, as O'Casey's revolutionaries try (and in O'Casey's eyes, fail) to become heroes/martyrs and Cuarón's Fishes try to steal Kee as a 'key' piece in some vast chess game with the British government.

The use of symbolism in both texts, whether it is subtle, overt, or downright manipulative (such as in the case of the Voice of the Man or the Fishes) increases the fascination I have with these works. It invites the most basic questions, like: what do I think is really happening here? What do I value? Is life a card game that needs a good shuffling, even if it means upheaval and suffering? Is life a series of chance happenings or is there a divine will playing out under all the chaos? I cannot think of more compelling questions than these, and I appreciate that neither text insults my intelligence by trying to answer them for me.

Guidelines for Answering Exam Questions: Comparative Study

1   In the examination you are asked to compare the texts under one of three different modes of comparison. Two of these modes will appear on the paper and you will be asked to select one and discuss it in relation to the three texts you have studied. You should write for about 65 minutes. The modes are as follows.

    A.   **Cultural Context:** The cultural context of any work of literature is the backdrop to the story. It refers to the 'world' in which the text is set.

    B.   **The General Vision or Viewpoint:** This relates to the author's/director's outlook on life. Their viewpoint influences our perspective of the text and its setting.

    C.   **Literary Genre:** This refers to the ways in which the story is told.

2   Comparison means both similarities and differences.

3   Texts must be discussed in relation to each other – identify and explore links between them.

4   Avoid summarising the stories of the texts that you have studied – your response should be analytical / discursive in approach.

5   There are two types of question – the single essay-type question and the two-part question.

6   The two-part question generally makes reference to a key moment / key moments. After you identify and describe a key moment, you may range through the text to establish the context and significance of this particular moment.

7   Where the essay-type question is concerned, address the question in your opening paragraph and outline your response to it.

8   Each paragraph in the essay-type answer should be based on one point of comparison between the texts. Aim to bring the different texts together in each paragraph with a view to producing a coherent comparative analysis.

9   The opening sentence in each paragraph should make the point of comparison.

10   Each point should be illustrated by relevant and accurate reference to (and possibly quotation from) the texts under discussion.

11   Refer back to the terms of the question at intervals to ensure that your response remains focused on the key issues.

12   As well as comparing the texts, show that you have engaged with them on a personal level – give your personal reaction to certain aspects of the texts that have come up for discussion in your response and that had an impact on you.

13   Write a brief conclusion.

14   Use the language of comparative analysis, e.g.:

–   *I noticed in both Text A and Text B that . . .*

–   *Text C differs from both Text A and Text B in that . . .*

–   *While both Text A and Text B highlight this issue, they treat it in a different manner.*

–   *In contrast to Text A, Text B . . .*

–   *Only in Text C do we see . . .*

–   *John in Text A reminds me of Peter in Text B because . . .*

–   *The manner in which A is portrayed in this text differs from its portrayal in my two other comparative texts . . .*

–   *I was struck by the sharp contrast between the responses of the protagonists when confronted by . . .*

–   *The worlds of both Text A and Text B have a number of common features.*

–   *The vision of society in Text A is much more positive than the vision of society in Text B.*

Poetry

Biography / Poetry / Sample Answers

John Keats

Biographical Note

Keats (1795–1821) was born in Finsbury, close to London, England. He was the eldest of five children. He was educated in a small, private boarding school. In 1804 Keats' father was killed in a riding accident. While Keats' mother, Frances, married again, her second marriage was unhappy and the children were raised by their grandparents. His mother suffered from depression and later contracted tuberculosis, dying in 1810. Keats, who had devotedly nursed her through her illness, was devastated. At just fourteen years of age, he was parentless. In 1811 Keats left school to take up an apprenticeship as a surgeon. However, he never had any real interest in this work, eventually feeling repelled by it. Poetry was becoming increasingly important in his life, and in May 1816 he had his first poem published in the *Examiner*, a sonnet entitled *O Solitude! if I must with thee dwell*. Keats' first volume of poetry, *Poems*, was published in 1817. Later that year, he wrote a four thousand word epic poem, *Endymion: A Poetic Romance*. The opening line of this famous poem remains instantly recognisable: 'A thing of beauty is a joy forever.'

On a personal level, Keats' life involved a great deal of pain and loss. His brother Tom contracted tuberculosis, dying from the illness in 1818. From a young age, Keats was fearful for his own life, as we see in his sonnet *When I have fears that I may cease to be*. Keats' greatest fear was that he would die before he had expressed all of the ideas that were teeming in his fertile imagination.

Keats produced the bulk of his poetic work in a highly productive four-year period between 1817 and 1820. One of his most famous achievements was his development of his theory of Negative Capability. In essence this theory suggests that the poet may harbour doubts and uncertainties, and not feel compelled to reach definite conclusions. Keats himself explained this theory as 'when a man is capable of being in uncertainties, mysteries, doubts, without any irritable reaching after fact and reason'. Keats, of course, belonged to the Romantic Movement, which began in the early nineteenth century and ended some fifty years later. Central to the Romantics' beliefs were the power of the imagination to see truths, the importance of man as an individual rather than as a social being, the need for man to re-establish an intimate relationship with the natural world and the necessity of developing a new poetic language that was as close as possible to everyday speech.

In 1820 Keats started to cough up blood and, with his medical training, immediately understood its grave implications. For a time he was looked after by Frances (Fanny) Brawne, the great love of his life and the woman to whom he was engaged, and her mother in their home in Hampstead. His friends advised a spell in Italy, as it was widely believed at the time that tubercular patients would benefit from being in a warm climate. However, Keats did not improve and he died in Rome in 1821. He was, remarkably, only twenty-six years old. At his own request, the following epitaph was inscribed on his tombstone: 'Here lies one whose name was writ on water.'

To one who has been long in city pent

The opening lines of this Petrarchan sonnet convey the contrast between the confinement of the city and the vast expanse of the beautiful sky. The sky is personified, with Keats speaking of 'the fair / And open face of heaven' and 'the smile of the blue firmament'. The restorative powers of nature are conveyed by the image of the poet, fatigued from life in the city, happily relaxing in the pleasantly long grass, reading 'a gentle tale of love and languishment'.

The sestet is dominated by a sense of melancholy as the poet returns home in the evening. As he hears the song of the nightingale ('the notes of Philomel') and watches the clouds sail by, Keats 'mourns' the rapid passing of the day. The closing lines compare the passing of this uplifting day to the falling of an angel's tear from heaven to earth.

References to breathing a prayer (presumably in gratitude for the beauty of the sky), heaven and 'an angel's tear' suggest Keats' awareness of a divine power behind the beautiful countryside.

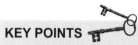

KEY POINTS

- Key themes are the rejuvenating powers of nature and the transient nature of beauty and happiness ('that day so soon has glided by').
- Effective use of metaphors and personification.

Ode to a Nightingale

In this poem we see Keats' deep desire to escape from the imperfect, transient physical world into the perfect, immortal world of the nightingale's song. For Keats the bird's song is a symbol of eternal beauty, happiness and freedom.

The opening stanza conveys the poet's gloom and lethargy: 'My heart aches and a drowsy numbness pains / My sense, as though of hemlock I had drunk.' Keats explains his feelings of despondency and inertia by means of a paradox: ''Tis not through envy of thy happy lot, / But being too happy in thine happiness'. The paradoxical notion that pain can be the result of excessive happiness startles and challenges the reader. The opening stanza contrasts the poet's melancholy with the joy and ease of the nightingale's song: the bird 'singest of summer in full-throated ease'.

The poet considers various avenues of escape from the grim world of reality. He considers the possibility of reaching the perfect world of the bird's song by means of alcohol: 'O for a draught of vintage!' The repetition of 'O' underscores his sense of longing. Keats describes the wine in the type of sensuous detail that is characteristic of his poetry. We can almost taste the wine, which has been 'cooled a long age in the deep-delved earth', and visualise 'the beaded bubbles winking at the brim'. The use of alliteration underlines the sensuous appeal of the wine by means of which the poet hopes 'to leave the world unseen' and fade away with the nightingale 'into the forest dim'.

The third stanza accentuates (emphasises) the pain and sorrow of the physical world from which Keats longs to escape. The poet thinks of physical life in terms of 'the weariness, the fever, and the fret'. The transience of life is vividly captured in a particularly grim image: 'Where youth grows pale and spectre-thin and dies.' The poet believes that Beauty and Love (their personification underlines their importance to Keats) cannot survive in a world of transience: 'Where Beauty cannot keep her lustrous eyes, / Or new Love pine at them beyond tomorrow.'

In stanza four Keats emphatically dismisses the idea of using wine to reach the perfect world of the nightingale's song, proclaiming that he will instead access it through the power of the imagination: 'Away! away! for I will fly to thee, / Not charioted by Bacchus and his pards, / But on the viewless wings of Poesy.' Through the power of his imagination, Keats finds himself in the world of the nightingale: 'Already with thee!'

Stanza five depicts the ideal world of the nightingale's song. This is a world rich in sensuous appeal, a world of darkness and tranquillity where the poet can smell the 'soft incense' that 'hangs upon the boughs', taste the 'dewy wine' and hear 'the murmurous haunt of flies on summer eves.' While the references to 'embalmed darkness' and to flies are suggestive of death and decay, Keats does not view death as something threatening – indeed at the start of the next stanza he even admits to having been 'half in love with easeful Death'.

The poet has considered the possibility of escaping harsh, painful reality through death. The idea of dying when the nightingale is 'pouring forth' his soul 'in such an ecstasy' appeals to the poet. As in *Bright Star*, he longs to forever capture a moment of perfect joy by dying when he is at his happiest. Here Keats sees death as a means of achieving total happiness. However, he realises that death is not the answer to his problems since it would deprive him of the perfect pleasure of the bird's song: 'To thy high requiem become a sod.'

In the seventh stanza Keats contrasts his own mortality with the immortality of the bird's song: 'Thou wast not born for death, immortal bird!' The beautiful song, which the poet has just enjoyed, has been experienced 'in ancient days by emperor and clown'. Keats suggests that the nightingale's song has had an uplifting and inspiring effect on people from ancient and biblical times through to the present. The song fires our imaginations, allowing us to experience a rare and special beauty: 'Charmed magic casements, opening on the foam of perilous seas, in faery lands forlorn.'

The word 'forlorn' acts as a reminder to the poet of the inescapable reality of loneliness and misery. It is like a tolling funeral bell signalling the end of the poet's imaginative experience. As the bird's 'plaintive anthem' fades, Keats realises that the imagination cannot offer him a lasting means of escape: 'Adieu! The fancy cannot cheat so well as she is famed to do'. The wonderful, magical experience stimulated by the bird's song is over and the poet returns to the world of reality. At the close of the poem Keats is back where he began, wondering if the power of his imagination has enabled him to experience a truly visionary moment or merely provided him with the means of temporarily escaping from reality: 'Was it a vision or a waking dream?'

KEY POINTS

- Key themes are the transience and pain of life and the poet's yearning to escape from reality into a world of lasting happiness and perfection.
- The contrast between the perfection and permanence of the bird's song and the imperfection and transience of real life is sharply drawn.
- Sensuous imagery – note stanzas 2 and 5 in particular.
- Symbolism: the bird's song is a symbol of lasting beauty and perfection.
- Sound effects: alliteration (e.g. 'Deep-delved', 'beaded bubbles'), assonance (e.g. 'blown . . . glooms'), sibilance (e.g. 'Singest of summer in full-throated ease'), etc.

On First Looking into Chapman's Homer

The reference to Homer in the title calls to mind his epic travel poems and, as we read into it, we see that this poem is dominated by images of travel and exploration. The 'realms of gold' in which Keats has travelled suggest the richness and power of the imagination. The 'many goodly states and kingdoms' and 'many western islands' he has seen represent the different poets whose work he has explored. Homer, whose wisdom is suggested by his 'deep brow', rules his own poetic realm, but Keats could never travel there because he did not understand Greek. However, Chapman's translation of Homer's classic opened the door to the latter's kingdom, enabling Keats to 'breathe in' its pure air: 'I heard Chapman speak out loud and bold'.

Keats draws an analogy between the excitement he felt on discovering Chapman's translation of Homer and that of an astronomer ('some watcher of the skies') on discovering a new planet ('When a new planet swims into his ken'). He also compares his feelings of elation to that felt by the Spanish explorer Cortes when he first set eyes on the Pacific Ocean. Like Cortes and his men staring silently and awestruck at this hitherto undiscovered vast expanse of water, Keats is moved beyond words by his own dramatic discovery of a whole new poetic world: 'and all his men / Look'd at each other with a wild surmise – / Silent, upon a peak in Darien'.

KEY POINTS

- Key theme is the excitement of reading poetry – this poem suggests that poetry opens up new worlds to the reader.
- The poem is dominated by metaphorical language of travel and exploration.
- Written in the form of a Petrarchan sonnet.

Ode on a Grecian Urn

This poem is similar in theme to *Ode to a Nightingale*. In both poems we see Keats' desire for permanence and immortality in a world of transience. The Grecian urn, like the nightingale's song, is a symbol of lasting perfection. However, in both poems Keats also acknowledges that he cannot remain forever in an ideal world conjured up by the imagination. In both poems he concludes that, having experienced perfect, timeless beauty, he must return to reality.

In the opening stanza Keats addresses the urn, which depicts pastoral (rural) scenes of a pagan festival. The metaphors of the 'still unravished bride of quietness' and 'foster child of silence' evoke the stillness and tranquillity of the urn. This sense of peace is reinforced by the sibilant 's' sound of the opening lines. Paradoxically, the silent urn can tell a tale more eloquently than the poet and his poem. There is a sense of excitement as Keats brings the lifeless urn to life by entering into the world of the story depicted on its sides: 'What men or gods are these? What maidens loth? / What mad pursuit? What struggle to escape?'

The second stanza opens with Keats asserting that art is superior to reality, that the world of the imagination is superior to the real world. He claims that the music that the piper on the urn is playing is more beautiful than real music because it appeals not to the ear but to the spirit or to the imagination: 'Heard melodies are sweet, but those unheard / Are sweeter.' He also suggests that the love depicted on the urn is superior to real love because it is forever beautiful and forever young. The 'bold lover' will never kiss the maiden he pursues (the repetition of 'never, never' is particularly emphatic) but, while he will never actually experience the 'bliss' of love, that love and her beauty will live eternally, untarnished by the harshness and disappointment of reality: 'For ever wilt thou love, and she be fair!'

The repetition of 'happy' (six times) and 'for ever' (five times) seems to underline the poet's belief in the superiority of art. We do however wonder if the poet is as convinced as he claims to be of the superiority of art over real life. As someone painfully aware of life's transience, Keats understandably delights in this vividly imagined world of eternal youth, timeless music and everlasting love. This perfect work of art has forever captured a variety of happy scenes, effectively freezing them in time. However, there is a suggestion that the love depicted on the urn lacks the vibrancy and warmth of real human passion: 'All breathing human passion far above that leaves a heart high-sorrowful and cloyed / A burning forehead, and a parching tongue.' While human love is subject to change and can involve sorrow and pain, Keats realises that art, although perfect and immortal, is also cold and lifeless.

In stanza four, Keats captures the ritual sacrifice of a heifer in a typically sensuous image: 'that heifer lowing at the skies, / and all her silken flanks with garlands dressed.' The image of the deserted, lifeless town reinforces the impression of the urn as a cold, lifeless object: 'And little town, thy streets for evermore will silent be.'

In the final stanza Keats moves from contemplating the scenes on the urn to reflecting on the urn itself. As he steps back and looks at the urn, he leaves the world of the imagination and returns to the world of reality. For all its timeless beauty, the urn is ultimately a lifeless artifact, as the poet's references to 'marble men and maidens', 'Thou, silent form' and 'Cold Pastoral!' clearly suggest. He admires the beauty of the urn and its capacity to 'tease us out of thought' (which is suggestive of its capacity to provoke an imaginative, as opposed to an intellectual or logical response). The urn remains 'a friend to man', reminding us that 'Beauty is truth, truth beauty'. While this equation of truth and beauty has provoked much controversy and debate, Keats seems to argue that what the imagination perceives as beauty must be truth.

As in *Ode to a Nightingale*, Keats accepts that he must return from a vividly imagined world of perfect, everlasting beauty to the world of imperfect, transient reality.

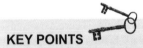

KEY POINTS

- Themes include Keats' desire to escape from transitory reality into a timeless world of enduring perfection.
- The contrast between art (perfect and everlasting, but cold) and reality (imperfect and transient, but living) lies at the heart of Keats' inner debate.
- Use of paradoxes, e.g. 'Heard melodies are sweet but those unheard are sweeter'.
- Memorable metaphors, e.g. 'unravished bride of silence', 'foster child of silence', etc.
- Sensuous imagery: e.g. Love is described as leaving 'a heart high-sorrowful and cloyed, / A burning forehead and a parching tongue'.
- The use of regular questions suggests the poet's imaginative engagement with the scenes depicted on the urn, e.g. 'What men or gods are these? What maidens loth?'
- Sound effects: alliteration (e.g. 'marble men and maidens', etc.), assonance (e.g. 'Sylvan historian', etc).

When I have fears that I may cease to be

In this sonnet Keats reflects on poetry, love and the transience of life. The repetition of the words 'when' and 'before' reflect his keen awareness of the passage of time. The poet's great fear is that he will die before he has achieved poetic fame or experienced perfect love. While the title of the poem underlines the poet's fear of death, this sonnet also expresses Keats' ambition and love of life.

Keats fears that death will prevent him from giving expression to all of the ideas in his fertile mind, and from realising his full potential as a poet. The metaphor of the harvest suggests the richness and fertility of the poet's imagination. He fears that he may not live long enough to harvest or express all of the ideas in his 'teeming brain'.

The second quatrain develops the idea that Keats may die before he has written all that he hopes to write. He appreciates and wishes to capture the beauty and mystery of the world, symbolised by the personified night sky ('the night's starred face') in his verse. He also wishes to write about the 'high romance', symbolised by the stars. The phrase 'the magic hand of chance' suggests the mysterious nature of the creative process. The references to night and shadows evoke the idea of death.

In the third quatrain Keats considers the possibility of time preventing him from experiencing the magical power of perfect love: 'Never have relish in the fairy power of unreflecting love.' However, he is also sharply aware of the transience of human beauty and of life itself: 'Fair creature of an hour.'

The poem concludes in a despondent manner in the rhyming couplet. When Keats considers 'love and fame' in relation to time, he is filled with a sense of gloom which is reflected in the image of the poet standing alone 'on the shore of the wide world'. Love and fame fade into unimportance or 'nothingness' when they are set against the grim, inescapable reality of life's transience.

KEY POINTS

- Key theme is the insignificance of love and poetic fame when set against the grim reality of life's transience.
- Effective use of imagery (e.g. 'on the shore of the wide world I stand alone'), metaphor (e.g. harvest metaphor), personificaton (e.g. 'the night's starred face').
- Uses Shakespearian sonnet form.
- Sound effects: assonance (e.g. 'fears . . . cease . . . gleaned . . . teeming'), alliteration (e.g. 'wide world') and end-rhyme (e.g. 'brain / grain', 'more / shore') give the poem a musical quality.
- Uses a euphemism ('When I have fears that I may cease to be') when speaking of his own death.
- Tone is ultimately one of despair.

La Belle Dame sans Merci

This poem is written in the form of a medieval ballad. It tells a story that is full of mystery, drama and uncertainty. As in other Keats' poems there is a contrast between the harshness of the real world and an ideal world of beauty and happiness.

This ballad consists of a dialogue between the knight and an unknown speaker. Stanzas 1–3 are addressed to the knight, while stanzas 4–12 express his reply. As in other Keats' poems, the real world is seen as a place of suffering. The knight looks sickly ('With anguish moist and fever dew), despondent ('So haggard and so woe-begone') and bewildered ('Alone and palely loitering'). The autumnal setting underlines the sense of desolation: 'The sedge has withered from the lake and no birds sing.' Long vowel sounds reinforce the bleak mood ('Alone . . . palely . . . woe . . . fading', etc).

The knight's meeting with this supernatural beauty ('a fairy's child' with 'wild eyes') seems to have been accidental. Everything about her is beautiful and the knight seems to be instantly enchanted by her: 'Full beautiful . . . / Her hair was long, her foot was light.' He immediately starts to woo her with garlands and bracelets of flowers: 'I made a garland for her head and bracelets too'. He put her on his 'pacing steed' and watched her 'all day long'. Once again, this poem is rich in sensuous detail: 'She looked at me as she did love / And made sweet moan . . . She found me roots of relish sweet, / And honey wild and manna-dew.' This mysterious woman speaks a strange language, yet the knight seems to understand her: 'she said / I love thee true.' Later, she took the knight to her mysterious fairy cave. The happy mood is dispelled when this enigmatic beauty is inexplicably overcome by sorrow: 'And there she wept, and sigh'd full sore'. After the knight attempts to console her 'with kisses four', she lulls him asleep.

The knight's strange experience has a nightmarish dimension – he has a vision of 'death-pale' kings, princes and warriors who warn him that he, like them, has been enslaved by 'La Belle Dame Sans Merci'. The image of their 'starved lips . . . gaped wide' is particularly grotesque and frightening. The beautiful, bewitching enchantress is closely associated with death, and may even be the embodiment of death.

At the close of the poem, the knight is back in the real world: 'And I awoke and found me here / On the cold hill's side'. He seems to have escaped from the nightmare, yet he can never escape the inevitability of death. The mood at the close of the poem is particularly bleak, with the knight isolated and seemingly without purpose or direction ('Alone and palely loitering'). The absence of birdsong ('And no birds sing') suggests that the happiness associated with birds singing is no longer possible.

Once again we see the contrast between the ideal world of beauty and happiness that the knight briefly experiences and the harsh world of reality to which he returns at the close of the poem. For a brief time the knight (perhaps representative of Keats) is captivated by a vividly imagined experience of an ideal world. However, like Keats, in both *Ode to a Nightingale* and *Ode on a Grecian Urn*, the knight, too, inevitably returns to reality.

This poem is gloomy in outlook since it suggests that love and death are inseparable. It is similar to *Ode to a Nightingale* in that both poems suggest the impermanence of love ('Where Beauty cannot keep her lustrous eyes, / Or new Love pine at them beyond tomorrow'). It resembles *Ode on a Grecian* Urn in that both poems suggest that love inevitably involves pain ('A burning forehead and a parching tongue').

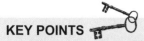

KEY POINTS

- Key theme is the contrast between the ideal beauty and happiness that the knight briefly experiences, and the harshness of the real world.
- A gloomy poem dominated by images and suggestions of death.
- The atmosphere of the poem is one of darkness and mystery.
- Vivid imagery.
- Repetition (e.g. first and last stanzas are largely similar).

To Autumn

While most poems on the subject of autumn tend to be largely gloomy reflections on death and decay, this poem celebrates the natural abundance of the autumn season. While there are suggestions of death and the passage of time, this is not a poem about life's transience; instead we see Keats delighting in the richness and beauty of the season. The sensuousness, which is a constant feature of Keats' verse, is strikingly evident in this poem. Each stanza deals with a different aspect of the autumnal world.

Stanza one opens with a wonderfully atmospheric description of autumn: 'Seasons of mists and mellow fruitfulness'. The alliterative 'm' ('mists . . . mellow . . . maturing') and repeated 'l' sounds ('mellow', 'apples', 'fill', 'shells', 'cells') suggest a sense of ease and harmony. Personified autumn is addressed in all three stanzas. In stanza one autumn is depicted as a co-conspirator with 'the maturing sun' in bringing about the seemingly unending fruitfulness of the season. Their shared work has an almost sacred quality as they 'load and bless / With fruit the vines that round the thatch-eves run'. Together, they are responsible for the weight of apples that bend the trees. The phrase 'budding more and still more' suggests unending abundance. Even the bees are deceived into thinking that this bountiful season will never end, with their hives full of honey ('For summer has o'er-brimmed their clammy cells'). Tactile imagery conveys the rich bounty of the season: autumn and the sun combine 'to swell the gourd,

and plump the hazel shells'.

In the second stanza autumn is personified as various people engaged in the diverse activities of harvesting. She is, in turn, a granary worker, a reaper, a gleaner and finally a cider maker. Autumn is largely inactive in this section of the poem. The images in this stanza are mainly visual. We see autumn 'sitting careless on a granary floor' with her hair 'soft-lifted by the winnowing wind'. The gentle, alliterative 'w' and assonant 'i' sounds create the sense of autumn's hair being lightly lifted by the wind. The image of autumn asleep 'on a half-reaped furrow' evokes a sense of ease. She is in no rush to complete the reaping and harvesting. Her lethargy suggests a sense of fulfillment. A sensuous image suggests how she is drowsy 'with the fume of poppies'. As a cider maker, autumn patiently watches over the production of cider from the abundant apples that had caused the trees to bend in stanza one: 'thou watchest the last oozings hours by hours.' The sibilance of this line underlines the sense of ease and tranquillity. Time is moving on: in the first stanza we could almost touch the ripening fruit, while in the second we can visualise the harvesting and processing of these fruits.

In stanza three time has moved on further and the harvest is done; all that now remains of it is 'the stubble-plains with rosy hue'. While this is a tactile-visual image, the imagery in this stanza is mainly aural. The poet listens to the plaintive music of autumn, the various sounds combining to create a veritable symphony: '. . . in a wailful choir the small gnats mourn . . . lambs loud bleat . . . Hedge-crickets sing . . . The red-breast whistles . . . And gathering swallows twitter in the skies.' There is a clear suggestion of death in this stanza with references to 'the soft-dying day', 'a wailful choir', the mourning gnats and the robin – a bird traditionally associated with winter. Keats is not despondent; he seems to be accepting of this natural process. He does not dwell on life's transience, but instead celebrates the distinctive beauty of autumn.

KEY POINTS

- Key theme is the abundance and distinctive beauty of autumn.
- Sensuous imagery present throughout.
- Sound effects: alliteration (e.g. 'mists and mellow fruitfulness', 'winnowing wind'), assonance (e.g. 'mourn', 'bourn'), sibilance (e.g. 'Thou watchest the last oozings hours by hours'), etc.

Bright Star

In this sonnet Keats is attracted to the permanence ('would I were steadfast as thou art') and 'splendour' of the 'bright star'. However, he is not enamoured of its detached, isolated existence. Keats describes the star as being hermit-like in its solitude: 'Like nature's patient, sleepless eremite'. Here we again see Keats' tendency to give human qualities to the natural world. As the sonnet develops, the words 'not' and 'no' make clear the poet's rejection of the star.

The star is depicted as watching over the 'moving waters' below. The poet's imagination infuses these waters with 'priestlike' powers as they cleanse 'earth's human shores'. The freshness and purity of the natural world is evoked by metaphor of the 'soft-fallen mask / Of snow upon the mountains and the moors'. Here the alliterative and sibilant 's' sound suggests the tranquillity of this winter scene, while the alliterative 'm' sound adds to the poem's musical qualities.

While the star is 'still steadfast, still unchangeable', it is also cold and remote. Keats is instead drawn to the transitory (transient or passing) but warm and vibrant world of human passion. The poet's idea of perfect happiness would be to be forever 'Pillowed upon my fair love's ripening breast, / To feel forever its soft fall and swell'. This sensuous image with its soft alliterative and sibilant 's' sound conveys the warmth of shared human love which contrasts with and highlights the cold isolation of the star. If the poet cannot forever experience this intensely passionate moment, then he would choose to 'swoon to death'.

In much of Keats' verse we see the tension between the poet's yearning for permanence and immortality, and his desire to enjoy the warm pleasures of real love.

While the transient physical world is a place of sorrow and pain, it is also the realm of passionate experience.

This sonnet resembles both *Ode to a Nightingale* and *Ode on a Grecian Urn* in that in all three poems Keats is drawn to the idea of an unchanging ideal world, before accepting the need to return to reality. Ultimately, permanence is not enough for the poet. The enduring splendour of the cold star, like the timeless perfection of the cold Grecian urn, cannot ultimately satisfy Keats who longs to forever savour the 'sweet unrest' of passionate love.

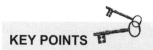

KEY POINTS

- Key theme is the contrasting attractions of the constant but cold star and the transient but warm world of human passion.
- Contrasting imagery: coldness and isolation of the star ('in lone splendour hung aloft the night') contrasted with the shared experience of warm human love ('pillowed upon my fair love's ripening breast, / To feel forever its soft rise and fall').
- Personification of nature: the star is 'like nature's patient, sleepless eremite'.
- Sound effects: Alliterative and sibilant 's' sound evokes the sense of perfect peace and happiness that accompanies the shared experience of human love.

Sample Answer

Explain why the poetry of Keats did or did not appeal to you.

The poetry of Keats greatly appealed to me for a range of reasons. Purely on a descriptive level, I love the way he uses sensuous imagery to convey the beauty of the natural world.

Few poets appreciate and celebrate beauty like Keats. On a deeper level Keats grapples with some issues of universal relevance in his work, reflecting on such matters as mortality, the pain of life, the search for permanence in a world of change and the power of the imagination. At the heart of much of Keats' poetry are the conflicting attractions of art and reality. While art is perfect and timeless, it can also be cold and lifeless. In contrast, while reality is painful and transient, it can also be vibrant and passionate. We can all relate to Keats' inner struggles as the issues that preoccupy him are universal and timeless. In the context of these inner struggles, another quality I greatly admire about Keats strongly emerges – his realism. Finally, I was impressed with the various sound effects Keats so effectively employs in his verse.

A simple poem that I greatly enjoyed is *To one who has been long in city pent*. Weary of the confinement of the city, Keats is rejuvenated by the natural world as he lies back in the long grass reading 'a gentle tale of love and languishment'. I like the way Keats regularly gives human qualities to the natural world, in this poem personifying the sky with his reference to 'the smile of the blue firmament'. However, his realism expresses itself before the sonnet ends when he reminds us of the transience of this uplifting day by comparing its passing to the fall of an angel's tear from heaven to earth.

In *Bright Star* Keats is attracted to the permanence and 'splendour' of the 'bright star'. However, he is not attracted to its detached, isolated existence. Keats sees the star as being hermit-like in its solitude: 'Like nature's patient, sleepless eremite.' The beauty of nature in winter is captured in the memorable image of the 'soft-fallen mask / Of snow upon the mountains'. The alliterative and sibilant 's' sound evokes a sense of perfect peace. While the star is 'still steadfast, still unchangeable', Keats is drawn back to the real world. His idea of perfect happiness would be to be forever 'Pillowed upon my fair love's ripening breast, / To feel forever its soft fall and swell'. This beautiful sensuous image with its soft sibilant and alliterative 's' sound conveys the warmth of shared human love that is ultimately more appealing to the poet than the existence of the immortal, but cold, star. The tension between Keats' yearning for immortality and his desire to enjoy the passionate pleasures of real love is apparent in much of his verse.

I regard *Ode to a Nightingale* as one of the truly great poems. In this poem we see Keats' intense desire to escape from the painful, transient physical world into the perfect immortal world of the nightingale's song. Like many people at difficult moments in their lives, Keats considers alcohol as a possible avenue of escape. He describes the wine in sensuous detail – one of the features of his verse that I particularly enjoy. We can almost taste the wine that has been 'cooled a long age in the deep-delved earth' and visualise 'the beaded bubbles winking at the brim'. The alliterative 'd' and 'b' sounds underscore the sensuous appeal of the wine, by means of which Keats hopes to fade away with the nightingale 'into the forest dim'. When he dismisses the idea of using alcohol to reach the perfect world of the nightingale's song, the poet finally accesses it by means of his imagination, flying there on 'the viewless wings of Poesy'. The world of the nightingale's song is rich in sensuous appeal. Here Keats can smell the 'soft incense' that 'hangs upon the boughs', taste 'the dewy wine' and hear 'the murmurous haunt of flies on summer eves'. However, we can sense the poet's realism asserting itself in the suggestions of death and decay to be found in the references to the 'embalmed darkness' and the murmuring flies. Ultimately, Keats realises that the imagination cannot offer him a lasting means of escape: 'Adieu! adieu! The fancy cannot cheat so well / As she is famed to do'. The wonderful, magical journey inspired by the bird's song is over and the poet returns to the world of reality. I can certainly understand Keats' longing to escape life's problems and transience, but I am impressed with the realism that brings him back to the physical world.

In *Ode on a Grecian Urn* we again see Keats' desire for permanence in a world of transience. The Grecian urn, like the nightingale's song, is a symbol of lasting perfection. The metaphors of the 'still unravished bride of quietness' and 'foster child of silence' effectively evoke the stillness and tranquillity of the urn. In the early part of the poem Keats asserts that art (symbolic of the power of the imagination) is superior to reality when he claims that the music played by the piper in one of the pastoral scenes depicted on the urn is more beautiful than real music because it appeals, not to the ear, but to the spirit or the imagination: 'Heard melodies are sweet, but those unheard / Are sweeter . . .'

Keats also suggests that the everlasting love of the figures on the urn is superior to real human passion. However, we get the impression that he 'doth protest too much' with the repetition of 'happy' when describing this love: 'More happy love! more happy, happy love! / For ever happy and still to be enjoyed.' There is a clear suggestion that the love depicted on the urn lacks the vibrancy and warmth of real human passion: 'All breathing human passion far above, / That leaves a heart high sorrowful and cloy'd, / A burning forehead and a parching tongue.' While human love is subject to change and can involve disappointment and pain, Keats realises that art, although perfect and timeless, is also cold and lifeless. Moving on to another scene portrayed on the urn, the poet captures the ritual sacrifice of a heifer in a typically sensuous image: 'that heifer lowing at the skies, / And all her silken flanks with garlands dressed.' In the final stanza, the poet leaves the world of the imagination and returns to the world of reality. For all its perfection, the urn remains a cold artifact, a mere reflection of real life as Keats' references to 'marble men and maidens', 'thou silent form' and 'Cold Pastoral!' clearly suggest. Another aspect of this poem that I enjoyed is the manner in which Keats leaves us grappling with his controversial declaration that 'Beauty is truth, truth beauty'.

The Keats' poem that I most enjoyed was *To Autumn*. While the title leads us to expect a despondent reflection on transience and death, what we actually get is a wonderful description and celebration of the overflowing abundance of the season. The sensuousness that I particularly admire in Keats' verse is again strikingly evident in this poem. The poem opens with a wonderfully atmospheric description of autumn: 'Season of mists and mellow fruitfulness, / Close bosom-friend of the maturing sun.' The alliterative 'm' ('mists . . . mellow . . . maturing') and repeated 'i' sounds evoke a sense of ease and harmony. Tactile imagery conveys the rich bounty of the season as autumn and sun combine 'to swell the gourd, and plump the hazel shells'. Autumn is brought to life as Keats personifies her as a variety of workers involved in the diverse activities of harvesting. The images in the second stanza of the poem are mainly, but not entirely, visual. We see autumn 'sitting carelessly on a granary floor' with her hair 'soft-lifted by the winnowing wind'. The gentle, alliterative 'w' and assonant 'i' sounds create the sense of autumn's hair being lightly lifted by the wind. The image of autumn asleep 'on a half-reaped furrow' evokes a sense of ease. Another sensuous image portrays her as being drowsy 'with the fume of poppies'. In the final stanza, the harvesting has been completed and all that now remains of the harvest is 'the stubble-plains with rosy hue'. While this is a tactile-visual image, the images in this stanza are predominantly aural. Keats listens to the plaintive music of autumn: 'in a wailful choir the small gnats mourn . . . lambs loud bleat . . . Hedge-crickets sing . . . The red-breast whistles . . . And gathering swallows twitter in the skies.' While the references to 'the soft-dying day', mourning gnats and 'a wailful choir' evoke the idea of death, Keats is not despondent. He is accepting of this natural process and does not dwell on the passage of time, choosing instead to celebrate the unique beauty and richness of autumn.

In conclusion, I would only like to restate my great admiration for and genuine enjoyment of the work of John Keats, a truly great poet.

Gerard Manley Hopkins

Biographical Note

Gerard Hopkins (1844–1889) was born to Manley and Catherine Hopkins. Gerard was the first of their nine children. Although he ultimately wrote no more than 40 mature poems, he is regarded as one of the major English poets. His parents were High Church Anglicans, and his father, a marine insurance adjuster, also published a volume of poetry. His talented family encouraged his artistic nature. In 1854 he entered Highgate School where he distinguished himself as a gifted student, winning a poetry prize after he began to write Keatsian nature poetry. He went on to win a scholarship to Balliol College, Oxford (1863-1867). At Oxford he searched for a religion that could speak with true authority – it was here that he came under the influence of John Henry Newman. In 1864 Hopkins was deeply moved by his reading of Newman's *Apologia Pro Vita Sua* which explained the reasons for his conversion to Catholicism. In 1866 Hopkins was received by Newman into the Catholic Church.

In 1868 Hopkins resolved to become a priest and he entered Manresa House, a Jesuit novitiate near London. Following three years of theological studies in St. Beuno's College in North Wales, Hopkins served as assistant to the parish priest in Sheffield, Oxford and London from 1877 until 1879 before going on to work as a parish priest in the slums of Manchester, Liverpool and Glasgow. Hopkins was appointed as Professor of Greek and Latin at University College Dublin in 1884. He taught there until he died of typhoid fever, after a long period of ill health, on 8 June 1889.

It is important to be aware of the unique features of Hopkins' style if his poetry is to be fully appreciated. Two key literary terms which Hopkins personally created must be understood. 'Inscape' refers to the essential inner nature of a person, an object, etc. For Hopkins, inscape is 'the species of individually distinctive beauty'. This term has also been defined as 'the revelation of God's energy to one's senses through nature'. The second poetic concept developed by Hopkins is 'sprung rhythm' which, in essence, relates to a new metre based on the counting of stresses rather than syllables.

God's Grandeur

Hopkins is a poet of intense emotions. This poem unifies feelings of both ecstasy and distress. Since this poem was composed in 1877, the year he was ordained as a priest, Hopkins is unsurprised that mankind may have disfigured and violated the earth, but contends that an unending freshness and a charged magnificence bring life to the natural world.

In the first quatrain of the octave in this sonnet, the poet portrays a natural world that is animated by God's existence. Similar to an electrical current, God's presence briefly develops into beams of light 'like shining from shook foil'. The poet goes on to compare the presence of God in the world to 'the ooze of oil /Crushed'. These clear and palpable demonstrations of God's existence in the world prompt the poet to pose a serious question which sees him wondering why we do not pay attention to God's authority, 'Why do men then not now reck his rod?'

Once again, the poet makes efficient and impressive use of both assonance ('ooze...oil') and alliteration ('reck his reed') – in this instance to underscore his serious, disheartened mood.

Onomatopoeia is also employed to good effect, with the repetition of 'trod' ('Generations have trod, have trod, have trod), conveying a sense of unending and tedious exertion.

This poem is written in the traditional form of a Petrarchan sonnet, with the octave normally setting a question or a difficulty and the sestet offering a decision on these matters that resolves them.

The theme that dominates this poem is the deep connection between man, nature and God. A related theme is the freedom Hopkins felt to resolve his religious faith with his love of nature. Indeed his capacity to see God in nature is also an obvious theme in many of his poems. Another theme of this poem that Hopkins explores is the contrast between the everlasting newness of nature and the deterioration of the appearance of the earth because of human behaviour.

The sestet displays Hopkin's intense belief in nature's capacity to regenerate itself. It also demonstrates his deep religious beliefs. The regeneration of nature imagined by Hopkins is controlled by the Holy Ghost, pondering over the earth with 'warm breast' and 'bright wings' and guaranteeing its productivity. As Hopkins puts it, in spite of all the oppression and misuse of the earth by people, 'nature is never spent'.

The closing image is not readily visualised. The enormous world has developed into the bird's nest and the warmth and sparkling contained within the image is comforting and consoling. The everyday language in the final lines heightens the accessibility of the poem, 'Oh, morning at the brown brink eastward, springs - / Because the Holy Ghost over the bent / World broods with warm breast and with ah! bright wings'.

KEY POINTS

- This poem shows us that Hopkins is a poet of deep emotions, with this poem combining feelings of both elation and despondency.
- In the first quatrain of the octave in this sonnet, the poet portrays a natural world that is enlivened by God's existence.
- Once again, the poet makes efficient and impressive use of sound effects.
- This poem is composed in the conventional form of a Petrarchan sonnet.
- A variety of themes are identifiable in this poem, particularly the poet's ability to see God in nature.
- The sestet displays Hopkin's intense belief in nature's capacity to regenerate itself.
- The closing image is not readily visualised.
- The everyday language in the final lines heightens the accessibility of the poem.

Spring

This is one of Hopkins' most renowned poems. It commences with an authoritative, forceful declaration that is incontrovertibly true, 'Nothing is so beautiful as spring –'.

This is then supported by a myriad of examples of nature's beauty and richness, '. . . weeds, in wheels, shoot long and lovely and lush; / Thrush's eggs look little low heavens, and thrush / Through the echoing timber does so rinse and wring / The ear, it strikes like lightnings to hear him sing'. Hopkins' willingness to commemorate weeds rather than flowers, for example, highlights his ability to see beauty in the everyday world.

There is an elated tone throughout the octave. Hopkins' control of sound effects is both efficient and impressive, 'When weeds, in wheels, shoot long and lovely and lush'. The alliteration of 'w' and 'l' in addition to the assonance of 'ee' and 'o' enhance this depiction of rich growth. We can visualise the wild flowers growing as we observe them.

The vitality of the new plants is captured in the verb 'shoot'. The beauty of the natural world has much to do with its eye-catching combination of colours such as the speckled appearance of the thrush's eggs (which are so impressive, they 'look little low heavens') and the variegated (multicoloured) blue and white in the sky. Once again, Hopkins' use of sound effects proves particularly effective, with the alliterative 'b', 'r' and 'f' sounds ('The descending blue; that blue is all in a rush / With richness; the racing lambs too have fair their fling') helping to convey nature's unique beauty.

Similar to virtually all of Hopkins' other poems, the impetus behind this one is essentially religious. Heaven and earth are brought closer together here; it is almost as if heaven is on earth. The advent of spring sets Hopkins thinking about Adam and Eve's loss of the Garden of Eden following their loss of innocence.

As is always the case with a Petrarchan sonnet, the descriptive octave is followed by a reflective sestet that analyses the ideas raised earlier. Hopkins associates spring with the youthful freedom from sin. This is why he appeals to Christ to watch over the young and to protect their innocence, or else they will become 'sour with sinning'.

In the concluding line Hopkins pictures Christ as a boy and Mary as a young maid, 'Most, O maid's child, thy choice and worthy the winning'.

KEY POINTS

- Poem opens with a dramatic declaration of the beauty of spring.
- There is an elated tone throughout the octave.
- Hopkins' use of sound effects is both efficient and impressive.
- The impetus behind this poem is essentially religious.
- As is always the case with a Petrarchan sonnet, the descriptive octave leads on to a reflective sestet.
- Among the broad themes in which Hopkins is interested are innocence and the physical demonstration of God's beauty in the human and natural worlds.

As kingfishers catch fire, dragonflies draw flame

This is a poem which commemorates uniqueness. Every natural thing is distinctive. The poem begins with memorably graphic images, 'As kingfishers catch fire, dragonflies draw flame; / As tumbled over rim in roundy wells'. In these lines Hopkins portrays the flash of the sun on the wings of the kingfisher and the dragonfly.

The sonnet confirms the uniqueness of every created thing. Hopkins portrays everything in the world around him from birds (kingfishers), insects (dragonflies) and inanimate stones to human beings trying to declare their identity. In doing this, everything gives glory to God. It is important to remember what, for Hopkins, makes his poetry so distinctive and special in terms of God and nature. For the poet, inscape is 'the species of individually distinctive beauty'. This term has also been defined as 'the revelation of God's energy to one's senses through nature'.

Aural imagery presents us with a range of everyday sounds that help to convey the distinctiveness of our existence and to see the individuality of everything around us as a manifestation of God's greatness. This is achieved through the use of onomatopoeia

('Stones ring') and, more particularly, alliteration ('fire... flame', 'rim... roundy... ring', 'tucked... tells', 'finds... fling', 'grace... goings graces', 'Lovely... lovely', 'Father... features... faces').

Once again, Hopkins employs the Petrarchan sonnet form. The theme of the poem is the physical demonstration of God's beauty in the human and natural worlds. At the heart of this poem is Hopkins' desire to give the reader a convincing example of his theory of inscape. He views God's sanctity (divinity) as the obvious and indisputable quintessence of His unique nature.

There is a striking contrast between the vividly descriptive octave and the reflective sestet. In the sestet of this sonnet Hopkins meditates on the distinctiveness of human beings. He believes that a human's most important quality is freedom of choice. They can select or reject the idea of giving glory to God. They communicate their individuality by complying with God's will, 'I say more; the just man justices; / Keeps grace; that keeps all his goings graces'. In agreeing with God's will, human beings make God present in the world.

KEY POINTS

- Key theme is the celebration of the uniqueness of every natural thing.
- Aural imagery provides us with a variety of everyday sounds that help to convey the uniqueness of our existence.
- Once again Hopkins uses the Petrarchan sonnet form, with the descriptive octave being followed by the reflective sestet.
- Hopkin's utilisation of sound effects (onomatopoeia and, more particularly, alliteration) proves to be highly effective.

The Windhover

The Windhover is a profoundly personal poem, with 'I' being the first word ('I caught this morning morning's minion') and 'my' featuring before the end of the octave ('My heart in hiding').

The opening line engages the reader's interest such is the sense of immediacy it creates: '... this morning morning's minion...'. Hopkins is exhilarated and strikingly affected by his encounter with the bird ('My heart in hiding /

Stirred for a bird…').

In this poem Hopkins commemorates the inimitable nature of the bird and the intensity of his relationship with 'Christ our Lord' (the poem's subtitle) – a relationship which develops through the poet's ability to see God in nature.

The bird's name derives from its habit of hovering in the air as it struggles to cope with the power of the wind, with its head in the wind. The windhover is a falcon which is likened to a knight. This image is developed by using the language of chivalry. The poet visualises the bird to be a knight on horseback fighting against the wind. The image of the windhover as a knight is also evocative of Christ, whom the poet names 'my chevalier', reflecting images of chivalry and knighthood.

This is certainly one of Hopkins' best-known, most discussed and best-loved poems. Hopkins himself described it as 'the best thing I ever wrote'. It is obviously open to a variety of interpretations, both literal and symbolic. There are even regular disagreements over the meaning of ambiguous words. One source of difficulty is Hopkins' use of the term 'Buckle!', the meaning of which is much debated – it could mean either 'collapse' or 'give way under pressure'. Another source of difficulty is the group of words 'To ring upon the rein', which may be a riding-school term, while 'to ring' is also a technical term of falconry.

The Windhover was written in Hopkins' final year of study in 1877 before being ordained as a priest. He expresses his respect and admiration for the beauty and wonder, strength and energy of the windhover, while also highlighting its praiseworthy individuality. The poem is dedicated to Christ, implying that while the poet is writing about nature, his primary theme is a spiritual one. This subtitle was added later with a view to accentuating the poem's religious importance.

Hopkins writes this poem in the form of a sonnet – a structure he commonly employs. He evokes the energy of the bird's movement by using alliteration and assonance, 'I caught this morning morning's minion, king- / dom of daylight's dauphin, dapple-dawn-drawn Falcon, in his riding / Of the rolling level underneath him steady air, and striding…'. The use of 'riding', 'rolling', 'striding' and 'wimpling' evoke the movement of the windhover in flight.

The vividly descriptive octave is followed by a discursive, analytical sestet. The falcon is juxtaposed to a knight. This image is advanced by using the language of chivalry. The poet pictures the bird as a knight on horseback fighting against the wind. The image of the windhover as a knight is also evocative of Christ whom the poet addresses as 'my chevalier'. Having portrayed the attractive nature of the bird's flight in the octave, Hopkins compares the beauty of the bird to that of Christ. He views Christ as 'a billion / Times told lovelier, more dangerous…' The image of the fire is indicative of Christ fighting against evil exactly as the bird fights against the wind. It is interesting to note that the octave may present the falcon as an emblem of Christ's sacrifice. The outstretched wings may symbolise the outstretched arms of Christ on the Cross.

In the sestet the fire image is introduced and continues to the final line. The embers appear lifeless, but when they collapse, the glowing heart of the fire is to be seen. The 'O my chevalier' develops into Christ in the hawk. In the concluding three lines the poet speaks of 'the sheer plod' of the religious life. The image of the ploughman showing the shine on the soil as he ploughs is comparable with the light which the demanding work of the religious brings to the poet. In the final two lines we have a suggestion of reward following labour as 'blue-bleak' develops into 'gold-vermilion'.

- A profoundly personal poem.
- The opening line engages the reader's interest, such is the sense of immediacy it creates.
- The intensity of the poet's relationship with God develops through his capacity to see God in nature.
- The poem is open to a variety of interpretations, both literal and symbolic.
- The poem is written in the form of a sonnet, with the vividly descriptive octave followed by the discursive and analytical sestet.
- The poem concludes on an optimistic note, with 'blue-bleak' being transformed into 'gold-vermilion'.

Pied Beauty

This is a shortened version of the conventional sonnet with ten and a half lines instead of the traditional fourteen. This is known as a curtailed sonnet form. In this poem man's presence is perceived to be in accord with God's creation. It starts and finishes with words of admiration, while advancing from the past ('brinded', 'plotted', 'pieced', 'freckled') to the present tense ('Who knows how?...Praise him').

Pied Beauty is a hymn of praise to God for the infinite diversity of nature. The opening line is filled with words of acclaim for God, 'Glory be to God for dappled things – '. This prayer-like beginning is then accompanied by a litany of vivid examples of the 'dappled' beauty to be located in the natural world. Hopkins includes the mottled blue and white colours of the sky, the 'brinded' (streaked) hide of a cow and the patches of contrasting colour on a trout. The chestnut presents us with a more complex and challenging image as we try to visualise its interior after it is compared to the coals in a fire ('Fresh-firecoal chestnut falls'), black on the outside and glowing within. The wings of finches are variegated, as is patchwork-like farmland. The final example is of the 'trades' (occupations) and activities of man, with their variety of materials and equipment, 'Fresh –firecoal chestnut-falls; finches' wings; / landscape plotted and pierced – fold, fallow and plough; /And all trades, their gear and tackle and trim'. Here we once again see Hopkins' effective use of alliteration enhancing the poem's musical qualities. More significantly, man is depicted as being in harmony with God's creation.

In the concluding five lines, Hopkins gives moral characteristics to the miscellaneous images on which he has expanded up to this point in terms of physical qualities. At this moment we are presented with a new idea or image: God is to be praised. Hopkins claims that the examples he has given are creations of God which highlight the unity and permanence of His power and inspire us to 'Praise Him'.

- This is a miniturised version of the conventional sonnet (also known as 'curtailed').
- It is a hymn of praise to God for the infinite diversity of nature.
- Effective use of alliteration.
- Man is portrayed as being in harmony with God's creation.
- God begins and ends this poem.

Felix Randal

This poem is written in the form of a Petrarchan sonnet and follows the traditional structure of this sonnet, with the descriptive octave followed by a reflective sestet.

Hopkins wrote this sonnet when he was working as a priest in Liverpool. This is one of the few poems in which he names an individual man and identifies his occupation, 'Felix Randal the farrier, O he is dead then? My duty all ended,'. The 'duty' to which the poet refers is the healing duty of the priest. In this poem, we see the ultimately fatal impact of a physical illness on the blacksmith, a strong, healthy man. The repetition of 'pining' evokes the gradual nature of this illness. Tragically, in addition to his physical decline, the poet's psychological health clearly deteriorated, '…watched his mould of man, big-boned and hardy–handsome / Pining, pining, till time when reason rambled in it…'. A combination of an unnamed four deadly ailments sadly caused the collapse of the blacksmith's balance of mind: '…and some / Fatal four disorders, fleshed there, all contended?'

Lines 5-9 open dramatically with the abrupt declaration, 'Sickness broke him'. The comfort that religion can bring is a significant feature of Hopkins' work. Perceiving himself to be primarily a priest in his poet-priest role, Hopkins recalls how he comforted and consoled the blacksmith, helping him to come to terms with the illness he had earlier cursed. He anointed Randal for the Last Rites before hearing his confession and giving him the Eucharist, '…I had our sweet reprieve and ransom / Tendered to him. Ah well, God rest him all road ever he offended!'

Following the traditional structure of the Petrarchan sonnet, the vividly descriptive octave is followed by the interesting observations of the sestet which focus on Hopkins' encounter with sickness and death. Tending the sick and looking after their needs encourages us to value them more. Hopkins recognises from his contact with Randal that there is a mutual exchange of love in hard times, with the terms 'touched', 'endures' and 'tears' conveying the profound nature of his emotions.

The poem concludes on an undeniably upbeat note with the underlying idea that Hopkins the priest becomes God's blacksmith, preparing shoes for the great dray horse for his journey into the next world. The final image of 'his bright and battering sandal!' is particularly optimistic, with the loud, alliterative 'b' sound suggestive of Hopkins' power and energy.

One of the most appealing features of this poem is the regular use of everyday language, 'Impatient he cursed at first, but mended / Being anointed and all, / Ah well, God rest him all road ever he offended!' Such colloquialisms ensure the accessibility of the content, themes and language of the poem.

KEY POINTS

- Written in the form of a Petrarchan sonnet.
- One of the few poems in which Hopkins names an individual man and identifies his profession.
- The poet suffers both physically and psychologically.
- Lines 5-9 open dramatically with the abrupt declaration, 'Sickness broke him'.
- Hopkins perceives himself to be primarily a priest in his poet-priest role.
- One of the most appealing features of this poem is the regular use of simple, everyday speech, which ensures it is readily accessible in terms of its content, themes and language.

- The poem concludes on an incontrovertibly optimistic note. The final image of 'his bright and battering sandal!' is particularly upbeat, with the loud, alliterative 'b' sound suggestive of Hopkins' power and energy.

Inversnaid

The inspiration for this poem originates in Hopkins' desire for the uncontrolled, tranquil and appealing world of the Scottish Highlands, where he sojourned only very briefly. The poem to some extent commemorates the unruly magnificence of the Scottish Highlands, a pleasing difference from the unattractive nature of such industrial cities as Liverpool and Glasgow where Hopkins served as a priest.

Hopkins' ability to see God in nature is an admirable feature of much of his verse. The poet tries to provide a precise portrayal of a highland stream, 'This darksome burn, horseback brown, / His rollrock highroad roaring down, / In coop and in comb the fleece of his foam / Flutes and low to the lake falls home'. Sadly, the poem's opening line evokes a similarly unappealing, disheartening world, with the dark water's implication of a polluted rural earth.

The effective use of alliteration evokes the speedy movement of the dark stream, '… burn… brown', 'rollrock… roaring', 'coop.,… comb', 'fleece… foam…/ Flutes…. falls'. The employment of onomatopoeia ('roaring') is similarly efficient and impressive in that it creates an aural image that enables us to imagine the distinctive noise of the Highlands.

The Scots-English nature of the language roots this poem in a quickly identifiable world, and results in the type of colloquial expressions that are easily comprehensible. Examples of such distinctive terms include 'burn', 'in coop and in comb', 'flutes', 'twindles', 'degged', 'groins of the braes', 'heathpacks', 'beadbonny ash' etc.

KEY POINTS

- This poem celebrates the natural world but, unlike so many other poems, this poem celebrates its creation, without speaking of God.
- The poet's use of sound effects is once again efficient and impressive.
- The Scots-English nature of the language roots this poem in a quickly identifiable world, and results in the type of colloquial expressions that are easily comprehensible.

I wake and feel the fell of dark, not day

This is one of the three sonnets known as the 'terrible sonnets' in which Hopkins plumbs the depths of despair. There is general agreement that this is the darkest of the terrible sonnets. This sonnet provides us with disturbing insights into the poet's primary psychological problem of severe depression. This poem portrays an inner world of gloom and hopelessness. In many respects, this is the most vivid of the terrible sonnets. The imagery deftly reflects the anguish of awakening in a state of total hopelessness. The initial image is palpable in nature, with the poet claiming to 'feel the fell of dark'.

The opening lines portray an experience familiar to depressives, many of whom awaken long in advance of the sun rising and endure anguish revealed in this poem in a frightening recomposition of an arousal from sleep in the blackness of night. We also perceive the poet's sense of an unseen evil around him. In this context 'fell' is a central term, with a double meaning – it may be interpreted as threat/ blow and also as an animal's skin, a truly horrifying image.

This sonnet evokes a sense of prevalent darkness. The poet awakens, anticipating the light of day, but discovers that he is engulfed by darkness. He clearly perceives the seemingly endless nightfall to be a threat, 'I wake and feel the fell of dark, not day. / What hours, O what black hours we have spent / This night!' The darkness of the night is evocative of the darkness of Hopkins' soul. The dark hours seem never-ending, '... where I say / Hours I mean years, mean life'. His cries for God's assistance are compared to unanswered letters, making God appear remote and coldly indifferent to his plight, 'And my lament / Is cries countless, cries like dead letters sent / To dearest him that lives alas! away'.

The traditional symbolism of light and darkness is very prevalent in this sonnet. While darkness indicates spiritual despair, daylight implies hope and consolation which are sadly regarded as far away.

The theme of the poem may be the poet's sense of being abandoned by God and lacking support. It also depicts his sense of self-loathing: In the sestet Hopkins attempts to explain why God has forsaken him, 'I am gall, I am heartburn'. He employs the image of yeast souring 'the dull dough' to show how his failings have soured his soul and have undermined his spiritual relationship with God.

KEY POINTS

- The key theme of the poem is spiritual suffering.
- The poem provides us with insights into the psychological problem of severe depression.
- This sonnet evokes a sense of prevalent darkness.
- The traditional imagery of light and darkness is very common in the poem.
- The conclusion of the poem reveals the poet's sympathy for others.

No worst, there is none. Pitched past pitch of grief

The poem opens with one of the most profound declarations of suffering ever made by a poet, 'No worst, there is none'. The use of the superlative persuades us that this is no overstatement, but a direct expression of reality.

This is one of the most dismal of the 'terrible sonnets'. This is a cry of despondency and spiritual agony. Hopkins conveys profound torment, believing that God has forsaken him. In this sonnet he is plumbing the depths of mental distress. There is no optimism and no spiritual sustenance. His only consolation is that death will bring a conclusion to his inner pain, while sleep offers him a brief break from his suffering.

In a memorable opening the poet declares that suffering has no limit and that pain will inevitably be heightened, 'No worst, there is none. Pitched past pitch of grief, / More pangs will, schooled at forepangs, wilder wring'. At this point Hopkins seeks assistance from the Holy Spirit, 'Comforter, where, where is your comforting?' The repetition of 'where' under-scores his despondency and communicates a sense of total dependency.

The deep inner suffering which the poet endures is revealed through his use of frightening, horrifying metaphors. His mind is a fathomless pit. He resembles a climber hanging over the edge of the steep, sheer face of a cliff. Alliteration underscores his cries for assistance, 'My cries heave, herds-long; huddle in a main, a chief / Woe, world-sorrow…'. Hopkins' feeling of abandonment is underlined by his direct appeals to the Holy Ghost and to the Mother of God, 'Comforter, where, where is your comforting? / Mary, mother of us, where is your relief?' He communicates here the sense of a man who believes himself unfairly treated and forsaken.

The sestet is a reflection on what has passed. The image of the mountain with the frail figure clinging to it, buffeted by the gales, and tempted to release his hold is suggested by the 'mountains' and the 'cliffs of fall'. These also symbolise the ups and downs of the spiritual life of mankind.

In the most renowned passage of the poem ('O the mind, mind has mountains; cliffs of fall / Frightful, sheer, no-man-fathomed, Hold them cheap / May who ne'er hung there'), we have the presentation of a terrified, despairing mind in terms of a mountain climber falling into an abyss.

The sonnet concludes on a hint of hope. Death ends even the most dismal life and sleep ends the most gloomy day, '…all / Life death does end and each day dies with sleep'.

KEY POINTS

- The poem opens with one of the most intense declarations of suffering ever made by a poet.
- This is one of the most dismal of the terrible sonnets.
- Written in the traditional form of a Petrarchan sonnet, with the descriptive octave followed by a reflective sestet.
- The poem concludes in a slightly optimistic mood.
- Key themes are mental and spiritual suffering and abandonment by God.

Thou art indeed just, Lord, if I contend

Although Hopkins had a strong religious faith, in this sonnet he wonders why his goodness goes unrewarded. In the opening two lines he acknowledges the righteousness of God when he complains to Him ('if I contend'), but believes that his questioning of God's justice is justifiable, 'Why do sinners' ways prosper? And why must / Disappointment all I endeavour end?'

He addresses God as 'Lord', accepting that he is fair-minded. But if he is genuinely fair, why does he allow goodness to go unrewarded? The poet has dedicated his life to God, while those who are the 'sots and thralls of lust' appear to prosper unscrutinised. If God was his enemy, Hopkins could understand why He has not in some way honoured him. On the contrary, God is his friend.

He is clearly hurt that God permits the wicked to thrive, while God's servants suffer. While recognising God's justice, he declares the justice of his own cause. The case is put respectfully ('Sir'), with the formal language of the courtroom being employed to evoke a sense of fairness. The questions he poses in the first quatrain reflect his sense of frustration. The questions continue in the second quatrain. If God was his enemy, he could not hurt him more. The drunkards and 'the sots and thralls of lust' can at least enjoy their sins, while he seemingly has no reward for his life of service. It is sadly ironic that those who gratify their sensuous desires appear to thrive, while he himself, who dedicated his entire life to God, appears to encounter only frustration, 'Oh, the sots and thralls of lust / Do in spare hours more thrive than I that spend, / Sir, life upon thy cause'.

In the sestet the poet contrasts the productivity of nature with his own infertility. Effective use of imagery conveys the rich abundance of the natural world, 'See, banks and brakes / Now leaved how thick! Laced they are again / With fretty chervil…'

The alliterative sound effects enhance the musical quality of the sonnet. The images of life, the growing plants and the nest-building birds highlight and sharply contrast with his own creative sterility, '…birds build – but not I build; no, but strain, / Time's eunuch, and not breed one work that wakes'. The cruel self-image ('Time's eunuch') may indicate his inability to find inspiration to glorify God through his poetry.

While God was reverentially referred to as 'my chevalier' in The Windhover, here the poet addresses him formally as 'Lord' and 'Sir'. We get the impression that Hopkins is placing himself at a distance from God.

There is a striking absence in this sonnet of Hopkins' positive spirituality as conveyed in his earlier poems. The image of the anvil contrasts with the use of a similar image in Felix Randal. In this poem there is the idea that the blacksmith is forging his soul into shape. Here, in contrast, Hopkins' soul is being battered on 'an age-old anvil'.

Although the poem may be interpreted as a complaint to God, it concludes in a serious prayer to God to make him fruitful, 'O thou lord of life, send my roots rain'. The image of a plant in need of rain is suggestive of Hopkins in need of creative sustenance.

KEY POINTS
- A deeply personal poem.
- Written in the form of a Petrarchan sonnet.
- Key themes are intense psychological suffering and his wrestling with his religious faith.
- In the sestet, the poet contrasts the productivity of nature with his own infertility.
- Effective use of imagery throughout the poem.
- The alliterative sound effects enhance the musical quality of the poem.

Sample Answer

A Personal Response

Notwithstanding the fact that he was born and died in the nineteenth century, Hopkins' poetry retains its relevance for the twentieth century reader. I admire many aspects of his style, particularly his creation of the inscape literary theory which refers to the essential inner nature of a person. It is good to be reminded that we are all unique in our own way. For Hopkins, inscape is 'the species of individually distinctive beauty'. He also defined this term as 'the revelation of God's energy to one's senses through nature'.

I also like Hopkins' use of the Petrarchan sonnet because it ensures variety in the content of much of his poetry, with the vividly descriptive octave being followed by a reflective sestet. It is interesting to note the variety of moods in his poetry. While many of his poems are downbeat in mood given that they are concerned with exploring the theme of depression, other poems are strikingly more optimistic. Another appealing aspect of his verse is the regular use of everyday language that ensures the accessibility of its content and themes. A final feature of his poetry that impressed me is his efficient use of sound effects.

With *Felix Randal* following the traditional structure of the Petrarchan sonnet, the vividly descriptive octave is followed by the interesting observations of the sestet which focus on Hopkins' encounter with sickness and death. Tending the sick and looking after their needs encourages us to value them more, while assisting us to respect our own innate worth. Hopkins recognises from his contact with Randal that there is a mutual exchange of love in hard times, with the terms 'touched', 'endures' and 'tears' conveying the profound nature of his emotions.

The poem concludes on an undeniably upbeat note with the underlying idea that Hopkins the priest becomes God's blacksmith, preparing shoes for the great dray horse for his journey into the next world. The final image of 'his bright and battering sandal!' is particularly optimistic, with the loud, alliterative 'b' sound suggestive of Hopkins' power and energy.

One of the most appealing features of this poem is the regular use of everyday language, 'Impatient he cursed at first, but mended / Being anointed and all, / Ah well, God rest him all road ever he offended!'. Such colloquialisms ensure the accessibility of the content and themes of the poem.

The Windhover is certainly one of Hopkins' best-known, most discussed and best-loved poems. Hopkins himself described it as 'the best thing I ever wrote'. It is obviously open to a variety of interpretations, both literal and symbolic. There are even regular disagreements over the meaning of ambiguous words. One source of difficulty is Hopkins' use of the term 'Buckle!', the meaning of which is much debated – it could mean either 'collapse' or 'give way under pressure'. Another source of difficulty is the group of words 'To ring upon the rein' which may be a riding-school term, while 'to ring' is also a technical term of falconry.

The vividly descriptive octave is followed by a discursive, analytical sestet. The falcon is juxtaposed to a knight. This image is advanced by using the language of chivalry. Hopkins' use of imagery is very effective. He pictures the bird as a knight on horseback fighting against the wind. The image of the windhover as a knight is also evocative of Christ whom the poet addresses as 'my chevalier'. Having portrayed the attractive nature of the bird's flight in the octave, Hopkins compares the beauty of the bird to that of Christ. He views Christ as 'a billion / Times told lovelier, more dangerous…'. The image of the fire is indicative of Christ fighting against evil exactly as the bird fights against the wind.

I wake and feel the fell of dark, not day is one of the three sonnets known as the 'terrible sonnets' in which Hopkins plumbs the depths of despair. There is general agreement that this is the darkest of the terrible sonnets, providing us with disturbing insights into the poet's primary psychological problem of severe depression, which sadly has become an extremely common problem in today's world. This poem portrays a sense of gloom and hopelessness. In many respects, this is the most vivid of the terrible sonnets. The imagery deftly reflects the anguish of awakening in a state of total hopelessness. The initial image is palpable in nature, with the poet claiming to 'feel the fell of dark'.

The opening lines portray an experience familiar to depressives, many of whom awaken long in advance of the sun rising and endure anguish after being awakened from sleep in the blackness of night. We also perceive the poet's sense of an unseen evil around him. In this context 'fell' is a central term, with a double meaning – it may be interpreted as threat/ blow and also as an animal's skin – a truly horrifying image.

Pied Beauty is a hymn of praise to God for the infinite diversity of nature. The opening line is filled with words of acclaim for God, 'Glory be to God for dappled things – '. This prayer-like beginning is then accompanied by a litany of vivid examples of the 'dappled' beauty to be located in the natural world. Hopkins includes the mottled blue and white colours of the sky, the 'brinded' (streaked) hide of a cow and the patches of contrasting colour on a trout. The chestnut presents us with a more complex and challenging image as we try to visualise its interior after it is compared to the coals in a fire, black on the outside and glowing within. The wings of finches are variegated, as is patchwork-like farmland. The final example is of the 'trades' (occupations) and activities of man, with their variety of materials and equipment, 'Fresh-firecoal chestnut-falls; finches' wings; /landscape plotted and pieced – fold, fallow and plough; /And all trades, their gear and tackle and trim'. Here we once again see Hopkins' effective use of alliteration enhancing the poem's musical qualities. More significantly, man is depicted as being in harmony with God's creation.

In the concluding five lines, Hopkins gives moral characteristics to the miscellaneous images on which he has expanded up to this point in terms of physical qualities. At this moment we are presented with a new idea or image: God is to be praised. Hopkins claims that the examples he has given are creations of God which highlight the unity and permanence of His power and inspire us to 'Praise Him'.

In conclusion, Hopkins' poetry remains relevant, ensuring that it continues to be well worth reading.

Robert Frost

Biographical Note

Robert Frost was born in San Francisco in 1874. His father died when Frost was eleven years old and the family moved to Massachusetts, New England where his grandparents lived. His poetry is associated mainly with the beautiful countryside of New England. At high school Frost studied a classical curriculum. He later attended both Dartmouth and Harvard, but did not enjoy college life and dropped out of both institutions. In 1895 he married Elinor White, a woman whom he had first met and fallen in love with in high school. Frost worked in a variety of jobs, including teaching and farming, both of which he enjoyed. He later became a lecturer in a college in New Hampshire. Frost lived in England from 1912 to 1915, returning to the US shortly after the outbreak of the First World War.

Despite the uncertainty surrounding his employment situation for many years, Frost was devoted to his poetry, having had his first poem published when he was sixteen years old. He read all of the great English poets, being particularly influenced by Wordsworth's belief that poets should write about everyday life in everyday language. His experience in a series of low-paid jobs meant that he was intimately familiar with the lives and concerns of ordinary people. Largely shunning the urban, industrialised world, Frost found his inspiration and his imagery in the world of nature. However, he rightly objected to being labelled 'a nature poet' because his poetry involves so much more.

As a poet, Frost achieved remarkable success, winning the Pulitzer Prize for his poetry on a record four occasions. However, his personal life was sadly marked by a number of personal tragedies which may account for the darkness that pervades some of his poems.

When you read the poetry of Robert Frost watch out for:

- His distinctive attitude to the **natural world**. He does not romanticise it, but rather sees in it a reflection of truth. It provides him with inspiration for many of his most philosophical poems.

- Frost reflects individuals as being essentially **isolated** and **lonely**, unable to fully communicate with their fellow human beings.

- Notice the use of very detailed, **vividly sensuous imagery**. This encourages the reader to participate in the scene – to be present, in a meaningful way.

- Several poems are strongly **narrative in style**. The perspective is often that of the 'I', or the poet himself, which gives an added sense of realism. Dramatic conclusions stimulate the reader to reflect on the poem's message.

- There is a wide **variation of tone** between the poems and even within the same poem. This also adds to the dramatic intensity of Frost's work.

The Tuft of Flowers

The two key elements (an isolated man, a rural setting) in this poem are typical of Frost's poetry. The central theme is man's relationship with his fellow man. Robert Frost said simply that this is a poem about fellowship.

This poem begins in a matter-of-fact, narrative manner. The speaker/poet describes how he went to turn cut grass so that it would dry in the sun, 'I went to turn the grass once after one / Who mowed it in the dew before the sun'. The scene that greets him is bleak, 'the levelled scene'. Conscious of his isolation, the speaker looks in vain for the mower, 'I looked for him behind an isle of trees'. The image of 'an isle of trees' suggests a sense of isolation and loneliness. The speaker longs to hear the comforting sound of another person, 'I listened for his whetstone on the breeze'. The speaker sadly concludes that the mower has left, leaving him isolated. The repeated long 'o' sound ('mown', 'alone') underscores the lonely mood. Isolation is seen as being inherent in the human condition, 'And I must be, as he had been, – alone'. The setting apart of the key word at the end of the line gives it greater emphasis. Being alone is seen simply as an unavoidable fact of human life, '"As all must be"/ . . . "Whether they work together or apart"'.

The word 'But' in line 11 indicates a change in direction, 'But as I said it, swift there passed me by / On noiseless wing a bewildered butterfly'. The personified insect is confused because it is searching for a flower it visited the previous day. The butterfly's plight mirrors that of the poet. Both insect and man are alone, searching for something comforting. The image of the butterfly searching without finding sets the speaker thinking about timeless philosophical questions ('questions that have no reply'). The butterfly's fruitless search for the flower may suggest the elusive nature of human happiness.

Line 21 signals another turning point in the poem,

'But he turned first, and led my eye to look / At a tall tuft of flowers beside a brook'. The butterfly draws the speaker's attention to a tuft of flowers. At this point nature seems to assume the role of spiritual guide to the speaker. The metaphor 'A leaping tongue of bloom' suggests how nature speaks to the poet. This is also an image with biblical/spiritual connotations, suggesting how man can be enlightened and inspired by nature. The mower had left the flowers 'to flourish' because he loved their beauty. Thanks to the butterfly, the speaker 'had lit upon /...a message from the dawn'. Here again we have an image suggestive of communication. Now the speaker sees the world around him in a new light as he hears 'the wakening birds around'. In his imagination he can hear the mower, with 'his long scythe whispering to the ground'. The gloom lifts as the speaker absorbs nature's 'message' – the speaker and the mower are spiritually connected by their shared love of natural beauty. Sensing the presence of 'a spirit kindred to my own', the speaker no longer feels alone.

In the final section of the poem Frost imagines himself working alongside this other man and sharing 'brotherly speech' with him. The closing couplet contradicts the earlier pessimistic assertion that man is always alone, '"Men work together"/...Whether they work together or apart"'. The speaker's revised viewpoint is optimistic and heartening.

KEY POINTS

- Key themes are human fellowship and man's ability to learn from nature.
- The poem is written in a series of rhyming couplets, but this formal structure does not detract from the naturalness of the language.
- Regular use of image and symbol means that this is a poem rich in suggestion.
- Contrast between gloomy opening and joyful conclusion.
- Sound effects include assonance ('mown...alone'), onomatopoeia ('whispering') and end-rhyme.

Mending Wall

This is another narrative poem which can be read on more than one level. The wall in the poem has a metaphorical meaning as well as being a physical reality. In this poem Frost explores an interesting philosophical question: Are walls and boundaries (symbolic of rules, regulations, conventions) necessary?

The early part of this poem is essentially descriptive. The opening statement ('Something there is that doesn't love a wall') suggests that gaps in the wall separating Frost's farm from that of his neighbour have been caused by some mysterious force. Of course, in reality, the greatest gaps are the result of the frost causing the ground under the wall to expand and then contract. The gaps in the wall are described, with some being so wide that 'even two can pass abreast'. Hunters have also caused an amount of damage to the wall.

With the advent of spring, Frost informs his neighbour about the condition of the wall. What follows seems to be a long-established annual ritual, 'And on a day we meet to walk the line / And set the wall between us once again'. It is ironic that the wall that divides the two men also brings them together, 'We keep the wall between us as we go'. Convention dictates that each man looks after the boulders that have fallen on his side of the boundary.

The poem has a humorous quality. The boulders come in various shapes, 'And some are loaves and some so nearly balls'. It seems that 'a spell' is needed 'to make them balance' because they seem to have a life of their own, obstinately refusing to stay where they are placed, '"Stay where you are until our backs are turned!"' The wall mending is described as 'just another kind of outdoor game, / One on a side'.

The poem becomes more interesting when Frost comes to a section where, in his view, 'we do not need the wall' since there are only trees on either side of the boundary. Frost makes a humorous observation, 'My apple trees will never get across / And eat the cones under his pines'. However, when he makes this point to his neighbour, the latter replies by reciting an old proverb, 'Good fences make good neighbours'. The mischievous side to Frost prompts him to question the validity of this received wisdom, '*Why* do they make good neighbours?' Frost accepts that walls are necessary in certain situations, such as containing animals. However, he goes on to state that before building a wall, he would ask 'What I was walling in or walling out, / And to whom I was like to give offence'. Here we see that Frost has an independent, questioning mind. He would also appear to be a considerate neighbour, anxious not to give offence. He tells his neighbour that 'Something there is that doesn't love a wall' (a reference to mysterious magical/supernatural forces or to nature itself?), hoping he might acknowledge the truth of this observation.

Frost concludes by portraying his neighbour as a Stone Age savage ('an old-stone savage armed') whose thinking has never evolved. Incapable of independent thought, he unquestioningly accepts the wisdom of an old proverb, 'He will not go behind his father's saying'. While Frost believes that his neighbour is enshrouded in a type of intellectual fog or mental darkness ('He moves in darkness'), it is significant that it is his neighbour who has the last word, stubbornly repeating the old proverb 'Good fences make good neighbours' as if he had coined the maxim himself.

KEY POINTS

- A narrative poem that can also be read on a metaphorical level.
- A poem that raises some interesting philosophical questions relating to boundaries.
- Repeated use of the first person ('I') underlines the personal nature of this poem.

- Humorous touches.
- Use of everyday language.
- Written in blank verse (unrhymed iambic pentameter).

After Apple-Picking

This is another Frost poem that has more than one level of meaning. On a surface level it is simply a nature poem celebrating the abundance of the harvest. On a deeper, metaphorical level it is a poem that explores the workings of the creative imagination. In this poem Frost adopts the persona of a farmer.

The poem opens in a clear, matter-of-fact manner as the farmer reflects on his day's work harvesting his apple crop, 'My long two-pointed ladder's sticking through a tree'. However, when he suggests that it is 'Toward heaven still', the symbolism of the creative ladder comes to mind. While some apples remain unpicked, the farmer is satisfied with his efforts, 'But I am done with apple-picking now'. The mood becomes lethargic, with the 'essence of winter sleep' on the night, 'The scent of apples' heavy in the air and the poet 'drowsing off'. The sibilant 's' sound, the repeated long vowel sounds ('bough... now... drowsing') and the slow rhythm combine to convey a pervasive sense of inertia.

The speaker recalls an experience earlier that morning when he looked at the world through a sheet of ice he had skimmed from a drinking trough. Looking through the sheet of ice transformed his vision of the world. Even though the ice has long since melted, the strangeness of the vision remains. Now, in his dream-like state, he continues to see the world in a new way. The familiar becomes strange, with 'Magnified apples' appearing and disappearing. His senses are sharper. Even the tiniest details on the apple are clear to him, 'And every fleck of russet showing clear'. The speaker is acutely aware of every sensation. His instep still aches and his foot feels as if it is still pressing down on the rung of the ladder. He imagines that his body is still

swaying with the ladder as the branches bend. He keeps hearing 'The rumbling sound / Of load on load of apples coming in'. This image suggests the richness and abundance of the harvest, with the repetition of 'load' being particularly effective. The image of 'ten thousand fruit' underscores the bountiful nature of the apple crop.

While the harvest was much anticipated, the speaker has had 'too much/Of apple-picking' and is 'overtired'. His love of the harvest is clear when he describes his experience of touching the apples and ensuring that they did not fall, 'Cherish in hand, lift down, and not let fall'. Every apple that falls – even if it is not visibly damaged – must go to the cider-apple heap. Now the speaker can think only of sleep. He wonders if his slumber will simply be 'just some human sleep' or will it resemble the hibernation sleep of the woodchuck? The closing lines suggest a sense of overwhelming exhaustion.

Like so many Frost poems, *After Apple-Picking* is open to more than one reading, since it can be read both literally and metaphorically. On a literal level the poem is a very realistic description of a farmer exhausted by his labours – realistic details include the enduring pain he feels in his instep from standing on the ladder. On a metaphorical level, harvesting the apples may be interpreted as the poet harvesting his creative imagination, with the opening image of the ladder suggestive of the creative ladder leading to the 'heaven' of poetic inspiration, and the sheet of ice representing the transforming power of the poetic imagination. The day's work from morning to night may be seen as a metaphor for the journey through life to death. Of course, sleep is commonly employed in poetry as a metaphor for death.

KEY POINTS

- A poem that has different layers of meaning.
- Use of simple, everyday language.
- Effective use of sound – sibilance ('Essence of winter sleep is on the night . . . scent of apples'), assonance (sticking . . . still . . . didn't fill'), end-rhyme.
- Repetition used to good effect – repetition of 'load' accentuates the abundance of the harvest, while repetition of 'sleep' underlines the drowsy atmosphere.

Birches

This poem begins in a casual, chatty manner with Frost describing birches bending against a background of upright trees. He would like to think that the trees were bent by boys engaged in the popular New England pastime of birch swinging, but knows that 'swinging doesn't bend them down to stay'. The phenomenon of the bending birches can only be explained by reference to the weather, specifically winter ice storms. Frost speaks directly to the reader, 'Often you may have seen them / Loaded with ice a sunny winter morning'. Frost goes on to describe the sounds of the frozen branches as their coating of ice begins to melt, 'They click upon themselves/... As the stir cracks and crazes their enamel'. The repeated onomatopoeic hard 'c' sounds enable us to hear the ice starting to melt on the trees. The image of the icy splinters combines the domestic and the heavenly, 'Such heaps of broken glass to sweep away, / You'd think the inner dome of heaven had fallen'. The effect of the winter ice storms is lasting. Weighed down for so long by the immense heaviness of the ice, the trees never recover. Their trunks are left forever bending, with their branches trailing the ground. Again the reader is directly addressed, 'You may see their trunks arching in the woods / Years afterwards'. A pleasant simile suggests that the arching trees are 'Like girls on hands and knees that throw their hair / Before them over their heads to dry in the sun'.

After giving us a factual explanation for the arching birches, Frost returns to his main topic of interest – swinging from birches. While he knows the reality behind the phenomenon of the arching trees, he prefers the imaginative explanation involving boys swinging from birches. The tone is casual and conversational, 'But I was going to say when Truth broke in...'. Truth is personified as that side of Frost that felt compelled to give the true reason for the bending birches. Frost's preferred explanation is a product of his fanciful imagination, 'I should prefer to have some boy bend them'. He imagines a boy 'too far from town to learn baseball' devising the game of birch swinging. This boy is described as having 'subdued his father's trees' by repeatedly swinging from them until 'not one was left/ For him to conquer'. Practising birch swinging teaches this boy some important lessons about life. This is a game that demands patience and judgement, 'He learned all there was / To learn about not launching out too soon'. It necessitates poise, 'climbing carefully / With the same pains you use to fill a cup / Up to the brim'. The actual jump obviously requires courage, 'Then he flung outward, feet first, with a swish'. The use of both alliteration and onomatopoeia gives this image an aural as well as a vivid visual quality.

In the final section of the poem, Frost recalls his own boyhood when he was 'a swinger of birches'. As he reminisces, the tone becomes nostalgic, 'And so I dream of going back to be'. Now when he is troubled, weary and directionless

('And life is too much like a pathless wood'), he longs to briefly escape, 'I'd like to get away from earth awhile ...'. He would like to return to begin afresh because 'Earth's the right place for love' and he does not know 'where it's likely to go better'. As a way of briefly retreating from the problems of life, Frost imagines himself climbing a birch tree. While he pictures himself climbing '*Toward* heaven', he has no desire to leave the real world permanently behind him. He would enjoy journeying toward heaven and journeying homewards, 'That would be good both going and coming back'. The closing line offers us some of Frost's admirable homespun wisdom, 'One could do worse than be a swinger of birches'.

As with so many of Frost's poems this poem can be read as a straightforward narrative poem, while also being open to a metaphorical interpretation. Birch swinging may be symbolic of the desire to briefly escape from life's difficulties. As such, it raises some interesting philosophical questions. Should we aim to escape from life when it becomes oppressive or problematic? Frost chooses a temporary retreat from life when he imagines himself climbing towards heaven – yet he insists that he always wants to return to reality. As a poet, Frost gets his inspiration from the world of reality. By climbing the creative / imaginative ladder toward heaven (the ladder pointing toward heaven is also an image that occurs in *After Apple-Picking*), the poet transforms reality in his imagination and achieves insight.

KEY POINTS

- Key theme is the desire to escape (temporarily) from harsh reality.
- Another Frost poem that can be read on both literal and metaphorical levels.
- Simple, everyday language conceals a depth and a complexity of thought – a poem that raises some interesting philosophical questions.
- Description leads to reflection and insight.
- Effective use of sound.
- Memorable visual and aural imagery.

The Road Not Taken

This poem is concerned with the nature and consequences of decision-making. It is dominated by the metaphor of the road. The image of travelling a road suggests the idea of journeying through life, while the idea of choosing a particular road is commonly symbolic of making an important decision, of choosing one path in life over another.

The speaker comes to a point in the autumnal woodland where two roads go off in different directions, 'Two roads diverged in a yellow wood'. He seems reluctant to make a decision, 'And sorry I could not travel both'. He looks down one road as far as he can to see if he can get some idea of what lies ahead. Having considered this option, the speaker decides to take the other road on the basis that it had 'the better claim / Because it was grassy and wanted wear'. We get the impression that he is an adventurous character, unwilling to travel the popular road. However, the next line seems to contradict what went before, stating that travellers 'Had worn them really about the same'. The contradiction is reinforced by the observation that 'both that morning equally lay/In leaves no step had trodden black'.

As the speaker chooses one road over another, he reflects that he may someday return to travel the other road, 'Oh, I kept the first for another day!' However, he reminds himself that such an eventuality is unlikely since one road leads on to another ('Yet knowing how way leads on to way') and it is unlikely that he will ever find himself in this particular situation again.

In the final stanza, the speaker imagines himself looking back on his life 'ages and ages hence'. He anticipates telling his story 'with a sigh'. The reader is left to consider whether this is a sigh of regret at having chosen the wrong road or a sigh of acceptance that decisions have to be made without the knowledge of what lies ahead. Certainly, these lines suggest the idea of a momentous decision, one that would have a great bearing on how his life would unfold. The closing lines underscore the significance of the speaker's decision, while reminding the reader

of the contradiction that lies at the heart of the poem, 'I took the one less travelled by, / And that has made all the difference'.

An initial reading of this poem seems to convey a straightforward message – in life you make your own decisions and travel your own road. However, it is the contradiction at the heart of the poem that makes it interesting. If both roads are essentially the same, does it matter which road he travels? Is there a suggestion that individual decision-making is not overly important since our lives are largely governed by fate? Or, as some commentators have opined, is Frost simply being mischievous, gently poking fun at those who are always looking for 'meaning' or a moral lesson in poetry?

KEY POINTS

- Key theme is the nature and consequences of decision-making.
- This simple narrative poem has another level of meaning – the metaphor of choosing a road suggests the idea of making an important, perhaps life-changing, decision.
- The poem is set in the beautiful autumnal woodlands of New England.
- Language is simple and direct.
- The poem has an appealing musical quality. A sibilant 's' sound pervades the poem, suggesting the tranquillity of this natural scene ('I shall be telling this with a sigh/Somewhere ages and ages hence'). Alliteration is also employed ('wanted wear', 'lay in leaves', 'way leads on to way'). Finally, the poem has a fixed rhyming pattern ('fair – wear – there', 'claim – same').

'Out, Out-'

This dramatic poem was inspired by a tragic real-life accident that occurred on the farm of one of Frost's friends in New Hampshire in 1910. The title of the poem recalls the lines from *Macbeth* which see the protagonist reflecting on the brevity of life, 'Out, out brief candle!'.

The poem opens to the dramatic sound of a snarling saw, 'The buzz saw snarled and rattled in the yard'. The image created is of a dangerous, savage animal. The use of onomatopoeia is particularly effective. The saw is cutting the

wood into 'stove- length sticks of wood'. Details such as this root the poem in the everyday world of a New England farmer. The alliterative phrase 'Sweet-scented stuff' suggests the appealing smell of the freshly-cut timber. The noisy saw interrupts the tranquillity of the surrounding countryside whose beauty is captured in a memorable image, 'those that lifted eyes could count / Five mountain ranges one behind the other / Under the sunset far into Vermont'. The peacefulness of this rural landscape is juxtaposed with the harsh sound of the saw, which becomes increasingly threatening. The repetition of 'snarled and rattled' evokes a sense of danger and fills the reader with foreboding. When we are told 'And nothing happened', our sense of anticipation is heightened.

The poet next speaks with the benefit of hindsight, 'Call it a day, I wish they might have said / To please the boy by giving him the half hour / That a boy counts so much when saved from work'. At this point in the poem, the reader's anticipation gives way to a sense of dread. The critical moment occurs when the boy's sister calls him for his supper and he is momentarily distracted, losing control of the saw. The wild animal image is developed as Frost describes how the saw 'Leaped out at the boy's hand'. This is the climax of the tragic drama. To add to the tragedy, the boy seems to have contributed to his terrible fate, 'He must have given the hand. However it was / Neither refused the meeting'. The short dramatic phrase 'But the hand!' conveys a sense of indescribable shock.

In a state of profound shock, the boy's first response is 'a rueful laugh'. Pathetically, he turns towards the other people who are around. The image of the boy 'holding up the hand, half in appeal, but half as if to keep / The life from spilling' is deeply poignant. In an instant the boy understands the awful reality: 'Then the boy saw all /...big boy / Doing a man's work, though a child at heart – / He saw all spoiled'. The boy lives in a harsh world where boys often do the work of men. He appeals to his sister not to let the doctor amputate his hand. Direct speech brings the terrible scene to life, 'Don't let him cut my hand off – / The doctor, when he comes. Don't let him, sister!' The heartbreaking truth was that 'the hand was gone already'.

When the doctor arrives, he puts the boy 'in the dark of ether' (ether was an early anaesthetic). Tragically, this is to be his final sleep. Short abrupt lines build up the tension, 'And then – the watcher at his pulse took fright. / No one believed. They listened at his heart'. A series of dashes suggests the inexorable ebbing away of life, 'Little – less – nothing'. The poem's final lines are deeply shocking in their suggestion of communal indifference to the tragedy, 'No more to build on there. And they, since they / Were not the ones dead, turned to their affairs'. Even allowing for the practicality that was part of the make-up of these farming people, this response is shocking and bewildering in its callousness.

KEY POINTS

- Key theme is the fragility of human life. Another theme is the harshness and injustice of a world where a child is expected to do the work of men.
- A dramatic poem, with a specific setting (a New England farm at sunset), 'characters', direct speech and tension.
- Memorable images evoke the beauty of nature, the threat of the saw, the horror of the accident and the indifference of neighbours.
- Effective use of sound – alliteration ('sweet-scented stuff'), assonance ('breeze drew across it') and onomatopoeia ('snarled and rattled').
- Punctuation used to good effect – regular full stops, dashes and exclamation marks convey a sense of mounting tension.
- Use of everyday language.
- Shocking ending.

Spring Pools

The main themes of this poem are transience and the unending natural cycle of life, death and renewal. Nature is seen to be both beautiful and harsh. Frost describes how the roots of trees soak up the water in spring pools, causing the flowers near them to wither and die. The opening lines evoke the beauty and tranquillity of nature as Frost describes how the spring pools perfectly mirror the sky, 'reflect / The total sky almost without defect'. Both the pools and the flowers that grow beside them 'chill and shiver'. These words have negative connotations, suggesting that the personified pools and flowers are aware that they are destined to shortly perish. The bleak mood is underlined when Frost states that both pools and flowers will 'soon be gone', reminding us that some of the most beautiful things in nature enjoy only a brief, precarious existence. Ironically, the pools and flowers must inevitably die so that the trees can produce their canopy of leaves ('bring dark foliage on').

The second stanza is dominated by the image of the trees which are portrayed as dark, threatening forces, 'The trees that have it in their pent-up buds / To darken nature . . .'. They have the power 'To blot out and drink up and sweep away'. The series of verbs accentuates the trees' destructive power. The poet warns the trees to 'think twice' before they use their power to destroy 'these flowery waters and these watery flowers'. The adjectives 'flowery' and 'watery' evoke the frail beauty of the flowers and pools, suggesting that they have no hope of resisting the powerful, oppressive trees. The short-lived nature of the spring pools is stated directly when Frost tells us that they were created 'From snow that melted only yesterday'. The closing line of the poem reminds us of the natural life cycle – the melting snow created the pools, which in turn nourished the flowers before both are obliterated by the trees. While life and death co-exist in the world of nature, the mood of the poem is essentially gloomy and the tone serious and regretful. The long lines (each stanza is based on a single sentence), the slow rhythm and the repeated long vowel sounds ('gone-on', 'away-yesterday') contribute to the solemn mood.

On a symbolic level, the delicate pools and flowers may represent the fragility of human existence. Just as the pools and flowers are erased by the trees, human life is blotted out by the passage of time. The trees may also be seen as being symbolic of those powerful forces in life that exploit, oppress and ultimately destroy the weak and the passive, symbolised by the flowers and the pools.

KEY POINTS
- Key theme is transience.
- A poem rich in symbolism.
- Gloomy mood, solemn tone.
- Use of everyday language.
- Musical qualities – end-rhyme, assonance ('chill and shiver'), sibilance ('These pools that, though in forests, still reflect / The total sky...').

Acquainted with the Night

This is one of the few Frost poems that has an urban setting. Written in sonnet form, the theme is the isolation and loneliness of the city dweller. The actual darkness of the night is suggestive of the speaker's inner, spiritual darkness. The speaker is a solitary figure walking through deserted city streets at night. The mood of the poem is relentlessly dark. The repeated use of 'I' indicates the personal nature of the poem, giving it a confessional quality. Frost experienced regular bouts of depression during his lifetime, many of which were associated with his rather tragic family life. His inner torment is such that he is unable to sleep and walks all night by himself.

The image of incessant rain establishes the bleak mood, 'I have walked out in rain – and back in rain'. Repetition suggests the monotony of urban life. The repeated long 'a' sound ('rain... rain... lane... explain') underscores the gloomy atmosphere. The physical journey that takes the speaker beyond 'the furthest city light' is symbolic of a spiritual journey that brings him to a dark place beyond all hope and comfort. The image of the speaker looking down 'the saddest city lane' heightens the melancholy mood.

The speaker is a solitary, uncommunicative figure. He has retreated into himself and is unwilling to communicate with the only person he meets, 'I have passed by the watchman on his beat / And dropped my eyes ...'. The only other indication of a human presence is the reference first to 'the sound of feet' and then to 'an interrupted cry', with the latter reference evoking the sinister, violent aspect of urban life. The cry he hears is 'not to call me back or say goodbye'. There is no connection between the speaker and any other person. He is completely alone as he wanders the city streets at night. The contrast between the isolation of the speaker and the sense of fellowship that lies at the heart of both *The Tuft of Flowers* and *Mending Wall* is very striking. The 'luminary clock against the sky' may be a metaphor for the moon, or it may be an actual clock. Either way, it suggests the passage of time. The statement that this 'clock ... / Proclaimed the time was neither wrong nor right' is rather cryptic, but possibly suggests the speaker's indifference to the world and time in which he lives. The repetition of the opening line at the close of the poem leaves us in no doubt but that the speaker, alienated and isolated, remains engulfed in his own spiritual darkness.

KEY POINTS

- A profoundly gloomy poem which explores the isolation and loneliness of urban life.

- The darkness of the night is symbolic of the darkness of the speaker's soul.

- A deeply personal poem inspired by Frost's own inner torment.

- Sound effects include assonance ('rain . . . lane'), alliteration ('I have stood still and stopped the sound of feet') and end-rhyme.

- Use of simple, direct language.

Design

The title refers to the idea that there is an order or design underpinning the workings of the universe. The order and beauty of the natural world are commonly seen as part of the design of a benign God. In this poem Frost questions this belief by presenting the dark face of the natural world. In the poet's view, either evil is intrinsic to the world in which we live (part of the design) or there simply is no divine plan or design governing our universe.

This poem is written in the form of a sonnet, with the octet (lines 1-8) being largely descriptive and the sestet considering some of the questions raised by the scene that is so vividly depicted in the octet. The opening image is unusual and unappealing, 'I found a dimpled spider, fat and white, / On a white heal-all'.

Normally a symbol of purity and innocence, white is, in this instance, linked with death and deception (the white flower camouflages the predatory spider). Ordinarily, a spider is black and a heal-all is a blue-coloured flower. The spider has a white moth trapped in his web. The moth is 'like a white piece of rigid satin cloth' – this simile is strongly suggestive of death (the lining of a coffin is commonly made of satin). Taken together, the spider, flower and moth are symbolic of death and disease, 'Assorted characters of death and blight'. Perhaps blight has caused the flower to be white rather than blue. Rather shockingly, Frost suggests that nature is driven by some evil force, comparing the spider, flower and moth to 'the ingredients of a witches' broth'. The closing image in the octet depicts the trapped moth being toyed with 'like a paper kite'.

In the sestet, Frost considers some of the questions arising from this incident in the world of nature. Speaking of the flower as if it were a living thinking entity, he asks why it used the colour representative of innocence to lure the moth to its death. The phrase 'the kindred spider' implies that flower and spider conspired to kill the moth. The poet wonders how the spider and the moth happened to end up on the flower at a particular point in time, 'What brought the kindred spider to that height, / Then steered the white moth thither in the night?' The verbs 'brought' and 'steered' suggest a guiding force behind events in the natural world. Frost concludes that everything that happened was nature's plan. In referring to a 'design of darkness' that has the power to 'appall' him, the poet clearly believes that the natural world is animated and guided by evil. The alternative, as Frost ponders in the closing line, is that there is no design – good or evil – governing the universe, 'If design govern in a thing so small'. The poem closes on this pessimistic note, with the sceptical poet wondering if there is a divine power with a grand plan or design for the world in which we live.

KEY POINTS

- A philosophical poem in which Frost questions the nature and indeed existence of a 'design' for the universe.

- Written in sonnet form – the octet is descriptive, while the sestet reflects on some of the questions arising from the natural scene depicted in the octet.

- An atmosphere of evil pervades the poem. Many words have dark, negative connotations: 'death', 'blight', 'witches', 'darkness', 'appall'.

- Images of beauty and delicacy (white satin, a snowdrop, a paper kite) are set alongside the harsh images in the poem (the fat white spider, the witches' broth, the blighted flower) to suggest how evil can be deceptive.

- A poem rich in irony – white, normally symbolic of innocence, is associated with deception and evil as the innocent-looking flower camouflages a white spider waiting to trap the moth. It is also grimly ironic that the heal-all, a flower associated with medicinal properties, plays a key role in bringing about the death of the moth.

- Effective use of simile (the moth is compared to 'a white piece of rigid satin cloth' and to 'a paper kite') and metaphor ('A snowdrop spider').

Provide, Provide

In this poem the speaker exhorts us to make provision for our old age and for unexpected eventualities. (Frost believed strongly in the concept of self-reliance). The opening stanzas describe how a once-beautiful girl ('The picture pride of Hollywood') is now 'The witch' or 'withered hag' who washes steps. The Old Testament beauty Abishag is a metaphor for the beautiful girl that the old woman once was. The references to the Old Testament and to Hollywood (a world renowned for its shallowness) remind us that certain truths are universal, timeless and immutable, foremost among them being the transient nature of youth and beauty. Sadly, when she was young and successful the charwoman failed to provide for herself financially. The speaker points out that this fate has befallen 'Too many' for the reader 'to doubt the likelihood' of it happening.

The first piece of advice the speaker offers in relation to avoiding similar misfortune is delivered in a tongue-in-cheek manner, 'Die early and avoid the fate'. However, if you are destined to lead a long life, he suggests that you acquire wealth ('Make the whole stock exchange your own!') or power ('If need be occupy a throne, / Where nobody can call *you* crone') since both can insulate you from an ignominious old age. The speaker suggests that we might learn from others who have relied on their worldly experience or simply on their honesty to avoid the hardship and suffering that often accompanies old age, 'What worked for them might work for you'. While there is no universal formula guaranteeing success in life and happiness in old age, one thing is certain: memories, no matter how glowing, will not protect a person when things get hard, 'No memory of having starred /.... keeps the end from being hard'. The speaker's final piece of advice is to buy friendship if necessary, 'Better to go down dignified / With boughten friendship at your side / Than none at all'. The poem ends with the exhortation that encapsulates the poem's key message, 'Provide, provide!'.

While the poem's emphasis on the need for self-sufficiency is admirable, some of the other values espoused are questionable. Although possibly lighthearted, some of the advice tends towards the materialistic, while more seems highly suspect – certainly many readers would have difficulty seeing how buying friendship could result in a dignified old age. The emphasis on the physically destructive effects of time points to a certain shallowness in the speaker, and many would find the language used in relation to old age ('The witch', 'the withered hag', 'crone') objectionable.

KEY POINTS

- Key themes include the destructive effects of time and the need for self-reliance.

- Images of youth and beauty ('the beauty Abishag', 'the picture pride of Hollywood') are juxtaposed with images of decrepit old age ('The witch', 'the withered hag').

- Language is simple and direct.

- Impersonal tone (no use of 'I').

- Frost's outlook on life in this poem is dark and cynical.

- Repetition underlines the urgency of the poem's message, 'Provide, provide!'

SAMPLE ANSWER

'Vivid descriptive, imagery that gives his poems layers of meaning and language that is very close to everyday speech are the primary reasons why readers enjoy the poetry of Robert Frost.'

Discuss the above statement with reference to the poems of Robert Frost.

The poetry of Robert Frost is certainly remarkable for its quality of detailed, vivid description, multi-layered imagery and language usage which is both accessible and clear. While his verse is vividly descriptive, it invariably moves beyond mere description, exploring important moral and philosophical issues. Frost reflects on isolation, loneliness, transience and death, as well as on such issues as the nature and consequences of choice. He uses imagery and symbolism to create layers or levels of meaning within his poems, which give them an intriguing quality – a sense that they are always on the verge of saying something more, but the readers must discover what this is for themselves. The use of language that is close to everyday speech creates a realism and authenticity which I found very appealing. This realism is often intense because although he appreciates the beauty of the world around him, he is keenly aware of its harshness. All of these key features contribute to the reader's enjoyment of the poetry of Robert Frost.

The Tuft of Flowers is an interesting poem which reflects on the nature of man's relationship with his fellow man. The language is wonderfully simple and accessible, 'I went to turn the grass once after one / Who mowed it in the dew before the sun'. The use of the first person in this narrative poem suggests its personal nature. The desire to establish contact with another human being is clear, ' I looked...I listened...'. The image of 'an isle of trees' suggests a sense of isolation and loneliness. The lonely feeling is underlined by the repeated long 'o' sound, 'But he had gone his way, the grass all mown / And I must be as he had been – alone'. The image of the 'bewildered butterfly' searching for a flower it visited the previous day suggests how man is often confused as he searches for happiness. We see how the butterfly sets Frost thinking about important philosophical questions, 'I thought of questions that have no reply'. I was fascinated to see how Frost's thinking is guided by the natural world, how the butterfly 'led my eye to look / At a tall tuft of flowers beside a brook'. Particularly striking is the image of 'A leaping tongue of bloom'. This image suggests how nature communicates with the poet. It is an image with biblical/ spiritual connotations, suggesting how man can be enlightened and inspired by nature. Frost realises that the mower left the flowers because he 'loved them'. The 'message from the dawn' is that the poet is not alone because he and the other man are spiritually connected by a shared love of natural beauty. The gloom of the first half of the poem is dispelled as a sense of isolation gives way to a sense of brotherhood. Poet and reader are heartened by the realisation that '"Men work together /... Whether they work together or apart"'.

Mending Wall is similarly enjoyable because it is another narrative poem that explores an interesting philosophical question: Are walls and boundaries (symbolic of rules, conventions etc) necessary? The poet describes how two farmers meet to repair a damaged wall, 'I let my neighbour know beyond the hill / And on a day we meet to walk the line'. Again, the use of the first person suggests the personal nature of the poem, and helps to 'connect' poet and reader. The repetition of 'between us' suggests how walls divide, yet the business of mending the wall brings the two men together. This poem has an appealing humorous quality. The boulders seem to have a mind of their own, '"Stay where you are until our backs are turned!"'. Frost questions the need for walls when they exist only to separate trees, 'My apple trees will never get across / And eat the cones under his pines'. While Frost believes that walls are not always necessary, his neighbour simply repeats the old proverb that 'Good fences make good neighbours'. I admire Frost's capacity for independent thought, his willingness to question the received wisdom encapsulated in the old proverb. I also admire his sensitivity to others, 'Before I built a wall I'd ask to know / What I was walling in or walling out / And to whom I was like to give offence'. In a memorable simile Frost compares his neighbour to 'an old stone-savage' because he seems to be incapable of thinking for himself. What I found most interesting about this poem is the unresolved conflict at its heart. We note that while Frost questions the need for walls, he nonetheless regularly repairs them. It is also significant that his neighbour has the last word.

The Road Not Taken explores an interesting theme: the nature and consequences of decision-making. This poem is based on the metaphor of life as a journey – a familiar image to which we can easily relate. The speaker describes how 'two roads diverged in a wood', compelling him to make a choice. The image of the poet looking down one road as far as he could suggests how we all try to anticipate the consequences of particular decisions. The use of the first person ('I' is used nine times) underlines the personal nature of this poem. The simplicity of Frost's language is an appealing feature of this poem also. What I found particularly intriguing is the contradiction that lies at its heart. An initial reading of the poem suggests that choosing the road 'less travelled' has 'made all the difference' to the speaker, implying that personal fulfilment can best be achieved by making our own decisions and by not conforming to everyone else's expectations. However, the idea that one road was 'less travelled' is clearly contradicted, '... the passing there / Had worn them really about the same / And both that morning equally lay / In leaves no step had trodden black'. I found this contradiction thought-provoking. Is Frost suggesting that it does not matter which road we choose since the course of our lives is pre-ordained? Such questions add to our enjoyment of the poem, as it encourages us to reflect on what the poem may be suggesting and we realise that there are several possible layers of meaning which can be explored.

Spring Pools is a meditation on spring and on the unending natural cycle of death and rebirth. What I found especially interesting about this poem was the layers of meaning created by Frost's use of imagery and symbolism. Sound is used very effectively in this poem. The sibilant 's' sound in the opening lines conveys the tranquillity of the natural world ('These pools that, though in forests, still reflect / The total sky...'), while the long vowel sounds in rhymes ('gone / on', 'powers / flowers' and 'away / yesterday') help to convey the serious, reflective mood. The images of 'flowery waters' and 'watery flowers' suggest the frailty of these beautiful pools and flowers. Frost uses personification to highlight the contrast between the vulnerability of the flowers which 'chill and shiver' and the power of the trees which 'blot out and drink up and sweep away' the forest pools and flowers. This series of verbs accentuates the destructive capacity of the trees. An initial reading of the poem suggests that in the world of nature death leads to rebirth – the pools and flowers must die so that the trees can grow. This image suggests how the powerless in human society are oppressed by the powerful. Also on a symbolic level, the delicate pools and flowers may represent our fragile human lives. We too are easily blotted out by the passage of time, a process that is as inevitable as tree roots soaking up forest pools.

I regard *Acquainted with the Night* as an important poem because it gives a voice to those alienated and bewildered by modern urban life. The repeated use of 'I' gives the poem a confessional quality. I like the way Frost uses simple language to ensure that this poem is readily accessible, for example, 'I have been one acquainted with the night'. Image and sound combine to convey the speaker's isolation and loneliness. The image of the speaker going beyond 'the furthest city lights' effectively conveys a sense of desolation. Images of rain and depressing alleyways ('the saddest city lane') suggest the speaker's despondency, while the actual darkness evokes the spiritual darkness that enshrouds him. The repeated long 'a' sound ('acquainted...rain...rain...explain...') underscores the lonely mood. The speaker does not 'explain' his plight to the watchman – the only other person visible in this grim urban landscape – or to the reader. The fact that the cry he hears in the night is not to call him back 'or say goodbye' underscores his disconnection from everyone else in the city.

Out, Out is perhaps the most shocking and unsettling poem of Frost's that I have read. It describes the unexpected, violent death of a boy, and reminds us how fate can cruelly alter our lives in a single moment. This is a narrative poem full of drama and tension. The scene is set in beautiful New England where one can see 'Five mountain ranges one behind the other / Under the sunset far into Vermont'. The tranquillity of this rural scene is disturbed by the buzz saw that 'snarled and rattled' in the farmyard. Frost's use of onomatopoeia conveys the harsh cacophonous sound of the saw. The portrayal of the saw as a dangerous 'snarling' animal immediately conveys a sense of danger. When Frost describes how 'nothing happened', we are filled with foreboding. This is a harsh world where a boy does 'a man's work', and the adult world is held partly accountable for the tragedy that occurs. When the boy is momentarily distracted by his sister calling him for his supper, the animal-like saw leaps out at his hand. The image of the boy holding up his hand 'to keep the life from spilling' is horrifying and deeply upsetting. I was taken aback by the manner in which the boy's neighbours react to his death. They coldly accept that there is 'No more to build on there' before turning 'to their affairs'. Perhaps they are not so much unfeeling as philosophical in their understanding that life must go on, but it is hard to believe that people could remain at an emotional distance from a tragedy such as this.

Reading the poetry of Robert Frost is an enjoyable experience. His vivid descriptions, superb use of imagery and accessible language make reading his poetry not only a pleasure but a quest for the meaning of human experience.

PHILIP LARKIN

Biographical Note

Philip Larkin was born in Coventry in 1922, the only son and younger child of Eva and Sydney Larkin. Anxious that his children should grow up in an environment that was intellectually stimulating, Sydney Larkin, a city treasurer, filled the house with books. Larkin did not find childhood a particularly happy time. Because his sister was ten years older, he felt like an only child, spending much of his time reading. He described his childhood home as 'dull, pot-bound and slightly mad'. His experience of his parents' marriage left Larkin convinced 'that human beings should not live together, and that children should be taken from their parents at an early age'. His views on the negative influence of parents on children were famously expressed in his poem *This Be The Verse*.

Short-sightedness and a bad stammer meant that school life was not enjoyable for the young Larkin, although his burgeoning writing talent was evident in his regular contributions to the school magazine, of which he became joint editor.

In 1940 Larkin went to St. John's College, Oxford, to study English. After graduating, Larkin went on to qualify as a professional librarian, all the while continuing to write and publish. In 1945 his first poetry collection, *The North Ship*, was published. Two novels, *Jill* and *A Girl in Winter* were published in 1946 and 1947 respectively. Larkin's professional career saw him work as Sub-Librarian at Queen's University, Belfast, before being appointed Librarian at the University of Hull. In 1955 *The Less Deceived* was published. His third collection, *The Whitsun Weddings*, was published in 1964, cementing his reputation as one of the foremost poets of the twentieth century. His last collection *High Windows* was published in 1974. Larkin's main interest was jazz and he wrote jazz reviews for *The Daily Telegraph* between 1961 and 1971. Larkin received many awards and prizes in recognition of his literary achievements, but declined the offer to succeed John Betjeman as Poet Laureate. While he had a number of relationships, he never married. He died in 1985.

Wedding-Wind

In this poem Larkin adopts the persona of a young woman who has just got married. The first section of the poem describes her wedding night. The repetition of 'wind' in the opening lines indicates how closely the woman associates it with both her wedding day and wedding night, 'The wind blew all my wedding-day, / And my wedding-night was the night of the high wind'. The language has an appealing conversational tone. The powerful wind interrupts her wedding night when it causes a stable door to bang 'again and again', prompting her husband to leave their marital bed in order to deal with the problem. The woman describes how he left her 'stupid in candlelight', suggesting that she was drowsy and in a daze. Her sense of confusion is evoked by the idea of seeing her face in the twisted candlestick,

'Yet seeing nothing'. When her husband returns and tells her that the horses are restless, we see the woman's kind nature and generosity of spirit when she feels sorry for the upset horses, 'I was sad that any man or beast that night should lack the happiness I had'. This is a beautifully simple expression of a newly-wed bride's feelings of perfect joy and contentment.

In the second section of the poem the woman reflects on the first day of her married life. 'Now' indicates that time and her thoughts have moved on, 'Now in the day / All's ravelled under the sun by the wind's blowing'. (The term 'ravel' is one of the few words in the English language that has opposite meanings – it can be interpreted as 'entangle' or 'disentangle'). The powerful wind has had an impact on the landscape and caused some damage to the farm. Even though she got married only the previous day, the farm work must be attended to. As a woman married to a farmer, she has new responsibilities which she willingly accepts, 'He has gone to look at the floods, and I / Carry a chipped pail to the chicken run'. The image of the 'chipped pail' evokes the ordinariness of her new life, but it is a life that she joyfully embraces. Even though the sun is shining and the wind has abated, it is still windy. The woman sets down her pail, in awe of the power and force of the wind that seems to rule earth and sky like an all-powerful hunter, 'All is the wind / Hunting through clouds and forests, thrashing my apron and the hanging cloths on the line'. The image of the forceful wind 'thrashing' the woman's apron suggests how marriage has invigorated her with a new energy and passion.

The wind now becomes a metaphor for the joy that will fill the woman's new life. She wonders if she will be able to bear the excitement and happiness that this 'wind of joy' has brought into her world. The question that starts with 'Can it be borne …?' suggests that her happiness is almost excessive. An interesting image underscores her sense of inexpressible delight – her every action will turn on this wind of joy 'like a thread carrying beads'. Her excitement is such that she wonders if she will be able to sleep 'Now this perpetual morning shares my bed?' The image of 'perpetual morning' suggests that every day of her new life will be fresh and exciting. She doubts if 'even death' could threaten her new-found joy, 'Can even death dry up / These new delighted lakes, conclude / Our kneeling as cattle by all-generous waters?' In attributing feelings of delight and generosity to the natural world, she imagines how the joy blowing through her life also fills the surrounding countryside. Significantly, the closing image is one of unity, with husband and wife 'kneeling' in gratitude for their marital love and for the joy that flows from it.

KEY POINTS

- Key theme is the transforming power of love and marriage.
- Poet speaks in the voice of a female persona.
- Language combines the conversational and the metaphorical.
- The wind is a metaphor for the joy that married life brings to the woman.
- Language / imagery has positive connotations: 'wind of joy', 'perpetual morning', 'delighted lakes', 'all-generous waters'.
- A wonderfully optimistic poem.

At Grass

In this poem Larkin contrasts the tranquil, anonymous lives of two racehorses at grass with their fame and glory filled pasts. The opening is quiet and unremarkable, with the speaker barely able to make out the individual horses as they shelter together in the 'cold shade'. Only when the wind 'distresses tail and main' does one horse move and start grazing, leaving the other standing 'anonymous again'. While the scene depicted is a pleasant one, it is not without a hint of darkness. The terms 'cold shade' and 'distresses' have negative connotations, possibly suggesting that the horses' lives are drawing to a close.

The poet now remembers the horses' earlier lives when they covered themselves in glory, winning 'Cups and Stakes and Handicaps'. Then, a race of 'two dozen distances' was enough 'to fable them'. The precise meaning of 'their names were artificed to inlay faded' is unclear – it may refer to their names being inscribed on a cup. The tone is nostalgic as Larkin recalls 'classic Junes'.

This tone is sustained in stanza three as the speaker vividly conjures up the excitement and glamour of a race meeting, 'Silks at the start: against the sky / Numbers and parasols: outside, / Squadrons of empty cars …'. Details such as the 'littered grass' surrounding the cars bring the scene to life. Larkin remembers 'the long cry' from the crowd that always followed the announcement of the winner. As the cry of the crowd fades, it is replaced by the cries of newspaper sellers on the street, 'Hanging unhushed till it subside / To stop-press columns on the street'. The contrast between the colour and excitement of the horses' racing years and the tranquillity and anonymity of their present lives is striking.

Larkin now indulges in some imaginative speculation, wondering if the horses are 'plagued' by memories, buzzing around their ears 'like flies'. The image of the horses shaking their heads suggests that this is not the case. The images that follow beautifully evoke the passing of time. This process is suggested by the image of shadows fading into the darkness. The horses' greatness gradually faded away as their power and speed diminished, and the world of racing became consigned to their past, 'Summer by summer all stole away, / The starting-gates, the crowds and cries'. Now, they know only the comfort of 'unmolesting meadows'. This image

suggests that the horses are untroubled and contented, with the demands of their racing years a thing of the past. Their names and achievements are recorded in the Almanac, an annual racing handbook.

Now the horses' racing names are no longer important, 'They have slipped their names'. Their racing years are long behind them. Their lives now are utterly different from what they once were and Larkin believes that it is a change with which they are happy. They 'stand at ease, / Or gallop for what must be joy'. In an earlier life they galloped home to the finishing line, spurred on by jockeys and closely observed by the crowd. Now, 'not a fieldglass sees them home' and no one is timing them with a stopwatch. Now, their lives are tranquil, unhurried, and anonymous, 'Only the groom and the groom's boy, / With bridles in the evening come'. The repeated long 'o' sound evokes a sense of quietness. Image and sound combine to create a sense of perfect peace. While the day drawing to a close may be suggestive of the horses' lives nearing their end, death is not seen in a threatening light – rather is it as natural as the groom waiting to put the horses' bridles on at the end of their day in the meadow.

KEY POINTS

- Key theme is the change brought about by the passage of time.
- Poem may be read on a symbolic level as a reflection on the meaning of life.
- Poem contrasts the horses' glory-covered pasts with the anonymous lives they now lead.
- Imagery deftly captures both the excitement of the races and the tranquillity of the horses' present lives.
- Tone is nostalgic – yet the poem also celebrates the contentment of the horses' present lives.
- Effective use of sound.

Church Going

The first two stanzas describe a man visiting a church and his observations on its interior. The speaker is the poet. As the poem develops, detailed description leads on to reflection, analysis and

philosophical speculation. The opening lines of the poem describe the speaker tentatively entering the church once he is 'sure there's nothing going on'. Onomatopoeia suggests the sound of the door closing behind him, 'letting the door thud shut'. The phrase 'another church' suggests that going into churches is something that the poet does regularly, while also evoking a sense of monotony (boredom). He looks around, taking in every detail, 'matting, seats and stone, / And little books'. The image of the 'brownish' flowers suggests the passing of time. The speaker's casual description of what he sees on the altar ('some brass and stuff / Up at the holy end') suggests his dismissive attitude towards the church. The language is colloquial, the tone informal. The speaker refers to 'a tense, musty, unignorable silence'. There is a touch of humour in the suggestion that only 'God knows how long' ago this silence was 'brewed'. Aware that people normally remove their hats in a church, the 'hatless' poet removes his bicycle clips in a humorously self-conscious gesture of respect ('in awkward reverence').

The second stanza sees the curious poet 'move forward' and run his hand 'around the font'. We see his observant eye as he wonders whether the new-looking roof was cleaned or restored. He takes the opportunity to step up to the lectern. Perusing 'a few hectoring large-scale verses', he cannot resist reading one aloud. However, he pronounces 'Here endeth' more loudly than he intended and the echo returns to him like a snigger. This is the only humorous note in a serious, meditative poem. The poet leaves, unimpressed with his experience. Cynically donating 'an Irish sixpence' at the door, he reflects that 'the place was not worth stopping for'. If he went into the church in search of some profound experience, he leaves disappointed.

At this point description gives way to reflection, questioning and speculation. Despite feeling 'at a loss' after every visit he makes to a church, the poet continues to be drawn to them. He is certain that churches will cease to function as places of worship and wonders what use they will be put to when they 'fall completely out of use'. The poet speculates that 'A few cathedrals' might function as museums. These will be places of curiosity without spiritual value. The image of 'parchment, plate and pyx in locked cases' underlines the poet's belief that churches will become spiritually

irrelevant and no longer function as living places of worship. He envisages some churches falling into a state of disrepair. The idea of letting the rest 'rent-free to rain and sheep' is humorous in a dark way but further reflective of his pessimistic vision of the future of churches. Larkin even considers the possibility that churches might come to be regarded 'as unlucky places' – a darker vision than churches simply becoming irrelevant and falling into disuse.

He imagines the empty buildings assuming a superstitious significance with 'dubious women' visiting them after dark 'to make their children touch a particular stone' or to see the ghost of a loved one. The poet goes on to reflect that 'superstition, like belief, must die'. When this occurs, he imagines the wholly abandoned churches becoming places of desolation, 'Grass, weedy pavements, brambles, buttress, sky'.

Larkin envisions the church gradually falling into ruin, becoming 'A shape less recognisable each week'. He now wonders 'who will be the last, the very last' person to visit this church. Will it be someone interested in church architecture ('one of the crew / That tap and jot and know what good roof-lofts were'), some antique lover, or some 'Christmas addict' anxious to imaginatively experience the rituals and atmosphere of that special season? Finally, he considers the possibility that the last person to visit this church might be someone like himself ('my representative') a 'bored, uninformed' atheist. A person like himself would be drawn to this cross-shaped building because it functioned for 'so long and equably' as a focal point in the lives of so many people, its rituals marking the key events in a person's life, 'marriage and birth and death'. Larkin acknowledges that the church's ceremonies gave order and meaning to human existence. His description of the church as a 'special shell' and an 'accoutred frowsty barn' reflect his ambivalent attitude towards churches. Despite his mixed feelings, the poet admits that he is pleased 'to stand in silence' in the empty church.

The closing stanza is, in contrast to the earlier part of the poem, solemn and dignified in tone.

The poet values the church because it is 'A serious house on serious earth'. In the church 'all our compulsions meet, / Are recognised, and robed as destinies'. He recognises that the Church is a serious place which lends a formality and a dignity to the key events in our lives – birth, marriage and death. The poet suggests that there will always be a need for such an institution, 'And that much never can be obsolete'. By honouring the key moments in our lives, the church fulfils our need to see meaning in such moments. A person's 'hunger … to be more serious' will see him drawn to this place ('gravitating … to this ground'). Despite predicting the demise of the church, the poet concludes that future generations will continue to associate the church with wisdom – a place 'proper to grow wise in'.

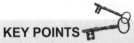

KEY POINTS

- Key themes include the role and importance of the church in the modern age and the human need for meaning in life.
- Poem moves from narrative/description to reflection and speculation.
- Tone varies from the indifferent and dismissive to the serious and dignified.
- Interesting metaphors: the church is 'this special shell' and 'this accoutred frowsty barn'.
- Language combines the conversational ('some brass and stuff', etc.) and the formal ('In whose blent air all our compulsions meet', etc.).
- Touches of humour.
- Use of rhetorical questions ('And what remains when disbelief has gone?', etc.).
- Sound effects include alliteration ('parchment, plate and pyx', 'dark … dubious', 'Stand in silence', etc) and assonance ('pipes and myrrh', 'for though I've no …', etc) and end-rhyme.

An Arundel Tomb

This poem was inspired by the ancient statue that decorates the tomb of the Earl and Countess of Arundel in Chichester Cathedral. The statue is unusual because the couple were sculpted lying side by side. Similar to *Church Going*, description leads on to serious reflection.

The opening stanza describes the statue in a direct manner, 'Side by side, their faces blurred'. The 'blurred faces' suggests how the passage of time has taken its toll on the statue. The couple are dressed in attire befitting their status ('proper habits'). The earl is wearing his armour, while his wife is wearing a stiff, pleated dress. The presence of two dogs at the couple's feet gives the cold, lifeless monument a warm, human touch. The poet is unimpressed with this aspect of the statue, describing it as 'that faint hint of the absurd'. He seems to regard the inclusion of the dogs in this commemorative monument as silly.

Larkin does not find the 'plainness of the pre-baroque' style sculpture appealing. However, his interest is awakened when he observes that the earl has withdrawn one hand from its gauntlet in order to hold his wife's hand. He describes the effect this image has on him as 'a sharp tender shock'. It is an image which suggests the power of love to outlive death.

The earl and countess never imagined that their monument would survive centuries, 'They would not think to lie so long'. Holding hands 'was just a detail friends would see', reminding them of the couple's love and faithfulness. The couple's names were carved on the base of the statue. The sculptor perceived that the loving gesture of the earl holding his wife's hand would 'prolong' these names by giving the statue a human quality that would draw people's attention to it, in this way helping to preserve the couple's identities and shared love.

At this point Larkin reflects on how time has changed both the statue and English society. The couple could never have guessed how early into its 'voyage' through the years their stone image would feel the destructive effects of time. The moisture in the air gradually eroded the sculpture, causing 'soundless damage'. Neither could they have imagined how soon after their deaths English society would begin to change. 'Turn the old tenantry away' may refer to social changes brought about by the demise of the feudal system or by the Reformation. Another social change the couple could not have anticipated was Latin falling into disuse, resulting in people looking at the statue, without being able to read the accompanying inscription, 'How soon succeeding eyes begin / To look, not read'.

Despite signs of decay, the sculpture has survived to the present day, 'Rigidly they / Persisted, linked, through lengths and breadths of time'. There is a suggestion here that the couple, frozen in their display of love, have transcended (risen above) time. While the passage of time is evident throughout the poem, it is most vividly evoked in stanza five. Seasons have inexorably come and gone, 'Snow fell undated. Light / Each summer thronged the glass'. The metaphor of 'a bright litter of birdcalls' strewing the cemetery (an image suggestive of spring) is particularly striking. While the landscape changes with the seasons, the 'Bone-riddled ground' remains an immutable reality. Each year new visitors ('altered people') arrive in an 'endless' stream to view the statue.

'Washing at their identity' suggests how this tide of people inadvertently wears away the monument. The effigies are 'helpless in the hollow of an unarmorial age' ('armorial' relates to knighthood). Defenceless in an age that is superficial and lacking in nobility, they are exposed to 'a trough / Of smoke in slow suspended skeins' (an image suggestive of the destructive effects of pollution). The passage of time has reduced their role in history to a footnote ('their scrap of history'). The closing line in this stanza ('Only an attitude remains') suggests how time has diminished the stone couple. The monument is associated more with the idea of immortal love than with their individual identities. The 'attitude' that remains is the statue's expression of love.

The poet declares that 'Time has transfigured them into / Untruth'. The statue has been transformed into a symbol of eternal love – a concept which the poet dismisses as false. Furthermore, the medieval couple never intended their monument to assume such significance, 'The stone fidelity / They hardly meant has come to be / Their final blazon'. Given our instinctive desire to believe that love can transcend time, we are inclined to view the statue as proof of this hopeful idea, 'to prove / Our almost-instinct almost true'. The use of 'our' and 'us' draws the reader into the poem. It is the phrase 'almost true' that qualifies the optimistic-sounding final line, 'What will survive of us is love'. The closing lines imply that love cannot survive the inexorable passage of time and the finality of death.

KEY POINTS

- Key themes include the passing of time, and the power of love to transcend time.
- Description leads on to reflection.
- Some memorable images ('A bright litter of birdcalls', etc).
- Fixed rhyming pattern.
- Pessimistic conclusion.

The Whitsun Weddings

This poem is based on a train journey Larkin made from Hull to London on a Whit Saturday. The weekend of Whitsun was a popular time for weddings, and Larkin observes various wedding parties seeing off the newly married couples as they board the train at different stops. Initially the detached observer, Larkin gradually becomes more involved with those he observes. Again we see how description leads to reflection and insight.

The poem opens in a conversational manner, 'That Whitsun, I was late getting away'. The image of 'the sunlit Saturday' sets the tone for the largely optimistic poem that follows. The 'three-quarters empty' train is warm, but airy ('All windows down') and Larkin settles into his journey. There is a sense of ease and relaxation, 'all sense / Of being in a hurry gone'. Vivid sensory details (the hot cushions, the blinding windscreens and the smell from the fish-dock) bring the poet's experience to life for the reader. Following the course of the river, the train races into the countryside 'Where sky and Lincolnshire and water meet'. This is an image of wonderful simplicity, evoking the beauty and harmony of the rural landscape. The poem is written largely in iambic pentameter (with the exception of the second line in each stanza which has four beats, all the others have ten beats) and this, along with the fixed rhyming pattern (ABABCDECDE) conveys the rhythm of the train.

Stanza two opens in an interesting way, personifying the weather, 'All afternoon, through the tall heat that slept / For miles inland'. The train journey is described as 'A slow and stopping curve southwards'. A series of images convey the contrasting rural and urban landscapes through which the train speeds: farms, cattle, hedges, a polluted canal, a greenhouse flashing in the sunlight. The new industrial towns hold no interest for the poet who describes them as 'nondescript' (featureless, dull). On the outskirts of one such town is a grim industrial wasteland 'with acres of dismantled cars'.

Newly married couples board the train at different stops. At first the poet does not notice the couples or the wedding parties that have come to see them off. Enjoying the sunshine and absorbed in his reading, he has little interest in what is happening in the shade of the platform. He mistakes the din ('whoops and skirls') created by the joyful wedding party for porters joking about ('larking with the mails'). Larkin only notices the wedding party as the train pulls away from the station. The women are happy ('grinning'), wearing perfume ('pomaded') and dressed in their finest clothes ('heels and veils'). The middle class poet displays a condescending attitude towards these working class women. In describing them as 'parodies of fashion' he suggests that their attire is only a cheap imitation of the latest fashion styles. As the train leaves, they seem to pose uncertainly ('irresolutely'), watching it go, waving goodbye.

His interest aroused by this experience, the poet looks forward to the next stop, anticipating another wedding party seeing off another newly married couple, 'Struck, I leant / More promptly out next time, more curiously'. Again, this group is described in a superior tone. The fathers wear the 'broad belts' of working men to hold the trousers of their suits in place, the mothers are 'loud and fat' and an uncle is stereotypically vulgar ('shouting smut'). The younger women with their 'jewellery-substitutes' are also described with a hint of arrogance. Stanzas one and two end with full stops, but from stanza three on the stanzas flow into each other as Larkin portrays one wedding party after another waiting at the various stops on the line to London.

In stanza five the poet's reflections extend beyond the platform scenes as he pictures wedding receptions throughout the countryside drawing to a close, 'from cafes / And banquet-halls up yards, and bunting-dressed / Coach-party annexes, the wedding-days / were coming to an end'. Here Larkin implies that these cheaper venues were all that working class people could afford. Again, we are made aware that the poet is far removed from – and feels far above – the world of the ordinary people who have now captured his interest. At every stop 'fresh couples' climb aboard the train with 'the last confetti and advice' being thrown. The coupling of 'confetti and advice' suggests the glib nature of the advice offered. It is interesting that from this stanza five on, Larkin speaks almost entirely in the first person plural ('And, as we moved …'), indicating his increasing involvement with the people he observes. The various expressions on the faces of those left on the platform reflect their feelings on the wedding they have just attended. With the day's excitement now at an end, bored children frown 'at something dull'.

The fathers are proud and delighted, never having known 'success so huge'. Married women, aware that married life would bring both joy and sorrow to the departing couple, 'shared the secret like a happy funeral' – a simile that perfectly captures their contrasting emotions. The young women are portrayed as 'gripping their handbags tighter', an image which suggests a combination of excitement and anxiety. They stare 'at a religious wounding' – a phrase suggestive of the pain that is an unavoidable part of marriage. Packed with married couples, the train recommences its journey. Interestingly, the poet now identifies with his fellow passengers, 'We hurried towards London'. The detached observer of the first half of the poem is now a participant in the scene. The image of 'shuffling gouts of steam' deftly captures the sight and sound of the train picking up speed. As the train nears the city, the landscape changes, 'Now fields were building-plots'. The onset of evening is suggested by the 'long shadows' cast by the poplar trees.

'Free at last', the newly married couples settle into the journey. For them, this journey is brief and unremarkable, 'Just long enough to settle hats and say / *I nearly died*'. The latter phrase conveys the nervous excitement of the couples as they recall the day's events. Larkin watches them as they watch the urban landscape flashing by – the train rushes past a cinema ('An Odeon'), a water tower and a cricket pitch ('someone running up to bowl'). He reflects on how none of them thought of the other couples. While they are naturally too absorbed in the excitement of their wedding day to think about anybody else, Larkin, the observer, considers how these couples' lives 'would all contain this hour'. In a striking image the poet gives the city of London an appealing rural quality, 'I thought of London spread out in the sun, / Its postal districts packed like squares of wheat'.

The poem ends with a moment of insight. As the train approaches the station ('past standing Pullmans, walls of blackened moss'). Larkin describes the twelve couples sharing the same train as a 'frail / Travelling coincidence'. It seems to the poet that the train is 'full of the power / That being changed can give'. Changed and energised by marriage, the couples are ready to release their new-found power into the world. There is a sense here of the unlimited possibilities for the couples embarking on the journey of married life. As the train shudders to a halt, the poet is thrown slightly forward, 'there swelled / A sense of falling'. The strange image of 'an arrow shower … becoming rain' evokes various ideas, in particular the power and energy of the newly married couples. It may also suggest the notion of Cupid's arrow of love and its ability to both inspire and injure.

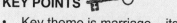

KEY POINTS

- Key theme is marriage – its joys, pain and power to change.
- Description leads on to reflection and insight.
- Imagery / description has a sensuous quality – engages our sense of touch ('all seats hot', etc.), smell ('a smell of grass / Displaced the reek of button carriage-cloth', etc.), sight ('A hothouse flashed uniquely', etc.) and sound ('whoops and skirls', etc).
- Language combines the conversational ('I was late getting away') and the metaphorical ('an arrow shower…becoming rain').

- Effective use of sound. The combination of iambic pentameter and the regular rhyming pattern conveys a sense of the steam train in motion. The use of onomatopoeia ('shuffling') suggests the sound of the train.
- Tone is initially detached, but the poet becomes increasingly involved in the scene he is observing.

MCMXIV

The Roman numerals that make up the title of the poem suggest a bygone age. This poem looks back on English society before the outbreak of the First World War. Stanza one opens with a description of men queuing in 'long uneven lines' to enlist in the British army. This image evokes the battlefields of the First World War. Patient and relaxed, they might have been queuing for a cricket game or a football match, 'As if they were stretched outside / The Oval or Villa Park'. The men are smartly dressed, wearing their 'crowns of hats'. The image of 'moustached archaic faces' underlines the sense that they belong to a time long gone. The sibilant 's' sound ('crowns ... hats ... moustached ... faces') conveys a peaceful mood. The image of the men 'Grinning as if it were all / An August Bank Holiday Lark' suggests a carefree world of innocence. The reader's awareness of the unspeakable carnage and horror of the war for which these men are enlisting charges this happy scene with irony. The men themselves are oblivious of the social upheaval that the impending war would bring – the world they know would be changed irrevocably.

In stanza two a series of visual details vividly evoke early twentieth-century English society. There are references to 'established names' on the sunblinds of businesses, the age-old English currency ('farthings and sovereigns'), children named after various royal figures and dressed in the black that children generally wore in that era, the antiquated 'tin advertisements' for 'cocoa and twist' (a type of tobacco) and 'the pubs wide open all day'. The overall impression is of a stable, unchanging, innocent society. Taken together, the images of smiling men, children happily playing and a sun-soaked town convey a sense of an idyllic world.

The opening lines of stanza three sustain the carefree mood. The luxuriant growth of the countryside covers place-names, 'And the countryside not caring: / The place-names all hazed over / With flowering grasses'. These lines suggest a sense of ease and abundance. The poet's use of alliteration, assonance and sibilance give these lines a pleasant musical quality. However, there is a change of mood at this point as sunshine gives way to shadow. The image of the fields 'Shadowing Domesday's lines' suggests how nature covers boundaries drawn up by William the Conquerer centuries earlier. However, the real significance of this image lies in its connotations – 'Domesday's lines' chillingly evokes images of doomed soldiers facing each other on the battlefield. The reference to 'wheat's restless silence' suggests a sense of foreboding, a threatening feeling of difficult times ahead. The closing lines in stanza three see Larkin focusing on the social divisions that were such a marked feature of English society at this time, 'The differently-dressed servants / With tiny rooms in huge houses'. Here we are reminded of the inequality and massive disparities in wealth that were inherent in a society divided sharply along class lines.

While aware that pre-war English society had its flaws, Larkin laments the innocence lost with the passing of that age. Repetition underscores the poet's belief that there has never been a time – before or since – to compare with it, 'Never such innocence, / Never before or since'. The image of 'the men / Leaving the gardens tidy' before departing for a war from which many would never return is poignant. The idea of 'thousands of marriages / lasting a little while longer' points to the heartbreak that lay ahead for so many. The repetition of the opening line at the close of the poem coveys the poet's conviction that this was a uniquely innocent age, 'Never such innocence again'.

KEY POINTS

- Key theme is the passing of an age of innocence.
- Use of simple language.
- Description of pre-war society has a strong visual quality.
- The enlisting men's innocence of the grim reality of the impending war gives the poem an ironic quality.
- Repetition used for persuasive effect.
- Poem consists of one long sentence without a main verb – a feature of style that conveys a sense of another era.

Ambulances

This is a gloomy poem that reflects on illness and death. Neither is mentioned directly, rather are they symbolised by ambulances. The simile with which the poem opens ('Closed like confessionals') suggests that ambulances are dark, closed and private. As ambulances 'thread' their way through urban traffic, they draw the attention of onlookers, suggesting our fascination with death. Ambulances 'absorb' the glances they get, giving back nothing in return. Here the mystery of death is evoked. The description of the ambulances' appearance ('Light, glossy grey, arms on a plaque') suggests their (and, by implication, death's) ordinariness. The closing lines in the opening stanza suggest that illness and death are indiscriminate (random), while death is inevitable, 'They come to rest at any kerb: / All streets in time are visited'.

Stanza two describes a scene from everyday life, 'The children strewn on steps or road, / Or women coming from the shops / Past smells of different dinners'. These lines give no hint of the drama that accompanies the unexpected arrival of the ambulance. The image of 'A wild white face' suggests a patient's terror when confronted with his/her own mortality. The image of red blankets has obvious connotations of blood. The tone of the closing line in this stanza is strikingly cold and detached, 'As it is carried away and stowed'.

As with so many of Larkin's poems, description leads to reflection. Having portrayed the ambulance's appearance and operation, the poem now explores its impact on onlookers. Their response to observing the ambulance is given a universal quality through the pronoun 'we', 'And sense the solving emptiness / That lies just under all we do'. The onlookers are now aware that the grim reality of death underlies all that we do. This moment of clarity and understanding came in an instant, 'And for a second get it whole'. They now see that the reality of death is 'permanent and blank and true' – beyond it lies only 'emptiness'. The implication of these lines is that Larkin does not believe in the idea of a spiritual afterlife and has a pessimistic view of human existence. When the ambulance leaves, the onlookers seem to sympathise with the unfortunate person in the ambulance ('Poor soul') but in reality, they are more upset at being reminded of their own mortality, 'They whisper at their own distress'.

The patient is 'borne away in deadened air', underlining the ambulance's association with death. The 'sudden shut of loss' suggests how, with the closing of the ambulance doors, the person inside is shut off from the world and from the life he knew. His life is 'nearly at an end'. This person was part of a family and of a particular society ('the unique random blend / Of families

199

and fashions'), but the links connecting him with family and society 'begin to loosen' in the ambulance. This sense of isolation (suggested by the earlier reference to the confessional) reminds us that everyone faces death alone.

The person in the ambulance is now cut off from interaction with loved ones, 'From the exchange of love'. He is 'unreachable' inside the 'room'

that is the ambulance. The importance of death is suggested by the image of traffic parting to let the ambulance go by. The ambulance brings its patient 'closer to what is left to come' – what is 'left to come' is death. The closing line reminds us that the experience of this one person awaits us all as we inexorably draw closer to the end, 'And dulls to distance all we are'.

KEY POINTS

- Key theme is the inevitability and finality of death.
- Description leads to reflection.
- Larkin offers us a bleak view of human existence.
- Tone is unemotional, detached ('… it is carried in and stowed', 'borne away', etc.), adding to the sense of bleakness.
- Poem is dominated by the metaphor of the ambulance.
- Imagery is drawn from everyday urban life: streets, traffic, women shopping, etc.
- Language combines the colloquial ('Poor soul', etc.) and the metaphorical ('the solving emptiness', etc.).

The Trees

This poem is concerned with the rebirth of nature in springtime and the transience of human life. The opening line depicts the advent of spring, a season associated with new life, 'The trees are coming into leaf'. The simile 'Like something almost being said' suggests that the process of foliation is not yet complete. It may also suggest that nature is communicating with us. The buds are personified, 'The recent buds relax and spread'. The sibilant 's' sound conveys the tranquillity of the scene. The first stanza closes with a strange metaphor, 'Their greenness is a kind of grief'. Budding leaves are normally a symbol of joy, hope and beauty rather than sorrow. Perhaps this grief is caused by the poet's awareness that, unlike nature, man cannot renew himself.

The poet teases out this idea in stanza two, posing a question, 'Is it that they are born again / And we grow old?' The poet's answer to this question is an emphatic 'no'. He points out that 'they (the

trees) die too'. Their new canopy of fresh leaves every spring is seen as a mere trick to deceive us into believing they are immortal, 'Their yearly trick of looking new'. In reality, of course, trees age (as the 'rings' in the trunk indicate) and die.

Yet, despite the poet realising that they are not immortal, the blossoming trees offer encouragement and hope to humans. In stanza three the trees are in full leaf, 'in fullgrown thickness', the castle metaphor suggesting their strength and grandeur. They seem to communicate a message to the human world in relation to how we should deal with the passage of time, 'Last year is dead, they seem to say, / Begin afresh, afresh, afresh'. The trees are admired for their determination to begin anew every spring. They exhort us to continually make a fresh start. Repetition adds to the persuasiveness of their message about beginning anew and living life to the full.

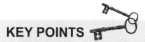

The Explosion

This is a narrative poem that describes a mine explosion in which many miners lost their lives. While the opening stanza depicts a quiet, sunny scene, it conveys a strong sense of foreboding. The shadows pointing 'towards the pithead' seem sinister, while the personified slagheap ('the slagheap slept') is a dark, threatening presence, conjuring up an image of a monster that might wake from its slumber at any moment. Of course much of the tension in the poem derives from our knowledge of the disaster that will occur.

Stanza two portrays a group of miners on their way to the pithead. A few details vividly conjure up the scene, 'men in pitboots / Coughing oath-edged talk and pipe smoke'. The miners, toughened by years of hard work below ground, smoke and swear as they make their way to work. Their coughing is the result of the unhealthy nature of their work underground. The miners are oblivious of the freshness and silence of the morning, 'Shouldering off the freshened silence'.

The poet then shifts his focus away from the group and on to an individual who chases after rabbits. He fails to catch them, but returns with a nest of lark's eggs. The image of the miner gently lodging the eggs 'in the grasses' suggests a gentleness and a delicacy that seems at odds with the rough and ready image of the miners in the previous stanza. This tender image heightens the poignancy of his death.

The phrase 'So they passed' suggests the idea of the miners unknowingly drawing closer to their grim fate. The reference to 'beards and moleskins' adds to the visual quality of the scene. United by bonds of family and friendship, the miners are a close-knit community, 'Fathers, brothers, nicknames, laughter'. Their innocent light-hearted banter contrasts with the looming dark shadow of imminent disaster. There is an ominous sense to the image of the miners walking 'Through the tall gates standing open'– it is as if they are marching into the next world. Long vowel sounds convey the solemn tone.

Stanza five deals with the terrible moment of the explosion. There are no graphic details of the carnage and devastation. The disaster is described in a detached manner. On the surface the explosion registers as 'a tremor'. The natural world registers the explosion in the cows' brief pause from their grazing. The fact that they stopped chewing for only 'a second' is a reminder that life goes on, regardless of such catastrophes. The image of the dimmed sun evokes the darkness of this dreadful disaster, 'sun, / Scarfed as in a heat-haze, dimmed'.

Stanza seven consists of a passage from the bible which holds out the hope of the dead enjoying the comfort of heaven and being re-united with friends and loved ones. It was reported that the wives of the dead miners saw this text 'Plain as lettering in the chapels'. The mystical experience continued with the wives having a momentary vision of their husbands. Some were 'Larger than in life', others bathed in a golden light ('Gold as on a coin') or 'walking from the sun towards them'. The account of these visions, with their suggestion of immortal life in heaven, gives the end of the poem a wonderfully uplifting quality.

The concluding line in the poem stands alone. In

one of the visions a miner was carrying the eggs he had found that morning, 'One showing the eggs unbroken'. The final image evokes the idea of new life and continuity in the face of tragedy.

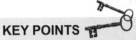

KEY POINTS

- Key theme is the possibility of life after death. Another key idea in the poem is the harshness of the miners' lives.
- Realistic details vividly depict the miners.
- Tone is generally detached, but Larkin's sympathy for the miners is clear.
- The full stops at the end of stanzas 1–5 create a sense of tension.

Cut Grass

The title of the poem suggests the idea of life brought to a sudden end. In this poem Larkin reflects on the natural cycle of death and renewal. The opening lines evoke the frailty and brevity of life, 'Cut grass lies frail: / Brief is the breath mown stalks exhale'. The breath 'exhaled' by the grass is the smell of freshly cut grass. Here Larkin gives human qualities to the grass. The image of cut grass may be symbolic of our mortality since death is often portrayed as the Grim Reaper with a scythe. Like the grass, we too will inevitably be cut down.

In contrast to the transience of life, death lasts forever, 'Long, long the death it dies …'. Death and new life co-exist in the beautiful summer countryside. The grass withers and decays 'in the white hours of young-leafed June'. While the grass is dying, the tone is not gloomy because the poet is everywhere reminded of the richness and abundance of nature. The countryside is covered in a blanket of flowers, whose freshness contrasts with the decaying grass. The fact that the flowers mentioned are predominantly white accentuates the sense of purity. White 'chestnut flowers' and 'white lilac' fill the poet's eye, hedges are covered in white blossom ('snowlike strewn'), while country lanes are decorated with 'Queen Anne's lace'. While all of these flowers will, like the grass, die, the mood is not bleak. On the contrary, poet and reader are cheered by the realisation that rebirth and renewal are constant features of the natural world. The repeated broad vowel ('frail… mown… exhale… snowlike… lanes… lace', etc) and 's' sounds ('With chestnut flowers, / With hedges snowlike strewn', etc.) help to convey the tranquil relaxed mood of a sunny summer's day. The closing image of the cloud gently blown by the summer breeze adds to the sense of perfect peace, further underlining the positive mood. The flowers are ephemeral, but more will replace those that wither and die. Life is transient, but it goes on, regardless of the demise of individual existences.

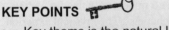

KEY POINTS

- Key theme is the natural life cycle of death and renewal.
- Poem may be read on a symbolic level – the ephemeral flowers may represent mortal man.
- Mood is essentially positive.
- Memorable natural images ('hedges snowlike strewn', etc.).
- A poem rich in musical qualities: alliteration ('Brief is the breath', etc.), assonance ('lanes of Queen Anne's lace', etc.), sibilance ('With chestnut flowers, / With hedges snowlike strewn', etc.) and end rhyme.

Key Points on Style: poetry of Philip Larkin
(Word Choice / Imagery / Sound Techniques / Contrast)

Word Choice
- Use of simple, accessible language. In 'Wedding Wind' for example, the poem opens with a statement of fact: *'The wind blew all my wedding day, / And my wedding night was the night of the high wind.'* Similarly, the opening of 'At Grass': *'The eye can hardly pick them out'*, referring to the retired race horses and the simple, conversational opening of 'Church Going': *'Once I am sure there's nothing going on / I step inside ...'* ; *'Someone would know: I don't'*. The language of all the poems is essentially down-to-earth and practical – the opposite of the more elaborate, ornamental style of the Romantic poets.
- Use of verbs to imply symbolic meanings: 'Borne', *'bodying-forth'*, in 'Wedding Wind', suggesting possible pregnancy in the future and regeneration – this is also linked to the image of the *'chicken-run'*. Changes of verb tense within a poem are significant. For example, in 'Church Going', the poem opens in the present tense, moves briefly to the past tense and then contemplates the future: *'I take off my cycle-clips ... run my hand around the font ... sign the book'* – then shifts to past tense: *'Yet stop I did'* and the remainder of the poem contemplates the future: *'When churches fall completely out of use / what we shall turn them into ... if we shall keep ...'*. The effect of these shifts in tense is related to the concept of the churches as they now are, what they were in the past and what they will be in the future.
- Use of words with positive and negative connotations: *'joy'*, *'delighted'*, *'all-generous'* are used in 'Wedding Wind' but are contrasted with words of negative connotation: *'banging'*, *'must go'*, *'twisted'*, *'restless'*, *'sad'*. This use of word choice creates contrast in tone, suggesting an ambiguity in the poem – joy in marriage but uncertainty, perhaps fear.
- Use of words with negative connotations are also apparent in 'At Grass':*'cold'*, *'distresses'*, *'anonymous'*, *'plague'*, *'shadows'*, 'Dusk' – the effect is to suggest that retirement is a prelude to death and anonymity.
- Use of word play in a poem like 'At Grass' to layer the meaning of the poem: *'distances'* is used to convey the length of the races run by the horses, but also conveys how they have become a distant memory *'They have slipped their names'*, *'The eye can hardly pick them out'*.

Imagery
- Use of nature imagery to indicate the strength of the speaker's passion. Notice this in 'Wedding Wind': especially the references to the strength of the wind – *'All is the wind / Hunting through clouds and forests, thrashing/ My apron'*. The violent nature of the energy of the wind – could this suggest an overwhelming love or a fear of the strength of her own passion?
- Use of very detailed description is common in all of the poems. Take for example 'Church Going' and its sensual appeal: we hear the door *'thud shut'* and the speaker *'pronounce Here endeth, much more loudly than I meant'*. We see the *'little books'*, *'sprawlings of flowers'*, *'an Irish sixpence'*. We smell

'*musty*' atmosphere, the '*whiff of gown-and-bands*', '*myrrh*'. We can almost feel the different textures of '*matting, seats and stone*', '*Grass, weedy pavement, brambles ...*' The effect of this richly sensuous imagery is to draw us into the poem, so that we experience what the poet is experiencing.

- The use of a cinematic technique is apparent in the detailed imagery and panning effect. A good example of this is in 'At Grass' – where the poet describes the races: '*Silks at the start: against the sky / Numbers and parasols*', '*squadrons of empty cars*', '*littered grass*', '*long cry*', '*stop-press columns*'.

Sound Techniques

- Larkin uses varied sound techniques which give a musical, lyrical quality to many of his poems. In 'Wedding Wind', many of these techniques are apparent – **Alliteration**: '*wind*', '*wedding*', '*wedding-night*', '*chipped* ' '*chicken-run*', '*borne*', '*bodying-forth*, '*beads*', '*bed*'. **Assonance**: '*My*', '*night*', '*high*'. '*again*', '*rain*', '*face*', '*came*'. : '*back*', '*lack*', '*sad*', '*had*', '*thread*', '*bed*'. No formal rhyme schemes are used, but the total effect is extremely musical and pleasing which emphasises the joy of the bride. Use of alliteration, assonance and rhyme also enhances the sound quality of the poem 'At Grass'. **Rhythm** cleverly brings out the fast pace of the races as opposed to the slow grazing of the horses.

Contrast

- Contrast is a stylistic technique used by Larkin throughout his poems. This can be seen in 'At Grass' where races and fame are opposed to anonymity and death. There is a contrast of time and seasons: '*faint afternoons*', '*faded, classic Junes*', '*Dusk brims the shadows*', '*Summer by summer*'. The effect is to focus attention on the transience of life and fame. Notice also the contrast of the peaceful meadows, '*unmolesting*', with the crowd's '*long cry*' and the excitement of the race. Contrast is also used effectively in 'Church Going' – faith is opposed to disbelief, the present to the future, the superstition is contrasted to the spiritual '*hunger*'.

Sample Answer

'Philip Larkin – An Introduction.'

Larkin believed that poetry should be accessible and enjoyable to ordinary people. He finds his inspiration in ordinary, everyday life. He said, 'I write about experiences, often quite simple everyday experiences which somehow acquire some sort of special meaning for me, and I write poems about them to preserve them'. Larkin's imaginative engagement with ordinary lives and commonplace situations leads him to reflect on a range of themes, notably love and marriage, nature, the passage of time and death. Even when he is not dealing directly with the transience of life, an awareness of death is invariably in the background of his poems. While Larkin deals with ordinary life, many of his poems are rich in philosophical ideas, with observation and description leading to reflection. His poems generally end in a memorable manner, with moments of truth and beauty often expressed symbolically. While Larkin's language is generally that of the ordinary man, it combines the colloquial with the descriptive and the metaphorical. The precise detail in his poems is testimony to his fascination with the everyday lives that are the stuff of his poetry. Larkin's rich, vivid images are often drawn from the natural world. A feature of his poetry is his use of regular rhyming patterns and stanza structures. Finally, many of his poems are written in the first person. While Larkin frequently adopts a persona, it is often difficult to distinguish between the voices of such personae and that of the poet. I will now discuss a number of Larkin's poems to illustrate these observations.

Larkin is often viewed as a bleak poet because of his preoccupation with death, but not all of his poetry is gloomy. Among his more optimistic poems are those dealing with the theme of marriage. Given his personal status as a confirmed bachelor, Larkin's preoccupation with this theme is a little unusual. In *Wedding-Wind* the poet assumes the persona of a young woman who has just got married – this is the first day of her new life as a farmer's wife. The conversational opening explains the title, 'The wind blew all my wedding-day, / And my wedding-night was the night of the high wind'. When the woman's husband returns from closing the banging stable door, he tells her that the horses are uneasy. In expressing her sympathy for the horses, the woman expresses a newly-wed bride's feelings of perfect joy and contentment, 'I was sad that any man or beast that night should lack the happiness I had'. As she goes about her chores on the farm, she is filled with awe at the power of the wind which now assumes a metaphorical significance, becoming the 'wind of joy' that blows through her life. The poem ends in a wonderfully uplifting manner, with the new bride's sense of perfect joy beautifully captured in an image personifying the world of nature. She doubts if even death could threaten her new-found joy, 'Can even death dry up / These new delighted lakes, conclude / Our kneeling as cattle by all-generous waters'.

The Whitsun Weddings also has an everyday setting, being based on a train journey from Hull to London on a Whit Saturday. Larkin observes various wedding parties seeing off the newly married couples as they board the train at different stops. In this poem we see how description leads to reflection. The poem opens in a typically conversational manner, 'That Whitsun, I was late getting away'. The poem is written largely in iambic pentameter and this, along with the fixed rhyming pattern (ABABCDECDE) conveys the rhythm of the train. As the journey continues, Larkin becomes increasingly absorbed in the lives of the people he observes at the different stops. The poet's detailed descriptions reflect his genuine interest in these people. The women are happy ('grinning'), wearing perfume ('pomaded') and dressed in their finest clothes ('heels and veils'). The fathers wear the 'broad belts' of working men'. Larkin becomes more meditative as the journey continues, imagining how the central characters in the wedding party feel on this special day. The fathers are proud and delighted, while the mothers, aware of both the joy and sorrow that lay ahead for the departing couple, 'shared the secret like a happy funeral' – a simile that perfectly captures their mixed emotions. The poem ends with a visionary moment. As the train approaches London, it seems to the poet that the young couples have been changed and energised by marriage (much like the newly married woman in *Wedding-Wind*), and are ready to release their new-found power into the world, 'Stood ready to be loosed with all the power / That being changed can give'.

Church Going is a poem inspired by an everyday happening. The opening stanzas describe a curious visitor entering a church and his observations on its interior. The speaker is the poet. Again we see how description leads on to reflection and philosophical speculation. The poem opens in a conversational manner, 'Once I am sure there is nothing going on / I step inside'. The poet looks around, taking in every detail, 'matting, seats and stone, / And little books'. After stepping up to the lectern and reading 'a few hectoring large-scale verses' aloud (a humorous touch), the poet leaves disappointed. Despite feeling 'at a loss' every time he visits a church, he continues to be drawn to them. Pondering the future role of churches, Larkin feels certain that, with the passage of time, churches will fall into disuse. He speculates that 'A few cathedrals' might function as museums in a post-religious society. Larkin imagines desolate, abandoned churches with 'grass, weedy pavements, brambles ...'. Despite his sceptical view of religion, Larkin values the church because its ceremonies lend a formality and a dignity to the key events in our lives: birth, marriage and death. A person's 'hunger ... to be more serious' will see them 'gravitating' towards the church, which he describes as a place 'proper to grow wise in, / If only that so many dead lie around'. The closing line reminds us that Larkin was always conscious of the dark shadow of death.

Ambulances reflects on Larkin's central preoccupation: the inevitability of death. The setting is the everyday world of the city and the central metaphor is a commonplace object – the ambulance is symbolic of illness and death. Imagery conveys the indiscriminate nature of illness and the inevitability of death, 'They come to rest at any kerb: / All streets in time are visited'. The image of 'A wild white face' evokes a patient's terror when confronted with his/her own mortality. As with so many of Larkin's poems, description leads to reflection. Having given us a visual image of the ambulance ('Light glossy grey, arms on a plaque') and described it in operation, Larkin goes on to consider its impact on onlookers. Their response to the ambulance is given a universal quality through the use of the pronoun 'we', 'And sense the solving emptiness / That lies just under all we do'. The onlookers are now aware that the grim reality of death underlies all that we do. They now see that the reality of death is 'permanent and blank and true' – beyond it lies only 'emptiness'. Larkin did not believe in the idea of a spiritual afterlife – this poem expresses a bleak view of human existence.

In *The Trees*, a commonplace scene prompts Larkin to reflect on the rebirth of nature in springtime and on the transience of human life. After describing the tress 'coming into leaf', the poet reflects on the difference between the trees and man, 'Is it that they are born again / And we grow old?' Larkin realises that the trees also age and die. Their fresh green canopy every spring is described as 'Their yearly trick of looking new'. Yet, despite the poet realising that they are not immortal, the blossoming trees offer encouragement and hope to humans. They seem to communicate a message to the human world in relation to the passage of time, 'Last year is dead, they seem to say / Begin afresh, afresh, afresh'. The poem ends on this memorably optimistic note, with the trees exhorting us to continually make a fresh start. Repetition adds to the persuasiveness of their message about beginning anew and living life to the full.

At Grass is a beautifully nostalgic poem that reflects on the changes brought about by the passage of time. The setting is an everyday rural one, with Larkin observing two retired racehorses grazing in a meadow. While the scene depicted is a pleasant one, it is not without a hint of darkness, with the image of 'the cold shade' suggesting that the horses' lives are drawing to a close. The poet remembers the horses in their golden heyday when they won 'Cups and Stakes and Handicaps'. Detailed description vividly conjures

PHILIP LARKIN – SAMPLE ANSWER

up the excitement and glamour of a race meeting, 'Silks at the start: against the sky / Numbers and parasols outside / Squadrons of empty cars …'. Larkin now indulges in some imaginative speculation, wondering if the horses are 'plagued' by memories buzzing around their ears 'like flies'. The image of the horses shaking their heads suggests that this is not the case. The image of shadows fading into darkness beautifully evokes the passing of time. While the horses' days of racing glory now belong to the past, the horses are contented and untroubled, enjoying the comfort of 'unmolesting meadows'. The day drawing to a close may suggest that the horses' lives are nearing their end, but death is not seen in a threatening light – rather is it as natural as the groom waiting to put on the horses' bridles at the end of their day in the meadow. In a memorable conclusion, image and sound (the repeated long 'o' sound) combine to convey a sense of perfect peace, 'Only the groom and the groom's boy, / With bridles in the evening come'.

John Montague

Biographical Note

John Montague was born in Brooklyn, New York in 1929. This was the year of the stock market crash that triggered the Great Depression in America. Montague's parents had emigrated to New York from their native Tyrone in search of a better life. However, the American dream never became a reality for the Montague family and they struggled to make ends meet. Grinding poverty had a terrible impact on family life. When John was four years old, his parents decided to send John and his two brothers back to Ireland where they would be raised by their relatives. Montague later described separation from his mother as the central event in his emotional life. To compound his misery, he was also separated from his siblings upon his arrival in Ireland. His grandmother looked after his brothers and his two aunts assumed the responsibility for raising John in the Montague family home in Garvaghey. His aunts were kind, supportive women and John loved exploring the rural landscape of Co. Tyrone, developing a love and an appreciation of nature. Montague later described the 'few years from four to eleven' as 'a blessing and a healing'. At the age of eleven Montague won a scholarship to St. Patrick's College, Armagh. While he felt cramped and unhappy in this school, it was here that he discovered his flair for writing. In 1946 Montague won a scholarship to study at UCD where he read English and History. Coming from a republican tradition, Montague had a particular interest in Ulster and Irish history. It was in UCD that his interest in writing really developed. Montague later went on to teach in a number of universities in the USA and Ireland. He also worked for a number of years as *The Irish Times'* French correspondent. He now lives in West Cork with his wife, the American novelist Elizabeth Wassell.

As you read the poetry of John Montague look out for the following features:

- For many poets, poetry is essentially a form of self-expression, an exploration of the self. For John Montague, however, poetry is a **means of communication**, an effort to understand, respond to and interpret the human experiences of those whom he encountered in life.

- He uses **experiences** of his own childhood, **loves** and **relationships** as a springboard to explore life. As a narrative poet, many of Montague's poems are descriptions of actual memories. His interest in Irish folklore and history are also represented in his work.

- Montague is a **lyrical** poet. Most of his poems are written from the perspective of 'I'. The speaker in most of his poems is generally himself, engaged in contemplating his **lived experience** and **direct observations**. This subjectivity, along with closely observed descriptions of the natural world and profound emotions, could be seen as aligning him with the Romantic poets of the nineteenth century.

- Montague's **language** is generally **direct**, personal and anecdotal. He addresses the reader in accessible, conversational English. His use of adjectives is noteworthy in their capacity to communicate meaning and express mood. Excellent examples of this feature can be found in *Windharp* and *The Wild Dog Rose*. His choice of verbs is powerfully evocative as we observe in *Killing the Pig* and *The Trout*. All of his verse is rich in **consonance** (repeating the same consonant in quick succession), **assonance** and **alliteration**, with **rhythms** based on **living speech**.

- One of the most remarkable aspects of Montague's poetry is his capacity to **sympathise with suffering**. We see this in poems like *Killing the Pig* and *The Trout*. His ability to move beyond his own personal suffering and sense of loss can be seen in poems like *The Locket* and *The Cage* where he contemplates compassionately the stresses which affected the lives of his parents. Often, the most eccentric of individuals become the subjects of his poetry, as we see in *Like Dolmens Round My Childhood* and *The Wild Dog Rose*, where he treats their eccentricity with gentle understanding.

- Wide **variations in tone** are apparent in Montague's verse. Tones range from pain to empathy, admiration, wonder, sarcasm and even guilt.

- Superb examples of **symbols** and **metaphors** can be found in Montague's poetry. His description of the train station in *All Legendary Obstacles* shows his ability to convey situation through images: 'water dripping from great flanged wheels… pale above the negro porter's lamp'. Other striking images are those of the cage in which his father was trapped in the subway stations of New York; the image of the wild dog rose as a symbol of human fragility and the locket as a symbol for his mother's love for a lost child.

Killing the Pig

This poem opens abruptly, with the opening line set apart from the rest of the poem: 'The noise'. The question that springs to the reader's mind is immediately answered – it is the sound of a pig being dragged to his death, 'He was pulled out, squealing'. The use of 'he' rather than 'it' gives the pig an individual identity. The image that follows is horrifying in its graphic detail, 'an iron cleek sunk in the roof / of his mouth'.

While some would dismiss this act of brutal violence on the basis that the pig is 'only' a dumb animal, Montague pre-empts such a response, '(Don't say they are not intelligent: / they know the hour has come / and they want none of it'. The implication of this is that the pig suffers both psychologically and physically. His desperate but futile resistance evokes the sympathy of the reader, 'they dig in their little trotters, / will not go dumb or singing / to the slaughter)'.

At this point the poet returns to 'the noise', describing the pig's squealing as 'That high pitched final effort'. In a final attempt to resist his imminent slaughter, the pig emits a sound that is truly unique, 'no single sound could match it'. The poet employs a series of metaphors in an attempt to convey a sense of this sound. The image of 'a big plane roaring off' conveys how the pig's final squeal filled the poet's head, drowning out all other sounds, while the

image of 'a *diva* soaring towards her last note' underscores its extremely high pitch. Two final aural images have disturbing connotations of violence: 'the brain-chilling persistence of an electric saw, / scrap being crushed'. However, in terms of conveying a sense of the pig's final squeal, none of these comparisons is adequate. The adjectives 'piercing and absolute' best describe this sound. 'Piercing' suggests the distressingly sharp sound of the pig's agonised squeal, while 'absolute' suggests that he puts his entire being into making this final, heartbreaking sound. This shrill, mind-numbing scream of protest demands attention, 'only high heaven ignores it'.

The cry is brought to an abrupt halt, 'Then a full stop'. Mickey Boyle (whose naming roots the poem in the real world) hits the pig 'a solid thump of the mallet / flat between the ears'. Onomatopoeia ('thump') and assonance (the repeated 'a' sound) combine to convey the sound of this sudden, powerful blow.

At this point the action speeds up dramatically as the stunned pig is butchered. Repetition underlines the sense of practised, detached efficiency, 'Swiftly the knife seeks the throat; / swiftly the other cleavers work'. Once the carving and slicing is complete, the pig is reduced to a carcass 'shining and eviscerated as / a surgeon's coat'. This simile again suggests the butchers' cold, clinical expertise.

The child (symbolic of life and innocence) is given 'the bladder to play with' – a gesture that appears to be part of the whole, unfeeling routine. This image suggests the theme of life and death, which daily co-exist on the farm.

The closing lines imply a contrast between the innocently happy child and the grim reality of death held forever in the farmyard walls, while reminding us that such death is an integral part of farmyard life, 'But the walls of the farmyard / still hold that scream, / are built around it'.

KEY POINTS

- A key theme is the disturbing indifference of human beings to the suffering of animals.

- Note how the first two words 'The noise' focus the attention of the reader on the pain which the animal is suffering by allowing us to hear before we see the pig. The 'squealing' of the pig lingers in the imagination even after the noise is quelled.

- Vivid detail captures the horror of the pig's death. The use of the phrase 'little trotters' evokes a compassion for the helpless animal, while 'will not go dumb or singing / to the slaughter' reminds us of young soldiers who marched heroically to certain death.

- A series of metaphors is employed to convey the idea of a uniquely extreme sound. Still concentrating on the noise, the poet compares it to 'a big plane roaring off, / a *diva* soaring towards her last note, ...an electric saw, / scrap being crushed'. All of these metaphors depict noises which are discordant to the human ear, thereby creating a feeling of horror and sympathy for the pig.

- Language is generally ordinary and matter-of-fact but is rich in suggestion and meaning. The phrase 'pulled out' indicates brutality and indifference to the animal's suffering. The imperative 'Don't say...' has a dramatic, disgusted quality.

- The naming of Mickey Boyle as the individual responsible for hitting the pig with the mallet adds realism and puts the emphasis on the human act of cruelty.

- The layout of the poem and regular use of full stops prompt the reader to pause and reflect on the different stages of the killing.

- The poet makes effective use of sound: the harsh 'k' sounds of 'cleek sunk' indicate the harsh coldness of the act. Onomatopoeia and assonance also contribute to the sound quality.

- Montague's sympathy for the pig is implicit throughout.

The Trout

This poem was inspired by an episode in Montague's childhood in which he caught a trout in a stream with his hands. As his vivid description indicates, the incident remains forever imprinted on the poet's memory.

Each step in the process demands complete concentration. The boy lies 'flat on the bank' and parts the rushes so that he can 'ease' his hands into the water 'without a ripple'. He does not want to signal his presence to the trout. Every move is executed with the greatest of care. His next step is to 'tilt' his hands 'slowly downstream / To where he lay'. Image and sound (the gentle assonant 'I') combine to suggest the delicacy of the fish, 'he lay, tendril-light'. In referring to the trout's 'fluid sensual dream', Montague attributes human qualities to the fish, evoking a sense of the trout's mysteriousness.

As he is poised over the trout, Montague is filled with a sense of his own power, seeing himself as a godlike figure, 'Bodiless lord of creation'. His approach has been so stealthy and so focused that he is almost unaware of his body, 'Savouring my own absence'. He is so absorbed in what he is doing that his senses seem sharper and everything seems to happen in 'slow motion'. While the reader would imagine the boy feeling nervous at this point, he is in fact perfectly composed before he makes his decisive move, 'the photographic calm / That grows before action'.

The boy unobtrusively brings 'the curve' of his hands under the trout's body. Again attributing human qualities to the fish, he describes him surging 'with visible pleasure'. Montague's view of himself as some kind of supernatural being is again apparent when he describes himself as being 'so preternaturally close' to the trout that he 'could count every stipple'. Still focused on the task in hand, he is careful to 'cast no shadow' that might panic the fish.

Finally he closes his hands to form a cage to trap the fish, still strangely motionless except for 'the lightly pulsing gills'. Leaning over the stream, he sees his reflection on the surface of the stream, 'my own enlarged / Shape, which rode on the water'. The moment of capture is conveyed in the dramatic phrase 'I gripped'. For the first time, Montague becomes aware of the impact of his actions on the fish, which is clearly panic-stricken. The image of the struggling fish lingers in his memory, 'To this day I can / Taste his terror on my hands'. The fact that he can recollect this experience so vividly underlines the extent to which Montague was affected by his encounter with the trout.

KEY NOTES

- This incident is captured in such a precise and detailed manner that it is almost recreated in the mind of the reader.
- Key themes are the beauty of nature and man's relationship with the natural world.
- Notice the flowing rhythm of the opening five and a half lines, which capture the flow of the water as the man slips his hands into the water.
- Montague's compassion for the suffering pig in 'Killing the Pig' is reflected in his sympathy for the terrified trout: 'To this day I can / Taste his terror on my hands'.
- The poet makes use of vivid imagery. The trout is described as being 'tendril-light' and existing in a 'fluid sensual dream'.
- He also uses alliteration ('Taste his terror', etc.) and assonance ('Flat on the bank', etc) to give the poem a musical quality.
- Montague makes effective use of punctuation. (The full stops in stanza four after 'gills', 'gripped' and 'hands' suggest the tension and excitement surrounding the capture of the fish.

The Locket

This poem describes the poet's strange, troubled relationship with his mother in a courageously honest manner. The opening lines suggest that it was his mother's death that prompted him to write this poem, 'Sing a last song / for the lady who has gone'. Montague describes their relationship as 'a fertile source of guilt and pain'. He feels guilty about the pain he caused his mother in the course of his birth, while their subsequent relationship involved a great deal of pain for him. His birth was a difficult one, a fact that his mother never tired of repeating: 'The worst birth in the annals of Brooklyn'. Montague flippantly describes his mother's claim as 'my first claim to fame'.

The poet explains how he was responsible for his relationship with his mother being fraught with difficulty from the beginning. His birth involved a 'double blunder' on his part. Firstly, his mother 'longed for a girl' and, secondly, his entrance into the world came by way of a breech birth, 'both the wrong sex, / and the wrong way around'. His mother seems to have been a complex, unnaturally cold woman. The baby's 'infant curls of brown' did nothing to assuage (diminish) her sense of resentment. His sins were 'Not readily forgiven'.

The emotional distance between mother and son grew wider in the months after his birth as a result of his mother's unusual unwillingness to nurse her new baby. The change in the way Montague refers to his mother underlines his enduring pain – having initially referred to her as 'she', he now addresses her directly, 'So you never nursed me'. Grinding poverty inevitably took its toll on family life. While his father tried to distract the family with his songs, there was no disguising the family's miserable circumstances. Montague recalls his mother's favourite saying, 'when poverty comes through the door / love flies up the chimney'.

In the poet's eyes the most straitened (impoverished) of circumstances could not justify his mother's decision to send John and his two brothers back to Ireland to be raised by relatives. The sense of hurt and sorrow is palpable, 'Then you gave me away, / might never have known me'. This feeling of abandonment was later compounded by his mother's unwillingness to reclaim him after she returned to Ireland from America.

In line 21 the poem moves forward in time, describing the poet's efforts to develop some kind of relationship with his mother. He reflects that if he had not made such an effort, '. . . you . . . might never have known me'. His eight-mile cycle to 'court' his mother recalls his parents' courting days. While the poet remains emotionally wounded by his mother's abandonment of him, the atmosphere between them seems relaxed as he recalls the 'wild, young days' of her youth. His sympathy for her is evident when he reflects that these carefree days 'didn't last long'. He realises that she was once a happy, popular young woman ('lovely Molly, the belle of your small town') before her life became a 'cocoon of pain'. The adjectives 'mournful and chill' suggest the sadness and harshness of her later life as she struggled to cope with an unhappy marriage, the demands of family life and extreme poverty.

Despite the pleasant nature of the poet's visits, his mother tells him to stop visiting her. She fears growing accustomed to his company and consequently missing him when he is no longer there, 'I start to get fond of you, John, / and then you are up and gone'. The poet recognises the 'harsh logic' in his mother's words – in order to avoid getting hurt, she chooses not to give their relationship a chance to develop, pre-empting any possibility of becoming emotionally attached to him. The poet perceives that his mother's difficult, disappointing life has left her emotionally damaged, 'a forlorn woman / resigned to being alone'. She does not possess the personal resources to 'connect' emotionally with her son.

Despite the poem's depiction of a strange,

problematical relationship between the poet and his mother, it ends with a sense of happiness and consolation. After his mother's death, the poet discovers that the locket she always wore around her neck contained a picture of him as a child,

'you wore an oval locket / with an old picture in it, / of a child in Brooklyn'. Montague describes this as a 'mysterious blessing'. The locket clearly symbolises his mother's love for him, but sadly she lacked the capacity to express that love.

KEY POINTS

- A key theme is the poet's problematic relationship with his mother. Another related theme is the effects of poverty.
- The tone of the poem is one of regret. Words like 'last' and 'gone' emphasise the finality of his mother's death. However, there is also a sense of distance from the mother who rejected him. He refers to her as 'the lady' and is clearly resentful of her rejection of him as a child. The poem ends on a more uplifting, poignant note, as he discovers that his mother wore a locket containing his picture. This seems to bring him consolation and a degree of closure.
- While this poem is primarily about Montague's own pain, he manages to create some sympathy for the mother who rejected him at different stages of his life.
- Direct speech brings his mother to life, communicating the essence of her personality. Her stated claim that his birth was 'The worst birth in the annals of Brooklyn' reveals an extraordinary insensitivity to the burden of guilt which she is placing on her child.
- The poem reflects the poet's sympathetic personality. He takes the initiative to visit his mother and is forgiving of the early rejection. He has sympathy for the early happy days of her youth 'which didn't last long'. He can view her as ' a forlorn woman / resigned to being alone'.
- Key adjectives underline the sorrow and harshness of his mother's life ('mournful and chill').

The Cage

This poem describes the poet's memories of, and relationship with, his father. James Montague was forced to leave his hometown in Garvaghey in Northern Ireland in the 1920s because of the high unemployment rate there at that time. He emigrated to New York, ending up living in the slums of Brooklyn. After his children and wife (in that strange order) returned to Ireland, he remained on his own in Brooklyn for the next 20 years. When he retired from his job in the underground he returned to Garvaghey. The title of the poem suggests the idea of imprisonment, its negative connotations setting the tone for the

largely bleak poem that follows.

The conversational tone of the opening lines draws us into the poem. The poet expresses his ideas in a simple, direct manner, 'My father, the least happy / man I have known'. The comma after 'my father' suggests a pause for reflection, as if in response to a question about the kind of man his father was. His father's face was unhealthily pale, retaining 'the pallor / of those who work underground'. His time in Brooklyn is described as 'the lost years'. His metaphorical prison is the ticket booth underground where

213

he worked. With its steel grille, this booth very much resembled a cage. These years were also irretrievably 'lost' to father and son, leaving them with no opportunity to develop a relationship. His father's life was dominated by the shuddering sound of the subway.

The poet describes his father as 'a traditional Irishman', a term suggestive of his rural Catholic background and fondness for alcohol. When he was 'released (a term with obvious connotations of imprisonment) from his grille', his father sought refuge from his misery in whiskey, drinking 'until / he reached the only element / he felt at home in / any longer: brute oblivion'. These lines evoke his father's sense of displacement and isolation. They also suggest that while he was imprisoned in the underground in his working life, he was enslaved to alcohol in his free time. The idea that his father only felt at home in a state of alcohol-induced unconsciousness sums up the personal tragedy that was his life.

Yet Montague admires aspects of his father's character, notably the resilience and spirit that enabled him to get up 'most mornings' and face the world with a spring in his step and a smile on his face, 'And yet picked himself / up, most mornings, / to march down the street / extending his smile / to all sides of the good, / (all-white) neighbourhood / belled by St. Teresa's church'. His father lived among fellow Irishmen, the reference to an 'all-white' district reminding us of the racism that was endemic in New York at that time, particularly in the Irish community.

His father eventually returned to his hometown after more than 20 years in America. Father and son went walking together through the local countryside, 'we walked together / across fields of Garvaghey / to see hawthorn on the summer / hedges'. The phrase 'as though / he had never left' relates to his father's familiarity with routes he has not walked in many years, 'a bend of the road / which still sheltered / primroses'.

Sadly, but inevitably, the 'lost years' in New York mean that father and son are separated by the type of emotional gap that is not easily bridged, 'But we / did not smile in / the shared complicity / of a dream'. Montague refers to the mythical tale of Odysseus and his son Telemachus to illustrate the difficulties facing his father and himself in their efforts to build a relationship. After leaving his wife and young son in order to go and fight in the Trojan War, Odysseus did not return home for 20 years. Just as Telemachus left home after his father's return, Montague also left his father shortly after his return to Garvaghey, going to America on a scholarship.

The final stanza moves forward in time. His father has since died. The poet is reminded of him whenever he descends into the subway or underground. It is sad that he associates his father primarily with this grim environment. The poet vividly imagines his father's ghostly presence, 'I see his bald head behind / the bars of the small booth; / the mark of an old car / accident beating on his / ghostly forehead'. Montague's depiction of his ageing father as a vulnerable, profoundly unhappy man trapped in a cage is very sad, but shows his compassion for him.

KEY POINTS

- A key theme is the poet's relationship with his father. It is a sad reflection on his father's loss of family life and the poet's loss of his father. The unhappiness of the exile far from home is another related theme.

- The poet describes his relationship with his father in an honest, open manner. His description of his father as 'the least happy / man I have known' is chilling in its bleak candour.

- The use of conversational language draws us into the poem.

- 'The cage' is the key symbol in the poem, suggesting both his father's daily physical imprisonment in the ticket booth and his sense of spiritual entrapment in an alien environment.

- The noisy, confined world of the underground – 'listening to a subway / shudder the earth', 'the bars of the small booth' – is sharply contrasted with the beauty, tranquillity and freedom of the Ulster countryside – 'we walked together / across fields of Garvaghey / to see hawthorn on the summer / hedges'.

- A classical allusion to the legend of Odysseus and Telemachus – 'when / weary Odysseus returns / Telemachus should leave' highlights the problematic nature of the poet's relationship with his father. The verb 'should' suggests an absence of choice, as though no possible relationship could ever exist between them.

Windharp

This short poem is composed of a single sentence that is broken up into lines of three or four words. A series of sensuous images evoke the impact of the wind on the Irish landscape. The 'windharp', also known as the Aeolian harp, requires no human hand to play it – its notes are sounded by the wind blowing through its strings. The bushes, grasses and tree branches of the rural landscape act as the strings of this metaphorical instrument, producing a variety of sounds that are distinctively Irish.

The opening line suggests that there are sounds that are unique to Ireland, 'The sounds of Ireland'. The poet describes the sound of the wind blowing through the Irish countryside as 'that restless whispering / you never get away / from'. Sibilance (using words that produce a hissing 's' sound) effectively conveys this 'whispering' sound. The breeze is described as 'seeping out of / low bushes and grass', with the sibilant 's' sound again creating its own distinctive music. The phrase 'heatherbells and fern' with its gentle assonant 'e' sound is particularly melodious. A visual image suggests the effect of the wind on the face of the landscape, 'wrinkling bog pools'.

The wind in the trees produces a harsh sound, 'scraping tree branches'. The verbs 'wrinkling' and 'scraping' have negative connotations, evoking the disturbing effect of the wind – Montague never idealises situations. In addition to affecting the landscape, the wind has an impact on the skyscape, with the phrase 'light hunting cloud' evoking an image of clouds racing across the sky. The verbs 'hunting' and 'hounding' ('sound hounding sight') suggest the wind's relentless quality.

The poet gives the wind a human aspect when he speaks of 'a hand ceaselessly / combing and stroking / the landscape'. This tactile image suggests the intimate relationship between the wind and the landscape. The poem ends with a wonderful simile, suggesting how the wind beautifies the countryside by putting a 'shine' on it similar to the glossy coat of a pony. The wind 'strokes' the countryside 'till / the valley gleams / like the pile upon / a mountain pony's coat'. Overall, the wind is portrayed as a positive force that breathes life into and energises the countryside.

All Legendary Obstacles

This is a love poem that tells of Montague being reunited with his lover. The poem is located in a train station in California where the poet waits for the woman who is crossing the American continent to be with him. The opening line conveys the sense of an epic tale, 'All legendary obstacles lay between / Us'. The 'obstacles' that separate the lovers are such natural barriers as the great American plains, 'the monstrous ruck of mountains', and 'The hissing drift of winter rain' that floods the Sacramento and San Joaquin rivers. The opening stanza may also be read on a symbolic level. The geographical distance that separates the lovers is suggestive of the emotional distance between them and the physical obstacles are representative of difficulties in their relationship.

Stanza two describes the poet waiting apprehensively for his lover's train to arrive. His anxiety is captured in the image of him 'shifting / Nervously from station to bar'. He watches edgily as another train, 'the San Francisco Chief or Golden Gate' (details that root the poem firmly in California), sails by.

Finally, his lover's train arrives. There is a cinematic quality to how the lovers are meeting on the platform at midnight. The woman is depicted as being 'pale / Above the negro porter's lamp'. What follows is far removed from the clichéd, sentimental image of reunited lovers rushing to embrace each other on a railway platform. Montague is typically honest: 'I was too blind with rain / And doubt to speak'. He reaches up to help the woman down from the carriage, 'Reached from the platform / Until our chilled hands met'. The references to 'doubt', 'rain' and 'chilled hands' may point to a problematic aspect to their relationship. Or perhaps the relationship is in its early stages and the lovers are, understandably, uncertain at this point.

The poem ends with an old lady viewing the departing lovers through 'a neat circle on the glass' of the train window. She sees the two lovers 'move into the wet darkness / Kissing, still unable to speak'. The ending of the poem is optimistic, but not totally so. The image of the lovers kissing is a romantic and suggestive of their growing closeness, but their inability to speak indicates that a certain communication gap remains. Montague portrays his relationship with his lover with typical honesty and realism.

they are vastly powerful forces.

- Use is made of varied tone. The poet is anxious, 'shifting nervously.' When the train arrives, instead of the moment of delight which we expect, we see a pale woman moving towards the poet, who is 'too blind with rain / And doubt to speak'. The climactic moment arrives when the two 'chilled hands' meet and the poem ends on a note of relief as the couple move away, 'Kissing, still unable to speak'.

- Effective use of sound: onomatopoeia ('hissing'), assonance ('hissing drift of winter rain') and sibilance ('to watch us / move into the wet darkness / Kissing, still unable to speak').

The Same Gesture

This poem celebrates a special kind of love. The 'secret room' referred to in the opening line is the room the lovers share. The 'golden light' in which this room is metaphorically bathed evokes the idea of a uniquely rich love. This is a room of intense passion 'where / everything – love, violence, / hatred is possible; / and, again, love'. While the poet acknowledges the complexity of this relationship, it is – as the closing words in stanza one indicate – characterised primarily by love.

The love that this poem celebrates is deep and meaningful. In this special room, the lovers achieve physical and spiritual union, 'Such intimacy of hand / and mind is achieved'. This total intimacy is realised under the room's 'healing light' – a mystical image that evokes the idea of the room as a sacred place. The love expressed here is portrayed in religious terms, e.g. the movement of the lovers' hands is described as 'a rite'.

The simile that compares the lovers' movements to 'court music' conveys the idea of something elegant and timeless. The lovers become so absorbed in each other that everything else is forgotten. They seem to lose themselves in each other, 'We barely know our / selves there though / it is what we always were – / most nakedly are'. The reference to nakedness reinforces the idea of the lovers' total intimacy. This nakedness is not just physical, but also a spiritual, intellectual, emotional nakedness. In essence, the lovers lay bare their souls to each other.

Eventually the lovers must leave their 'golden' self-contained world of love and return to the reality of their individual daily lives, 'we leave, re- / suming our habits / with our clothes'. The poet evokes the humdrum routine of daily life with typical economy, 'work, phone, drive / through late traffic'.

Driving through late traffic, the poet carries memories of this special experience with him. Something in the mundane functional action of changing gears reminds him of the loving movements that had earlier brought a sense of total contentment to his lover, 'changing gears with / the same gesture as / eased your snowbound / heart and flesh'. The poem ends with the poet savouring a beautiful moment in a deeply loving relationship.

KEY POINTS

- A key theme is love – the poem celebrates a special romantic relationship.
- This is a deeply personal poem.
- The poet uses 'we' rather than 'I', underlining the strength of the bond connecting the lovers.

- The language used combines the ordinary/everyday with the metaphorical ('a secret room of golden light', etc.).
- The poem has an economic style.

Like Dolmens Round My Childhood

The dolmens (large boulders used to mark ancient burial sites) mentioned in the title symbolise some of the old people who lived near the poet when he was a child. The title suggests how these elderly neighbours dominated his young life. Stanzas 1–6 provide the reader with vivid pen pictures of some of these old people, each of whom is distinctive and memorable. We are first introduced to Jamie MacCrystal, a contented old man who 'sang to himself'. He is depicted in a sympathetic light as a kindly character who gave the poet 'a penny every pension day'. His considerate, gentle nature was also reflected in his feeding of the birds in winter. However, the world he lived in was a harsh one and as soon as it was known that he had died, thieves ransacked his cottage, 'Mattress and money-box torn and searched'. The final image in stanza one evokes his lonely, isolated existence, 'Only the corpse they didn't disturb'.

Maggie Owens is remembered as an eccentric old woman, surrounded by animals, 'Even in her bedroom a she-goat cried'. She is portrayed as a poisonous gossiper, 'a well of gossip defiled, / Fanged chronicler of a whole countryside'. The phrase a 'fanged chronicler' suggests that her storytelling had a dangerous, vicious quality. She was reputed locally to be a witch. However, the poet, even as a boy, had the good sense and compassion to see beyond such superstitious notions to the reality behind the somewhat sinister image, 'all I could find / Was her lonely need to deride'. Her disparagement (belittling/mocking) of others was the result of being embittered by loneliness.

Stanza three describes a family who 'lived along a mountain lane'. The Nialls were surrounded by the beauty of nature ('heather bells ... clumps of foxglove'), but were unaware of it because

they were all blind. Their only means of support was the 'Blind Pension' and their only form of entertainment was the 'wireless' (radio). The image of 'dead eyes' that 'serpent-flickered' suggests that as a child the poet was slightly frightened of this family whenever he entered the house to take shelter from 'a downpour of mountain rain'. Yet the idea of a door ever open to neighbours suggests the warm hospitality that was traditional in rural Ireland at that time. The image of 'the muddy sun' evokes a world enshrouded in darkness and shadow.

Mary Moore 'lived in a crumbling gatehouse', whose 'leaning gable' is humorously compared to the Leaning Tower of Pisa. The reality of Mary's harsh, unglamorous life is captured in a visual image, 'Bag-apron and boots, she tramped the fields'. Like the other characters already mentioned, Mary had to cope with poverty, struggling to make a living from her small farm, 'Driving lean cattle from a miry stable'. In her solitary battle to survive, Mary became hard – her name was 'A by-word for fierceness'. Yet, as is so often the case, there was more to her than her image suggested, 'she fell asleep' reading love stories. Her fierce exterior disguised a lonely heart yearning for love and romance.

The sectarian realities of Northern Ireland are apparent in the poet's memory of 'Wild Billy Eagleson', a Protestant loyalist who married a Catholic girl. The poet recalls himself and his young friends dancing around the old man shouting 'To Hell with King Billy'. Billy was abandoned by both sides of the community, but his isolation was really only brought home to him during the Orange marching season, 'Forsaken by both creeds, he showed little concern / Until the Orange drums banged past in the summer'.

The characters who were depicted individually

in the preceding stanzas are now discussed collectively, 'Curate and doctor trudged to attend them'. The verb 'trudged' suggests a long, tiring journey. The remoteness of these old people's dwellings is conveyed by the image of a 'main road' becoming a 'lane' and, finally, a 'broken path'. The arduous nature of the journey undertaken by curate and doctor is clear from the image of these men, 'Gulping the mountain air with painful breath'. Sometimes these elderly characters were found dead by neighbours, sitting lifeless by 'a smokeless hearth'. Having lived alone, they sadly died alone. Loneliness and isolation were the grim realities of these people's lives and deaths.

The closing stanza opens with an abrupt statement, 'Ancient Ireland, indeed!' Here the poet seems to dismiss idealised versions of Ireland's past. He had first-hand experience of this Ireland. He was there and knows the truth, 'I was reared by her bedside'. The reality of that earlier Ireland was superstition ('The rune and the chant, evil eye and averted head'), fierce family and local feuds, poverty, loneliness and isolation. The final lines of the poem return to the characters depicted in the first six stanzas, 'Gaunt figures of fear and of friendliness'. This paradox suggests that they were both frightening and friendly. These figures haunted him ('trespassed on my dreams') for years before an unexplained change occurred and he 'felt their shadows pass'. The fact that he no longer felt haunted by them was probably the result of growing up, maturing and acquiring a clearer perspective on the past.

KEY POINTS

- A key theme is the reality of the Ireland in which Montague grew up – a world of poverty, loneliness, superstition and sectarianism.

- The poet portrays a variety of old characters from his childhood. They no longer have the power of fear over him as he now views them with compassion and sympathy.

- The language used combines the conversational ('Jamie MacCrystal sang to himself') and the descriptive ('Dead eyes serpent-flickered').

- The poet makes use of memorable imagery. The major image is that of the dolmens. These ancient stone structures stand out on the landscape, in the same way as the old people stood out in the poet's childhood – dominating and haunting his imagination. As the poem progresses, the dolmens become less symbolic of terror as he feels 'their shadows pass / Into that dark permanence of ancient forms'.

- Note the effective use of sound: alliteration ('Fomorian fierceness of family and local feud'), onomatopoeia ('Orange drums banged', etc.) and sibilance ('Silent keepers of a smokeless hearth').

The Wild Dog Rose

The central character in this poem closely resembles the old people in *Like Dolmens Round My Childhood*. In both poems we see that outer appearances do not always reflect underlying realities. The first section of the poem opens with the poet going to say goodbye to an old woman known as the cailleach (two meanings – 'old woman', 'witch'). She was another of those figures who 'haunted' his childhood. As an adult, he no longer thinks her 'harsh', recognising that she is just a human being who has had a hard life and been 'hurt by event'. The old woman's cottage is described in detail. It is remote ('circled by trees') and unwelcoming (the adjective 'admonitory' suggests that it warns people to stay away). Its dilapidated condition is suggested by the description of how it 'straggles' into view. The fields surrounding the house are neglected, full of 'rank thistles' and 'leathery bracken'.

Our first glimpse of the cailleach explains why she inspired such fear in the poet when he was a child. A vivid metaphor conveys her ragged appearance, 'a moving nest / of shawls and rags'. Detailed description paints an off-putting image of the old woman, 'the great hooked nose, the cheeks / dewlapped with dirt, the staring blue / of the sunken eyes, the mottled claws / clutching a stick'. She is surrounded by a 'retinue of dogs' that emits 'savage, whingeing cries' as the poet approaches. When he first sees her, Montague once again experiences 'the terror of a child'. However, that instinctive response does not last as the adult poet has dispensed with the superstitions of childhood. His changed attitude towards her is apparent when the old woman stares at him and he returns her gaze 'to greet her, / as she greets me, in friendliness'. Sharing memories of the past, the two achieve 'reconciliation'. Their new closeness is conveyed by a simile, 'like old friends, lovers almost'. They talk about neighbours, many of whom 'now lie in Garvaghey graveyard'. The old woman confides in the poet, telling him how she turned down a proposal of marriage in her youth because she did not want to leave her own community ('and go among strangers – / his parish ten miles off') and how 'For sixty years / since she had lived alone'. The poet feels 'honoured' at being taken into the old woman's confidence. The verb 'idle' ('I idle by the summer roadside, listening') suggests how Montague is now perfectly relaxed in her company. He understands that it is loneliness (which he describes as 'The only true madness') that prompts the old woman's endless stream of talk as she goes on to tell of 'the small events of her life'. However, we soon realise that one of these events is anything but 'small'.

While the second section of the poem opens with an image of natural beauty ('the dog rose shines in the hedge'), what follows is a reminder of the ugly deeds of which man is capable. In this section the old woman tells a story 'so terrible' that the poet struggles to cope with it, 'I try to push it away, / my bones melting'. The story describes the attempted rape of the seventy-year-old woman. She recounts how late one night 'a drunk came beating at her door / to break it in'. The repeated loud 'b' sound conveys a sense of terrifying noise. The poet's use of onomatopoeia enables us to almost hear 'the bolt snapping'. The viciousness of the intruder is immediately obvious in his response to the barking dogs, 'he whirls with his farm boots / to crush their skulls'. In the chaotic scene that follows, the old woman struggles on the floor with her assailant. The poet's description of the old woman and the drunk as 'two creatures crazed / with loneliness' is an attempt to understand – without in any way condoning – this appalling act. The drunk's brutal, sordid actions are vividly depicted, 'his body heavy on hers, /... he rummages while / she battles for life'. The old woman desperately tries to fend him off, the unequal battle suggested by the image of her 'bony fingers' pressing against 'his bull neck'. She prays to the Blessed Virgin to help her to break the drunk's grip on her neck. She eventually succeeds and 'he rolls / to the floor, snores asleep'.

The third section of the poem returns to the present to a description of the flowers mentioned earlier in the poem, 'And still / the dog rose shines in the hedge. / Petals beaten wide by rain, it / sways slightly'. The frail but resilient flower may be symbolic of the frail but resilient old woman. The cailleach explains the flower's significance to her. Pointing out how it is the only type of rose that does not have thorns, she tells the poet, 'Whenever I see it, I remember / the Holy Mother of God and / all she suffered'. The closing image evokes the fragility of the rose, 'that weak flower ... crumbling yellow cup ... pale bleeding lips ... each bruised and heart-/shaped petal'. This image suggests how the vulnerable old woman has been 'bruised' or wounded by life. It recalls the poet's description of her in the opening section of the poem, 'a human being / merely, hurt by event'. Significantly, the rose continues to shine despite being beaten by the rain, just as the old woman endures in the face of hardship, loneliness and violence.

This poem is open to a symbolic reading. In Irish folklore Ireland is often portrayed as an old woman. The attempted rape of the old woman may be symbolic of the British Empire's violation of Ireland.

KEY POINTS

- A key theme is the power of faith and the capacity of the human spirit to experience trauma and endure.
- The poem is divided into three distinct sections. We see Montague's changed attitude to an old woman who he once considered to be a witch. The second section deals with the account of an attempted sexual assault. The third section explores the strength which the old woman derived from the symbolism of the dog rose.
- The poem may be read on a symbolic level. The old woman may be the symbol of Ireland violated by British colonisation.
- The poet uses memorable descriptions: the 'rank thistles' and 'leathery bracken'; the 'cheeks / dewlapped with dirt', the 'bones melting', etc.
- Montague makes effective use of metaphor ('a moving nest of shawls and rags') and simile ('like old friends, lovers almost').
- There is also effective use of alliteration ('beating . . . break . . . bolt') and onomatopoeia ('snapping', 'yelping').
- The tone is sympathetic towards the old woman, who was previously a source of fear to the author.

A Welcoming Party

The title of the poem is rather misleading in that it suggests a joyful occasion. Far from being joyful, the experience that inspired this poem was in fact harrowing (distressing) for the poet. The poem opens with a question in German which means, 'How was it possible?' At the end of the Second World War cinemas throughout the western world showed newsreels depicting the unspeakable horrors of the Nazi concentration camps. The young Montague and some of his teenage friends went to see such a newsreel, 'That final newsreel of the war: / A welcoming party of almost shades / Met us at the cinema door'. The phrase 'almost shades' suggests that those incarcerated in the camps were so emaciated (starved) that they were no more substantial than shadows. The poet was so affected by images of these shells of humanity that they filled his mind, leading to his picturing them meeting himself and his friends 'at the cinema door'. The image of skeletal figures 'clicking what remained of their heels' is strange and grim – it is suggestive of the prisoners' attempt to display their gratitude to their liberators.

With the sickening newsreel images etched indelibly on his memory, Montague depicts the obscene reality of the death camps. The metaphor of 'nests of bodies' conjures up an image of prisoners packed tightly together, indistinguishable from each other. This is an image of dehumanising degradation. The image of 'insectlike hands and legs' underscores the prisoners' deathly thinness. The poet can still hear their heart-rending wailing, 'And rose an ululation, terrible'. The most tragic aspect of these camps was that so many children were numbered among their victims. Children who should have been in school learned only about death, 'Children conjugating the verb 'to die'.'

Stanza three opens with an oxymoron (a phrase containing terms that contradict each other, e.g. a friendly fight; genuinely fake): 'One clamoured mutely of love' ('Clamoured' means 'to make a loud noise', while 'mutely' means 'silently'). This may refer to an excited child greeting his liberators, with the image seemingly being recorded without the accompanying sound. The simile that compares his mouth to 'a burnt glove' is disconcerting (disturbing), with its obvious connotations of suffering. Other children raise their hands 'bleak as begging bowls', pleading for help. The alliterative 'b' sound accentuates the gloomy mood. These innocents are not begging for anything of a material nature – they

are asking for 'the small change of our souls'. In other words, they are looking for a little humanity and compassion.

The poet is deeply affected by this image and, drawn into the world on the screen, imagines some prisoners smiling at himself and his friends as if they were their 'protectors'. However, the poet seems to have little to offer them. Overwhelmed by what he has seen, he wonders incredulously how these meagre forms are still alive, 'Can those bones live?' The poet is acutely aware of his own inadequacy in the face of such mind-numbing horror, 'Our parochial brand of innocence / Was all we had to give'. The scenes depicted on the screen were completely beyond his narrow, limited experience of life.

The scenes described in stanzas 1–4 set the young Montague thinking about his place in the greater scheme of things. Ireland's neutrality during the global conflict meant that the country was far removed from the harsh realities of the war, 'To be always at the periphery of incident / Gave my childhood its Irish dimension'. Consequently, the war had no significant impact on the young Montague – it was a 'drama of unevent'. While the newsreel images affected him on an emotional level, he feels helpless and can do nothing about them, 'Yet doves of mercy, as doves of air, / Can falter here as anywhere'.

In the final stanza, the poet reflects on the whole day. He has acquired a chilling insight into the grim reality of modern war and its total disregard for innocent men, women and children, 'I learnt one meaning of total war'. The final image of the young poet going into his school and belting a football through the air suggests how frustrated he feels at his helplessness.

KEY POINTS

- A key theme is the horror of the Nazi concentration camps and man's inhumanity to man. Another theme is Ireland's isolation from the rest of Europe.
- The language combines the conversational and the metaphorical.
- Imagery in the poem is unusual, often challenging.
- The tone varies from one of horror to one of frustration.

Sample Answer

"John Montague explores intensely personal experiences with insight and compassion"

You have been asked by your local radio station to give a talk on the poetry of John Montague. Write out the text of the talk you would deliver in response to the above title. You should refer to both style and subject matter. Support the points you make by reference to the poetry on your course.

Good evening listeners and welcome to tonight's programme which is one of a series dealing with the work of modern Irish poets. The focus of my talk tonight is on the poetry of John Montague. I will be looking specifically at the manner in which the poet explores intensely personal experiences with insight and compassion and will also be examining some of the features of style which has gained him recognition as one of the foremost poets of our times.

John Montague was born in Brooklyn, New York in 1929 and spent the first four years of his life there. With the family struggling to survive, his mother took the extraordinary decision to send John and his two brothers back to Ireland to be raised by their relatives. It is not surprising, therefore, that his poetry explores such early personal trauma and his childhood in Garvaghey with an intensity born from a deep sense of rejection. However, he manages to create a detachment in his treatment of these subjects and never dissolves into self-pity or unrelieved bleakness. In terms of his style, his images are often striking and memorable and his descriptions are vivid and concise. Like most modern poets, much of his language has an appealing conversational quality which engages the reader and creates a sense of personal intimacy.

Two poems of heart-breaking intensity are *The Locket*, and *The Cage*, where the poet's unusual, difficult relationships with his parents are described with admirable honesty. In *The Locket* Montague details how his relationship with his mother was problematic from the beginning. Firstly, his mother had been hoping for a girl; secondly, he entered the world by way of a breech birth, 'both the wrong sex, / and the wrong way around'. The sense of hurt and abandonment that the young boy felt is palpable throughout the poem. His sense of rejection was later compounded by his mother's unwillingness to reclaim him after she returned from New York. Despite such cold-hearted treatment, Montague later made a great effort to get to know his mother, an effort which was not fully successful. One cannot but admire Montague's understanding and compassionate nature – he reflects on how his mother's painful, disappointing life left her emotionally wounded, 'a forlorn woman / resigned to being alone'. The discovery of the locket, 'with an old picture in it, / of a child in Brooklyn', could easily allow this poem to collapse into a sentimental portrait of a mother's hidden love for an abandoned child. However, Montague is too direct in his approach for this to happen. By stating that he was 'not readily forgiven' for something that was totally beyond his control, he provides a sharp, direct criticism and reveals a measure of the hurt that was inflicted. He states the facts in a stark, uncompromising manner, which shocks the reader –'You never nursed me...Then you gave me away.' I am sure most of you listening tonight to these accusing, abrupt lines can sympathise with the complex tangle of love and resentment which Montague felt. It is astonishing that he

223

is capable of offering us at the same time an intriguingly compassionate insight into his mother's behaviour.

The Cage is a similarly intensely personal poem that provides an insight into the poet's relationship with his father, a man who spent over 20 years working in the New York underground. The title suggests how his father felt physically confined and spiritually imprisoned during these years. Montague vividly recreates a life of isolation where the pain of loneliness is deadened only by whiskey. The conversational, yet dramatic style of the opening draws us into the poem, 'My father, the least happy / man I have known'. The phrase 'lost years' captures the denied opportunity to develop a relationship. When his father eventually returned to his hometown, father and son 'walked together / across fields of Garvaghey / to see hawthorn on the summer / hedges'. Montague's honest portrayal of their relationship is admirable – as in *The Locket*, he does not idealise it, 'But we / did not smile in / the shared complicity / of a dream'. Now, whenever the poet descends into the subway or underground he is reminded of his father, 'I see his bald head behind / the bars of the small booth'. With compassionate insight he realises that his father was a trapped and vulnerable figure.

Montague writes about romantic relationships with the same honesty that characterises his portrayal of his relationship with both his mother and father. *The Same Gesture* is a poem that celebrates a special kind of love that finds expression in a 'secret room'. One can imagine this room being bathed in a metaphorical 'golden light' – an image that evokes the idea of a rich and warm love. Montague's realism recognises the complexity of love; in this room of intense passion 'everything – love, violence, / hatred is possible'. The poet's admirably economic style is apparent in his description of the lovers' deep and meaningful love, 'Such intimacy of hand / and mind is achieved'. The idea of the lovers eventually having to leave their 'secret room' and return to humdrum reality is described with similar economy and elegance, 'we leave, re- /suming our habits / with our clothes'. Montague writes about love with tenderness and sensitivity, as we see in the poem's memorable final lines. Something in the mundane, functional action of changing gears reminds the poet of how he had earlier helped his lover to achieve an elevated state of contentment and offers us an insight into their relationship, 'changed gears with / the same gesture as / eased your snowbound / heart and flesh'.

Not all of Montague's intensely experienced memories are associated with relationships. His fascination with nature also inspires his work and offers many profound insights into man's relationship with other living creatures. *The Trout* was inspired by a childhood memory of the poet catching a trout in a stream with his hands. The scene is depicted so vividly that the poet draws us into his childhood world. Each step in the process demands complete concentration. The boy lies 'flat on the bank' and parts the rushes so that he can 'ease' his hands into the water 'without a ripple'. His next step is to 'tilt' his hands 'slowly downstream to where he lay'. Image and sound (the gentle assonant 'i') combine to suggest the delicate beauty of the fish, 'he lay, tendril-light'. The boy unobtrusively brings 'the curve' of his hands under the trout's body. Attributing human qualities to the fish, he describes him surging 'with visible pleasure'. He is so absorbed in the task that it is only when he finally grips the trout that he becomes aware of the impact of his actions on the fish, which is clearly panic-stricken. Montague's compassionate nature is reflected in his enduring memory of the trout's panic, 'To this day I can / Taste his terror on my hands'. The same compassion for another vulnerable creature is apparent in a disturbing poem entitled, *Killing the Pig*. This poem provides an insight into the capacity for human beings to be oblivious to the suffering of animals. A series of vivid comparisons appeal to our sense of hearing as the pig's screams are likened to a 'big plane roaring off...the brain-chilling persistence of an electric saw...scrap being crushed'. All of these sounds are painfully intense and evoke a deep compassion for the animal. I think that most of you listening tonight will agree that this poem challenges us to question our own attitudes and behaviour towards other life species. Montague certainly offers us a chilling insight into an inhumane act and raises moral dilemmas associated with it.

Many of Montague's intensely explored experiences are related to a strong sense of place and of the past. As we have seen in the last two poems, much of his poetry is rooted in his childhood memories in Garvaghey. His depiction of the local eccentric characters in *Like Dolmens Round My Childhood* are interesting, vivid pen-pictures offering us insights into Irish social history. His portrayal of the characters who dominated his young life is compassionate and genuine. Jamie MacCrystal is remembered as a kind character who gave the poet 'a penny every pension day'. His gentle, sensitive nature was reflected in his feeding of the birds. Maggie Owens was a poisonous gossiper, 'a well of gossip defiled', reputed locally to be a witch. However, even as a boy, the poet had the insight and compassion to see beyond such superstitious notions and perceive the lonely person behind the rather sinister image, 'all I could find / Was her lonely need to deride'. Her belittling of others was the result of being embittered by loneliness. In the closing stanza the poet abruptly dismisses idealised versions of Ireland's past, 'Ancient Ireland, indeed!'. He was there ('I was reared by her bedside') and knows the truth. The reality of that earlier Ireland was superstition ('The rune and the chant, evil eye and averted head'), fierce family and personal feuds, poverty, loneliness and isolation. This poem vividly conveys these harsh social realities in its depiction of the eccentric characters who dominated the poet's childhood. In this poem we can see Montague's narrative technique – his capacity to capture a character and a place with dramatic intensity while providing profound insights into human loneliness and sorrow.

The Wild Dog Rose is yet another example of an old woman who closely resembles the old people in *Like Dolmens Round My Childhood*. This poem similarly offers us a window into the past. A vivid metaphor conveys the old woman's ragged appearance, 'a moving nest of shawls and rags'. Detailed description explains the fear that she inspired in the poet when he was a child, 'the great hooked nose.../ the sunken eyes, the mottled claws / clutching a stick'. Of course as an adult, the poet is no longer fearful of her. He knows now that she is simply another person wounded by life, 'a human being / merely, hurt by event'. Sharing memories of the past, the two achieve 'reconciliation'. Their new closeness is conveyed by a lovely simile, 'like old friends, lovers almost'. The poet's compassionate nature is again evident in his perception that it is loneliness (which he describes as 'The only true madness') that prompts the old woman's endless stream of talk. The graphic description of her attempted rape by a drunk who broke down the door of her house is chilling in its intensity. However, the image of the rose beaten by the rain but still shining suggests the resilience of this old woman in the face of hardship, loneliness and violence.

I think there is no doubt that the poetry of Montague is a poetry inspired by and emanating from his own intensely personal experiences. In this talk, I have confined myself to this aspect of his work in order to emphasise the importance of how memories rooted in childhood continuously float to the surface of consciousness. Memories can offer insights into the individual life and the lives of others while drawing on a deep well of human compassion. We see this stylishly presented in the work of John Montague.

I hope you will tune in again at the same time next week when I will be continuing an examination of the poetry of John Montague with particular attention to the poems inspired by Irish history and the situation in his native Northern Ireland.

Thank you and goodnight.

Eiléan Ní Chuilleanáin

Biographical Note

Eiléan Ní Chuilleanáin was born in Cork in 1942, the daughter of author Eilís Dillon and Professor Cormac Ó Cuilleanáin, a writer and a professor who fought in the Irish War of Independence. She studied English at University College Cork before continuing her academic education at Oxford University. Her upbringing and experiences in Cork had a tremendous effect on her literary output.

Regarded by many as one of the most important contemporary Irish female poets, Ní Chuilleanáin explores a variety of themes in her poetry. She is interested in Irish history and social issues, the power of religious belief, love, transience and loss. Many of her poems link historical and modern events in an original and compelling manner.

In an interview in 2009, Ní Chuilleanáin stated, 'The question I ask myself constantly is "is this real? Do I really believe this, do I really feel this?" But that is a question I cannot answer except by trying again in a poem.' The result of this search for truth gives rise to many thoughtful and complex poems which can be challenging for the reader.

On the occasion of her being awarded the 2010 Griffin Poetry Prize, the judges observed that, 'She is a truly imaginative poet, whose imagination is authoritative and transformative. She leads us into altered or emptied landscapes... Each poem is a world complete, and often they move between worlds... These are potent poems, with dense, captivating sound and a certain magic that proves not only to be believable but necessary, in fact, to our understanding of the world around us.'

Eiléan Ní Chuilleanáin is not only a poet, but an accomplished translator of poems from other cultures and editor of the literary magazine *Cyphers* and the *Poetry Ireland Review*. She has taught English in Trinity College Dublin since 1966. With her husband, the poet Macdara Woods, she divides her time between Ireland and Italy.

When you are reading the poetry of Eiléan Ní Chuilleanáin watch out for the following:

- A **deceptively simple style**. Most of her poems deal with complex and obscure themes. Her poems are enigmatic (mysterious, challenging to interpret) in quality.

- A preoccupation with **transitions** or **translations**, for example from the physical to the spiritual worlds or from past to present, is common in her work.

- A tendency to use simple narration as a means of entry into a poem which then becomes **more obscure** as the poem progresses.

- The poet's interest in and knowledge of **history** and **architecture** is apparent in her work.

- References to **myth**, **legend** and **folk tales**. This assists detachment and helps universalise themes.

- The **poet's mother** Eilís Dillon was a writer of children's stories and this influence is apparent in some of the poems.

- Use of **vivid imagery** which is richly **sensual** in quality and often drawn from the natural world.

- **Abstract thoughts** which are expressed through concrete images.

- Her main themes deal with **life** and **death**, the dramatic differences in the power wielded by males and females throughout history, historical shifts in power from empires to revolutions – with a recurring reference to Ireland's history – and a **spiritual versus physical view** of the world.

Lucina Schynning in Silence of the Nicht

The unusual title of this poem is taken from a Middle Scots poem by a Scottish poet, William Dunbar (1460-1517). 'Lucina' is another name for the goddess of the moon (also called Diana).

The theme of the poem deals mainly with a reflection on the desolation which followed the Cromwellian invasion of Ireland in 1649 but also provides an insight into the resilience of the human spirit.

Stanza one opens with a direct translation of the first two lines of Dunbar's poem. An atmosphere of silence and stillness is created as we imagine the moon 'schynning' (shining) in the 'silence of the nicht' (night). The night is clear as the sky is 'all full of stars'. Description then gives way to a dramatic monologue as an unidentified speaker relates how he/she was in the 'ruin' of an ancient building, reading a book by the light of a 'sour candle'. The use of the word 'sour' suggests bitterness, which is extended further by the reference to the fact that the speaker has no food or drink, no protection against the elements and none of the entertainment which would usually accompany life in a fine castle or hall: 'without roast meat or music / Strong drink or a shield from the air'. The desolation reaches a high point of intensity in the description of the window as being 'crazed'. This could mean broken or cracked, but also has connotations of being mad or insane. Ní Chuilleanáin may be depicting symbolically the suffering and desolation which followed the Cromwellian invasion of Ireland in 1649. It is interesting to note that the speaker is not identified. It could be somebody living in the seventeenth century, enduring the devastation and oppression of the time or, alternatively, it could be the poet herself adopting a persona in order to communicate her own feelings about such horrific historical events, or indeed as a means of exploring personal grief. In a typical manner, Ní Chuilleanáin's poetry is obscure in meaning after a fairly simple narrative opening. Despite the depressed mood, there is some relief in the fact that the clouds have cleared and the speaker felt, 'Moonlight on my head, clear after three days' rain'. The sensuous imagery employed in this stanza draws the readers into the scene, allowing them to experience the bleakness and harshness of the setting.

The second stanza continues the narrative as the speaker washed in 'cold water' which had been 'channelled down bogs' and dipped between 'cresses' or sharp-tasting plants. The fact that the water was 'orange' in colour could be because it was bog water, but this could also be a reference to the Battle of the Boyne in 1690, when William of Orange defeated the army of the Catholic King James II of England. Perhaps the poet is also thinking of the conflicts between Protestants and Catholics in the more recent past, which are often resurrected during the Orange parades in the North of Ireland every year. There is no doubt that the speaker feels dispossessed, homeless and oppressed. As in the first stanza, the mood changes slightly from hardship to relief as the speaker slept 'safely' while bats flew through the room by night. There is no disturbance or interruption of the surrounding calm as only sheep grazing nearby observed the speaker awakening in daylight.

In an almost dream-like vision, the third stanza depicts scenes of horror and death. Without knowing exactly which historical events are being recalled, the reader can assume that the history itself is one of terrible suffering: 'Behind me the waves of darkness lay'. Plagues of mice and beetles crawl out of the 'spines of books'. It is not certain if the speaker is reading about the atrocities of the past from history books and recalling such events or if the plagues are symbolic of present suffering; certainly death is evoked in the 'pale faces with clay' and the reference to the 'disease of the moon gone astray'. There is no relief as the mood of despair and desolation is maintained to the end of the stanza.

In a sudden shift of tone, the fourth stanza opens in direct contrast to the preceding stanza. Gone are the plagues of mice and beetles and the faces of the dead. In their place are the wonders of nature. The speaker is able to relax and contemplate the 'sky growing through the hole in the roof". In a wonderful image, personal amazement is compared to that of 'mosaic beasts on the chapel floor' who had been deprived of communication with the natural world. When the roof fell in, after the Cromwellian invasion, they could then observe the sky with awe and wonder. It is interesting to note that the word 'desert' is now used instead of the bogland setting of the second stanza. The word 'desert' suggests that which is barren and lifeless and also has connotations of a wilderness, deserted by human beings. There is undoubtedly a sense of alienation and loneliness in the poem which has been dramatically presented in each of the stanzas. However, this stanza prepares the reader for the poem's generally positive conclusion.

The final stanza is a celebration of the natural world. The rain, wind and cold water of the opening stanzas is now replaced with reference to the grasshopper, lark and bee all of which suggest the warmth of summer days. The lark is a bird traditionally associated with hope because it rises at dawn and soars high into the sky. Bees are associated with summer as they gather honey from flowers. All of nature seems to embrace the speaker – 'Sheepdogs embraced me' – as he/she looks far down the road, 'between hedges of high thorn' and observes a hare 'absorbed, sitting still / In the middle of the track.' Although there is a sense of calm and relaxation in the entire scene, there is also a suggestion of vulnerability. Ní Chuilleanáin used this image of the hare in the poem *On Lacking the Killer Instinct,* which deals with the death of her father. The final image in the poem emphasises however a new-found confidence and belief in the future which is captured in the sound of the 'chirp of the stream running'. Perhaps the poet is saying that all sorrows and losses pass with time; that we must face the future with hope and confidence. The running stream might symbolise the energy and life force which gives resilience to the human spirit and a capacity to move forward and leave what is past in the past where it belongs.

KEY POINTS

- The poem is set in a ruin somewhere in Ireland, after the Cromwellian invasion of 1649. However, the poem is not simply a meditation on an historical event but has layers of meaning, both historical and personal. Meaning is suggested rather than stated.

- The use of a dramatic monologue recreates the sense of alienation and desolation felt by Irish people after invasions, famines and other devastating events.

- The speaker, surrounded by living creatures, under an open sky, becomes part of the surrounding life but is also identified with the crumbling ruin and the people who were cruelly dispossessed and butchered during the invasion.

- Despite its dark subject matter, the poem is life-affirming and demonstrates the resilience of the human spirit. The final image of the running stream is evocative of life continuing.

- Notice the assonance on the 'i' sound in the opening line of the poem: 'Moon shining in silence of the night'. This helps to create the atmosphere of calm stillness as it slows the line down. It is also very musical and harmonious in sound quality. The sibilant 's' sound also creates the hush of the silent night.

- Alliteration adds to the music of the poem and helps to connect related words: 'reading...ruin', 'meat...music', 'slept safely. / Sheep stared', 'hedges of high thorn' etc.

- Excellent use is made of repetition to give emphasis to key words: 'plague' is repeated three times in the third stanza and contributes to the overpowering sense of suffering and oppression. The moon is referred to twice in the first stanza and again in the third stanza.

- Unusual word choice contributes to a sense of the surreal. The candle is 'sour', the windows 'crazed', the moon is a 'disease', the bogland becomes a 'desert'.

- The poet employs contrast effectively to show the connections between animate and inanimate nature. Animal images abound: bats, sheep, mice, beetles, sheepdogs, lark, bee and a hare. The sky, moon, stars, air, rain and water all signify the constant world of nature. These images contrast with the ruin, book, window, roof, the 'pale faces' of the dead and the inanimate 'mosaic beasts' who adorn the chapel floor. The speaker is connected to both the living things of nature, the ruin and the constancy of sky, stars and stream. The major contrasts are those between the darkness of the opening with the more confident, upbeat ending and the fine balancing of the still sky and stars with running streams, air blowing, bats flying etc.

The Second Voyage

The title of this poem refers to the Greek hero Odysseus, whose first journey was an epic and constant battle with the sea; now exhausted by the struggle against the forces of nature, he decides his second voyage will be on land and therefore less difficult.

The theme of the poem is related to transitions, a subject of particular interest to Ní Chuilleanáin. Past and present are explored as Odysseus learns to overcome frustration and accept that he cannot detach himself from the challenges offered by the sea.

The opening stanza of the poem is quite amusing in the way that the heroic Odysseus is presented. Ní Chuilleanáin almost cartoonises Odysseus resting 'on his oar', contemplating how the waves lack even the 'decency' to acknowledge his triumph over them. The personification of the waves adds to the humour and also brings out the conflict between the hero and these opponents. They are described as having 'ruffled foreheads' – a wonderful image of their rippled, foaming surface – and are also depicted as 'Crocodiling and mincing past' as Odysseus rams his oar 'between their jaws'. The choice of verbs here gives the impression that the waves are actually

teasing him by refusing to be 'ridged / Pocked and dented with the battering they've had'. As the hero looks into the depths of the 'simmering sea' with its 'scribbles of weed', he wonders why the waves of the ocean lack the personality of the beasts named by Adam, who was given dominion over the creatures of the earth by God in the book of Genesis. Adam could salute a new beast or look with admiration on a 'notorious' creature, but the waves 'Have less character than sheep and need more patience'.

Having expressed his dissatisfaction with the element he has spent his life navigating, Odysseus decides that the time has come for him to abandon the sea and start a new career on dry land. The narrative now has all the quality of a quest or a journey. The hero states that he will 'park' his ship and 'walk away' from the life he has known. With his oar as his companion, Odysseus imagines travelling inland, past riverbeds and herons who 'parcel out the miles of stream', moving 'Over gaps in the hills' and 'through warm / Silent valleys' until he will meet a farmer. With keen humour Ní Chuilleanáin presents the boastful arrogance of Odysseus as deciding that he will plant his oar, (his former weapon against the waves) as a 'gatepost or a hitching-post', in a place where someone is 'Bold enough to look me in the eye' and to ask him where he is 'off to with that long / Winnowing fan over your shoulder'. He will then, he imagines, be ready to 'organise' his house and settle down.

However, it is not quite that easy for Odysseus to leave 'the profound / Unfenced valleys of the ocean' for the limitations of the land. He considers all the ways that water is controlled by man in fountains, kettles, lakes, muddy puddles, horsetroughs and canals. He feels the salt taste of his own tears as he realises that the sea is his true home, regardless of the 'insults' of the waves. He can never abandon the freedom that the ocean offers him and the challenge that it presents.

KEY POINTS

- A keen sense of humour is apparent in this poem where the epic hero Odysseus is depicted as conversing with his oar, being outraged at the disrespect shown to him by the waves of the ocean and his arrogant awareness of his own importance: 'when I meet a farmer / Bold enough to look me in the eye'. The portrait is engaging through this use of comedy.

- Notice the contrast between the confined landscape and the boundless sea. The 'Unfenced valleys of the ocean' symbolise challenge and freedom, which Odysseus cannot abandon.

- This poem, like several others on the course, deals with the notion of transition or change and the obstacles and difficulties of such transitions.

- Personification is used very effectively, giving a life-force to inanimate things like the waves, the oar and the sea.

- Richly sensuous images create vivid pictures in the imagination of the reader.

Deaths and Engines

This is a poem which provides a context for the poet's experience of her father's death which took place in 1970 – a time when many lives were lost during the political conflict in Northern Ireland. One could view the poem as dealing with an individual, personal death as well as the universal experience of death, whether due to natural causes or as a result of violence.

Simple narrative opens the poem as the poet recalls the descent of a plane to an airport in Paris. 'We came down' suggests that a journey is reaching its ending. The plane, driven by an engine moves 'In a stiff curve', a phrase which evokes a sense of the inevitable and a certain unease regarding the landing. The sighting of the wreckage of another plane on the snowy landscape also adds a chill to the experience. It first appears as 'an empty tunnel', isolated: 'nobody near it' and finally, 'Tubular, burnt-out and frozen'. This could be read metaphorically as the poet's awareness that life is a journey from which we eventually descend into the cold reality of death. Passing through a tunnel is an image commonly associated with dying and the stark juxtaposition of 'black' with the whiteness of the snow adds a sense of drama to the event. Stanza two continues the narrative as the plane faces 'The snow-white runways in the dark'. Nothing can be heard except the 'sighs / Of the lonely pilot'. The description in these two stanzas have a chilling effect on the reader as there is nothing to relieve the mood of foreboding encapsulated in the image of the 'frozen' wreck.

In the third stanza, the poet focuses on the shape and coldness of the 'metal wings' of the plane describing their chill as being 'contagious'. This

231

may be a reference to the cold acceptance that the journey of life comes to an end in death for everybody. Nobody escapes. She then addresses an unidentified person, perhaps her dying father, noting that he will need wings of his own. Multi-layered images representing 'Time and life' abound in this stanza. The metal wings of the plane are likened to a knife and fork, meeting as they cross. The lifeline in the palm of the hand 'breaks' and the curved line of the plane's descent meets the 'straight skyline'. All of these images show a connection between two things which bring about an ending. The 'lifeline in your palm' suggests that our time in life is laid out for us since birth; it has an inevitability. The placing of the word 'Cross' at the beginning of the fifth line, with its Christian connotations, might also indicate the journey of suffering which precedes death.

An apparent change of tone opens the fourth stanza as 'images of relief' appear. An image of a wounded man with 'a bloody face' dressed in hospital pyjamas and 'Sitting up in bed, conversing cheerfully' seems to offer hope of survival, of continuing life. However, the harsh reality of the final line of this stanza dismisses the illusion that death can be evaded: 'These will fail you some time.'

The descent of the plane which was so graphically depicted in the opening stanza is now recalled in the fifth. Again the poet addresses the dying person, likening the death to the landing of a plane and its unstoppable career. She tells him that he will be alone, like the 'lonely pilot' of the second stanza, and will find himself 'Accelerating down a blind /Alley, too late to stop'. Despite the inevitability of these final moments however, there is a ray of hope as death is described as being 'light'.

The final stanza is both disturbing and consoling. The body will be 'scattered like wreckage' but out of this ruin, the memories of the dead loved one will 'spin and lodge in the hearts' of all those who are left behind. Memory can keep alive those whom we are destined to lose. Here we see another reference to the powerful bonds which join family members. Ní Chuilleanáin returns to this theme in many of her poems.

KEY POINTS

- In this poem the poet contemplates death using the metaphor of a plane making its descent from the sky to the land.
- Notice the image of the wreckage of the plane, which has similarities with ruined or deserted buildings in some of the other poems.
- Poem opens with simple narrative but becomes more obscure as it continues.
- Use is made of contrast to create a dramatic impact. The white snow serves as a backdrop for the burnt-out wreckage. The passengers faced 'snow-white runways in the dark'.
- Unease and tension is communicated through the use of descriptive phrases: 'a stiff curve', ' an empty tunnel', ' nobody near it', 'No sound came over / The loudspeakers...lonely pilot'.
- Notice the repetition of words relating to coldness: 'snow', ' frozen', 'cold of metal wings', which create a chill of foreboding.
- The metaphor of the wrecked plane is connected to the death of her father: 'Accelerating down a blind / Alley, too late to stop'.
- Note the use of images of things crossing or meeting: a knife and fork, a lifeline in the palm which breaks and creates a junction, a plane's curved track against a straight skyline.

- Suffering and death are contrasted with relief and lightness: 'Hospital pyjamas', 'conversing cheerfully' are juxtaposed with 'A man with a bloody face...cut lips', 'You will be scattered like wreckage'.
- Run-on lines, particularly in the fifth stanza, convey a sense of powerlessness, of losing control as inevitable death approaches.
- The poem ends on a positive note as Ní Chuilleanáin assures her father that he will live forever in the memories of those who love him.

Street

The poem opens with a narrative concerning an unidentified man who falls in love with a butcher's daughter. This woman obviously works with her father as she wears the 'white trousers' commonly worn by butchers and has a 'knife on a ring at her belt'. The poet places the word 'Dangling' at the start of the third line which suggests that the knife is, somehow, an invitation or enticement to follow – think of dangling a carrot in front of a donkey! There is, however, something repellent in this image of a tool used to butcher animals. The hypnotic fascination of the man as he stares at 'the dark shining drops on the paving-stones' is both revolting and mysterious, leading to countless questions in the mind of the reader. Is he attracted to the woman because of her ability to inflict death in order to make a living? Is this a normal source of attraction? Why is her beauty or the lack of it not mentioned? Does she know he is watching her? The mystery builds up and compels the reader to read on in order to discover more.

The second, longer stanza continues the narrative with a build-up of tension as the man secretly follows the woman: ' One day he followed her'. We can almost see him, half-concealed as he moves through the 'slanting lane at the back of the shambles' (a place for slaughtering animals). We wonder why he is so secretive and why she is so elusive. The gentle downward movement, 'slanting', may suggest a gradual entry into a kind of netherworld or hell. Next, he arrives at a door which 'stood half-open'. This detail invites us to wonder if the door has been deliberately left half-open so that he can continue to follow her or if it has been half-closed in order to deter

him from doing so. Certainly the door represents some form of barrier which must be overcome just like the stairs. Most intriguing of all perhaps is the fact that having removed her shoes, the woman climbs the stairs leaving the faint, fading 'red crescent' of her heel marks on each step. Her shoes are paired neatly at the foot of the stairs, but the neatness of her shoe placement contrasts with the fact that she must be standing in so much gore during her work that blood still gets inside to stain her feet. As she rises up, away from the world of dead or dying flesh, her physical trail vanishes, leaving the man behind in the mortal world. Is this woman perhaps a goddess of sorts? One who has power, who can leave behind the physical world, transcending it?

At this point the narrative abruptly stops. We never discover the identity of either the man or the woman. We never discover if they met or even if he continued to follow her.

Street is an unusual variant on the quest type of fairy-tale. The domestic normality of the images conceals the strangeness of the attraction. The man is prepared to follow the woman in a manner that is almost menacing. He 'fell in love with her' when he saw her wearing the clothing and bearing the knife of her trade. He appears more fascinated with the drops of blood on the ground and with her bloodied heel prints (a lot of blood must have been spilt if it actually seeped into her shoes!) than he does with her personality or actual beauty.

There is no doubt that in this poem Ní Chuilleanáin dangles a story before the bewildered eyes of the readers and allows them to ponder its mystery for themselves.

KEY POINTS

- *Street* is a short lyric poem which explores edges, boundaries and the mystery which lies beyond that which seems familiar.

- The entire poem has a dream-like quality with some elements of nightmare as the woman carries a 'knife', the man gazes at the 'dark shining drops' of blood, and follows the woman down the slanting lane.

- Three things are revealed about the butcher's daughter:

1. She wears white. White is often associated with purity, sanctity, or cleanliness.

2. She is 'dangling a knife on a ring at her belt'. The word 'dangling' suggests a dancing or playful quality. It also suggests the blade is currently uncontrolled or bouncing in any direction. This may imply a threat: anything (or anyone) could find themselves on the wrong end of it. In some cultures, goddesses play double roles as sanctified, compassionate beings yet also bringers of bloody death and destruction. The woman's knife means death for the animal, but food (or life) for the townspeople. This duality (as a bringer of both life and death) suggests that the woman with the blade enjoys a certain degree of power, which the man may find profoundly attractive.

3. She leaves a trail of blood from dead animals in her wake. The man stares at 'dark shining drops on the paving-stones'. *Staring* means he is fascinated by this trail – it matters to him. A trail can be signs left by a wounded animal, something vitally important to a hunter for survival as a way to track and kill their prey. Trails can also be paths made by humans in a wilderness guiding them back to civilisation. This second meaning of a trail, as a guiding path to save people from becoming lost in the wild, again implies a life-saving property.

- Details are revealed to arouse interest and a desire to know what is going to happen, but we are given no details as to the outcome of this event. Perhaps this is why this most impressive poem feels so obscure. It shows us how profoundly unknown, though not necessarily unknowable, our actual lives may be.

- The atmosphere is one of suspense and intrigue.

- Because this poem is from a collection called *The Magdalene Sermon*, it may have some religious significance, but its obscurity makes it impossible to neatly connect to any religious message.

- Notice the use of the run-on lines in the first stanza which create a sense of urgency and immediacy. The second stanza also uses this technique and after the first sentence, employs only one, powerfully driven sentence which spills over into the third stanza.

Fireman's Lift

Ní Chuilleanáin has said that she was thinking of the death of her mother, (the writer Eilís Dillon) when she wrote *Firemen's Lift*. The setting for the poem is the cathedral in Parma, Italy whose dome features Italian Renaissance artist Correggio's fresco of the Virgin Mary's assumption into heaven. Ní Chuilleanáin had visited this cathedral in 1963 with her mother. The art and architecture of the dome, the 'big tree of the cupola', became a reminder of her mother's recent death. Ní Chuilleanáin focuses on the struggle of the angels to lift Mary into the heavens. This struggle is also connected to the labour and wonder of a mother giving birth – another passage from one form of life to another. The poem therefore works on several levels. The poet has said that the care given to her dying mother by nurses, who lifted and supported her during her last illness, is also part of the inspiration of the poem. A 'fireman's lift' refers to a certain method of supporting the full weight of another person on your shoulders.

In a typical narrative-style opening, the poet addresses her mother as she recalls a shared memory. The wonder and awe that mother and daughter felt in Parma is graphically captured in the description of the domed roof of the cathedral, the cupola, which appears to grow like a tree and then 'splits wide open to admit / Celestial choirs'. It is almost as if the barrier which is the roof of the cathedral has been swept away to allow the earthly to meet the heavenly. The phrase 'fall-out of brightness' captures the splendour of the occasion depicted in the fresco.

The second stanza continues the narrative. Energetic verbs convey the effort needed as the Virgin's body is 'Hauled up in stages', 'spiralling' towards the heavens. 'Teams of angelic arms' lift, support, heave and crowd around her body, passing her ever upwards towards the waiting Christ. This imagery reminds us of the energetic efforts made by firemen, working in teams, to haul people from a place of suffering to a place of safety. Collective effort produces the desired end.

Ní Cuilleanáin then recalls how she and her mother stepped back to see the masterpiece in its totality. This is something which the painter would have longed to do as his own arm 'swept in the large strokes', but this pleasure would be denied or at least deferred for him. The artist must wait for the completion of his work of art before he can truly see it.

The poet describes seeing the angels and watching saints: 'Melted and faded bodies... Loose feet and elbows and staring eyes / Floated in the wide stone petticoat / Clear and free as weeds'. Here, art and architecture meet and are blended together. Within this image of the dome, fringed with a 'petticoat' of plasterwork, Ní Chuilleanáin stresses the interrelationship between architecture and the figures in the painting as she describes the angels and saints bending over the ascending Virgin as she passes into another life.

These details present a vivid sense of reality even though the mists obscure the vision somewhat as it moves further towards the top of the dome.

The fifth stanza marks a turning point as the poet reflects on the necessity of letting her mother go, of setting her spirit free. Ní Chuilleanáin realises that like the teams of angels who pass the Virgin from one level to the next level of waiting hands (just as firemen may need to do on occasions), so she must pass her mother on to eternity. It is a burden for her to do this, but one she must lovingly bear. 'This is what love sees,' she tells us, referring to the 'branch loaded with fruit'. This image of the tree bearing fruit could be symbolic of her own essential bond with her mother. She was the fruit of her womb, as Jesus was the fruit of Mary's womb. The natural cycle involves birth, life and death and the labour to bring a child into the world involves a letting-go – a separation of sorts. In the same way, death demands separation and loss. The image of the tree laden with fruit could also be applied to the 'big tree of the cupola' mentioned in the first stanza which 'splits wide open' to allow the brightness to enter. Mary bore Christ. The tree of the cross bore Christ whose suffering led to resurrection. The poet's mother bore her, nourished her mind and body and now, after the suffering associated with death, must be passed on, aided in her transition from life to death.

Images of art and architecture blend magnificently in the next stanza. The limbs of the assisting angels who labour to lift the Virgin heavenwards are blended into the fresco. We see a 'jaw defining itself, a shoulder yoked', images of effort and determination. The pillars are likened to supporting arms; the roof made from a back; a bridge from legs while the lifting hands function like a crane offering not only support and height but also gently cradling the body. The Virgin's face is like a 'capital'.

Ní Chuilleanáin has said that much of the poem's inspiration came from the loving support and care given by the nurses who looked after her mother in her last illness. She now sees these nurses as being similar to the supporting angels in the fresco, 'Their heads bowed over to reflect on her...As she passed through their hands'. Her mother's endurance is reflected in the 'muscles' which 'clung and shifted' as she moved ever closer to the 'edge of the cloud'. At this point, the Virgin Mary, a mother, is blended with the image of her own departing mother. There is the same mystery of what lies beyond the cloud which acts as the boundary between what is known and what cannot be known or fully understood.

KEY POINTS

- The poet and her mother first visited Parma Cathedral in 1963. The poet recalls the visit during the illness and death of her mother in 1994. As in so many of her other poems, the closeness and importance of family relationships are emphasised.

- The poem juxtaposes powerlessness and power. The assumption of the Virgin Mary – who is symbolically connected to the poet's dying mother – is described in earthly, concrete terms. She is lifted and passed upwards to meet Christ by 'teams' of angels. (Firemen lift bodies to safety by working in teams, passing the person from one to the other and to eventual safety. The bearing of the full weight of another on your back or shoulders is known as a 'fireman's lift').

- The poem celebrates the skill needed by nurses in lifting fragile, sick and powerless people. Powerful verbs depict the energy and effort required, which is also depicted in the teams of angels: 'Teams of angelic arms... heaving, / Supporting, crowding her' as she is 'Hauled up in stages'. Ní Chuilleanáin herself noted how, when she saw Correggio's fresco, 'I could only concentrate on one aspect, the way it shows bodily effort and the body's weight'.

- Note the striking use of vivid descriptive detail to create the fresco in the mind of the reader.

- The run-on lines of the opening stanza are replaced by a more disjointed rhythm as the efforts of the angels are described.

- Symbolism is extensively used throughout the poem.

- Art and architecture blend seamlessly in this poem connecting the concrete reality of the building with the spiritual vision of the artist and his depiction of the Assumption of the Virgin Mary.

All for You

All for You is taken from Ní Chuilleanáin's collection entitled *The Brazen Serpent.*

The poem begins with a short three-line stanza written in deceptively simple language. Some travellers arrive at a 'strange stableyard' and 'dismount'. We are never actually told the identity of these travellers.

'The donkey walks on...And sticks his head in a manger'. Echoes of Christ's nativity scene are hard to ignore here, given the mention of strangers arriving after a long journey on a donkey and the specific word 'manger', although the text is never explicit as to whether this arrival is a holy one or not.

The voice in the second stanza changes from the inclusive 'we' to an exclusive 'you'. Suddenly the reader is transported to what sounds like a mansion: 'The great staircase of the hall slouches back/Sprawling between warm wings. It is for you'. The verb 'slouches' suggests negativity – something corrupt here – and the verb 'sprawling' implies a form that has lost control of itself. Nonetheless, 'warm wings' embrace the visitor. The use of the verbs to describe the steps as they 'wind and warp' connote being misled somehow. Winding paths are confusing; warped things are misshapen and deviant. The house acts like a body, grossly enveloping the wanderer who enters it. 'Among the vaults, their thick ribs part...'. Here are images of solidity – vaults suggest huge arched roofs or massive chambers to guard valuables. The 'thick ribs' imply a massive creature, monstrous in scale, opening to receive this visitor and house them. There are vast ovens heating the mansion.

The third stanza repeats the phrase 'It is for you'. We are shown images of vast reserves of food and drink. The visitor lies down to sleep, a mysterious key still in their pocket, unused. Although the poem resists a straightforward interpretation, it may be an imaginative reading of the three temptations Satan inflicts on Jesus in Luke's gospel. In this gospel, Jesus wanders out into the desert for forty days. Toward the end of his fast he is starving. His defences against temptation

are extremely low. Satan appears and suggests that Jesus magically turn a stone into food. Jesus refuses, claiming 'Man shall not live on bread alone'. Then the devil shows Jesus all the nations of the world and promises that if Jesus will simply worship him, 'it will all be yours'. Once again, Jesus rejects Satan's claim that it is 'all for you', and says: 'Worship the Lord your God and serve only him'. Finally, the devil transports Jesus to the highest point of a temple and tells him to throw himself off, claiming that God will command his angels to 'guard you carefully; they will lift you up in their hands, so that you will not strike your foot against a stone'. Jesus answers: 'Do not put the Lord your God to the test'.

We may see here the three temptations implied in line 8: 'The doors/Of guardroom, chapel, storeroom/Swing wide...'. The storeroom contains vast amounts of food so the wanderer will not go hungry. The chapel (or temple) is right next to the 'guardroom', a room that contains guardians (or angels) that will see the wanderer will come to no harm. The echo 'It is for you' winds through the poem, a possible refrain welcoming the visitor to great power and wealth.

But what of the 'rage of brushwood'? Perhaps the answer lies in another biblical text, the Book of Isaiah. This book features a furious god who has kept itself hidden from the people of earth because it despises their sin. The writer of that passage implores god to return and punish humanity: 'As fire burns brushwood...' Isaiah 64:2 (NKJV).

The writer of the Book of Isaiah goes on to claim: 'All of us have become unclean, and all our righteous acts are like filthy rags; we all shrivel up like a leaf, and like the wind our sins sweep us away.' Isaiah 64:6

Perhaps the image of the vast 'ten-pound jars/ Rich with shrivelled fruit' is an allusion to those who have succumbed to the temptation of power. Fruit here is rich in the sense of being sweet, but can also refer to wealth. The fruit is a kind of flesh and it is 'shrivelled' in the manner implied by the writer of Isaiah as something corrupted, broken down, rotten. This 'rage of brushwood' is a furious but absent god, angry about how the living 'roots' of the spirit have been 'torn out and butchered' – recalling the suffering and crucifixion of Jesus.

At any rate, the wanderer seems unworried by the heat of this raging fire flowing out to meet him. 'Where better to lie down / And sleep…?' the visitor asks. Sleep here could imply a lack of awareness of the deeper reality being suggested here. Despite the promise of order ('the labelled shelves'), the house is wrapping itself around the figure, imposing itself, suffocatingly hot, warping in all directions, constantly promising 'It is for you'. The sleeping figure forgets all about the key in their pocket. Is this key perhaps suggesting that there is a way out?

In Matthew 16:19, before Jesus dies, he makes the apostle Peter head of the church, and says: 'I will give you the keys to the kingdom of Heaven'. Again, in the Book of Isaiah, faith is seen as a key, 'He will be the sure foundation of your times, a rich store of salvation and wisdom and knowledge; the fear of the Lord is the key to this treasure'. Such a key is a symbol for knowledge – a way to wake up, to see through and escape corrupting power. But the figure in the poem seems very comfortable with their choice to enter this mansion. They seem pleased with access to a vast storehouse, reassured by the guardhouse, comforted by the seething fire. It's all for them, after all. However, it is also a far cry from the simplicity of the stable of Bethlehem which was referred to in the opening stanza.

In a nutshell, we could interpret the poem as contrasting the temptations of a worldly, self-indulgent life and the opportunity to exchange it for a life of simple spirituality which offers hope and redemption.

(Eiléan Ní Chuilleanáin had three aunts who were nuns and she had a certain fascination with those who surrender the things of the flesh for those of the spirit.)

KEY POINTS

- Like many of Ní Chuilleanáin's poems, this poem is open to different interpretations, but there is no doubt about the biblical connotations. According to an Old Testament story, God told Moses to make a serpent out of bronze which would save repentant sinners if they looked at it. The Serpent of bronze in the Old Testament is familiar to Christians because of the reference to it by Jesus in St John's Gospel: 'As Moses lifted up the serpent in the wilderness, even so must the Son of Man be lifted up, that whoever believes in Him should not perish but have eternal life' - (John 3:14-15). However, traditionally, Christians have associated the serpent with Satan and evil. Satan, brazenly, tried to tempt Jesus to embrace a life of power and ease, rather than crucifixion, death and resurrection, but failed to do so.
- Notice the sudden shift of setting in the second stanza which transports the reader to a surreal environment.
- The plural 'we' used in the first stanza suddenly shifts to the singular 'you' in the second stanza.
- There is an abundance of descriptive detail but the full significance or meaning of the staircase is never revealed. As is typical of this poet, a certain air of secrecy surrounds the poem.
- The imagery is dramatic and powerful throughout the poem with constant appeal to the senses. We are invited to see the interior of the building, feel the heat of the great ovens, smell the fragrance of tea

chests and almost taste the shrivelled fruit.

- Notice the ferocity of certain images: 'thick ribs part', 'rage of brushwood', 'torn out and butchered'.

- The tone of the final stanza is less intense than in the second stanza. Just as the donkey in the opening stanza naturally went towards food and presumably rest, so does the 'you' persona find the storeroom and a place to rest.

- One could read the poem as having some reference to those who decline a life of comfort and ease in order to follow a spiritual life. This could be a reference to the poet's aunts who surrendered the opportunity to become mothers ('shrivelled fruit') but who, nevertheless, preserve the life of the spirit ('the key still in your pocket').

- Notice the architectural images throughout the poem which are typical of Ní Chuilleanáin's poetry.

Following

Like much of Ní Chuilleanáin's work this poem has a dream-like quality and presents us with the difficulties of a woman trying to pursue the ghost of her father. The first stanza contains hints of an *aisling* or dream-vision, where a beautiful woman or an animal such as a cow were symbolic of Ireland.

It opens with what seems to be a young girl desperately following her father's 'trail' through a crowded cattle fair. He keeps disappearing into the throng, always just out of reach, and doesn't seem overly concerned if she can keep up with him or not. We never see his whole figure; instead he is reduced to flashes of tiny detail: 'a glimpse of a shirt-cuff, a handkerchief'. The final description conveys two noteworthy elements: '…the hard brim of his hat, skimming along'. His hat is 'hard-brimmed', suggesting a tough exterior, and it 'skims' along, implying a fast-moving creature – a strong, quick mind that rises above the crowd. She has to shoulder 'past beasts packed solid as books', and we see here a familiar Ní Chuilleanáin motif (a recurring idea or image): a blurring of the realms of word and flesh. The cattle are crammed together like heavy books on a library shelf. Since the poet's father (Cormac O'Chuilleanáin) was a professor and writer himself there may be a hint that, even though the opening stanza is set in a cattle fair, it is really illustrating how her father was swallowed

up by vast libraries of learning during his life. In this dream-memory of the cattle fair everything is solid flesh, and reluctant to give way to her chase. The 'dealing men' who act as barriers are as big and unyielding as the cows they sell: 'A block of a belly, a back like a mountain, / A shifting elbow like a plumber's bend'. Of course, adults typically seem like giants to young children, but there is something nightmarish about the size and solidity of these characters. They are the obstacles of an adult world, always holding her apart from her father who seems perfectly at home in a world of giants, whether these are enormous books, cows or powerful men.

The second stanza moves from a relatively simple – if stressful – anxiety memory about losing her father in a crowd to a more unnerving dreamscape. Her hunt continues, and she is 'tracing light footsteps/Across the shivering bog by starlight'. Unlike the cattle fair, a scene set during the day but heavy with the weight of his work as both a scholar and a soldier, this night scene seems weightless and lit with a strange light. Her father's corpse has floated up from the wakehouse (a place where dead bodies are held while people mourn them), and is now 'Gliding before her in a white habit.' Where everything in the landscape of the first stanza holds her back and away from him, now everything beckons her forward: 'The ground is forested with gesturing

239

trunks'. Being held back in a dream is frustrating but when the landscape starts calling you forward things feel eerie. Despite the 'gesturing trunks', the other images seem even more nightmarish than the giants of the first stanza: 'Hands of women dragging needles/Half-choked heads in the water of cuttings, / Mouths that roar like the noise of the fair day'. It may be that these are images from the Irish War of Independence, or the civil war that followed. Women were traditionally the sewers and needleworkers of the day, and many lost sons and husbands to the fight. Men were hanged ('choked') or in other ways cut down for their part in the conflict. The imagery here suggests a whole nation of suffering, roaring like the noise of the hidden aisling implied by the 'fair day'.

The third stanza finally allows her to reach what seems to be the ghost of her father. He waits for her, with two glasses of whiskey poured. Whiskey comes from the Irish phrase *uisce beatha*, meaning 'water of life'. Ironically only one of them is alive, and the other is still disappearing. His body once again vanishes or translates itself into various parts: a clean bright library and a set of neat, laundered clothes. The interiors (i.e. pages of the books and linings of clothes) become hard to distinguish – both are 'Ironed' down and give away so little of themselves. 'The smooth foxed leaf has been hidden/In a forest of fine shufflings'. A foxed leaf is a page that has developed brown discoloured spots over time; the same happens on human skin in old age.

'The square of white linen/That held three drops/ Of her heart's blood is shelved/Between the gatherings/That go to make a book –.' Again, we see blood (or the body/flesh) fusing with another kind of text – in this case linen. The linen that preserves the small stain of her blood is hidden inside the pages of another text: a book. The collection of individual pages is called a 'gathering'. Such a term contains echoes of meetings of men who assembled to fight for a different type of gathering, a nation. Just as pages standing together compose a book, so people standing together make up a nation. This book of a nation contains traces of innocent blood – not only the minor hurt of the poet herself, who perhaps felt she never got close enough to her father because of his own various pursuits, but the blood of many that is often spilled to create a nation.

The final two lines of the poem are particularly, dense: 'The crushed flowers among the pages crack/The spine open, push the bindings apart'. Crushing a flower inside the pages of a book is a crude way to preserve it. The flower becomes a museum piece, held in a living death, like a ghost. We can retain the beautiful thing, but its life is flattened out of it. Perhaps this is a metaphor for the martyr. Those brave souls who fought for a nation and who were flattened by the history-makers, are beautiful, their memories preserved to some extent. But their suffering, placed at the heart of our history, troubles the living. It threatens to 'crack the spine' of any text (or nation) built around such a 'terrible beauty', to borrow a phrase from W.B. Yeats. The paradox here is that the horrors of our shared history bind together the text of our nation, while simultaneously pushing those bindings apart.

Finally, as her father went before her at the fair and into death, Ní Chuilleanáin realises that she must follow – death also awaits the living.

KEY POINTS

- The opening of the poem is deceptively simple and narrative in style.
- The first stanza contains hints of an *aisling*. An aisling is a poem dating back to a time when Ireland was colonised by the English. Poets would write in secret code about fighting for a free nation, and Ireland was often depicted as a cow or a beautiful woman. Cormac O'Chuilleanáin was not only a writer and scholar but also a fighter in the Irish War of Independence. It may be that these giant 'dealing men' are selling giant

symbolic cows or ideas of Irish freedom. Their mountainous dimensions might remind the poet of how fierce her father's associates seemed to her as a child, and how they threatened to take him away from her forever.

- The reference to the women's 'needles' in the second stanza may also be applied to textiles. The word textile is derived from the Latin root *textere* which means a weaving. So, our modern word text (meaning a book or anything written or composed) comes from the same root as our word for clothing or cloth. Here, we see Ní Chuilleanáin engaging in a symbolic blending of the weaving of history, writing, and her own poetic creation.

- The idea that the past is never forgotten but remains as a shaping force in the present is evident in this poem.

- The run-on lines, commas and dashes in the first stanza suggest the difficulty of following the 'trail' of her father's coat as they moved through the fair.

- Notice the effective use of alliteration and consonance: 'a block of a belly, a back like a mountain'. The recurring 'b' sound and the harsh 'ck' consonants emphasise the stress endured by the following child.

Kilcash

During the era of the Penal Laws (1695-1800), British colonisers felled many of the woods in Ireland to provide timber to make ships for the British navy and to deprive native Irish revolutionaries of the opportunity to hide in the dense forests. Many of the Irish Earls took flight to France and Spain and the old castles fell into ruin.

This poem is a translation from the anonymous Irish nineteenth century ballad, *Caoine Cill Chais*. The original poem is a lament for the ruination of the castle of Kilcash, its woodlands and the life of gentility and grandeur which was once lived there. The great house, which was situated in Clonmel in Co. Tipperary, was owned for several generations by the Butler family who are referred to in Ní Chuilleanáin's poem, but the main focus of interest is Margaret Butler, Viscountess Iveagh, who died in 1744. The Butler family were originally settlers from the time of the Anglo-Norman invasion of the twelfth century who became 'more Irish than the Irish themselves' and who were, unlike most planters, Catholic. One of the Butler family, a brother-

in-law to Lady Iveagh, was even a Catholic Archbishop. This family, who took over Kilcash in the sixteenth century, were great patrons of music and culture and provided support for bards (poets and minstrels). The woodlands of Kilcash were sold in 1797 to Anglo-Irish settlers. Ní Chuilleanáin's translation is true to the original but emphasises the mistreatment of nature and its impact on political and social life.

The theme of the poem deals with dispossession and loss. There may also be an underlying message that those who were once the oppressors and outsiders have themselves fallen to another wave of invaders. One could therefore detect a slight disapproval regarding the willingness of the native Irish to accept and become dependent on those who dispossessed them throughout history.

The opening stanza opens with a speaker, probably a bard, wondering how the local population will manage for 'timber' because of the levelling of the woods. Traditionally, the great woods which surrounded the castle provided timber to the locals. The Butler family has gone, the great house is never mentioned and the bell which once rang out is now silenced. Having described such desolation, the speaker lavishes praise on Viscountess Iveagh, a woman of renown and 'honour' who attracted 'Earls' who 'came across oceans to see her'. The reference to the 'sweet words of Mass' indicate that, unlike many other settlers, the Butlers were Catholics (although Thomas Butler, the husband of Lady Iveagh was nominally a Protestant) and more absorbed into the Irish culture. Despite the obvious praise, it is possible to detect a slight sarcasm in the fact that the native Irish are so dependent on the landed gentry.

The lament continues in stanza two as the speaker recalls the 'neat gates', the 'long walks', the 'avenue' and the 'fine house', all of which are, like those who once lived there, gone. As the speaker sees the old buildings 'knocked down', the trees that once offered 'shade' felled and the Butlers 'depressed and tamed', he cannot but feel a deep sense of 'affliction' and loss. However, again there is a hint of irony in the fact that these colonisers, who once took the land from the native Irish, have been cut down like the woods around Kilcash.

Stanza three focuses on the silence of the natural world which reflects the silencing of the domestic life of the great house. The 'commotion' of ducks and geese, the 'eagle's shout' and the humming of bees are heard no more. The deserted beehive, once a 'honey store', is a reminder of the rich life and 'sweet words of Mass' which have disappeared. Because of the felling of the trees the 'musical birds are stilled'. Even the cuckoo, a bird associated with the hope of spring, is 'dumb in the treetops' and cannot sing its 'lullaby' to the world. Ironically, the cuckoo is a bird that lays its eggs in another bird's nest. When the young cuckoo hatches it dispossesses the original brood by throwing them out of the nest!

The fourth stanza continues the description of Kilcash, abandoned by the herds of deer and those who once hunted them. They have moved to higher ground and look with 'pity' on those who have been abandoned. The destruction of the way of life once lived by the Butler family is conveyed in the contrast between the 'smooth wide lawn' which is now 'broken' and the fact that the house, once a shelter and refuge, is now vulnerable and exposed to 'wind and rain'.

A deeper and more threatening desolation is depicted in the fifth stanza. Now the deserted landscape and ruin are situated in an almost surreal environment. 'Mist hangs low on the branches' while nature itself reflects the surrounding gloom: 'Darkness falls among daylight /And the streams are all run dry'. The alliteration on the hard 'd' sound creates an atmosphere of harshness and links the darkness with the dryness of the streams and the absence of daylight. The repetition of the word 'no' to describe the disappearance of the hazel, holly and berries conveys a profound mood of negativity. Both hazel and holly bushes were associated with good luck, prosperity and had spiritual associations. 'Bare naked rocks', the 'leafless' forest and the 'game gone wild' all emphasise the barrenness which has replaced life and a loss of order and control. The mood is one of total despondency.

Having described the disastrous changes which have befallen Kilcash and its surroundings, the speaker now addresses the 'worst' of the 'troubles' – the descendants of Lady Iveagh no longer inhabit Kilcash. The 'gentle maiden' of this stanza is probably the wife of the eighteenth Earl of Ormonde, a countess who was 'the poor souls' friend' and who 'never preyed on the people'. Those who knew her now lament her leaving. Given that this lady is referred to as 'She', and the only other woman in the poem is Lady Iveagh, it is probable that her identity is being fused with that of her predecessor so that she becomes symbolic of the ancient order and the Butler family itself.

The final verse takes the form of a Catholic prayer, as it is addressed to 'Mary and Jesus'. The speaker longs for the old way of life to be restored, that the 'house will rise up / Kilcash built up anew', never again to be 'laid low'.

KEY POINTS

- This poem is a translation from an Irish nineteenth century poem, so it does not share many of the more obscure features of Ní Chuilleanáin's poetry.

- The reference to the earls who came to see Lady Iveagh from 'across oceans' is a reminder of Irish Catholic resistance during this historical era.

- Notice how the desolation of the landscape reflects the desolation of the speaker. The use of repetitive negative phrases gives emphasis to this mood: 'No hazel, no holly or berry'.

- Regular metre creates a repetitive, heavy effect in keeping with the heavy-heartedness of the speaker.

- Despite the tone of hopelessness and despair which runs through each of the preceding stanzas, the final stanza ends on a note of hope, with a prayer that Kilcash will regain its former glory. From the perspective of the present time, we can see that this hope was actually futile because Kilcash is in a dangerous state of decay and will never attain its former state. In addition, the Butler family never returned to this ancestral home.

- It is not clear from the translation if Ní Chuilleanáin is actually sharing the same feelings as the speaker. It is possible to pick up a sense that the pathetic state of the dependent peasants is something of which she would disapprove. References to the deer and hunters looking down at the people 'with pity' and the description of the 'gentle lady' as 'the poor souls' friend' emphasise the level of dispossession and dependency which was the order of the day. Ní Chuilleanáin would also be well aware that the Butlers were not actually dispossessed but sold the lands for profit to the Anglo-Irish.

On Lacking the Killer Instinct

On the surface this is one of the more accessible of Ní Chuilleanáin's poems. There are three layers of narrative and three protagonists: the first narrative concerns a female hare being coursed (i.e. being chased by greyhounds for sport); the second regards the poet's father as a young freedom fighter during the Irish War of Independence, being pursued by British soldiers; the third involves the poet herself as she 'fled up into the hills' in an attempt to escape the enormity of her now-elderly father's impending death in hospital.

The opening stanza fuses the fleeing hare's predicament with the poet's. As the narrator retreats into the hills in a desperate and irrational attempt to hide from her father's sickness, she finds the hare 'absorbed, sitting still/Right in the grassy middle of the track'. The memory of the hare and of the poet's own attempt at 'escape' in the hills have been evoked by 'the morning paper's prize photograph:/Two greyhounds tumbling over, absurdly gross/While the hare shoots off to the left'. Note the mention of the word 'prize' in describing the photograph. The photographer has hunted down the image – he/she has won it. Despite the cruelty of hare coursing, perhaps this photographer has the 'killer instinct' to ignore the moral drive to oppose the pastime, and instead captures their prize: this glorious image.

The photo depicts the greyhounds in that instant as huge and powerful, but also as clumsy, outclassed and utterly defeated by their smaller, smarter quarry (i.e. the creature they are chasing). The dogs are 'absurdly gross'. Gross means large, even monstrous, but it can also mean the purely physical, as in the phrase 'gross anatomy', like when one cuts into a specimen to see its bodily structure. The opposite of gross is subtle. There is an implication that the dogs are a crude physical force, whereas the hare is something more rarified: a subtler kind of body, perhaps even spiritually energised.

The term 'absurd' is often used to mean simply ridiculous or silly, but it is a profound concept. It means the complete absence of any ultimate (or final) sense. The absurd is really a state where there is no meaning or reason to anything. Life and death, otherwise known as the human condition, can also be seen as absurd. We struggle to survive and then we die, and at times of the death of a loved ones, people can find themselves asking: 'Well what was the point of living, and making so many little escapes from danger, if we're only going to die in the end. It's absurd'. But the poem seems to suggest, if there is any meaning to life, perhaps it is in those stolen moments when we achieve a type of glory. The hare, for instance, lives a short brutal life of fear, but in the instant when she outsmarts the hounds we see in the photo 'her bright eye/ Full not only of speed and fear/But surely in the moment a glad power'. This is a special power: the hare cannot attack the hounds outright –they will always be larger than her – but she can elude them. Similarly, our bodies will all succumb to death eventually, but until then we may be fully alive if we are aware of the presence of death, and feel its breath on our neck.

The hare may even represent the soul, eluding physical death (the absurd gross body that eventually tumbles and falls) and skipping on into a higher state of glory.

The poet recalls that her father has had a taste of this 'glad power' himself when he eluded capture from a 'lorry-load of soldiers' which was 'growling' as it hunted him down. The single man being pursued by such a large force presents us with a mirror of the small revolutionary force of Ireland being opposed by the vast might of the British empire. Perhaps by comparing her young father and his fellow revolutionaries to the hare, the implication is that the Empire is a spiritually dead thing, a powerful but crude physical mechanism, whereas the revolutionary is infused with some manner of grace. The notion of chance is raised here. How did he know he could get away with hiding in the house? What would happen to the others if he had been caught? But the kindness and courage of the house-owners is part of the grace her father seems to be able to tap into, just as the hare knows how to move at just the right moment to evade her enemies.

The symbolism of the hare and the revolutionary seems straightforward enough, but why is it called "On lacking the killer instinct?" On a basic level, the coursing hounds are a special breed of hunter: they naturally possess the killer instinct but perhaps because they are muzzled or simply clumsy they often overtake the hare without killing it. (Even so, the effect of coursing is terrifying for the hare.) Who else lacks a killer instinct in the poem, and is its absence automatically a good thing? Certainly the soldiers could have pressed the people in the house harder to admit they were harbouring a fugitive. Her father, after all, presumably had a killer instinct, which is why he is being chased in the first place. The poem implies that what is right to do in one circumstance is right to avoid in another. The hare is right to run, but the poet sees her own flight as immature: 'And I should not/Have run away'. Instead, she returns to the hospital to face the very monster she is hiding from: death itself. She goes 'washed in brown bog water'. This water may be a baptism of sorts, a paradoxical cleansing of the soul with the dirt of the physical, natural, corruptible world. The enigmatic final line is haunting: 'And I thought about the hare, in her hour of ease'.

What might it mean for the poet's own 'hour of ease'? If the hare achieves liberation by letting the dogs tumble and fall, does this mean that the poet herself cannot find 'ease' until her father dies. If so, by the end of the poem does she really lack a killer instinct? At the start she was fleeing from death, but by the closing lines she walks toward her father's mortality. She is not literally killing him, of course, but perhaps she realises she needs his physical body to die before she can be released from her anxiety about his suffering.

Her own 'blissful dawn' may never come, but the last line implies a hope that it may. If a hare can win over such impossible odds, if there can be a moment of glory or 'gladness' in the absurd struggle that is life, maybe there's hope for any of us. Perhaps the question is: when to avoid death and when to seek it out.

KEY POINTS

- Notice how the poet varies the sense of time and setting in this poem. There is a blending of past and present as the poet engages in the triple narration.

- The frantic pace of the flight from reality of the poet, the flight of the hare from the hounds and her father's flight from his pursuers is reflected in the breathless pace of the run-on lines. The first sentence is actually 14 lines long! The use of commas in phrases of varied length captures the sense of dodging in and out which accompanies a chase.

- The whole point is that, taken on face value, we always assume that the lack of a killer instinct is commendable, but the reality is far more complicated as we see in nature and in war. It is natural to try to hide from death, our own or others, but we eventually have to face the inevitable.

- Contrast is effectively used as the fleeing poet is juxtaposed with the hare 'sitting still'. The sibilance in this phrase suggests a state of calm acceptance and repose.

- The poem is rich in alliterative phrases: 'sitting still', 'borne back', 'paper's prize photograph', 'nineteen twenty-one, nineteen years old, never / Such gladness' etc. These alliterations add to the musical quality of the poem but also serve to link key words and related ideas.

- Bearing in mind the historical references in this poem and in particular her father's escape from his pursuers, one could read the poem as exploring the role played by chance in the shaping of a nation's history and future.

The Bend in the Road

Poems dealing with transience, grief and loss recur frequently in the poetry of Eiléan Ní Chuilleanáin. In this poem she shows how a specific location can hold a memory and evoke a past event.

The poem opens with a demonstrative 'This' to describe an actual place – a bend in a road. This bend marks the spot where a child became unwell during a car journey and it became necessary to stop there for a while to allow him to recover. As the other passengers, mysteriously referred to as 'they', wait 'in the shadow of a house', the speaker refers to a tree 'like a cat's tail' which appears to be waiting also. After a while the child recovers. What is unusual about this description is the fact that we are never told who the speaker is. It could be the poet herself, the mother of 'the child', (who is also not identified) or some other individual who may not necessarily have been present since the speaker uses 'they' instead of 'we'. Despite the simple, conversational tone, several details alert the reader to the fact that something important is happening or is about to happen. The 'shadow' in which they waited, watched by a personified tree, which 'waited too,' builds up a sense of anticipation.

In the second stanza, the speaker reveals that the incident happened 'Over twelve years' earlier. The tone becomes less detached as the child is now addressed directly and told that the bend in the road is 'the place / Where you were sick one day on the way to the lake', as though such a commonplace incident had some special significance. Since then, the child has grown; he is 'taller now than us'. Here the use of the word 'us' creates the impression that the speaker was indeed in the car that day and remembers how

'silent' the road was. Time has passed and some things have changed: 'The tree is taller', like the child, 'the house is quite covered in / With green creeper'. Only the bend in the road remains as it was in the past. A reader cannot but be intrigued by the mysterious suggestion of the house being 'covered in', while the reference to a 'creeper' might indicate that time has crept up silently, initiating change, perhaps even a type of decay. There is no doubt at this point that the entire incident has taken on some special significance, not only for the speaker but for the family. It is a shared moment of their history, forging a bond between them. Clearly the bend in the road is a place which is often passed.

Stanza three now explores the idea that a particular place has the power to evoke and capture memories of the living and the dead. These memories are 'Piled high, wrapped lightly' like a large 'cumulus cloud' in a perfect sky. The scene becomes somewhat surreal in quality, as if the cloud is storing the past, packing it softly away, preserving it in the 'air', like the spirits of the dead – the 'absences'. Some of those who 'breathed / Easily' earlier in the poem are now dead and their memories linger in this place where they once stopped for a sick child.

On a different level, the cloud also suggests the pillows and coverings of the dying, who 'wrapped and sealed by sickness', know that they cannot carry on for long, burdened with the 'weight' of human suffering. Just as a cloud cannot bear the weight of the moisture it absorbs and must release its burden, so the dying find release in death. Their 'presence' remains in the air of this place, this bend in the road, where the tree still stands, casting its shadow and waiting.

KEY POINTS

- A sense of mystery is created from the beginning as the reader is not clear about the identity of the speaker, the child or the people referred to as 'they'. The mysterious images of the 'shadow of a house' and the tree 'like a cat's tail' waiting while 'nothing moved' also emphasise the strangeness of the occasion, even though stopping a car for a sick child is a very commonplace event.

- Symbolism is very effectively used to suggest meaning. Concrete realities like the bend in the road may represent life's journey, where we cannot see what is ahead but must travel on, accepting what may be around the next corner. Air also has a symbolic meaning. Those who are now dead once 'breathed / Easily' at that exact spot where their 'presence' is now stored 'in the air'. The air has become a repository for memory; it holds the 'cumulus cloud', which, although a concrete reality is itself another abstract symbol which is rich in suggestion. In these symbols we can see the poet's technique of using concrete images to suggest abstract concepts.

- Notice how each stanza refers to sickness. Initially it is a child who becomes 'sick', but who soon gets 'better'. The next stanza recalls the memory of that sickness: 'The place where you were sick', while the poem ends with a reference to family members who become 'wrapped and sealed by sickness', which became too much for them to bear. The words 'sick' or 'sickness' therefore, act as a type of motif, linking the thought process of the poem.

To Niall Woods and Xenya Ostrovskaia, married in Dublin on 9 September 2009

This poem was written on the occasion of the wedding of Eiléan Ní Chuilleanáin's son, Niall, to Xenya Ostrovskaia in 2009. It has an almost fairy-tale quality as it describes two people starting out on a quest or life-journey together. As is common in many of her poems, the poet links past and present by referring to legends and myths from both Russian and Irish folklore, showing the blending of two cultures.

In the first stanza the poet addresses the young couple, advising them to 'look out across the fields' and to 'see the same star'. One could imagine that like the magi of old who followed the star that led them to a divine revelation, so these young lovers will follow their own star and observe it pitching itself 'on the point of the steeple'. The poet offers her son and his wife her blessing, reminding them sensibly to make provision for the journey by taking 'half a loaf' with them. This image is thought-provoking as there is a suggestion that they will have to provide now for themselves, that her work as a parent and provider is over. An atmosphere

of loving warmth pervades this stanza. Notice the use of the run-on line which conveys the long and winding path which lies before them. Alliteration adds to the music of the stanza and links key words together: 'same star', 'Pitching... point...'.

The second stanza opens with a command: 'Leave behind the places that you knew'. Perhaps the poet is attempting to impress on the couple that life has now changed and that they must accept such change in order to fully unite. Reassurance is also offered when she tells them that all that they leave, they will 'find once more'. The truths and moral lessons learned in childhood from fairy tales, such as the 'sleeping beauty' will always be theirs like a fountain of knowledge from which to draw strength and inspiration when needed. The story of the sleeping beauty is, of course, one which conveys the awakening power of love and the obstacles which must be overcome for that love to be realised. A very important character in Irish legend is the King of the Cats. The legend says that the cat keeps his identity hidden, but if one were to cut off a part of his ear, he would quickly claim his exalted title, perhaps telling some disagreeable home truths. By introducing the 'talking cat', Ní Chuilleanáin is humorously preparing the young couple for the discoveries they will make about each other's weaknesses and foibles. The entwining of the two stories into one, as the cat stays beside the sleeping beauty, 'Solid beside her feet' is wonderfully evocative as the reader considers how closely united love and truth really are.

Stanza three is whimsical and clever as the 'talking cat' is described as waking up and telling stories from the different traditions of the bride and groom. The Russian legend concerns a hero who must journey forth to catch a firebird who steals 'golden apples' from the garden of the Emperor. Like the Prince in the sleeping beauty tale, the hero will have many obstacles to overcome before he can be victorious. The stealing of the apples is also frustrating as it happens 'every morning'. Perhaps the poet is suggesting that every journey of love requires some struggle and much courage and determination is needed if happiness is to be achieved. The reference to the ancient Irish myth concerns the King of Ireland's son who

fell in love with an enchanter's daughter whom he later lost. Perhaps love should never be taken for granted! By weaving these tales together and giving them to the talking cat to tell, Ní Chuilleanáin acknowledges the different cultures and traditions of the couple and the richness of the past which they can now share.

The final stanza deals with a story which, the poet assures us, the talking cat will 'not know'. This story is taken from the Bible and concerns Ruth, a woman who married outside her tribe and went to live in a different land with her husband. When her husband died, Ruth remained with his people and helped to harvest the crops. Although lonely for her own homeland, out of respect for her mother-in-law, she 'stood by her word'. Ruth 'trusted to strangers' and was rewarded by marrying the owner of the 'barley field' – a field where she helped to harvest the crop.

In the final line, we are told that the story of Ruth ended on a positive note: 'she lived happily ever after'. Love and sacrifice are always repaid. In one sense, we could view Ní Chuilleanáin herself as being somewhat like the King of the Cats, with her mysterious tales and expression of the truth. She ends the poem by asking the young couple to trust her when she says that Ruth 'lived happily ever after'.

KEY POINTS

- Language is conversational in style and deceptively simple. Many layers of meaning underlie the simplicity of the diction.
- Run-on lines in each verse convey the sense of forward movement, a journey of an idea to its conclusion. This is a metaphor for the quest or journey on which the young bride and groom are setting forth.
- Notice the personification of the star in the first stanza which adds to the sense of awe and wonder.
- Alliteration is used effectively in the opening stanza. The sibilant 's' sound on 'see...same...star...steeple' creates an atmosphere of hushed wonder.
- The references to fairy tales and legends is very appropriate in this poem. Apart from the obvious associations of fairy tales with magic and romance, there is also the added advantage that the poem is not over-personalised. It could be a poem for any young couple setting out on a new journey in their lives.

- Fairy tales and legends are also used to link the two cultures in a very effective manner.
- All of the fairy tales and legends mentioned emphasise the importance of courage and perseverance in order to achieve happiness.

Translation

The word translation can mean many things: to change words from one language into another; to move the bones of a holy person, such as a saint, from one resting place to another; to transport someone from earth up to heaven without leaving the body behind; to transform a body from one state to another (like water into steam); to reach a spiritual state of ecstasy, where the mind leaves the body. All of these meanings combine in this poem.

The poem opens with a dedication: 'for the reburial of the Magdalenes'.

The Magdalenes were young women who worked in slave-labour laundries run by the Catholic church in Ireland from the eighteenth to the twentieth century. Typically, the girls were described as "fallen women" because many had become pregnant outside of marriage. Many were subjected to psychological and physical abuse and were not paid for their work. In 1993 the bodies of 155 laundry workers were found buried in a mass grave under a convent in north Dublin. The bodies were exhumed (dug up) and cremated. This poem was recited by Ní Chuilleanáin as their ashes were reburied at Glasnevin cemetery.

Interestingly, the name Magdalene comes from St. Mary Magdalene. She has been unfairly represented in art through the centuries as a prostitute or a "fallen woman" despite there being no biblical evidence she was ever anything but a beloved and important follower of Jesus.

The opening stanza implies two instances of translation: moving the girls' bodies from under the laundry floor to the cemetery, and transforming them from flesh into ashes. Mixing the remains together into the soil 'evens the score', suggesting that no matter what your background is, everyone is equal in death.

The second stanza is a flashback to life in the laundry. 'White light blinded and bleached out/ The high relief of a glance'. White light can be associated with holiness, but here such light is blinding. It's the glaring white of endless laundry work. The girls are so controlled as to be denied the relief of even looking at each other as they bleach stains out of other people's dirty sheets.

Another instance of translation occurs in the imagery of water turning to steam. The steam exhibits qualities of young carefree girls: it 'danced' around cold stone drains that swallow water into an underworld of sorts. Steam doesn't fall – it rises and escapes. We are told it 'giggled and slipped across water'. The spirit of the young girl escapes being drawn down into any dark cold drain, or grave.

The third stanza becomes a prayer – 'Assist them now', and imagines the girls' spirits set free through their bodies being buried properly. It imagines the spirits entering an afterlife and searching for their long-dead parents, and a memory of their own names. The phrase 'under the veil' is an obscure one. It may mean being held under the thumb of veiled nuns at the laundry. But a veil is also a common metaphor in Christianity, meaning a kind of blindness that prevents us from seeing through time, or human life, to perceive heaven (or God, or eternity) as it really is. To be 'under the veil, shifting' might mean that they are still restless spirits, trying to pierce through the veil to find peace everlasting. They are still confused and upset at what has happened to them in life, and so is society as a whole.

The different ways in which words and bodies can be translated has been discussed in the opening paragraph. The term 'translation' blurs the distinction between word and flesh, and according to Christian belief our human world is the word of God made flesh. But this poem tracks an uneasy relationship between human identity and the world of the spirit. 'The edges of words grinding against nature' sounds difficult, even painful. Stanza four shows us that if steam (or the spirit) rises, water (or the body) sinks or falls: 'As if, when water sank between the rotten teeth/Of soap, and every grasp seemed melted'.

The paradox here is that soap is meant to clean things, but instead it absorbs the filth of everything it cleans. The girls live in abject poverty, cleaning everyone else's filth and being regarded as filthy themselves. The irony here is that the 'rot' is in the society that incarcerated these girls away from the world in an endless cycle of cleaning. As soap melts in their hands, they feel their grasp on life itself is melting away. Now that they are dead, the poem implies that they are still haunted by, and haunting the world that treated them so badly. One girl seems to be tormented by the cry of steam: 'Until every pocket in her skull blared with the note – / Allow us now to hear it, sharp as an infant's cry'.

She may have become pregnant once and been put in the laundry as penance. The poet invites us to hear the cry of steam or infants, 'While the grass takes root, while the steam rises'. Now they are buried and surrounded by the grass of graves, we imagine the roots of grass growing down into fresh-dug soil and the steam, or spirits, rising.

The final stanza changes voice from the narrator to one of the spirits. It says: 'Washed clean of idiom • the baked crust/Of words that made my temporary name'. Playing on the laundry imagery, the spirit says it has washed off the 'idiom' (a word so specific to a place it cannot be translated) of its earthly form. Word and dirt make us a 'baked crust' of a 'temporary name'. The idea that the spirit was a filthy girl, a small helpless thing, is a delusion – a 'parasite that grew in me – that spell lifted'. The spirit sees through the illusion, or veil, that kept her from seeing what she truly is. The image of a parasite growing inside her may also allude to how she might have been led to see her baby, and how she was forced to give it away and work in the laundry.

'Let the bunched keys I bore slacken and fall'. Keys to locked doors are a common motif in Ní Chuilleanáin's poetry. Bunched keys suggest a life with many locked doors. There are no locks now, so let the keys fall away. The soul rises like steam, liberated, but even in liberation it forms a cloud, darkening the society that allowed this shame to happen. Only in death can the women find their true identity. (Each woman was given a temporary name, to conceal their true identities when they were in the laundry.)

KEY POINTS

- This poem is typical of Ní Chuilleanáin's style. The symbols are complex and open to different interpretations.

- Some interpretations of the poem suggest that the person who bore the bunched keys is actually one of the nuns who had power over the women who worked in the laundry. However, the statement that 'I lie in earth sifted to dust' seems more likely to be spoken by one of the Magdalenes, as the poem was composed for the occasion of the burying of their remains.

- Note the detailed, sensuous images which evoke the atmosphere in the laundry, particularly in stanzas two and four.

- The harshness of the lives lived by the women is captured in the sounds and meaning of certain words: 'grinding', 'rotten teeth,' 'grasp', 'skull blared', 'sharp as an infant's cry', 'bunched keys'.

- The poet juxtaposes sounds with silence. Notice how it is the 'steam' which 'danced....giggled...slipped', not the young women. They worked in silence. However, these verbs remind us of their youth and the life they should have been enjoying. We are invited to hear the 'shuffle and hum' of the movement of the women and the machines. The note which 'blared' inside a woman's skull was not allowed to be heard and silence of steam rising replaces the remembered sharpness of 'an infant's cry'.

- Take particular note of line length in this poem. Each of the first two stanzas makes a complete statement while the next three stanzas prepare for the voice speaking in the last stanza. The final stanza has an unusual punctuation. Notice how the phrases are separated by dots as opposed to full stops, giving the sense of fragmented speech to reveal fragmented lives.

- Alliteration on explosive 'b' sounds in stanza two reflect the energy involved in the work: 'Blinded and bleached'; hard 'd' and 'g' sounds reflect the harshness of the environment: 'glance...giggled', 'danced... drains'.

Sample Answer

The poetry of Eiléan Ní Chuilleanáin is challenging but ultimately rewarding. Discuss.

Eiléan Ní Chuilleanáin's poetry is certainly very challenging but absolutely rewarding for the reader who invests the time and effort to understand and engage with her complex, multi-layered images and themes. I found the study of her poetry an unusual experience as she opens many avenues of thought, provokes many interesting questions and encourages the reader to form a personal response to her work.

Ní Chuilleanáin appears to speak in simple natural language. With only a few exceptions, like *Lucina Schynning in Silence of the Nicht*, her titles tend to be short and direct: *Street, All for You, Following, Translation, The Bend in the Road* and so on. Her opening lines also typically display a colloquial storyteller's voice getting ready to recount an anecdote. *Deaths and Engines,* for instance, opens with: 'We came down above the houses/In a stiff curve, and/At the edge of Paris airport/Saw an empty tunnel'. The image, and the language recounting it, seem commonplace, almost mundane. *Street* presents us with yet another bald opening: 'He fell in love with the butcher's daughter/When he saw her passing by in her white trousers'. Likewise, *All for You* begins with an abrupt three-line stanza about people arriving at a 'strange stableyard' and a donkey going into a manger: 'The donkey walks on... And sticks his head in a manger'.

At first sight, we might see some of these openings as part of a cosy folk tradition or the familiar modern language of personal anecdote. Either way, we relax into the sense that this is going to be an easy read: a little tale we can pick up and carry around in our pocket, as light as lint. So part of the challenge in reading Ní Chuilleanáin for the first time is how this apparent simplicity and directness can suddenly give way without warning, after a line or two, into the mysterious abstract language of dream or supernatural belief or the alien scope of ancient world-views or history. Our sense of being in a comfort zone of that which we know is shattered as we move from the stable in the opening of *All for You* to the strange interior of a great hall which 'slouches back' and where steps 'wind and warp', beckoning us into hidden depths of meaning. The silence and calm of the night in *Lucina Schynning in Silence of the Nicht* is suddenly replaced with the nightmare images of plagues of mice and beetles 'Crawling out of the spines of books'. We move from the world of the Cromwellian invasion of Ireland, through horror and death, to 'the chirp of the stream running' – a strange, mysterious journey which challenges and surprises us but is ultimately rewarding in its hope for the future.

Another challenging aspect in reading Ní Chuilleanáin is the dramatic shift in tone from the commonplace to the sinister or nightmarish. A sense of threat seems to hang over most of her poems I have read. Consider the love-struck voyeur in *Street* admiring from afar the butcher's daughter and her white trousers. By the third line his (and our) gaze is directed to her 'Dangling a knife on a ring at her belt'. The fourth line subtly guides him to the trail of 'dark shining drops' she leaves behind. Are these drops of blood? It seems so. The poem has barely begun and already we are set spinning in a world of paradox: here is an object of attraction that comes across like an image of death or slaughter itself. Even the trail she leaves behind her is a paradox, being both 'dark' and 'shining'. What kind of love story is this? All the comfort and cosiness promised by the opening (boy-meets-girl) is whipped out from under us. The man follows the girl, seemingly obsessed by the paradox of beautiful horror she presents to him, and we are just as helpless, following Ní Chuilleanáin's lead, equally attracted and threatened by the capricious 'Dangling… knife' of her verse.

If Ní Chuilleanáin keeps her individual word choice simple (I never had to look up any of the words she used in a dictionary), her themes are vast and forbidding. Her main themes deal with life and death, the dramatic differences in the power wielded by males and females throughout history, historical shifts in power from empires to revolutions – with a recurring reference to Ireland's history – and a spiritual versus physical view of the world. This last theme is probably the most challenging, especially for a modern secular teenager like myself, although it is a mystery that has perplexed people since the dawn of time. Consider her poem *Fireman's Lift*: It seems to be about one of the most solid and physical of disciplines, architecture, but as we consider the fresco on the church wall, we realise that it depicts the physical body of the Virgin Mary being 'lifted' up into the non-physical world of heaven by angels. The physical opening at the top of the cupola in the cathedral almost suggests that anyone could float up out of the weighty human world of apses and arches and into another rarified world.

This unnerving marriage of the comprehensible, human, engineered world and the spirit realm reappears in *Deaths and Engines* when the poet imagines her own death in a fiery airplane explosion: 'The cold of metal wings is contagious: / Soon you will need wings of your own.' The image of needing wings to enter the afterlife is almost comical, like a cartoon angel, but Ní Chuilleanáin isn't laughing. In fact, she implies that this is exactly what happens to all of us: we all float out of this world one way or another, whether it is dramatic like a plane crash, or the subtle vanishing footprints of the butcher's daughter as she ascends a staircase and her trail disappears from the view of her worldly admirer.

I find this threshold between two worlds a tough thing to contemplate, partially because I do not like regarding my own death or the death of loved ones, and partially because I do not know what happens when we die. The notion of an afterlife throws me back on myself and forces me to ask what I really believe we are, and what the mortal world means. In the mad dash to secure points for college, relax with friends on weekends and obsessively keep up-to-date with social media, there is very little in my life that demands me to contemplate these intimidating questions. However, having explored such issues in the work of this poet, I find that the effort is ultimately very rewarding.

Finally, despite the energy of the scenes Ní Chuilleanáin depicts (terrified hares being coursed, Irish freedom fighters being hunted down by a 'growling' lorry of soldiers, Odysseus fighting back against a 'simmering sea') there is a quietness to her endings. Where many of her poems drop us into weird worlds, or explore complex themes or layered narratives, by the end of each work we find the various strands or layers come to some tentative resolution. This calmness is a strange reward, because it doesn't always seem convincing to me. But there is an excitement of going through a confusing experience (like dying itself maybe?) and then finding yourself in a cool space, all anxiety put aside for the time being.

Reading the poetry of Eiléan Ní Chuilleanáin is not like going on a holiday to some faraway paradise and then finding yourself safe back home. Instead, it is as though she takes you across a threshold of some sort, familiar at first but increasingly strange. Whether you like where you end up or not, you have to admit that you are somewhere new.

Eavan Boland

Biographical Note

Eavan Boland was born in Dublin in 1944. Her father's career as a diplomat saw the family living in both London and New York before she returned to Dublin, aged 15, and completed her secondary education. Boland went on to attend Trinity College, graduating with a first class degree. Her peers at Trinity included other gifted poets such as Michael Longley, Brendan Kennelly and Derek Mahon. Boland lectured for some years at Trinity before devoting herself fulltime to her writing. She got married in her mid-twenties and her subsequent move to the suburbs had a major impact on her poetic development.

Though removed from Dublin's vibrant literary scene, Boland found inspiration in her experience of the suburban world. After much travelling, she appreciated the stability that married life in the suburbs brought. Realising that a predominantly male poetic tradition did not regard motherhood and the life of a housewife as 'fit material for poetry', Boland drew on her own experience as mother and housewife to give a voice to the thousands of women living in housing estates in the suburbs. Love, marriage, motherhood and the suburban experience now became her central poetic preoccupations. On the international stage, such poets as Sylvia Plath and Adrienne Rich were also using their experience of marriage and motherhood as subject matter for their poetry. Boland also explores such themes as Irish identity, the nature of the Irish historical experience and the role of the female poet in society.

The War Horse

This poem was inspired by a commonplace incident that occurred in the suburban estate in which the poet lived. Image and sound combine to draw the reader into the poem. It is a 'dry night' and a horse is wandering around the estate in which Boland lives. The horse has escaped from 'the tinker camp on the Enniskerry Road'. Onomatopoeia enables the reader to hear the 'clip, clop / Casual iron of his shoes', 'his breath hissing, his snuffling head'. The horse is regarded as a threatening, destructive presence 'as he stamps death / Like a mint on the innocent coinage of earth'. When Boland surveys the damage done after the horse has passed her home, she is relieved to see that 'no great harm is done'.

The poem becomes more interesting when Boland uses the language and imagery of war to describe the damage done by the wandering horse. A torn leaf is described as 'a maimed limb'. A destroyed rose is depicted as a 'mere line of defence', and as a 'volunteer' that is 'expendable'. The connection between the damaged plants and the human victims of violence is very clear in the following image: 'a crocus, its bulbous head / Blown from growth'. The long 'o' sound helps to evoke a solemn mood. The crocus is depicted as 'one of the screamless dead'.

Boland's use of the terminology of war to portray the destruction wrought by the horse suggests that this suburban incident has prompted her to reflect on broader issues relating to our attitudes towards the threat and violence of war. When this poem was written in the mid 1970s, the violence in Northern Ireland was threatening to spill over into the Republic. When the threat of destruction has passed, the poet's feeling is one of relief, 'But we, we are safe'. The repetition of 'we' suggests the insular (inward-looking), self-absorbed mentality that prevails in this suburban estate. As the 'huge, threatening horse' ambles on, neighbours hide behind curtains. The destruction done by the horse may be seen as a symbol of the violence in Northern Ireland, while the refusal of Boland and her neighbours to confront the threat of the horse suggests the unwillingness of people in the south of Ireland to confront the violence that was blighting life in the North at this time. A rhetorical question sets readers thinking about our attitudes towards violence, especially the violence on our own doorstep: 'why should we care / If a rose, a hedge, a crocus are uprooted / Like corpses, remote, crushed, mutilated?' The adjectives 'distant' and 'remote' imply that we in the Republic of Ireland regard the Northern problem as being very far removed from us. Selfishly indifferent, we lack the 'fierce commitment' necessary to involve ourselves in a potentially dangerous situation.

The poem ends with Boland feeling a connection with her ancestors, who faced threatening, violent situations in earlier times, 'And for a second only my blood is still / With atavism . . . /recalling days of burned countryside'.

KEY POINTS

- Key theme is outsiders' detached, insular attitude towards the violence in Northern Ireland.
- An unremarkable incident that occurs in Boland's suburban estate prompts her to reflect on our attitude towards violence and war.
- The poem is written in a series of rhyming couplets.
- The language and imagery of war indicates that the poem is not just about the minor damage done by a wandering horse.
- Repeated use of 'our' and 'we' underscore our insular attitudes ('our laurel hedge', 'our house', 'our short street', 'we, we are safe').
- Other sound effects include internal rhyme and assonance ('hock and fetlock', 'blown from growth').
- Use of onomatopoeia enables us to hear the horse ('clip clop casual iron of his shoes. . . hissing breath . . . snuffling head).
- Rhetorical question prompts the reader to reflect on our attitude towards violence and war, particularly the violence on our own island ('why should we care if . . . ?').

Child of Our Time

This poem was inspired by the harrowing image of a dead child being carried from the rubble following a bomb explosion in Dublin in 1974. The title of the poem suggests that this innocent child was a victim of the times in which we live. This poem is both elegy (lament) and lullaby. A series of antitheses (contrasting ideas) in the opening stanza suggests how the tone of the poem alternates between tenderness and outrage. The antithetical style contributes towards the creation of a balanced tone. The opening stanza reflects Boland's desire to create some sort of order and harmony from the terrible chaos and 'discord' of the child's death, 'This song, which takes from your final cry / Its tune, from your unreasoned end its reason / Its rhythm from the discord of your murder'. Boland underlines the tragedy and terrible finality of the child's death, 'your final cry . . . your murder . . . the fact you cannot listen'.

In the second stanza the poet reflects on the failings of the adult world that contributed to the death of the child. The collective 'we' suggests a sense of collective responsibility, 'We who should have known'. The world of childhood is evoked by references to rhymes, soft toys

255

and legends. Our duty was to create a safe environment in which this child could grow and learn. Ironically, the adult world must now learn from the dead child, 'We . . . must learn from you dead'.

The final stanza holds out the hope that we might learn from the child's death and rebuild around the child's 'broken image'. Boland attributes the child's death to our inability to communicate with each other ('our idle talk')

and exhorts (encourages) us to find 'a new language'. Images and language ('idiom') relate to our culture, values and attitudes. The adult world stands accused, 'Child / Of our time, our times have robbed your cradle'. The final line has a prayer-like tone, expressing the hope that the death of the child – who may be taken to represent all innocent victims of violence – will awaken the world to the need for change, 'Sleep in a world your final sleep has woken'.

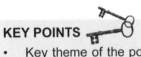

KEY POINTS

- Key theme of the poem is the unspeakable tragedy of a child's violent death and Boland's desire to put some sort of meaning on this senseless tragedy.
- The poem's long lines reflect the sad, solemn mood.
- The poet involves the reader in the poem in stanzas 2–3 ('We . . . our').
- Although the tragedy had its origins in the Northern conflict, politics do not enter into this poem, and names and places are not mentioned. In this way Boland highlights the universality of this tragedy.

The Famine Road

In this poem Boland reflects on the famine, the darkest and most traumatic period in Irish history and on the theme of colonial injustice. What is particularly unusual about this poem is the analogy that Boland draws between the suffering of the famine victims and the anguish of a barren woman. This is a dramatic poem with specific settings, 'characters', different voices and an element of conflict and tension.

The poem opens with Colonel Jones, an English official in Ireland, reading a letter from Lord Trevelyan. In a classic example of racist stereotyping, Trevelyan arrogantly dismisses the entire Irish nation as being 'as idle as trout in light'. He rejects the idea of giving the starving people any kind of charity, suggesting that both their bodies and weak characters would benefit from hard work. The 'toil' he has in mind is road building. These public works schemes were the government's response to the desperate plight of a famine-stricken nation. The infamous 'famine

roads' rarely served any purpose other than sapping the little energy the starving people had, 'roads to force / from nowhere, going nowhere of course'. The image of the blood red seal on the letter suggests the callous indifference of the English administration.

The repeated harsh 'k' sound ('fork, stick . . . rock, suck') also suggests the harshness of these officials, who are happy that starving people 'suck April hailstones for water and for food'. An image suggestive of cannibalism underlines the desperation of the starving people, 'each eyed – / as if at a corner butcher – the other's buttock'.

Disease was as great a killer as starvation. Boland highlights the misery of a typhoid victim who becomes an outcast ('a typhoid pariah') because of others' fear of contracting the highly contagious, deadly disease. The extent to which people are dehumanised by starvation is powerfully conveyed when Boland describes how the unfortunate man is left to die alone, with no one to say even a prayer, 'No more than snow / attends its own flakes where they settle / and melt, will they pray by his death rattle'.

Jones' letter to Trevelyan is smug in tone. The public works programme went better than they expected because the famine victims were too exhausted to even contemplate any kind of rebellion, 'sedition, idleness, cured / In one . . . / the wretches work till they are quite worn'. The image of corn being marched to the ships when people were starving to death dramatically highlights the theme of colonial injustice. The image of Jones coldly viewing the bones of famine victims from the comfort of his carriage underscores the heartless detachment of these officials.

Intertwined with the dramatic portrayal of the suffering of the famine victims is the depiction of the suffering of a barren woman. In the italicised verses the woman is addressed by a doctor who unfeelingly quotes statistics when discussing her infertile state, 'one out of every ten and then / another third of those again'. The voice becomes even more insensitive and upsetting, 'You never will, never you know'. The repetition of 'never' is particularly hurtful and the advice he offers ('grow / your garden, keep house') hollow and meaningless to the devastated woman. The unfeeling voice of the doctor reminds us of the callous tones of the English officials. The famine road is a symbol of the futility of the lives of both the famine victims and the barren woman. The poem reminds us that those in positions of authority are often lacking in humanity and compassion.

KEY POINTS

- Theme is the suffering of famine victims and the callousness of the English administration.
- Boland draws an analogy between the suffering of the famine victims and the anguish of a barren woman.
- The famine road symbolises the futility of the lives of both the famine victims and the infertile woman.
- A dramatic poem with specific settings, 'characters', different voices and an element of conflict and tension.
- The adjectives 'sick, directionless' aptly describe the plight of the starving people.
- The image of the blood-red seal suggests the cruelty of the English administration.
- Repetition of harsh 'k' sound evokes the harshness of the ruling regime ('fork, stick . . . rock, suck').

The Shadow Doll

In this poem Boland reflects on the nature and meaning of marriage. The poem was inspired by a Victorian porcelain doll that the poet viewed in a museum. The doll, a miniature bride, would have been sent by a dressmaker to a bride to help her decide on the design of her dress. As in *The Black Lace* *Fan My Mother Gave Me*, a concrete object prompts Boland to reflect on a range of issues associated with the particular object. The view of marriage expressed in this poem is very dark. Basically, marriage is perceived to be a form of imprisonment that confines, constrains and silences women.

In lines 1–9 the doll is described in a series of concrete images. The detailed description suggests the special, delicate beauty of the dress, 'They stitched blooms from the ivory tulle / to hem the oyster gleam of the veil'. However, the language used in relation to the doll evokes a sense of repression and containment, 'stitched', 'neatly sown', 'airless glamour', 'under glass, under wraps'. The doll would have been kept by the married woman and would have witnessed her unfolding life, complete with its 'visits, fevers, quickenings and lusts' (suggestive of sex, pregnancy and childbirth). Boland personifies the inanimate doll when she describes it as 'discreet'. Here she may be suggesting that women remain silent about their personal lives.

Lines 10–15 focus on the Victorian bride herself. As the bride-to-be views the doll in all its artificial perfection ('the shell-tone spray of seed pearls, / the bisque features'), she has a vision of herself in the place of the porcelain doll, 'she could see herself / inside it all'. Here she seems to gain a frightening insight into the restrictive nature of marriage.

The poem's final section (lines 16–21) switches focus from the Victorian bride-to-be contemplating her shadow doll to Boland on the night before her own marriage. Her endless repetition of her vows suggests her feelings of apprehension. A list of various items ('cards and wedding gifts – / the coffee pots and the clocks') suggests the typical pre-wedding clutter. Significantly, the closing image is one of confinement, 'the battered tan case full of cotton / lace and tissue paper, pressing down, then / pressing down again'. The repetition of 'pressing down' suggests a growing sense of claustrophobia at the prospect of the confinement of marriage. All of the suggestions of oppression and imprisonment culminate in the poem's final three words, which are set apart for emphasis, 'And then locks'. The clear implication of these words is that, where women and marriage are concerned, little has changed since Victorian times.

KEY POINTS

- Key theme is the way in which marriage represses and confines women.
- It is in examining a concrete object (the porcelain doll) that Boland is prompted to meditate on the nature of marriage from Victorian times to the present.
- Various images of imprisonment: the 'airless' glass dome that houses the doll, the locked suitcase, etc.
- Much of the poem's language has connotations of confinement: 'stitched', 'under wraps', etc.
- Repetition is used for emphasis ('pressing down, then / Pressing down again').

White Hawthorn in the West of Ireland

This poem describes a journey that Boland makes from her suburban Dublin home to the West of Ireland. This personal experience leads to the poet reflecting on the contrast between the confinement and boredom of the suburban world and the vastness and magic of the natural world. While Boland is a poet who regards life in the suburbs as suitable material for her poetry, her portrayal of the suburban world in this poem is distinctively negative.

The conversational tone of the opening lines draws the reader into the poem, 'I drove west / in the season between seasons. / I left behind suburban gardens./ Lawnmowers. Small talk'. This imagery evokes a dull, restricted, monotonous world. The regular full stops underscore the confinement and rigid order of the suburbs.

The contrast between Boland's normal humdrum environment and the wild landscape of the West is sharply drawn. The image of 'splashes of coltsfoot' with its sibilant 's' sounds suggests the beauty and tranquillity of nature. The oxymoron 'the hard shyness of Atlantic light' suggests the mysterious, indefinable nature of the light in the West of Ireland. (An oxymoron is a figure of speech which involves contradictory terms being used in conjunction with each other). The phrase 'the superstitious aura of hawthorn' suggests that there is something mysterious about hawthorn. Boland has a longing to fill her arms with the hawthorn's 'sharp flowers'. She yearns to embrace the hawthorn and become one with the natural world, 'be part of that ivory downhill rush'. This image sharply contrasts with the images of confinement in the first stanza.

However, the poet's knowledge of the folklore relating to hawthorn causes her to pause and hold back from embracing the plant. In Irish folklore many superstitions surround hawthorn. Linked with the world of the fairies, hawthorn is associated with death and bad luck, 'the custom was / not to touch the hawthorn / . . . a child might die, perhaps'.

So the poet leaves the hawthorn 'stirring on those hills / with a fluency / only water has'. Here the hawthorn is seen as a mysterious, living entity. An energetic life force, it has the ability 'to re-define land'. Visitors are struck by the abundance of hawthorn in the western landscape. Boland states that 'for anglers and for travellers', it is 'the only language spoken in these parts'. The hawthorn now assumes a symbolic significance, representing the unique culture of the West of Ireland. Just like the other visitors, Boland cannot become part of this world, no matter how much she is drawn to the idea.

KEY POINTS

- This poem celebrates the unique beauty of the West of Ireland.
- Repetition of 'I' underscores the deeply personal nature of the experience at the heart of the poem.
- Poem contrasts the confinement of the suburbs with the freedom of nature.
- While regular full stops suggest the enclosed world of the suburbs, run-on lines evoke the unrestricted western landscape.
- Use of memorable visual imagery ('splashes of coltsfoot', 'that ivory downhill rush').
- Sound effects: – the sibilant 's' sound suggests the peacefulness of the West ('Under low skies, past splashes of coltsfoot').

Outside History

The theme of this poem is history's exclusion of the voiceless. In writing this poem, Boland remembers and honours those forgotten people who have remained 'outside history'. The poem opens with a factual statement, 'There are outsiders, always'. The natural image that follows depicts the stars ('those iron inklings of an Irish January') as being far removed from the reality of human life. They 'have always been / outside history'. The stars may be seen as symbols of myth – the idealised versions of Irish history. Under the stars real human history in all its pain and darkness unfolds, 'Under them remains / a place where you found / you were human, and / a landscape in which you knew you were mortal'. Boland sees history in a very negative light, describing it as an 'ordeal'.

Faced with the choice of myth or the real, painful world of history, Boland chooses the latter. It seems that she is 'only now' becoming aware of the 'darkness' of history. The image of 'roads clotted as / firmaments with the dead' suggests the devastation of the Great Famine. The image of people slowly dying underlines the terrible suffering that people endured throughout our history. The poet's compassionate nature is highlighted when she imagines us kneeling beside these dying people and whispering in their ear. The closing line reminds us that while we may remember and honour the forgotten victims of history, we cannot change or undo the wrong that was done to them. The closing line points to our collective responsibility for their suffering, 'And we are too late. We are always too late'. The repetition of 'too late' underscores the regretful tone. It seems that we are always too late in learning the lessons of history.

KEY POINTS

- Key theme is the forgotten lives of the voiceless.
- Effective use of imagery ('roads clotted as firmaments with the dead')
- Repetition of 'too late' conveys regretful tone
- Key words express the poet's deeply negative view of history, 'pain', 'ordeal', 'darkness'.

The Black Lace Fan My Mother Gave Me

Similar to most poets, Boland writes regularly on the themes of love and relationships. This poem was inspired by a black fan given to Boland by her mother. This fan had originally been given as a gift to her mother by the man who later became her husband. It was in fact the first gift that Boland's father gave her mother and is seen as a symbol of their love. Typical of Boland, she does not attempt to idealise or sentimentalise her parents' relationship. She describes their love in an honest, realistic manner. The fan represents the joy and stability of their love, but also its imperfection.

The opening line gives a sense of personal history being recollected, 'It was the first gift he ever gave her'. Its importance is underlined by the fact that its exact cost ('five francs') and the place where it was purchased ('the Galeries') are clearly remembered. Sensuous imagery evokes the atmosphere of pre-war Paris, 'It was stifling. A starless drought made the nights stormy'. A few crisp sentences give us a glimpse of their individual personalities, 'They met in cafés. She was always early. / He was late'. This particular evening, his purchase of the fan meant that he was even later than normal. Detailed description helps us to picture Boland's impatient mother looking down Boulevard des Capucines, before ordering more coffee and standing up as if to leave. Boland imaginatively recreates the scene, using sensuous imagery, 'The streets were emptying. The heat was killing. / She thought the distance smelled of rain and lightning'. The reference to the threatening weather may suggest that the relationship was problematical in some way or that the woman had doubts or worries in relation to the future of the relationship.

Stanza three gives us a vivid image of the fan. It is appropriately decorated with roses, the traditional flowers of love. The skilled craftsmanship that went into its creation is suggested by verbs and adverbs, 'darkly picked, stitched boldly, quickly'. While Boland appreciates the delicate beauty and elegance of the tortoise-shell, she is aware of the 'violation' of the tortoise that facilitated the creation of this love token. The description of the tortoise-shell as 'a worn-out gold bullion' suggests the rich, enduring nature of her parents' love. However, the following lines recall the dark hints of the opening stanza, 'The lace is overcast as if the weather / it opened for and offset had entered it'. The fan represents the beauty, longevity and imperfection of her parents' love. Put simply, it is a symbol not just of the romance of their early romantic days together, but of the real lifelong relationship – complete with all its ups and downs – that they have shared.

Stanza five returns to the scene of that stifling Parisian night. Thunder is in the 'airless dusk' – again, perhaps hinting at a stormy relationship. There is a sense of drama and anticipation, 'A man running. / And no way now to know what happened then – / none at all – unless, of course, you improvise'. Boland knows the history of the fan, but the story of her parents' love is incomplete, known only to her parents themselves. All we can do is 'improvise' or imagine how her parents got on through their years of marriage.

The final stanza is dominated by the image of a blackbird – the bird is another traditional symbol of love. The image of the blackbird is highly evocative. While the fan is beautiful, it has been affected by the ravages of time ('worn out'). It is, of course, also an inanimate object. In contrast, the blackbird is, like her parents' love, vibrant and alive. This closing image means that the poem ends on a triumphant, celebratory note, 'Suddenly she puts out her wing – / the whole, full, flirtatious span of it'. Her parents' love has weathered various emotional storms and survived. The adjectives 'whole, full' suggest a love that is balanced and complete, while the adjective 'flirtatious' suggests that the romance in their relationship remains intact. Sound effects (the alliterative 'full, flirtatious' and the sibilant 'flirtatious span') contribute to the upbeat mood at the close of the poem.

KEY POINTS

- Key theme is the nature of Boland's parents' relationship and love.
- The fan is a symbol of their love, as is the blackbird later in the poem.
- Sensuous images evoke the atmosphere in pre-war Paris.
- The story of her parents' early love is told in a clear, crisp manner (stanzas 1–2).

This Moment

This poem celebrates a special moment in everyday life. While *White Hawthorn in the West of Ireland* presents suburban life in a negative light, this poem suggests that everyday life in the suburbs has its moments of beauty. The opening lines set the scene, 'A neighbourhood /At dusk'. The mood is peaceful. There is a sense of anticipation, 'Things are getting ready / to happen / out of sight'. The natural world seems to wait in expectation, 'Stars and moths./ And rinds slanting around fruit'. The stars will shortly rise, the moths flutter and the apples sweeten. However, for the moment, everything in the natural world seems to pause 'But not yet'. The sense of anticipation intensifies. The next image is beautifully simple and vivid, 'One tree is black. One window is yellow as butter'. This domestic simile is very apt.

The moment at the heart of the poem occurs when a child runs into the arms of his mother, 'A woman leans down to catch a child / who has run into her arms / this moment'. By referring to 'a neighbourhood', 'a mother' and 'a child', Boland suggests the universality of this special moment. The natural world seems to respond to and celebrate the moment when mother and child are re-united, 'Stars rise. / Moths flutter./ Apples sweeten in the dark'. The sibilant 's' sound that dominates the poem conveys a sense of perfect peace. The natural imagery evokes a sense of universal harmony. The short lines and regular full stops encourage the reader to read through the poem slowly, and to reflect on the special beauty of a commonplace event.

KEY POINTS

- Key theme is the beauty of the mother-child relationship.
- Vivid images.
- Economic style.
- Use of simple, everyday language.
- Effective use of sound.
- Mood is quiet and reflective.

The Pomegranate

The theme of this poem is the mother-daughter relationship and the manner in which it inevitably changes over time. Boland draws on the myth of Ceres and Persephone to underline the universal relevance of her own personal experience. The poem is written in blank verse which is similar to a natural speaking voice. This is appropriate for a poem in which Boland is clearly speaking from the heart.

The legend of Ceres and her Persephone tells of the abduction of young Persephone by Pluto, god of the underworld, who wanted her to be his wife. Devastated by the loss of her daughter, Ceres searched everywhere for her. As goddess of vegetation, Ceres threatened to interrupt all growth in the world until Celeus, the King of Eleusis, identified Persephone's abductor. Ceres went to reclaim her daughter from the underworld, only to discover that, having eaten some pomegranate seeds, Persephone would be forced to spend half of each year in the underworld. When Persephone is with Ceres, everything grows, but as soon as she returns to the underworld everything starts to wither and die.

As a child, Boland was drawn to this legend ('The only legend I ever loved') because, as a child in exile in London ('a city of fogs and strange consonants'), she could relate to Persephone's exile in the underworld. Later, as an adult and mother, she could relate to the feelings of Ceres when she had to go out on a summer's evening searching for her own daughter at bed-time, 'When she came running I was ready / to make any bargain to keep her'. However, Boland realises that the special relationship between mother and daughter inevitably changes over time, 'But I was Ceres then and I knew / winter was in store for every leaf / on every tree on that road'. Boland is keenly aware of the universal, inexorable nature of the ageing process. Time would inevitably change the nature of her relationship with her daughter – this was an 'inescapable' reality.

Line 24 marks a turning point in the poem, with the movement from the past to the present. This section of the poem has a dramatic quality. The scene is set: it is winter, a starless night and Boland climbs the stairs. As she watches her teenage daughter sleeping, she is filled with conflicting emotions. The teen magazine and can of coke are typical of a teenage bedroom. It is symbolically significant that her daughter also has a plate of uncut fruit because this represents the pomegranate. In the context of this poem, eating the fruit symbolises leaving the world of childhood behind and entering the world of adulthood. The idea of eating the fruit also has obvious biblical connotations involving the loss of innocence. Boland now considers how things might have turned out if Persephone had not eaten the pomegranate, 'She could have come home and been safe / and ended the story and all / our heart-broken searching'. The use of 'our' indicates that Boland is speaking for Ceres, for herself, and for all mothers. However, she knows that the relationship between mother and daughter must inevitably change. Just as Persephone 'reached out a hand and plucked a pomegranate', so will Boland's own daughter inevitably enter the world of adulthood and so change their relationship forever.

Aware of the kind of experiences awaiting her daughter in adulthood, Boland wonders what she should do, 'I could warn her'. While the poet recognises that the suburban world in which they live is far removed from the world of Greek legend ('It is another world'), she knows that even this world can be harsh, 'The rain is cold. The road is flint-coloured'. However, if she postpones the grief, she 'will diminish the gift' – perhaps a reference to the freedom to live her own life that she will grant her daughter. Every world has its share of pain and sorrow and, while Boland would like to insulate her daughter from the harsher aspects of life, she accepts that she too must live her life and learn through personal experience the things that Boland herself now knows, 'The legend will be hers as well as mine. / She will enter it. As I have'. These lines suggest an unending, universal, natural process. When her daughter wakes in the morning, she will put the pomegranate to her lips. The poet resolves to 'say nothing'.

KEY POINTS

- Key theme is the changing nature of the mother-daughter relationship.
- A personal poem to which every parent and child can relate.
- Mythical allusions suggest the universality of the poet's experience and feelings.
- The harshness of the modern world is evoked in vivid, dark images ('The rain is cold. The road is flint-coloured').

Love

This is a deeply personal poem, the theme of which is the changing nature of love. It was prompted by a visit to a 'mid-western town' in Iowa in the United States where Boland and her husband lived in the early years of their marriage. The reference to myths suggests the extraordinary, magical nature of their love at this time. The reference to the bridge 'the hero crossed on his way to hell' derives from a tale in Virgil's Aeneid that describes Aeneas crossing the bridge into hell to see his dead comrades. In this instance Aeneas may be seen as a symbol for Boland's husband who often crossed this bridge over the River Iowa to visit their seriously ill infant daughter in hospital. That period in the family's life might certainly be described as hellish – Boland states that her infant daughter was 'touched by death'.

The family's old apartment is described in detail, 'We had a kitchen and an Amish table./ We had a view'. The language here is simple and crisp. A memorable metaphor suggests the strength and gentleness of the love that Boland and her husband shared at this time, 'And we discovered there / love had the feather and muscle of wings'. The wings image further suggests the power of love to elevate and inspire. The poet suggests the powerful, elemental force of their love when she personifies it as 'a brother of fire and air'.

Boland remembers how her ill daughter was 'spared'. When the poet again refers to the myth of Aeneas, she describes how, when his comrades hailed him, 'their mouths opened and their voices failed' – an image suggesting the impossibility of expressing intense emotion. This mythical allusion implies that Boland was unable to articulate the depth of love that she felt at this special time in her life. Just as nostalgia for his previous life spurred Aeneas on to visit his former comrades in hell, Boland is filled with longing to return to the earlier life that she and her husband shared.

Boland now reflects on the present state of their love, 'I am your wife./ It was years ago. / . . . We love each other still'. The latter line clearly implies that their love is not the same as it was during that traumatic period in their lives, although it continues to survive, 'Across our day-to-day and ordinary distances / we speak plainly'. Boland longs to return to that earlier time to once again experience that uniquely intense love, 'And yet I want to return to you / on the bridge of the Iowa river as you were with snow on the shoulders of your coat and a car passing with its headlights on'. This romantic image has a cinematic quality. At that time the poet saw her husband 'as a hero in a text'. Now she longs to 'cry out the epic question' and ask him if they will 'ever live so intensely again'. Boland uses an apt adjective to sum up the strength of this special love, describing it as 'formidable'. Drawing again on Greek mythology the poet depicts love as a male god, 'it offered us ascension / even to look at him'. The use of the religious term 'ascension' suggests the spiritual quality of their powerful love – this image connects with the earlier 'wings' metaphor, underlining the idea that love has the power to elevate and inspire, enabling Boland and her husband to transcend the problems of everyday life.

The closing lines underline the impossibility of the poet returning to that earlier time in her life or articulating the uniquely intense love that she and her husband once shared, 'But the words are shadows and you cannot hear me. / You walk away and I cannot follow'.

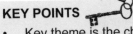

KEY POINTS

- Key theme is the changing nature of love.
- The language combines the conversational and the metaphorical, with mythical allusions suggesting the depth and complexity of their love.
- Use of memorable imagery.
- Tone is nostalgic

Sample Answer

Write out the text of a talk that you would deliver to your class, outlining your response to the poetry of Eavan Boland.

Good afternoon classmates,

I found Eavan Boland's poetry to be original and thought-provoking. While female readers in particular appreciate Boland's poems on marriage, motherhood and the place of women in society, her work also has a wide appeal. She writes about history, violence, love and suburban life in a way that is fresh and interesting. I like the way she often uses a personal experience to reflect on an issue of universal importance. I admire her obvious compassion for all victims of violence and oppression and her anger at those who visit suffering and misery on innocent people. She has great powers of description and her verse has an appealing visual quality. Her use of sound effects to evoke particular moods is also very effective. I especially like her use of everyday, conversational language – Boland deals with issues that matter in language that we can understand.

I would first like to talk about *This Moment*, a poem of wonderful simplicity which conveys the magic of an everyday event. We could all relate to the heartwarming image at the heart of the poem: 'A woman leans down to catch a child / who has run into her arms / this moment'. Boland cleverly underlines the universality of this moment by writing of 'A neighbourhood . . . a woman . . . a child'. The poem's short lines and regular full stops create a sense of anticipation, while encouraging us to pause and reflect on the power and beauty of this moment. This poem contains one of my favourite images: 'One tree is black./ One window is yellow as butter'. This is a wonderfully simple, vivid image. I liked Boland's repeated use of the sibilant 's' sound to convey a sense of perfect peace. The way nature seems to respond to and celebrate the meeting of mother and child ('Stars rise. / Moths flutter. / Apples sweeten in the dark') underscores the naturalness of this special moment. There is a lovely sense of universal harmony in this poem.

I enjoyed reading the poem *Love* because it set me thinking about the way love changes over time. Again, the theme of this poem is both personal and universal. I admire the honest way Boland writes about her relationship with her husband. She seems to confide in the reader. She describes how her love for her husband was intensified by the traumatic experience of nearly losing her sick child. Simple details of her life in Iowa draw us into her domestic world: 'We had a kitchen and an Amish table./ We had a view'. I really like the image that she employs to suggest the beauty and strength of their shared love, 'And we discovered there / love had the feather and muscle of wings'. Her description of their mutual love as elemental ('a brother of fire and air') was memorable. I think you will agree that, as a class, we found the reference to an episode from Virgil's Aeneid quite challenging. However, when we teased it out, we discovered that by employing this mythical allusion, Boland was suggesting how it can sometimes be impossible to express intense emotion. Like Aeneas' comrades in hell, her feelings were too intense to be expressed: 'their mouths opened and their voices failed.' While the mythical allusions mean that this poem has its share of metaphorical language, more of the language has a lovely simplicity and conversational flow: 'I am your wife./ It was years ago. / . . . We love each other still.' Here Boland reminds us that love can grow and change over time. This poem contains another memorable visual image – that of her husband crossing the bridge with snow on the shoulders of his coat 'and a car passing with its headlights on'. I could almost picture this image on a big cinema screen. Many of us can relate to the idea of idealising a person you love: 'I see you as a hero in a text – / the image blazing and the edges gilded.' I think 'formidable' is an apt adjective to describe a really powerful type of love. Boland offers us some words of wisdom at the close of the poem when she suggests the impossibility of returning to the past: 'You walk away and I cannot follow.'

One of the reasons Boland appeals to so many readers is that she writes about life in the increasingly populated suburbs. In *White Hawthorn in the West of Ireland*, she highlights the contrast between the suburban and rural worlds. A few well-chosen words suggest how the suburbs are both physically confined and spiritually stifling: 'I left behind suburban gardens./ Lawnmowers. Small talk.' I love the way Boland combines visual imagery and the sibilant 's' sound to suggest the freedom, wildness and tranquillity of the western landscape, 'Under low skies, past splashes of coltsfoot'. I can see why she longs to become one with nature, 'be part of / that ivory downhill rush'. Boland's use of punctuation in this poem is very effective. Regular full stops underscore the confinement of the suburbs, while run-on lines suggest the unconfined freedom of nature. I like the way she portrays the West as a special, magical place where one cannot but be aware of 'the superstitious aura of hawthorn'. I noticed how she draws a sharp contrast between the fixed, orderly suburban gardens and the seemingly fluid, shifting landscape of the West where the hawthorn is 'stirring' on the hills and has 'a fluency only water has'. I was struck by the way she presented the hawthorn as a symbol both of the West's wild beauty and unique culture, 'the only language spoken in these parts'. I like the way she celebrates all that is special about the West, while at the same time, setting us thinking about the quality of modern day suburban life.

Boland is again critical of the suburban mentality in *The War Horse*. Again, I admire her ability to use a personal experience to reflect on an issue of wider importance. I like the visual and aural imagery that draws us into the scene: 'the clip, clop casual / iron of his shoes / . . . his breath hissing, his snuffling head.' An original simile captures the damage that the wandering horse does to a manicured suburban garden: 'he stamps death / like a mint on the innocent coinage of earth.' This poem becomes more interesting as Boland uses the language and imagery of war to describe the destruction done by this frightening invader – a damaged leaf is compared to 'a maimed limb', while an uprooted crocus is 'one of the screamless dead'. The destruction done by the horse becomes a symbol of the violence in the North, while the image of Boland's neighbours hiding behind curtains suggests our insular, uncaring attitude towards the violence in our own country. The use of repetition effectively underscores our selfish indifference: 'But we, we are safe'.

Classmates, most of us share Boland's interest in our past. I admire the compassionate way she writes about the famine, the worst catastrophe in Irish history in *The Famine Road*. Her use of dialogue really brings home the indifference and harshness of the English regime. We can almost hear the arrogant Lord Trevelyan casually dismissing an entire nation as worthless, 'Idle as trout in light'. Boland makes effective use of sound, with the repeated harsh 'k' sound ('fork, stick . . . rock, suck') accentuating the harshness of the officials responsible for 'managing' the famine. Boland's use of a familiar image to suggest the horror of cannibalism is particularly disturbing: 'cunning as housewives, each eyed – as if at a corner butcher – the other's buttock.' The image of the typhoid victim dying alone is also very shocking, suggesting how the famine dehumanised its victims, draining them of any sympathy for others. Our entire class was outraged at Jones' callously pragmatic view of the famine as a cure for Irish rebelliousness. One of the most interesting features of this poem is the way Boland compares the suffering and oppression of the famine victims with the pain and humiliation of an infertile woman. The doctor who coldly quotes statistics and glibly suggests that this unfortunate woman look after her house and garden is as arrogant and as unfeeling as Jones and Trevelyan. Boland reminds us that those in positions of power and authority are often lacking in humanity and compassion. The famine road metaphor effectively suggests how the lives of the famine victims and the infertile woman are similarly futile, 'what is your body now if not a famine road?'

Child of our Time is similarly powerful and thought-provoking. This is a poem that really sets us thinking about the violence in our own country and about our responsibility for that violence. Boland was inspired to write this poem by the harrowing image of a dead child being carried from the scene of a bomb explosion in Dublin. I admire Boland's desire to create some sense of order and harmony from the chaos and 'discord' of the child's death. I was struck by the irony of the adult world learning from a child: 'We who should have known how to instruct . . . / . . . must learn from you dead.' Boland rightly encourages us to 'learn' from and 'rebuild' around the child's 'broken image'. She points to our collective guilt for this tragedy when she refers to our inability to communicate ('our idle talk'). Classmates, we should respond to Boland's exhortation to develop 'a new language' of reconciliation. We all share the hope expressed in the poem's poignant closing line that tragedies such as this will wake us up to the need for change: 'Sleep in a world your final sleep has woken'.

In conclusion, my overall response to Boland's poetry is very positive. She addresses issues that are relevant and important to the modern reader, giving us much food for thought. Memorable images, conversational language and effective use of sound add to the appeal of her verse. Thank you for your attention.

Paul Durcan

Biography:

Paul Durcan was born in Dartmouth Square, Dublin on 16th October 1944, the eldest of three children. His father, John, was a teacher who later became a barrister and then a circuit court judge in the west of Ireland. Durcan's youth was spent mostly between Dublin and Turlough, Co. Mayo. He claims that relations with John became strained when his father changed from being a humorous man to being a stern, demanding and distant father. Durcan blames this in part on the loneliness of the judicial career.

His relationship with his mother was warmer. Sheila MacBride Durcan came from a family famous for its literary and political heritage. Major John MacBride, a leader and martyr of the 1916 Rising, was Paul's granduncle. John MacBride was married to Maud Gonne (a woman who was loved by WB Yeats and who inspired much of his finest poetry). Sean MacBride, the son of the marriage, was Durcan's godfather. Sheila Durcan was in the legal profession too and performed extremely well in her law exams. She was obliged, however, by the customs of the day to stop working when she married.

Durcan began to study Law and Economics at UCD, but at 19 years old he was committed by his family to St. John of God psychiatric hospital. Durcan believes the fact that he didn't conform with his privileged middle-class family led them to take this step. He later attended a Harley Street Clinic, where he was treated with electroshock and barbiturates, and claims he narrowly escaped being lobotomised. He was incorrectly diagnosed as suffering from schizophrenia. He believes he was not suffering from any mental illness prior to this experience but his treatment left him with recurring depression and a permanent sense of isolation and loneliness.

Durcan spent three years in and out of various mental institutions until he ran away and began to associate with the poet Patrick Kavanagh, who served as a mentor to him.

Durcan's poetry owes a great debt to Kavanagh, fusing as it does the mythic and the commonplace, direct (even blunt) language, and the linking of loneliness with revelation. In 1967, attending a wedding at the Shangri-La Hotel in Dalkey with Kavanagh, Durcan met Nessa O'Neill, his future wife. They lived in London and raised two daughters, Sarah and Siabhra. In 1970 they moved to Cork, where Nessa taught in a prison. Their marriage ended in 1984.

It has been said of Durcan that:

'Poetry can often seem remote and removed from the real world but the beauty about Durcan's poetry is that it is of this world and, in particular, very much of Ireland.'

Nessa

Nessa is a love poem about the poet's wife, Nessa O'Neill. It opens with two facts: the date he met her and the place in which he met her. But the factual world of dates and places blurs into the mythic by the second line. The hotel (Shangri-La) is an allusion to a mythical place (it's from a novel by James Hillman), loosely based on the Buddhist paradise Shambala, where people are enlightened and live incredibly long blissful lives. The term roughly correlates to 'cosmic peace', a notion mentioned in another Durcan love poem, *The Girl with the Keys to Pearse's Cottage*. The Himalayas as a site of enlightenment is also alluded to in *Windfall,* a poem that charts the collapse of Durcan's marriage.

In the opening stanza of *Nessa*, the woman is presented as taking the lead: 'She took me by the index finger/And dropped me in her well'. The index finger may be sexually suggestive and being dropped in her 'well' may mean an initiation into sex. The young man seems overwhelmed and even spellbound by her power; the comparison to a well is striking. Wells are dangerous structures and have drowned many people in rural Ireland. They are also often associated with myths and fairytales, and they boast wish-fulfilling properties. The deep 'well' of Nessa's love is not calm or still; it is a 'whirlpool', a place of incredible energy and chaos, and the poet claims in a repeating refrain that 'I was very nearly drowned'.

Durcan often slips deftly from mythical visions to ordinary or even blunt dialogue. The second stanza opens with a direct order from his lover: 'Take off your pants, she said to me'. His awe is such that 'I very nearly didn't'. What follows may be a comic change of direction – she's offering to go for a swim – or it may be another sexual metaphor. Though there are some significant exceptions, water imagery is often used in Durcan's poetry as a token of the most sublime happiness and reassurance. The invitation to swim in the Irish Sea here could be an invitation to 'hop' into the sea of love itself. But again the refrain tells us that the sea is not calm but in chaos, a whirlpool that nearly drowns him.

The third stanza advances the dramatic verbs of the first two stanzas (took, dropped, hopped) by claiming he 'fell' in a field. She falls (in love) beside him, and he wishes to remain 'in the grass with her all my life'. The refrain returns, but now 'that was a whirlpool' has subtly changed to 'she was a whirlpool'.

The final stanza changes the tone as the poet addresses Nessa directly. Possibly in a sly allusion to the ancient Greek myths about mermaids and sirens, the poet's address comes complete with antique diction: 'O Nessa my dear'. Here it is unclear who is playing the role of siren singer, threatening the death of the unsuspecting sailor who hears it. The poet seems to be calling her into the sea now, to live with him 'on the rocks'. He asks her to let her 'red hair down'. Red hair is associated with mythic Irish ideals of feminine beauty, and letting one's hair down is a relaxing of all restraint and defence. It is to luxuriate in sensual play.

The closing four lines are especially charged, as they suggest that the couple will actually 'drown' each other in love, and then their ghosts will 'ride into Dublin City/In a taxi cab wrapped up in dust'. The fatalist tone is borne out by the closing refrain, which has shifted from the past tense of reminiscence, to the present tense: 'you are a whirlpool', and the almost-gleeful anticipation of the final line: 'And I am very nearly drowned'.

KEY POINTS

- The factual world of places and dates blurs into the mythical world in this poem.
- Note the deep significance of the image of the well.
- Water imagery is often used in Durcan's poetry as a token of the most sublime happiness and reassurance.
- Notice the change in the use of verbs and the change of wording in the refrain to mark the development of the relationship.
- Poet addresses Nessa directly in stanza four. This marks a change in the direction of the relationship.
- Note the variation of tense in the refrain in the final stanza.

The Girl with the Keys to Pearse's Cottage

Pádraig Pearse was a poet, barrister, and one of the leaders of the 1916 Rising, a role for which he was executed along with Durcan's uncle, John MacBride. (Durcan writes about this famous branch of his family in *The MacBride Dynasty*.) During the Rising, Pearse read aloud the Proclamation of the Irish Republic on the steps of the GPO, a document Durcan ironically alludes to in *Windfall*. Pearse also gave a speech/eulogy at the funeral of the fenian Jeremiah O'Donovan Rossa, an event referenced in Durcan's *Six Nuns Die In Convent Inferno*.

In his role as a member of the Gaelic League – an organisation that promoted the Irish language – Pearse built a modest cottage in Rosmuc, Connemara, where this poem is set.

On the surface, *The Girl with the Keys to Pearse's Cottage* is about unrequited teenage love. The poet (typically male in this genre) loves a girl from afar, but for unstated reasons does not – or cannot – bridge the divide between them. This fits with a larger pattern in Durcan's work, that of a man trying and failing to communicate across great gulfs of time (personal or national history), space (the Atlantic Ocean) or emotional distance (the anxiety that otherworldly beauty can evoke in a young man).

Thinking of the cottage, he visualises 'two windows and cosmic peace'. The home is presented here as a place to gaze out from, and in doing so, receive a kind of grace, not unlike the window of the poet's own home in *Windfall*. The cottage is humble: 'bare brown rooms and… whitewashed walls'. It is adorned with some heroic remnants: 'Photographs of the passionate and pale Pearse'.

However, as with hero-worship in general, the cottage looks better from a distance: 'I recall wet thatch and peeling jambs/And how all was best seen from below in the field'.

Fields are often used as symbols of a rural and romantic Ireland, and it is in such a romantic setting that the young trainee poet can be found practising his alliteration: 'Compiling poems of passion for Cáit Killann'.

It's never explained why Ms. Killann has the keys to the cottage, but she seems an appropriate keeper for the spiritual home of such an intense figure as Pearse. The girl herself cuts a striking figure, composed as she is entirely of contrasts: 'Her dark hair was darker because her smile was so bright', and dressed 'In sun-red skirt and moon-black blazer'. If there is symbolism attached to the clothing, it is unclear what it might be, but the red of the skirt may allude to the blood shed for Irish freedom, and the black to death. Or it may be a contrast between the 'cosmic' rotations of day and night (sun and moon).

Cáit is a virtual alien in her own land. She looks 'toward our strange world wide-eyed./Our world was strange because it had no future'. The 'our' is also unclear here. It could refer to the futureless romance between her and the poet, or it could mean 'our' in the sense of people living in the West of Ireland, or Ireland in general. This poem was written in the 1970s when Ireland was on the brink of a significant economic recession. Many people would soon have 'no choice' but to emigrate to countries like England or, in Cáit's case, America.

The final stanza aches with the pang of dashed teenage love, but also with the heartache of losing so many fellow countrymen and women to other shores. The notion that she has 'gone with your keys from your own native place' suggests that the emigrants have taken something with them, and left both the emigrants and those who remain somehow locked out of the home that should be the source of cosmic peace to all.

Durcan's taste for mingling painters into his own poetry emerges again – as in *Windfall* – when he references El Greco, the nickname of a genius artist who left his native Crete in Greece to live in what were then the centres of power (Venice and Rome) and who died in Spain far from his native land. His figures were known for their extreme elongated features and other-worldly appearance. Durcan blends the otherworldly character of Cáit's eyes with the 'Connemara postman's daughter's proudly mortal face'. Even though the young poet is tempted to celebrate her as a mythic being – or an ideal frozen in time like Pearse – it is her humanness, her grounded working-class roots, that ultimately speak to him. Her face is 'mortal', meaning that unlike a symbol, it will suffer and die. Perhaps here there is more than a celebration of the living over the legend.

KEY POINTS

- A recurring idea in Durcan's work is that of a man trying and failing to communicate across great gulfs of time (personal or national history), space (the Atlantic Ocean), or emotional distance (the anxiety that otherworldly beauty can evoke in a young man).
- Note the small details in the description of Pearse's cottage.
- There is a suggestion that the reality of the cottage is not quite as perfect as the image of cosmic peace which the poet remembers.
- Excellent use of alliteration and symbolism.
- The use of bright, dramatic colour makes the figure of the girl, Cáit Killann, stand out and may have symbolic connotations.
- The necessity of emigration in order to survive is alluded to in the poem – this was not the dream of Pádraig Pearse!
- The fact that the girl still holds the keys of the cottage suggests loss. Those left in Ireland are somehow locked out of their rightful heritage.
- Although Cáit is presented as an almost mythic character and associated with the work of great artists, the final picture is one of a real woman who was forced to emigrate. This can be read symbolically as a representation of the ideals of Pearse and the reality of modern Ireland.

The Difficulty that is Marriage

The opening line of this poem hits us with hard alliterative 'd' sounds: 'We disagree to disagree, we divide, we differ…'. The reader is thrust into the scene: a married couple in discord. Even the familiar phrase of reconciliation ('agree to disagree') is rejected and mangled into a deliberately confusing double negative – people disagreeing to disagree could be read as always choosing to agree, but this is not the case here. From the outset, the claim strains our sense of logic: do they fail even to 'disagree' in the sense that they don't fight openly, and instead 'divide' or 'differ' into the protective realm of their own silent, private opinions? It's hard to answer because Durcan doesn't show us the couple in action. Instead, we are transported from the opening line to what seems to be a nightly ritual: the poet regarding his wife as she lies 'curled up in sleep'. He describes her as 'faraway', and this is an important motif in Durcan's poetry: much of his work seems to struggle with conveying a message from across a vast gulf: a sea; sleep; death; memory; a foreign land; the tightlippedness of a remote loved one or family member.

The restless speaker arranges 'a mosaic of question marks' across the bedroom ceiling. He does this most nights so we assume he is disturbed, but then the tone of his inquiry seems joyous: 'How was it I was so lucky to have ever met you?' Again, we are thrown back on ourselves as readers – here is a man who is troubled, who can't sleep, can't find any middle ground with his wife, and cannot figure out how he is so lucky to find himself in this bind.

The difficulty of this paradox makes us notice the form of the poem. It's a sonnet – it has 14 lines and a natural break after the 8th line.

Traditionally, sonnets can be intellectual exercises that introduce a problem or riddle and then try to solve it.

In the second line, Durcan claims to 'lie in bed' each night. The word 'lie' here could have a double meaning. He literally lies in bed beside his wife but may also be involved in a 'lie' about their relationship. Is this line an admission that he is struggling to make his own double claim: I love you and feel lucky to be with you, but I feel lonely and removed from you at the same time? Certainly, by the end of the poem he is making paradoxical statements: 'You must have your faults but I do not see them'. It's a contradiction: I know you're not perfect, but I think you're perfect. It is as if by day he differs and divides from his wife, but by night his mind is differing and dividing within itself. He claims he doesn't place her on 'a pedestal or throne' but in the same breath says he would 'rather live with you for ever/Than exchange my troubles for a changeless kingdom'. To give up a kingdom (presumably the eternal paradise promised in Christianity) in favour of the company of one's wife here on a 'changeling earth' (a corrupt substitute for heaven) is placing her on something of a pedestal, surely.

There is another difficult paradox here. The issue of mortality is a recurring theme in Durcan's work. Let us look at it more closely:

'I am no brave pagan, proud of my mortality'. The meaning of 'pagan' is unclear here. It's a word typically used to describe tribes of people who don't belong to Christianity (or the other religions of Judaism or Islam), and who believe in a spiritual existence where gods live in various elements of the natural world—like water, air, fire, or plants and animals. Some pagans believe in a personal afterlife (as the Greeks and Romans believed in hells and heavens) but others don't, believing instead in reincarnation or oblivion. Durcan here describes his ideal pagan as 'brave', which might suggest he considers wishing for effortless eternal life next to a Christian God as, in some way, less than brave. Does he see a truly rewarding life as one of struggle and maybe even discord?

Besides paradoxes, sonnets often concern themselves with romantic love. But this 'sonnet' is caught between romantic love and modern rejection of such a quaint notion. Metrical rhymes are discarded in favour of unrhymed blank verse, suggesting a kind of chaos or randomness even in this traditional poetic form.

Given the density of paradoxical claims being made in the poem, the title needs to be read very carefully. Note that Durcan doesn't call it The Difficulties of Marriage which would be banal and simply mean that marriage has difficulties in it. No, he implies here that marriage is difficulty. The difficulty is not simply that tension can emerge between two people who live together, but rather the sweet and subtle trap, or riddle, that is intense love. Perhaps the speaker doesn't love his wife in spite of their demanding relationship, but because of such demands. It is interesting to compare Durcan's poem *Nessa* here, where he explicitly pairs intense love with 'drowning'. He suggests that if they stay together they will 'ride into Dublin City/In a taxi-cab wrapped up in dust' possibly implying that they will become ghosts ('dust') and haunt the human world. He presents her as a whirlpool drawing him into her depths. This is not the language of a man who loves in spite of the whirlpool of fear or anger or difficulty, but because of it.

KEY POINTS

- Note the use of alliteration on the hard 'd' consonant which strikes a note of discord from the outset.
- Some confusion and ambiguity is created with the interplay of 'agree' and 'disagree'.
- Much of Durcan's work is concerned with the struggle to convey a message from across a vast gulf: a sea; sleep; death; memory; a foreign

land; the tightlippedness of a remote loved one or family member.
- Note the paradoxical nature of some lines where the poet suffers in the relationship yet feels happy to have found his wife.
- The issue of mortality is a recurring theme in Durcan's work and is evident in this poem.
- The poet seems to suggest that a truly rewarding life is one of struggle and maybe even discord.
- The poem is a sonnet. Metrical rhymes are discarded however in favour of unrhymed blank verse, suggesting a kind of chaos or randomness even in this traditional poetic form.
- Careful attention needs to be paid to the multi-layered meaning of the title of this poem.
- The poem has parallels with the poem *Nessa*.

Wife Who Smashed Television Gets Jail

The tabloid-headline-style title launches us into a first-person voice. Lines 1-21 are the husband speaking directly to the judge who is evaluating the case of the smashed TV. The opening lines present the wife as being aggressive and threatening without any context for why she might be frustrated. The speaker is careful to use deferential phrases like 'my Lord' and clumsy, legal-sounding phrases like 'peaceably watching' to curry favour with the magistrate.

He claims they were simply enjoying the 1970s detective show *Kojak,* and that at the same moment that Kojak shoots a character with the same name as the defendant ('Goodnight, Queen Maeve'), the wife flies into a rage and smashes in the box.

The reference to Queen Maeve is particularly loaded. Maeve (or Medb) was a powerful and ambitious 'Warrior Queen' of ancient Connacht. She features in a cycle of myths, and is depicted as a complex character: forceful, sexual and uncompromising. She murders her rivals and takes many husbands and lovers – some of whom she kills or abandons. Her name may be associated with the English word mead, which is a sweet wine. As such, Maeve takes on the role of a goddess of sexuality, violence and intoxication. The violence is humorously echoed

in the modern context by her way of taking on her 'rival' for affection and attention: the TV. Her mythical connection with intoxication is re-visited, again in a humorously petty way, when she suggests that 'We'd be much better off all down in the pub talking…'. This 'queen' has fallen a long way from her origins in Irish myth. But the presence of a powerful and uncompromising woman is still threatening to the judge. He is paraphrased (possibly by a reporter) in lines 22-26, and his argument is far more bizarre and illogical than anything Maeve has said or done. Justice O'Brádaigh trots out the well-worn claim that families are the 'basic unit of society' but then mangles that by arguing the TV may be a 'basic unit of the family.' Following his twisted logic, any wife who prefers playing games in a pub over watching the family TV is a threat to the fabric of society! He orders her to be locked up and refuses any legal appeal, seemingly oblivious to the fact that in doing so he has broken up the actual human family by removing the wife and mother.

Looked at one way, this could be a darkly comical tale about how a cruel and disloyal mythical queen gets reincarnated in the 20th century and frightens some petty men into locking her up. But on a more serious level it depicts the power of unbalanced and self-important judges to split up families and incarcerate people for petty crimes. The poet seems worried about the

Establishment's tendency to side with property concerns over human concerns, such as Durcan's on-going hunger for deep communication. He seems to be presenting the TV as something that can interfere with real family communication and corrode the deep ties that form when people play and talk together.

Given the mythical name of the wife and the Gaelic spelling of the judge's surname, there may also be a tension being set up between the Irish background of the speakers in this poem and the American culture of the TV shows they are watching. Perhaps the poet is implying that traditional Irish culture is being sold out in favour of foreign – and particularly American – passive pleasures.

KEY POINTS

- Note the tabloid-style title and the use of first-person narration. This creates immediacy and a sense of drama.
- In Irish myth, Queen Maeve is depicted as a complex character: forceful, sexual and uncompromising. The use of the name for the wife is powerfully symbolic. The violence is humorously echoed in the modern context by her way of taking on her 'rival' for affection and attention: the TV.
- Note the irony of the fact that the judge breaks up the family unit himself by removing the wife and mother.
- Durcan presents the TV as something that can interfere with real family communication and corrodes the deep ties that form when people play and talk together.
- The explicit references to the Irish names of Maeve and O'Brádaigh form an ironic contrast to the imported American TV series *Kojak* which was interrupted by the wife's actions.

Parents

Durcan's poems often display unusual titles, like *Madman* or *Six Nuns Die in Convent Inferno,* but *Parents* has a deceptively simple title, so our guard is down when we read the stunning opening line: 'A child's face is a drowned face'.

On a purely literal level, this probably means that a newborn's features, recently freed from the aquatic environment of the mother's womb, can look scrunched up and alien, like a watery corpse. But the deeper import of the line is that first-time parents, who are still overwhelmed by the enormity of their new role, tend to investigate their unnervingly calm sleeping baby at night-time and wonder if it is dead. The use of the verb 'stare' rather than 'gaze' or 'admire' takes us to an animal place of amazement and primal concern with keeping their vulnerable infant safe.

Like the sleeping wife and fretful-yet-loving husband in *The Difficulty that is Marriage,* this poem relates a scene of people trying – and failing – to communicate across a mysterious gulf or distance. The parents here are 'Estranged from her [the baby] by a sea'. The sea could represent sleep, but also the sheer difference between the consciousness of an infant and an adult.

Initially, the baby is presented as an exotic sea creature, something alien, being observed by the creatures that live on solid land: the grown-ups. But in the uneasy world of the poem, even this relation is not fixed. Everything reverses whenever the baby wakes: 'If she looked up she would see them…mouths open/Their foreheads furrowed –/Pursed-up orifices of fearful fish –/Their big ears are fins behind glass'. The baby's weak eyesight renders the image of her guardians as warped and muted, but even she could make out that these are worried fish watching her.

In another unexpected reversal, even though the baby is asleep, she is active, 'calling out to them', but despite their 'big ears' they 'cannot hear her'.

The theme of isolation, or the unbridgeable gap that can exist between family members even when they love and need each other, mingles with another related Durcan anxiety: the fear of homelessness. The new parents find themselves 'locked out of their own home', and that is what the arrival of a new baby can do:

displace old comforts with new roles and scary new concerns. This mysterious sea creature has pushed the couple out of their familiar world and onto a strange isolated island. They are 'stranded' in the night, staring with awe at the marvel of their alien visitor. Note the repetition of key words: 'sea' ends the third, fourth, fifth, sixteenth and seventeenth lines; 'Father, Father/ Mother, Mother' echo in a ghostly manner, as if the child is calling out to them not from sleep but from the death the parents fear so deeply. In this manner, the poem conveys the intensity of the parents' love for their child without ever succumbing to sentimentality.

KEY POINTS

- The title of this poem is deceptively simple.
- The overwhelming responsibility of new parents when faced with a newly born child is explored in this poem.
- Like the sleeping wife and fretful husband in *The Difficulty that is Marriage*, this poem relates a scene of people trying – and failing – to communicate across a mysterious gulf or distance.
- Note the use of unexpected reversals in the viewpoints expressed in the poem (parents vs child).
- Themes of isolation, anxiety and homelessness are explored in this poem as they are in several other poems by Durcan.
- The poem conveys the intensity of the parents' love for their child without ever succumbing to sentimentality.

'Windfall', 8 Parnell Hill, Cork

Section 1 (Lines 1-37):

On the surface, the title is simply the poet's old address where he lived with his wife and daughters, but the house name (Windfall) can be understood to have two meanings at least. The first is that of a lucky win, something like a lottery, or the grace of God: a gift that lands in your lap regardless of whether you deserve it or not. The second meaning of windfall refers to fruit that has dropped from a tree without being chosen or picked, and in that sense may imply randomness, chaos or even an expelled quality. The first meaning – that of a jubilant lottery win – informs the first 112 lines of the poem (i.e. the

vast bulk of it).

Durcan repeats 'home' six times in seven lines, as if turning the familiar word around and around until it becomes alien, exotic – like repeating your own name until it becomes strange. This de-familiarising of the basic stuff of life is something poetry has great power to do, and certainly Durcan is interested in helping us see how the profound and sublime can be found in even the most ordinary scenes and phrases. He claims that the throwaway statement 'Well, now, I'm going home' makes him feel 'sovereign' (like a king). In lines 8-14 he converts the view from his window – the seeming ordinariness of industrial Cork – into something worthy of great painters like Cezanne. Another painter, Goya, is referenced also, but this is more foreboding; Goya was famous for painting dark images of cruelty, madness and abandonment in places like war zones and lunatic asylums. There is a note of hyper-self-reflectiveness here, as Durcan shows us himself 'Dreaming that life is a dream which is real/The river a reflection of itself in its own waters/Goya sketching Goya among the smoky mirrors . . .'.

His tone lightens as he sketches a scene of domestic bliss: TV watching with the kids, wife knitting on the couch. The other houses have picturesque or sentimental names (meaning 'with love', 'without cares', 'little peace', 'little mountain', etc.) but their house means Pure Luck.

'It is ecstasy to breathe if you are at home in the world' (Line 19). This line connects to the reference to '. . . Buddhist Monks/In lotus monasteries' (Lines 24-25), because Buddhism teaches that letting go of egotistical struggle and self-regard is the key to happiness. Monasteries are seen as places for refugees from that worldly struggle for power or fame. The poet seems to be saying that as long as he has his home and family, he wants for nothing and so enjoys a profound calm. The lotus is a sacred flower that grows out of the muck of a lake, and Durcan presents his freedom of mind as blossoming out of the muck of 'homicidal' Cork City. In Buddhism, being born human (as opposed to animal) is considered a 'windfall' because you have a chance to 'wake up' from the whirlpool dream of life and death and achieve Nirvana, as Durcan puts it: 'A chance in a lifetime to transcend death'. Transcending death, in a Buddhist context, doesn't mean literally living forever; it means seeing through the illusion of the grasping ego that makes you feel separate from the world, and which holds onto anger, lust, envy, loneliness, fear etc. But even in his 'lotus monasteries' there are still dark thoughts, as Durcan sneers at the gap between the dreamy language of Ireland's Proclamation of Independence (our own country's claim to sovereignty), which promises to cherish each child equally, and the reality 'where the best go homeless'.

Section 2 (Lines 38-75):

This section opens with another scene from his 'high window' and again we see notions of connection to all of reality: 'shipping from all over the world'. The river Lee, like the poet-turned-family-man, is 'busy, yet contemplative'. The house is covered in prints of fine art, but mixed with the famous paintings is the even finer art of personal photos, the life and times of family members played out in holiday snaps doing 'ordinary' things like building sandcastles or camping. There are a few references to religious ceremonies (First Holy Communion, Confirmation Day) but there's no indication these holy rites are any more or less sacred than the other memories. The poet tells us he 'pored' over these images with his children often, suggesting that recollection is important to both him and them. This 'ritual' of remembering is presided over by the mother 'from a distance –/ The far side of the hearthrug'. Although she is watching 'proudly', there may be a hint of a gradual drifting apart taking place.

Section 3 (Lines 76-101):

Water imagery changes from river to sea. The children's home is 'Their own unique, symbiotic fluid'. Durcan's use of symbiotic is itself unique, because the term 'symbiotic' refers to the relation between species who mutually support each other. Because he's applying it to a medium here (water) and in the context of something being unique to each child, the mind naturally thinks 'amniotic', the womb sea we all float into the world through. If we allow this reading, the house is a great womb indeed, because even the parents partake in this 'private sea'.

Repetition is used ('a sea of your own' appears twice) to reinforce this notion of sovereignty. The family house is a place of playful inversions. You can 'hang upside down from the ceiling... hands dangling their prayers to the floorboards'. Here, prayers are grounded, and go down to the solid base of the home instead of up to a cloudy pie-in-the-sky heaven. All this playing is done with equanimity – a meditative trait of being able to find balance in even the most chaotic environments – in front of postcards from Thailand, a Buddhist country.

The sea world of the house breaks down into the minutiae (tiny details) of 'sands underneath the surfaces of conversations, / The marine insect life of the family psyche'. The family's life is being depicted as a rich and complex ecosystem enjoying a very fine but delicate balance.

This ecosystem seems complete into itself, like a meditating monk. The parents ignore the phone, disconnecting from superficial conversation so as to connect more thoroughly with each other. This is a kind of asylum, 'In which climbing the walls is as natural/As making love on the stairs'. 'Natural' is a strange word here, and may mean 'instinctive' or 'impulsive', implied by the act of having sex on uncomfortable stairs. 'Climbing the walls' sounds fun, but contains hints of going mad. Perhaps there are echoes here back to Goya's paintings of asylums, or Durcan's own psychiatric incarceration in his youth, but here the asylum lives up to its name: a shelter for refugees from the world.

The section ends with a curious claim: 'The most subversive unit in society is the human family'. This is an inversion of the usual 'family values' claim that the family is the basic unit of society. How and what does Durcan's happy family subvert? Perhaps there is something about love, fun, relaxation and instinctive life that is a threat to some other imposing project he sees at large in the world, like the global industrial activity he can see from his window.

Section 4 (Lines 102-113):

This section is composed of echoes of statements he or the children have made over the years regarding home. What's notable is how ordinary they sound; there's nothing here you haven't said a million times yourself. But by seeing the word 'home' appear on the page again and again, you begin to realise how inextricably linked the language of home and reassurance prove to be.

Section 5 (Lines 114-126):

The tone drastically shifts – suddenly Durcan enters into a confessional mode. He never states what he did, other than he was 'put out of my home' with 'good reason'. The third line inverts 'windfall' from happy win to becoming 'fallen' or 'felled'. Without the protective refuge of his family's home, he seems to cease being a human. He is relegated to 'creeping, crawling' about the 'alien' city of Dublin. He becomes restless as a bird 'beyond all ornithological analysis'. His chance to meditate in his monastery, to escape the endless cycle of rebirth, has been lost. He tumbles from 'Bed-and-breakfast to bed-and-breakfast', a creature of the wind.

Section 6 (Lines 127-137):

After imagery of water and wind, the final image is that of fire. He peers into 'other people's homes' and sees the family hearth as a primal need, something gathered around by every tribe known to man, from the ancient Native Americans to the modern middle class nuclear family. Even the TV functions as a fire of sorts, a light to gather around. His final lines are cold and technological, a radio operator trying and failing to speak from one side of the word Windfall to the other, from the sad to the happy, from the present to the past, from the isolated father to the unified family: 'Windfall to Windfall—can you hear me?' No answer.

His last line is a recycled one. The 'pet' suggests it was originally aimed at one of his children. Now he uses it to reassure himself, not a domestic 'pet' but a lonely animal lost in the street.

KEY POINTS

- Durcan is interested in helping us see how the profound and sublime can be found in even the most ordinary scenes and phrases
- Note the repetition of the word 'home' in the opening section of the poem.

- He converts the view from his window – the seeming ordinariness of industrial Cork – into something worthy of great painters.

- The poet suggests that as long as he has his home and family, he wants for nothing and so enjoys a profound calm – like that enjoyed by Buddhists.

- The poet emphasises the importance of recollections to himself and to his family as he pores over old photographs of major family occasions.

- Note the repetition of sea and water imagery and its connection to life. The family's life is being depicted as a rich and complex ecosystem enjoying a very fine but delicate balance.

- Note the dramatic shift in tone as Durcan is put out of his home and becomes homeless.

- Durcan uses the image of fire symbolically. It represents warmth, energy and togetherness.

- The final image of the poet as a lost 'pet' animal is deeply moving.

Six Nuns Die in Convent Inferno

The title of this poem reads like a dramatic newspaper headline, but the dedication beneath it contains the confounding pairing of the phrase 'happy memory' with a reference to nuns burning to death sometime after midnight on a specific date. This fusing of factual detail with dramatic flourish and sombre image with joyous language sets the complex tone for what follows.

Part 1, Section 1 (Lines 1-62):

The poem is narrated by one of the six deceased, though we never learn which one. Her opening lines are factual and simply locate where the nuns lived in Dublin city centre. However we quickly see a playful spirit emerge as she turns the grandiose description of Grafton Street as a paseo into a verb 'where everyone paseo'd'. A paseo can mean an elegant boulevard to stroll through, but originally it meant an entrance into a bullfighting arena – a place of combat and struggle and danger. The notion of struggle is touched on deftly in the very next line, as she remembers often passing the 'great patriotic pebble of O'Donovan Rossa'. Rossa was a member of the Fenians. He fled to New York in the 1870s to work as a journalist and to raise

great sums of money to set up a 'dynamiters' school' to organise the bombing of British cities. Referring to his large stone monument as a 'patriotic pebble' seems to deflate that kind of martyr in the nun's eyes. Perhaps she is implying that we all seek freedom, but violence is a spiritually petty route to take.

She remembers passing 'tableaus' (a striking image of a group of people; often they are showing a scene from history, such as Jesus surrounded by his apostles at the Last Supper) of punks. The punks are rebels and freedom-seekers too, idealistic young people who find themselves self-exiled from the middle-class world of shopping and commerce that Grafton Street represents. They are like nuns or monks with 'half-shaven heads' or soldiers in 'martial garb', but the nun sees how 'vulnerable' they are, 'Clinging to warpaint and to uniforms and to one another' in much the same way as militants of all kinds and in all times have done. Although nuns are typically viewed as humble and meek, the punks' reactionary pose is nothing compared to how rebellious the nun sees herself: 'The wild woman, the subversive, the original punk'. One of Durcan's favourite words, 'subversive', is here, so we know he has warm feelings for her.

The nun seems surprised at her ability 'To opt

out of the world and to/Choose such exotic loneliness/Such terrestrial abandonment'. This homelessness is the flipside of Durcan's lonely character who tumbles lost through the Dublin streets by the end of *Windfall*. Here the nun celebrates her 'exotic' choice to turn her back on the instinctive life of sex and childbirth. Even so, she notes how banal her 'weird bird' life is, using 'A lifetime' three times to describe her humble bike, galoshes stored away, umbrella drying out – evidently a lot of time spent outdoors in miserable weather.

The nuns' dormitory high up in the convent is as 'eerie an aviary as you'd find/In all the blown-off rooftops of the city'. Her freedom is complex and not without conditions, because she returns every evening to an aviary (a large cage for birds) – one from which they cannot escape on the night of the fire.

As well as the bird image, she likens herself and her sisters to the crew of a nineteenth-century schooner. The image is of brave, tough voyagers – people without roots. The specific nature of the vehicle also echoes back to exiles like O'Donovan Rossa who set sail for cities like New York en masse in the nineteenth century, hunting for freedom of one sort or another. The nun and her sisters use their 'schooner' to follow an ancient 'young man' who 'lived two thousand years ago in Palestine'. She notes that he was a 'subversive' too, and 'died a common criminal' in the eyes of his prosecutors.

Section 2 (Lines 63-84):

Suddenly the narrator takes us into the terrifying heart of the fire, but the language is not that of fear. Even the flames are 'the arms of Christ'; the fire is likened to its opposite – the cooling waves of the sea (a common Durcan motif for comfort). The burning nun's mind is chaotic as she hops from the 'disintegrating dormitory' to a beach excursion 'the year Cardinal Mindszenty went into hiding'. Mindszenty was a Hungarian who opposed fascism and communism and believed in religious freedom. He was labelled 'subversive' first by Nazis, who imprisoned him, and then by communists, who locked him

up for even longer. He was finally stripped of his titles by the Pope and took refuge in the US embassy in Budapest. He died in exile in Vienna. Through his various trials he clung to his title of 'Prince Primate', much as the punks do to their safety pins and warpaint. There is thus a marked twinning of courage and vulnerability throughout this poem.

As she burns, the narrator's mind darts between her happy beach memory, the allusion to the trials of Mindszenty, and the nuns' banal fantasies of darning that fugitive-martyr's socks. It's difficult to know if the effect is meant to be comical or disturbing. Is this a clever wit, or the rambling of a mind scared out of its wits?

Section 3 (Lines 85-131):

Durcan's fascination with water and joyous drowning is revisited as he manages to turn a fire victim into someone reflecting on how 'Christ is the ocean . . . We are doomed but delighted to drown' (compare the poet relishing his being swallowed into the whirlpool of love in *Nessa*.)

Looking back on her terrestrial life, the narrator concludes that she and her celibate sisters are 'furtive' rebels, 'mothering forth illegitimate Christs/In the street life of Dublin city'. She is careful to use the word 'illegitimate' here, making a point that the law of the land rarely if ever overlaps with the law of Love, and that the spiritual life is often rebellious or subversive. The narrator is profoundly unselfish, not even grasping onto her own life. She reflects on what a 'refreshing experience' it is to lose things: 'How lucky I was to lose…my life'. This stands in stark contrast to the married man in *Windfall*, whose 'luck' falls away once he loses his place in the world, even though he lives on.

The nun's mind makes a characteristic dart from profundity to the small detail as she remembers the book she was reading that fateful night: Conor Cruise O'Brien's *The Siege*. O'Brien was a diplomat and scholar of sectarian unrest. His own relationship with Ireland's struggle with English colonialism was uneasy, and he switched from Nationalism to Unionism later in life. *The Siege* is about sectarian conflict in the Middle East, Jesus' birthplace, between Palestinian Arabs and Zionist Jews seeking refuge in their own state after the horrors of the Holocaust. Oddly, the nun mentions only the price tag of the book. Perhaps this is a sly allusion to the materialism that Durcan's subversives are always fighting against in some way.

Section 4 (Lines 132-147):

This short surreal section shows us the nun drawing the fire dragon to her breast, ecstatic in death. The imagery focuses pointedly on her fulfilling the biological function of giving birth that she has foregone in her celibate life, but here all the nuns are 'frantically in labour' to their deaths. Before the fire she describes them as 'sleeping molecules', implying they are part of a larger fabric. The crisis of death serves to wake them up to a higher reality. A blur of figures attend to them: phantom doctors and nurses help them 'giving birth', while Christ alternates as an 'Orthodox patriarch' and a fireman 'splashing water on [their] souls'.

The six names of the deceased are presented as a memorial in text. The closing image is of joyous innocence: frisky kittens in the sun.

Part II—Section 5 (Lines 148-154):

The second part shifts to an omniscient narrator. It tells of Jesus listening to the Grafton Street punks, and then addressing them in astonishment: 'I tell you, not even in New York City/Have I found a faith like this'. Whether he is referring to the faith of the nuns or the punks is not clear. The reference to NYC seems arbitrary, but could be an ironic allusion to O'Donovan Rossa, who managed to drum up huge sums of money in New York to fund a bombing campaign in England.

Section 6 (Lines 155-165):

The final section shows us the nuns' ghosts after the park is locked and the whole world has receded. They kneel by the Fountain of the Three Fates, an ironic spot as it refers to pre-Christian (Norse) characters called Norns, who control the fates of gods and men. The monument has a deeper significance, as it was a gift from the German people to Ireland for giving shelter to their war refugee children during World War II. Moving back further in time, St. Stephen's Green was a site for public executions – often in the form of burnings. Reciting the Agnus Dei (Lamb of God) conveys its own irony, not only because it refers to letting Christ in 'under my roof' (as the nuns burned under their own roof), but also because the words are attributed in the Gospel of Luke to a Roman centurion – a representative of power and war. Durcan refers to the recitation as a 'torch song'– the allusion to fire is obvious, but a torch song is often a song about unrequited love. Were the devoted nuns truly loved by a god who let them burn? Perhaps we all feel unworthy of love to some extent, but the closing lines (from an ancient soldier to an ancient punk) suggest that we are all refugees in some way, and behind all the uniforms and poses of power, the only thing we have to cling to at last is the 'aid' of love itself.

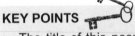

KEY POINTS

- The title of this poem reads like a dramatic newspaper headline. Note how tragedy and happiness are mixed in the language of the opening.
- Complex, symbolic images are used throughout.
- Note the unusual linking of the speaker with punks. Although nuns are typically viewed as humble and meek, the punks' reactionary pose is nothing compared to how rebellious the nun sees herself: 'the wild woman, the subversive, the original punk'. Christ is also seen as a

subversive in this poem.

- Repetition is used effectively. 'A lifetime' is repeated three times to describe her humble bike, galoshes, umbrellas drying out – evidently a lot of time spent outdoors in miserable weather.

- The description of the fire uses language associated with comfort rather than fear.

- The reference to Cardinal Mindszenty, a subversive, helps to link the notions of courage and vulnerability throughout this poem.

- Surreal, multi-layered imagery is effectively used to describe the nuns' deaths.

- The closing lines (from an ancient soldier to an ancient punk) suggest that we are all refugees in some way. Behind all the uniforms and poses of power, the only thing we have to cling to at last is the 'aid' of love itself.

Sport

Like many of Durcan's poems, *Sport* is autobiographical but differs from his typical approach in its directness. There are no flights of fancy, no surprising combinations of metaphors, images or scenes. Instead it recounts a single memory: the day the poet played in goal for his hospital's Gaelic Football team. As a young man, Durcan had been committed to St. John of God psychiatric hospital against his will. His internment is ironically 'celebrated' in this poem again and again as he uses the now-defunct phrase 'Mental Hospital' six times while describing his impressive performance on the day of the match.

He uses the second person ('you') to speak to his father, a stern circuit court judge whom Durcan believed was profoundly disappointed in him. The opening lines are achingly sad: 'There were not many fields/In which you had hopes for me'. The term 'fields' can mean 'areas of expertise' but here we see the poet setting the scene on a literal field – a playing pitch. He notes that his father took the effort to drive him fifty miles to the game, and this detail can be read as thanking his father for the opportunity, or illustrating how driven and demanding his father was to see his son excel at something. He says his father stands on the sidelines to

'observe me'. Unlike the verbs 'cheer' or 'support', 'observe' is a detached, clinical word. 'Sidelines' sound removed, distant, far from the action. The poet seems to be grouping his father with the psychiatrists and other authority figures who feel responsible for his well-being, but don't love him.

Durcan describes the huge, almost animal-like men he is defending the goal against: 'gapped teeth, red faces/Oily, frizzy hair, bushy eyebrows … over six foot tall/Fifteen stone in weight… All three of them, I was informed,/Cases of schizophrenia'. He is presenting these men as monstrous, and this is often how society regards the spectre of mental illness itself – something looming, threatening, dangerous. These men are the faces of chaos.

The poet notes that no one knows the truth of anyone else on the field: 'There was a rumour/That their centre-forward… Had castrated his best friend'. This extreme action (which may or may not have happened) is attributed to a 'misunderstanding'. The poet makes use of extremely vague language, such as 'rumours' and 'misunderstandings'. Perhaps Durcan is implying that everyone committed to a psychiatric ward – or at least in his case – is there due to a breakdown in communication. Certainly there is no real or effective communication between himself and his father, who only manages a terse 'Well played, son' at the end of the match. Even though the poem is directed to 'you' there is a tired sadness in the tone that suggests this message is too late to reach its real audience. It feels like a letter he has written but knows he'll never send.

But there is euphoria here too, and moments of pride. The speaker surprises himself at his courage and skill in the heat of the game: 'I made three or four spectacular saves'. He attributes his father's presence as giving him 'That will to die/That is as essential to sportsmen as to artists', but this is a very loaded compliment. The phrase 'will to die' could mean a burst of courage and selflessness – of self-sacrifice – but it could also mean a self-destructive drive that draws you into acts of masochism or self-damage. He says he wanted to 'mesmerise' and be 'mesmeric'; both verb and adjective are derived from an infamous eighteenth-century hypnotist called Franz Mesmer. Mesmer was a 'quack' doctor who used a variety of bizarre techniques to 'heal' his patients, many of

whom were hysterics. One method involved the patients swallowing a fluid containing metal while Mesmer ran magnets over them to create a healing 'magnetic tide'. His theories of animal magnetism were discredited as 'imagination', and he spent the last twenty years of his life in self-imposed exile, a recurring theme in Durcan's work. The poet might be taking a dig at the psychiatric professionals here, although it's possible he is simply using a word we hear often in the context of great performances in art and sport: the audience feels lifted up by an other-worldly spectacle of grace under pressure.

Despite the elements of wry humour and fleeting pride, the underlying tone in *Sport* is one of sadness, not only the personal sadness of being seen as a disappointment, but also the general poignant 'spectacle' of mental illness, and the gaping hole that is left when communication breaks down. All we have left to separate the 'winners' from the 'losers' are numbers on a scoreboard.

KEY POINTS

- Note the unusually direct approach in this poem which focuses on a single memory.
- The repetition of the words 'Mental Hospital' emphasises the sense of stigma Durcan felt at that stage of his life.
- The poet's uneasy, detached relationship with his father adds a poignant tone to the poem.
- Durcan presents his fellow inmates as being monstrous. This is often how society regards the spectre of mental illness itself – something looming, threatening, dangerous.
- The underlying tone in *Sport* is one of sadness, not only the personal sadness of being seen as a disappointment, but also the general poignant 'spectacle' of mental illness.

Father's Day, 21 June 1992

This poem shows Durcan as an emotionally complex writer. It fuses comedy and wit (and shades of farce) with genuine poignancy. It opens on a naturalistic scene: a man frazzled as he rushes to pack and run out the door to his waiting

taxi. It is at this most frantic and inconvenient moment that his wife chooses to spring a request on him: bring a huge threatening-looking axe with him down on the train to Cork to loan to her sister. He protests, suggesting his sister-in-law settle for a 'simple saw'. How does an axe differ from a saw? Is one more 'simple' than another?

One difference that jumps to mind is that the action of an axe seems more violent. One hits the tree repeatedly until it falls.

The speaker seems paranoid about his neighbours, claiming that 'the whole world' is 'inspecting' the waiting taxi. This may imply that he's already worried about how his marriage (and his character) might come across to others. His anxiety seems unfounded until we learn later that his relationship with his wife is indeed in trouble and doesn't hold up under scrutiny.

His wife, for her part, seems cool to the point of being cold. Despite his show of fluster and hurry, she keeps her request firm, and her language simple: 'Yes, if you wouldn't mind, that is'. The pronounced politeness – her show of reasonableness – could be interpreted as a technique called 'passive-aggression'. This is when a person puts pressure on someone to do something, but acts as if they are being perfectly calm and polite, making the put-upon person feel like they themselves are being unreasonable. It works on her husband; he folds under her request like a sofa bed: 'I decided not to argue the toss. I kissed her goodbye'.

The axe in question is set up 'behind the settee'. This is significant: not only is the axe (an implement of violence) hidden from plain view until the last second, but the location is also noteworthy. For Durcan, the couch (or settee) is a stand-in for the heart of the home. It is where the family gathers to lounge and live their comfortable, instinctual life. The tool of destruction lurks right behind where he tends to relax the most.

She presents the axe to him, 'neat as a newborn babe'. It is naked, as painful truth is always naked. The comparison to the baby is comical, but there's a sadness under this wit too. As we saw in *Parents*, having a child can be traumatic

in a way. It alters the nature of the couple's relationship forever. Durcan may be suggesting through this linking of images (axe=baby) that having children changed them from a 'couple' to a 'family' (it is Father's Day, after all), but once those children grow up and leave the house, the father and mother must rediscover who they are, and if they do not like who they find themselves to be, the tree of family life may suddenly transform into an axe ready to split the man and woman apart.

The second part of the poem is set on the train to Cork. He claims the whole way down he is beset by 'Guilt feelings', but we don't know why he should feel guilty until he confesses to his fellow traveller, a stranger in the seat near him: 'I am feeling guilty because she does not love me'. This is the irrational language of love. In his mind, the speaker believes it his own fault that he is not loveable, and lists off some feeble attempts to explain it to himself: he takes up too much of the bed; he is 'coarse' in his attempts to have sex with his wife; he eats pasta the wrong way. This is a man struggling and failing to communicate with the passenger on the train, with his wife, even with himself. He doesn't even choose to speak, instead he 'overheard' himself talking to the passenger, as if he is purely passive and has no control over what he does or how he does it. When the passenger eyes the axe and departs the seat without leaving the train, we see a comic scene (He's mistaking the author for a crazy man!) but really there is the spectre of depression looming in the final stanza. The speaker feels isolated: 'we sat alone/The axe and I'. Outside, the 'green fields' – symbols of youth and fertility – flee from him. He is not young, he will have no more children, and the daughters he does have are 'gone away' too. Unlike the frenzy of the opening lines, there is a quietness to this end, but it is a desperate one.

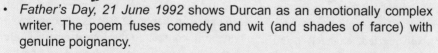

KEY POINTS

- *Father's Day, 21 June 1992* shows Durcan as an emotionally complex writer. The poem fuses comedy and wit (and shades of farce) with genuine poignancy.

- 'The axe behind the settee' is a significant image, not only for its connection to violence but because it is hidden behind a piece of furniture usually associated with relaxation and calm.

- An excellent simile occurs when the poet describes his wife presenting the axe to him, 'neat as a newborn babe'. It is naked, as painful truth is always naked.
- The final image in this poem is that of the poet struggling to come to terms with the breakdown in his marriage and feeling unable to communicate.
- Despite moments of brilliant wit, the poem is profoundly sad and disturbing.

The Arnolfini Marriage

Ekphrastic art is art that describes the beauty of a detailed object, often a painting or sculpture. The word 'ekphrastic' comes from the Greek 'ex' + 'phrazein' = to point out or explain. It has a rich history, going all the way back to the epic poet Homer, for instance, who could describe the beauty of an ornate shield. In modern English, ekphrastic poetry is typically poetry about visual art. It aims to interpret a painting or sculpture, and sometimes speaks as if it were the voice of the original work talking to us as a character; it was a popular genre of poetry in the nineteenth and twentieth century among scholar-poets.

Durcan's *The Arnolfini Marriage* is from his collection of ekphrastic poems *Give Me Your Hand* (1994), loosely based on paintings in London's National Gallery. Considering most people feel lost when looking at 'official' art, Durcan's book title suggests reassurance: perhaps he is offering his hand as a guide. Or perhaps the paintings are reaching out to the poet, asking him to have faith and follow them into their mysteries.

The Van Eyck painting which this poem describes is a tangle of uncertainties. We know it was painted by Dutch artist Jan Van Eyck in 1434, but almost every other detail is disputed. For instance, scholars disagree on what the title should be: 'The Arnolfini Portrait/Marriage/Wedding/Bethrothal/etc.' are just some suggested names. Experts differ on whom it depicts (which Arnolfinis? There are a few candidates), their relationship (are they married, engaged?) and even whether the woman is pregnant or not (the bulging of her dress may suggest wealth or

fertility rather than an actual pregnancy).

Durcan's interpretation starts with the title; obviously he has decided this is a portrait of a married couple. The poem speaks to us in the cool measured tones of the wealthy subjects on the canvas. Everything about them is measured, even their speech, which unpacks in neat three-line stanzas.

Whether due to historical uncertainty about their exact identity, or from a detached aristocratic attitude, they keep their introduction simple: 'We are the Arnolfinis'. They follow this greeting with a terse cautioning: 'Do not think you may invade/Our privacy because you may not'. Already the poet has pulled the rug out from under us; the couple send mixed messages, inviting us into their home (into their marriage), but immediately telling us not to get too comfortable. The purpose of this painting, Durcan suggests, is not to invite outsiders in, but to show them what they are missing out on. It's all an elaborate boast. Theirs is 'The most erotic portrait ever made'. They appeal to the artist not to portray them with sentimentality, but for that cooler intellectual virtue: to do justice to their 'plurality,/Fertility, domesticity, barefootedness'. The plurality may refer to the prospect of offspring – thereby increasing the number of Arnolfinis – or it may be the more abstract boast of how they enjoy a distinctness from each other (note the physical distance between the man and woman) while still being able to claim the sovereign sense of 'we' that is celebrated in *Windfall*. Boasts of 'domesticity' may be in contrast to the robust farm labourers of the day – who would be red-faced and large like the huge schizophrenic country men we see attacking the goal in *Sport* – and not pale and slender-fingered like this couple.

They present their bed 'As being our most necessary furniture'. Again, this could be a sexual boast, but it may also allude to a convention of the time where guests were received onto the bed as if it were a couch. Couches feature in Durcan's poetry as a kind of 'heart' or centre of a living room.

'Our brains spill out upon the floor'. This confounding line in stanza 5 throws us back on ourselves. Since the terrier is sniffing the 'minutiae of our magnitude', it may mean that the couple's greatness is manifest in small details. These people must have substantial resources. Perhaps the 'brains' here mean that their intellect is expressed in the profusion of rich materials (dress fabric, curtains, bedsheets) that 'spill' out before us. Like most wealthy people, they think they have come by their good fortune through their own brilliance.

Stanza 6 could have come from *Windfall* – it is the closest to warm and intimate that the speakers attempt. But there is a smugness underlying it, as if they were rare creatures to enjoy intimacy: 'Most people are in no position to say "we"'. Again, this is the language of implied exclusion. And by stanza 7 the exclusion turns explicit and personal. They are virtually pointing a finger at the divorced poet, and accusing him of being a failure: 'Are you? Who eat alone? Sleep alone?'

The final stanza seems to be a different speaker, or at least a radical break in the tone of the poem. TV programmes on RTÉ are still interrupted to make way for the Angelus, a call to prayer and reflection. This poem plays on the notion of reflection, hinting at the literal reflection of the self-aware painter who worked himself into the mirror on the wall between the figures of man and woman. Durcan is hinting at how he has worked his own concerns into this poem about one of the most famous self-referential paintings in art history. The term 'reflection' could also be used in the sense of a meditation: 'To do justice to our life as a reflection'. The reader might find an echo here back to *Windfall* when the poet reflects, yet again, on famous painters, and considers how life is a dream that is also real.

The final two lines are enigmatic: 'Here you have it:/The two halves of the coconut'. A coconut is another exotic food, like the oranges in the painting. It is a sphere, and sometimes spheres and circles are symbols of the perfection of God – consider the domed (half-sphere) mirror on the wall surrounded by a circular frame made up of tiny religious scenes.

Coconuts, like the mysteries of religions and marriages, are hard to crack open and get inside. But if you are smart or strong enough to get within that rough, resilient exterior, there is rich food indeed, and a sea of warm nourishing milk awaiting you.

KEY POINTS

- The poem speaks to us in the cool measured tones of the wealthy subjects on the canvas. Everything about them is measured, even their speech, which unpacks in neat three-line stanzas.
- The poem is an elaborate boast as the couple in the painting appear to be taunting the viewers. They introduce themselves but also insist on maintaining a distance.
- Like most wealthy people, the Arnolfinis think they have come by their good fortune through their own brilliance. Unusual images are used to indicate their brains.
- The language used by the Arnolfinis is that of exclusion which has a rather smug tone.
- The final stanza seems to be a different speaker, or at least a radical

- break in the tone.
- Durcan hints at how he has worked his own personal concerns into this poem about one of the most famous paintings in art history.
- Coconuts become symbolic of the mysteries of religion and marriage – tough exteriors but warm, nourishing centres.

Rosie Joyce

On the surface, this poem is a joyous three-part ode to the birth of the poet's granddaughter. But there are layers here that delve beneath the birth of the child, touching on ancient history and reach up into the possible shoots of future political growth.

Part I:

The opening image is one of birthing labour, as the 'hot sun pushed through the clouds,' and the child is born. The second stanza paints a world where everyone seems to be celebrating, setting out bright china on picnic rugs.

The first explicit religious allusion is when Durcan notes Rosie was born on the Christian holy day: Sunday. Durcan is in the middle of a mock-epic journey through Ireland when he learns of her 'incarnation' (a metaphysical term for when a god takes human form on earth). The intensity of this mystical language is offset by the perfunctory notice he gets from his son-in-law (whose name – Mark – is coincidentally that of one of the apostles) announcing the great event. It simply conveys the child's gender, weight and birth time, and affirms that all is well.

Part II:

The first four stanzas of Part II are an extended representation of the world breaking into bloom in celebration of their god Rosie's arrival. This is followed by the poet making his way to Dublin, a city that has been presented by him in other poems as the site of his 'homelessness' since his divorce. Now the city is a source of fortune to him, and he refers to 'Each canal bridge' as 'an old pewter brooch'. The reference to pewter may be significant given that it immediately precedes his sudden flashback to his father making such an epic journey himself, the judge/father 'relishing his role as Moses'. Pewter was an alloy technique used in the making of metal, weapons, ornaments etc. It was devised in ancient Egypt, and Moses was the leader of the oppressed slaves out of Egypt under the guidance of a benevolent god. The theme of escape from oppression (via a god's assistance) may be implied here. However, where the poet's father asserts a 'Great Divide' between the people, be they Egyptians and Jews, or East Coasters and West Coasters in Ireland, Durcan counters this with an alternative vision of reality:

'There are higher powers than politics/And these we call wildflowers or, geologically, people.'

The poet seems to be claiming that political divisions – those that have woven our history – are imaginary or at least petty, whereas nature (our mountains, rivers, flora etc.) is real. He uses the term 'geologically' to make us think of timescales. People are geological (in the sense of occupying a huge stretch of time) relative to the lifespan of flowers. And of course our greater environment (rivers and mountains) dwarfs the lifespan of humans, likening us, and even the incarnation Rosie, to ephemeral wildflowers.

Durcan alludes to the journalist Jonathan Philbin Bowman's show *Daymaker,* which focused on events that made people's day. But Durcan is exclaiming this phrase in a new way, as if the child's birth is a celestial event, like the god of Genesis who makes/creates the day. For Durcan, Rosie makes – or renews – life. With her birth, the poet's three-year long depression breaks and lifts: 'But you saved my life'.

Section III

This short final section is laden with allusions. Two of the main ones are considered here. On his return from Dublin to Mayo, Durcan meets

John Normanly, a man he is obviously friendly enough with to stop and talk to and mention by full name in his poem. He points out that John (another apostle but also a possible allusion to John the Baptist) is an 'organic farmer' and that he is connected with the 'Western Development Commission'. That organisation is an ecologically conscious attempt to create sustainable farming and energy practices in the West of Ireland, and plays into Durcan's belief that it is the land itself, the living things on it, that matter. This idea of the hopeful eco-politics of Rosie's (rosy?) future is presented in contrast to the old corrupt cronyism of Irish party politics. Durcan uses Pádraig Flynn, an Irish politician whom Durcan considers corrupt, as an example of political cronyism.

Normanly and Durcan 'wet our foreheads' (baptise themselves/get drunk) in a discussion of John Moriarty's autobiography. Moriarty was a mystic and philosopher who travelled widely and practiced a variety of jobs, including teaching English literature and being a live-in gardener for a monastery in Oxford. The autobiography Durcan and his friend are discussing is called *Nostos,* which is Greek for 'homecoming'. Durcan references the book here because he feels himself returning to full human life (coming home), redeemed by the 'incarnation' of new life that is his grandchild. But there may be more implied by the literary allusion. Moriarty is something of a nature poet himself, and mentions in the book that he would prefer to celebrate the mountain itself rather than cheer a Moses on top of it. This may be a subtle rejection of Durcan's own judge father as Moses, holding up the tablets of the Old Testament. Rosie is presented instead as an avatar of a New Testament, which may be love of the true things of life: wildflowers, people, clean water and fertile soil, and the ancient dark mountains that stand firm before the dawn.

KEY POINTS

- This poem is a joyous three-part ode to the birth of the poet's granddaughter.
- Christian images, heavy with allusion, are interspersed with prosaic details about the child's weight, height and time of birth.
- In the second part of the poem the poet seems to be claiming that political divisions – those that have woven our history – are imaginary or at least petty, whereas nature (our mountains, rivers, flora etc.) is real.
- For Durcan, Rosie makes – or renews – life. With her birth, the poet's three-year-long depression breaks and lifts: 'you saved my life'.
- The short final section is laden with allusions.
- Rosie is presented as being a symbol of love and of life.

The MacBride Dynasty

Durcan's poetry verges on prose in this piece. Durcan was related to both the MacBride and Gonne families on his mother's side. *The MacBride Dynasty* is more telling than showing, as the speaker remembers a visit to his grand-aunt (and one-woman national institution) Maud Gonne when he was a young boy and she was an elderly woman. Taking a mythical cue from Yeats, Durcan likens his own mother to a 'vengeful goddess/Spitting dynastic as well as motherly pride'. A dynasty is a line of rulers or other prominent and powerful people, and it is clear in the poem that the MacBrides consider themselves to be an 'alpha' family in Ireland. His mother is going to 'show off' her 'walking, talking little boy' to Maud Gonne, referred to as 'the servant of the Queen'. This title works in two ways, as Gonne claimed to have received a vision of the mythical 'Queen' of Ireland, Cathleen Ní Houlihan, as if to imply she had been chosen to follow the path that best served the creation of an Irish sovereign state. The title of 'servant' also works ironically, because Gonne – born in England – chose to reject rule by the British monarchy, and is hardly servile in her manner at all. If anything, Gonne is depicted as enamoured with her role as a cultural treasure, 'keen as ever to receive admirers'.

Durcan mocks her as a vain and even ludicrous old dame of the theatre, noting that 'Only the previous week the actor MacLiammóir/Had been kneeling at her bedside reciting Yeats to her/His hand on his heart, clutching a red rose'. The scene is overwrought with forced artfulness and reverence. W.B. Yeats was a poet, playwright, and statesman, an obsessive admirer of Maud Gonne, and one of the founding 'myth-makers' of the emerging Irish republic. He stands as a giant in the history of Irish mythic poetry, and one imagines that the subversive Durcan would have an uneasy relationship with such a figure, given Durcan's own love of mythic imagination, but distaste for official state propaganda.

The young boy views the aged Gonne through a nightmarish lens: 'sticking out her claws/To embrace me, her lizards of eyes darting about/ In the rubble of the ruins of her beautiful face'. This could be read as a cruel rendering of an old woman, or simply an honest recreation of the emotional outbursts very young children are given to. He flees, and is found and 'quieted' by his cousin Séan.

From line 26 on there is a vague but sustained attack from Durcan's mother on Maud Gonne. She is accused of being 'disloyal' to her husband (Durcan's mother's uncle, John MacBride) but it is never explained what she did. In point of fact, Maud Gonne separated from John MacBride and accused him publicly of drunkenness, domestic abuse and molesting Iseult, her 11-year-old daughter from a previous marriage. This airing of 'dirty laundry' in public may be the greatest offence to insular family consciousness, especially dynastic consciousness. The grandmother's voice chimes in here like a ghost, singing John's praises, and the poet describes him as the 'pride of our family'.

Instead, the ire is focused on Gonne, who is described as 'not worthy of Mummy's love'. The idea of being 'worthy' (or not) of love is something that haunts much of Durcan's poems. He struggles to be worthy of his father's love in *Sport* and struggles to be worthy of love from his wife in *Windfall* and *Father's Day*. *Rosie Joyce* is about being redeemed by a love that forgives and accepts unconditionally. But none of that is made explicit here. Instead, the closing lines are hard and cold. The collective pronoun 'we' is used to envelop and warm members of a family, but also to exclude others. Here, 'We', the dynastic family, will 'tolerate' Maud. She may remain as a central prop in the propaganda of the early Irish state, but 'we would always see through her'. This dismissive tone may be an ironic attack on insular family politics, or it may be a sincere and direct attack on the use of self-aggrandising myths in political art. Given that the poem is being recounted from the perspective of a young child, it's hard to know exactly how much we should take its claims at face value. One thing is certain: the vagueness of the accusations and the cold judgemental quality of the tone – so out of place in a Durcan poem – suggest we should tread carefully in how we read what is being said.

KEY POINTS

- Notice the prose-like quality of the style in this poem.
- Maud Gonne is depicted as enamoured with her role as a cultural treasure, 'keen as ever to receive admirers'.
- Note the poet's use of irony throughout the poem.
- There is a mocking tone as Durcan describes Maud receiving the

attentions of the actor MacLiammóir.

- The physical description of Maud Gonne has a nightmarish quality.

- The idea of being 'worthy' (or not) of love is something that haunts many of Durcan's poems. Here, Maud is seen as being unworthy of love because of her separation from and allegations against John MacBride.

- Note the use of the collective pronoun 'we' to include the members of the family, but to exclude Maud Gonne.

- The poem has a cold, judgemental quality which is not very typical of Durcan and may be more of a reflection of the views of others towards Maud. It is almost as though Durcan remembers being a child and absorbing the attitudes of his mother and grandmother.

Sample Answer

What I like and/or dislike about the poetry of Paul Durcan.

Write a personal response to this statement supporting the points you make with reference to the poems of Durcan on your course.

(Intro: Personal initial reaction to poems)

On first reading, I confess I found Paul Durcan's poetry confusing, and even a little slapdash. The conversational, colloquial tone felt like it clashed with the weird imagery, which hopped from idea to seemingly-unrelated idea. The images and metaphors were certainly striking, but I struggled to make sense of it all. Now, having read the poems several times and considered motifs that occur consistently, what emerges isn't confusing, but is instead a complex portrait of a complex man: The Difficulty That Is Paul Durcan.

(2nd para: consideration of titles, introduction to mix of tones/modes: factual, subversive, mystic, comic)

The first thing that might throw the average unsuspecting reader is how Durcan mixes up a few registers, or voices, that you don't usually find together. For instance, his titles often read like tabloid headlines: *Six Nuns Die in Convent Inferno, Wife Who Smashed Television Gets Jail, Sport, Madman*. Others are banal, like addresses (*Windfall, 8 Parnell Hill, Cork*) or dates (*Father's Day, 21 June 1992, Ireland 2002*) or simply names (*Nessa, Rosie Joyce*). But then we read the poems, and the bland – or tabloid – titles don't prepare us for what comes next. Far from factual or journalistic detail, we encounter a mix of political subversion and mystical comedy.

(3rd para: Durcan as 'subversive')

Let us consider the subversive aspect first. Durcan, as far as I can tell, isn't a satirist and never seems to attack any particular political party or social movement. Instead, his upset is a more general grudge against suffering from – or himself being – a vague historical disappointment. In *Sport*, he addresses his father directly and says outright that 'I was fearful I would let you down'. He manages to do a good job in goal, but keeps underlining that he was playing for a 'mental hospital', and that, even considering how lowly he felt by being committed against his will, 'Seldom if ever again in your eyes/Was I to rise to these heights'. I think this poem is subversive because mental health – even today – is stigmatised. Most individuals and their families keep any hint of depression, anxiety etc. hidden from public view. But Durcan lays it all out for us. It's extremely confessional. This level of honesty, of admitting not only to having been committed, but wanting approval from Daddy so badly (and failing to get it) is unsettling. And it's moving, because any time an adult man takes off the mask of strength or certainty it is a kind of political act. Anyone who says: let's stop pretending everything in our personal life or in our nation is fine – is being subversive.

(4th para: Developing 'subversive' reading and adding 'mystic')

Durcan keeps returning to the twin themes of privacy and family throughout his writing.

In *The MacBride Dynasty* he pulls out more dirty laundry when he reveals the way his mother's family closed ranks on Maud Gonne, his grand-aunt. They are punishing her for 'disloyalty' to John MacBride when she publicly humiliated him by accusing him of drunkenness and abuse of her daughter. The MacBrides allow the living legend, Gonne, to remain part of their 'dynasty', but they secretly reject her: 'For dynastic reasons we would tolerate Maud' but she will always be 'not worthy of Mummy's love'. Again, I think there's something subversive and even angry about the notion of being 'worthy' of love. This is a strikingly candid portrait of how ugly family politics can get behind closed doors. Because of the family ties to the Easter Rising and the birth of the Republic, *The Girl with the Keys to Pearse's Cottage* still feels personally subversive. Durcan describes Pearse's tourist-attraction cottage as having 'wet thatch' and 'peeling jambs', and points out how it's better viewed from a distance than up close. Symbolically through the cottage, Durcan is presenting the national martyr-hero as a stand-in for all official propaganda: glorious from afar, but not holding up well upon close inspection. The girl he fancies from a distance has to leave the country and move to America because Ireland cannot support its young. More disappointment, more imagined failure in the eyes of elders.

This fusing of personal and national and/or historical disappointment bleeds into *Windfall* too. Durcan paints a cosy portrait of enjoying a loving family (stealing 'a subversive kiss' with his wife while ignoring the ringing phone) only to lose that love and find himself 'homeless'. In a moment of foreshadowing this exile, he takes another dig at the language of the Proclamation, claiming he lives 'In a country where all the children of the nation/Are not cherished equally'.

(5th para: painterly quality of mystic writing—motif of water)

But countering this epic disappointment is the cool, painterly, even mystic element of the poet's work. For all the restless movement of Durcan's poems, he seems to find brotherhood with painters: people who show us a still scene. *Windfall* likens the view of Cork from Parnell Hill to something Cezanne or Goya would produce. *The Arnolfini Marriage* lets the painting of the austere couple speak back to us from across the centuries. *Nessa* paints idyllic scenes of a young couple falling in love in a field, and *Rosie Joyce*, about the birth of his granddaughter, shows us a joyous portrait of 'sky blue-and-white china in the fields/ In impromptu picnics of tartan rugs'. Present in most of these poems is the motif of water. It takes many forms and can be a chaotic whirlpool of love in *Nessa* or a private sea of intimacy in *Windfall*. Durcan's use of water imagery is as complex as the man himself. In *Windfall* he hits us with this cosmic head-scratcher describing the Lee: 'The river a reflection of itself in its own waters'. Even the fire in *Six Nuns* becomes water, which becomes Christ Himself: 'Christ is the ocean…Christ is the fire in whose waves/We are doomed but delighted to drown'.

(6th para: resilient [humour] and self-pity)

Shades of self-pity can creep into Durcan's work at times. Even though he attributes the phrase 'Exotic loneliness' to a dead nun, we get the impression he sees himself as being a romantic exile. First his parents cast him out (as in *Sport*) and even in maturity he presents himself as 'creeping, crawling' and 'homeless in Dublin' in *Windfall*. In *Father's Day* he acts as if deserted by daughters: 'all the green fields running away from us/All our daughters grown up and gone away'. But even so, I can't reduce the man to being merely a martyr.

I can't imagine what it's like to be committed to a mental hospital as a teenager or to get electroshock therapy either. Perhaps the most likeable element of Durcan's work is how he weaves humour into so much of his poetry. We get absurd scenes of accompanying an axe on a train, and a weird 'aviary' of the nuns. There's the crazy and yet impressive Queen Maeve of *Wife Who Smashed Television Gets Jail,* and the smug enigma that is the couple in *The Arnolfini Marriage.*

What I like and respect most about Durcan's poetry is that it isn't used to hide from reality or soften it. His absurdities and playful images come across instead as a way to explore the awesome mysteries and crippling disappointments of life a bit more safely, like the way divers use their tanks to go deeper into dark waters.

Guidelines for answering exam questions: Poetry

Type of Questions

Leaving Certificate Higher Level Poetry questions tend to be general in nature. Questions essentially look for a candidate's personal response to a poet's work. Personal engagement with the text must be supported by detailed textual knowledge.

Examples:

(a) Write a personal response to the poetry of Eavan Boland.

(b) Write an introduction to the poetry of John Montague.

(c) Account for the popularity of Robert Frost's poetry.

(d) Explain what you liked and / or disliked about the poetry of Paul Durcan etc.

If a question is slightly more specific, the terms of the question must be addressed and kept in focus. However, at the heart of all poetry questions is the idea of personal engagement with the text.

The following are examples of slightly more specific poetry questions:

1. Write an article for a school magazine introducing the poetry of John Montague, to Leaving Certificate students. Tell them what he wrote about and explain what you liked in his writing, suggesting some poems that you think they would enjoy reading.

2. What impact did the poetry of Eiléan Ní Chuilleanáin make on you as a reader? Your answer should deal with the following: (a) Your overall sense of the personality of the poet, (b) The poet's use of language/imagery.

What does personal engagement with the text involve?

* Comment on themes, subject matter.
* Comment on the relevance of a poet's themes.
* Explain why a particular poem is worth reading.
* Say why you can relate to or 'connect' with certain themes.
* Discuss how particular poems had a particular impact on you.
* Explain why a personal poem has a universal appeal.
* Say which poems you most enjoyed.
* Comment on aspects of a poet's style:
* Language: accessible? simple/complex? etc.
* Imagery: vivid? precise? unusual? etc.
* Sound effects: alliteration, assonance, onomatopoeia, rhyme, etc.

Note: Your personal response must be grounded in the text – support your points by appropriate reference to and/or quotation from the poems on your course.

EXAMPLES OF THE LANGUAGE OF PERSONAL ENGAGEMENT

- *I can relate to this poem because . . .*
- *This poem remains relevant because . . .*
- *I enjoyed this poem because . . .*
- *What I liked / disliked about this poem was . . .*
- *This is my favourite poem because . . .*
- *This poem opened my eyes to . . .*
- *This poem helped me to understand . . .*
- *This poem had a profound impact on me because . . .*
- *This poem offers interesting insights into . . .*
- *This poem set me thinking about / made me aware of . . .*
- *I particularly like the image of . . .*
- *The image of . . . effectively conveys the idea of . . .*
- *The image of . . . is particularly striking.*
- *The vivid imagery fires my imagination . . .*
- *I like the way the poet compares . . .*
- *The poet employs a powerful metaphor to . . .*
- *This unusual simile is effective because . . .*
- *The poet's use of sound is particularly effective here because . . .*
- *The use of everyday, conversational language made the poem very accessible . . .*
- *I love the poet's wonderful use of detail . . .*
- *The poet's eye for detail brings the character / scene to life . . . etc. etc.*
- It is also important to write in the appropriate form and to employ the appropriate register (type of language).
- For example, you may be asked to write your response to a poet's work in the form of a letter in which you speak directly to the poet.
- If your response takes the form of a speech/talk, use conversational language / employ a chatty tone, etc, etc.

STRUCTURE YOUR ANSWER
- Brief introduction, addressing the question and outlining your response to it.
- One point (for example, a poet's use of imagery) or one poem per paragraph. Brief conclusion, referring back to the question.

Remember:
- Avoid summarising poems – remain focused on your key points. Aim to be analytical / discursive in responding to a poet's work.
- The emphasis throughout your response should be on personal engagement grounded in the text. Regularly quote from and refer to text to support points made.
- You do not have to discuss a fixed number of poems, but it is difficult to produce an impressive response discussing fewer than three poems.

RESPONDING TO THE UNSEEN POEM

In responding to this question, you must display an ability **to personally 'connect'** with the poem and the poet. You are expected to make intelligent use of the text to support your interpretation.

Look at the **shape of the poem**. Is it organised in stanzas? Is it written in sonnet form? Are any lines set apart from the rest of the poem? For example, the final line in Philip Larkin's *The Explosion* stands alone to emphasise the final image of 'eggs unbroken', evoking the idea of new life and continuity in the face of tragedy.

Note the **title** of the poem – it has not been chosen at random. What does the title suggest? Does the poem fulfil the expectations suggested by the title? For example, the title of John Montague's *A Welcoming Party* suggests a poem about a joyous occasion, but instead the poet recounts his shock at watching newsreels showing the horrors of Nazi concentration camps. In contrast, when we read Gerard Manley Hopkins's *God's Grandeur*, we expect – and get – a poem portraying a natural world enlivened by God's existence.

It is important to remember that a poet chooses his/her **words** very carefully to express his/her feelings. Words may be used literally or metaphorically ('I turned to ice', etc). They may be selected for their connotations / associations ('The waters of the canal pouring redemption for me' suggests the idea of an experience that is almost religious, etc.). Words may also be selected for their sounds.

Make a note of **your first impression** which will, naturally, be general in nature. What did you think of the poem's opening and closing? Did anything in particular strike you? A word? A phrase? An image? Were certain words suggestive of a particular mood or idea? Did the poet make use of repetition? Was the imagery primarily visual or did it appeal to a range of different senses? Are there any colours in the poem? If so, what feelings do you associate with these colours? Does the poem make use of contrast?

Your **second reading** of the poem will need to be more focused. Try to identify the dominant feeling in the poem and make a note of the key words and images that convey this feeling.

How would you describe the **language**? Is it formal or colloquial / chatty? Modern poets use the language of the modern age, ensuring that their poems are readily accessible. Is there any unusual use of language? For example, in Eavan Boland's *The War Horse*, the poet uses the terminology of war ('mere life of defence', 'a maimed limb') to describe the destruction wrought by an escaped traveller's horse to a suburban estate. In Paul Durcan's *Parents*, the poet uses unexpected reversals (the baby is asleep yet is 'calling out' to her parents; despite their 'big ears' they 'cannot hear her') to convey the intensity of the parents' love for their child.

Discuss the poet's use of **imagery**. Are certain images particularly effective? An image is basically a word-picture which may consist of a single word or a number of lines. Similes and metaphors are types of images. Does the poet make use of comparisons and, if so, are they effective in conveying a particular idea?

Consider the poet's use of **punctuation**. For example, regular full stops can serve different purposes. In her poem, *This Moment,* Eavan Boland makes regular use of full stops to create a sense of expectation. Regular full stops also help to create a reflective mood. A full stop at the end of a poem suggests a sense of closure, while its absence suggests the idea of something unresolved. Emily Dickinson often ends a poem with a dash or a question mark. Regular question marks suggest uncertainty.

What happens between the beginning and end of the poem? How do the poet's thoughts and feelings **develop**? Does he/she achieve some **insight** as the poem develops?

Consider the poet's **use of sound** (alliteration, assonance, onomatopoeia, rhyme, etc). Different sounds help to suggest different moods. For example, an alliterative 'b' sound can suggest a noisy atmosphere, a repeated 'd' sound a gloomy one and a repeated 's' sound a sense of peace. Are certain vowel sounds repeated and, if so, to what effect? For example, the repetition of broad vowel sounds helps to convey a serious, sad or lonely mood ('Alone, alone, all alone', 'staring face to face', etc.

Key Points – Mention the following:

- Title of poem.
- Key theme.
- Shape.
- Opening.
- Key words / phrases / images.
- Way in which ideas develop.
- Use of sound.
- Conclusion.

Remember:

- Your response to the poem must be supported by intelligent use of the text.
- Show an awareness of literary terms in your response.

Key Literary Terms

ALLEGORY – A piece of writing that has both a surface meaning and another, deeper meaning. The purpose of an allegory is often to illustrate a moral or truth. *Example:* On the surface George Orwell's *Animal Farm* is a simple tale of animals taking over and running the farm on which they live. On a deeper level, this tale highlights the corrupting effects of total power. (Orwell had the old Soviet Union in mind when he wrote this novel.)

ALLITERATION – A run of words (usually consonants) starting with the same letter. *Examples:* 'Billy Brennan's barn' – Patrick Kavanagh. 'In the sun the slagheap slept' – Philip Larkin.

ALLUSION – This occurs when a writer refers to a well-known character, event, historical happening or work of literature. *Examples:* In *The Pomegranate* Boland alludes to the myth of Ceres and Peresphone. In *The Cage*, Montague refers to Homer's poem *The Iliad*, '…for when / weary Odysseus returns / Telemachus should leave'. In *September 1913* Yeats refers to Irish history, 'Was it for this the wild geese spread / The grey wing upon every tide?'

AMBIGUITY – This occurs when a word, phrase or sentence is open to more than one interpretation. *Example:* 'I am king of banks and stones and every blooming thing' – Patrick Kavanagh.

ANALOGY – A comparison made to show how two things are similar. Similes and metaphors are based on analogy. *Example:* 'Hope is the thing with feathers / That perches in the soul' – Emily Dickinson.

ANTITHESIS – This refers to the juxtaposition of contrasting phrases or ideas. *Example:* My words fly up, my thoughts remain below' –

ARCHAISM – This refers to a writer's use of old-fashioned (archaic) language.

ASSONANCE – This occurs when a vowel sound is repeated in words close to each other. *Example:* 'But ranged as infantry / and staring face to face' – Thomas Hardy.

BLANK VERSE – This is unrhymed iambic pentameter (each line consisting of ten syllables). *Example:* 'Your batman thought you were buried alive / Left you for dead and stole your pocket watch' – Michael Longley.

CLICHÉ – This refers to a well-worn, overused expression or phrase. *Examples:* 'Tomorrow is another day', 'raining cats and dogs', 'a crying shame'.

CLIMAX – This refers to a moment of great intensity in a play or dramatic poem. *Example:* Having reflected deeply on the plan to murder Duncan, Macbeth decides not to go ahead with it. However, Lady Macbeth intervenes and Macbeth succumbs to her powers of persuasion. At the close of a very tense scene, Macbeth declares: 'I am settled and bend up each corporal agent to this terrible feat.'

CONCEIT – This is an unusual metaphor or comparison used especially by metaphysical poets such as John Donne. *Example:* Donne compares his lover and himself to the two legs of a mathematical compass to suggest how they will never be separated, even when he embarks on his travels, 'As stiff twin compasses are two, / Thy soul the fixed foot, makes no show / To move, but doth, if th'other do'.

COUPLET – This refers to two successive lines of verse, usually rhymed and of the same metre. *Example:* 'I lift the window, watch the ambling feather / Of hock and fetlock, loosed from its daily tether' – Eavan Boland.

DIALECT – This refers to a form of language spoken in a particular geographical area, which contains words and expressions not found in the standard language.

DRAMATIC IRONY – This occurs in a play when the audience knows more than a particular character. It is very ironic that having been betrayed by the Thane of Cawdor, Duncan then bestows this title on Macbeth, little knowing that his apparently loyal and trustworthy kinsman plans to muder him.

ELEGY – This is a poem of lamentation, a poem mourning the dead.

EMOTIVE LANGUAGE – This is language that evokes an emotional response in the reader. *Example:* 'I touched his head, his thin head I touched' – Michael Longley.

EPIGRAM – This is a concise (short) and witty saying. *Example:* 'But wild ambition loves to slide, not stand / And fortune's ice prefers to vertue's land' – John Dryden.

EPIPHANY – This refers to a moment of insight / understanding, such as Elizabeth Bishop achieves in the closing lines of *The Fish.*

EUPHEMISM – This is a gentle or indirect way of expressing something drastic, offensive or unpleasant. *Example:* He passed away.

FIGURATIVE LANGUAGE – This refers to language which makes use of simile and metaphor to express an idea. To speak figuratively is to speak metaphorically.

FREE VERSE – This is verse that is unrhymed and unmetered. It is widely used by modern poets. *Example:* 'I caught a tremendous fish / and held him beside the boat / half out of the water, with my hook / fast in the corner of his mouth'. – Elizabeth Bishop.

HYPERBOLE – This refers to the deliberate use of exaggeration or overstatement to emphasise a point. *Example:* 'Ten thousand saw I at a glance / Tossing their heads in a sprightly dance' – Wordsworth.

IMAGERY – This is a general term which embraces similes, metaphors, symbols. Basically, it refers to any type of word-picture.

IRONY – Verbal irony occurs when one thing is said, while the opposite is meant. *Example:* 'For men were born to pray and save' – Yeats. Irony of situation occurs when a situation is very different from what the protagonist believes it to be.

LYRIC – This refers to any short poem which directly expresses personal feeling.

METAPHOR – This is a type of image that directly compares two things, without using 'like', 'as' or 'than'. *Examples:* 'I turned to ice' – Derek Mahon. 'a leaping tongue of bloom' – Robert Frost.

MOTIF – This refers to a recurring theme or feature in a writer's work.

ONOMATOPOEIA – This occurs when the sound of the word suggests the sound being described. *Examples:* hissing, sizzled, clanging.

PARADOX – This refers to a statement that appears to be, but is not, a contradiction. *Example:* The freezing ice burnt my hand.

PATHOS – This refers to a quality in literature that evokes a deep, sympathetic feeling in the reader.

PERSONA – This refers to the voice or speaker in a poem. The persona is usually – but not always – the poet.

PERSONIFICATION – This is a technique whereby a writer attributes human qualities to an animal, object or idea. *Example:* The happy sun smiled down on us.

PETRARCHAN SONNET – This refers to a sonnet which consists of an octave/octet (set of eight lines) and a sestet (set of six lines). The octave presents us with a situation or problem which is resolved in the sestet.

QUATRAIN – This is a four-line unit of verse.

RHYTHM – This refers to the movement or flow of words.

SHAKESPEARIAN SONNET – This consists of three quatrains and a rhyming couplet.

SIBILANCE – This is a whispering/hissing 's' sound. *Example:* 'Its surface seems tilted / To receive the sun perfectly' – Longley.

SIMILE – This is a type of image which compares two things using the words 'like', 'as' or 'than'. *Example:* 'One window is yellow as butter' – Eavan Boland.

STYLE – This refers to a writer's individual way of expressing his/her ideas.

SYMBOL – This is a word or phrase which represents something real and concrete, but also represents something other than itself. *Examples:* A dove is a symbol of peace, a flower a symbol of beauty.

THEME – This refers to a key idea in a piece of writing. (There may be more than one theme.)

TONE – This is the attitude of the writer towards his/her subject. A tone may be joyful, angry, bitter, self-pitying, etc. etc.

SAY NO TO BULLYING
NOBODY DESERVES TO BE BULLIED
TELL AN ADULT YOU CAN TRUST

This Anti-Bullying campaign is supported by the Department of Education and Skills with the co-operation of the Irish Educational Publishers Association